Advances in Artificial Intelligence in Education

Volume 3

This book series focuses on using artificial intelligence (AI) in educational contexts, providing the venue to showcase the latest developments in this rapidly moving field. From personalised instruction to adaptive assessments and immersive learning experiences, AI tools and technologies can revolutionise education and empower educators, students, and decision makers.

A wide range of topics surrounding the use of AI in learning and teaching are explored, covering global perspectives from different communities and disciplines. The book series approaches the use of AI in education with caution and addresses ethical considerations such as data privacy, algorithmic bias, and transparency. By examining AI socially responsible and inclusively, AI's full potential shall be unlocked and create a future of education that is personalised, engaging, and equitable for all learners.

The titles in the series cover the use of AI within K-12 through tertiary settings and in other domains such as professional, lifelong, and work-integrated learning. The series accepts monographs and edited volumes that fit the scope mentioned above and covers various topics, including (but not limited to) tutoring systems, adaptive learning, feedback provision, learner modelling, assessment analytics, as well as teaching and learning support. The series also includes titles covering related issues of ethical and responsible use of AI, data privacy, bias and transparency, educational design, institutional adoption, and inclusion.

Please contact Professor Dirk Ifenthaler at dirk@ifenthaler.info if you wish to discuss a book proposal for the series.

Guy Tchibozo
Editor

International Perspectives of Generative AI in Education

Insights from Research in Diverse Educational Contexts

Springer

Editor
Guy Tchibozo
LISEC UR2310
University of Strasbourg
Strasbourg, France

ISSN 3004-9903 ISSN 3004-9911 (electronic)
Advances in Artificial Intelligence in Education
ISBN 978-3-031-99803-4 ISBN 978-3-031-99804-1 (eBook)
https://doi.org/10.1007/978-3-031-99804-1

This Springer imprint is published by the registered company Springer Nature Switzerland AG
The registered company address is: Gewerbestrasse 11, 6330 Cham, Switzerland

Acknowledgments

This book was published with the support of Analytrics (www.home.analytrics.org).

The authors of this book would like to thank the reviewers and the series editors for their constructive comments.

Contents

Part I Introduction

1 **From Technology-Centric AI Conversations to Avenues in Educational GenAI** 3
Guy Tchibozo

2 **A Brief Overview of Foundations and Advances in Programming with AI** 11
Rutwa Engineer and Ibrahim Nantomah

Part II Caught Off Guard by GenAI: Teachers' and Learners' Needs, and Ways for Readiness

3 **Bridging the Gap: Exploring the Aspirations and Realities of AI Acceptance Among Secondary School Teachers in Luxembourg** 19
Daniela Hau, Robert A. P. Reuter, O. Mariño, and Claude Houssemand

4 **What Is AI? The Need for AI Literacy in Education** 47
Lesley Wilton, Clare Brett, Stephen Ip, Rutwa Engineer, and Athena Tassis

Part III Improving Pedagogy and Instruction: Potential and Issues

5 **Development of Academic Discourse Through Generative Artificial Intelligence-Enabled Transmediation** 79
Heather Cato and Amy Burke

6 **Information Literacy in the Age of Large Language Models** 101
Benjamin Bewersdorf and Ryan Mitchell Wittingslow

7 **Can AI Enhance Teaching and Learning in Physical Education?** . . . 115
Hock Beng Tommy Ng

8 AI-Generated Images for Linguistically Responsive and Multimodal Elementary Literacy Curriculum and Instruction 129
Gayoung Choi and SungEun Min

9 Towards AI Didactics: Call for Teachers to Train Large Language Models for Research Writing in Higher Arts Education 149
Lauri Väkevä and Heidi Partti

10 Updating the Research-Teaching Nexus Framework in the Age of Generative AI: Prioritizing GenAI-Proof Research Tasks 169
Bérangère Laroudie and Guy Tchibozo

11 Simulation in Mixed-Reality Learning Environments: Safe Spaces for Pre-Service Teachers to Practice Classroom Management 187
Therese M. Cumming, Hee Min Lee, and Jordana F. Hoenig

12 Generative AI Cascading Effect Framework for the Global South: Exposing Pedagogical Gaps in Teacher Education 207
Matthew Nyaaba

Part IV Planning Lessons and Assessing Knowledge While Reducing Burnout and Increasing Productivity

13 Generative Artificial Intelligence as a Collaborative Lesson Planning Tool for Novice Teachers: Emerging Perspectives 227
Beverly B. Ray and Esther Ntuli

14 Empowering Teachers Through GenAI-Created Lesson Plans 245
Domenica Spadoni and Gina L. Solano

15 An Exploratory Study on the Use of GenAI in Higher Education as Support for Teachers' Feedback of Written Assignments 263
Stefanie A. Hillen

16 Identifying GenAI Effectiveness: Grading Elementary Writing 285
Tyler Harnish and Gina L. Solano

17 Utilizing AI to Mitigate Teacher Burnout 297
Austin C. Ross

18 Teacher Perspectives on Using Generative Artificial Intelligence to Improve Productivity in Lesson Planning, Rubric Creation, and Assessments 307
Shelby Grosso and Gina L. Solano

Part V Students, AI, and GenAI: Identity Formation and Perceptions

19 The Impact of Generative AI on Student Identity Formation 327
Ezechiel Thibaud

20 Future Teachers' Perspectives on AI in Education: Insights from Bethlehem University Students 345
Alejandro González Cerna

Part VI Taking a Critical Step Back

21 Critical Generative AI Literacy in Education: Inter/National Perspectives from Teacher-Research 359
Michael Singh, Lìpíng Niú, and Xiǎo-Lí Lǐ

Part VII Conclusion

22 Educators and GenAI: Harnessing a Power, Not Bowing Down to Some Cryptic Deity 383
Guy Tchibozo

Index 391

Editor and Contributors

About the Editor

Guy Tchibozo holds a Ph.D. in Economics. From 1990 to 2020, he worked at the universities of La Réunion, Limoges, and Strasbourg (France), serving first as an Associate Professor in Economics and then as a Full Professor in Education. His teaching focused on the economics and politics of 'education and the labor market'. He was also, in parallel, an expert with the European Centre for the Development of Vocational Training (Cedefop, in Thessaloniki, Greece), between 2007 and 2020. He is currently pursuing his research at LISEC UR2310, the educational research center at the University of Strasbourg. Professor Tchibozo has a long-standing research interest in education policy and quantitative analysis, focusing particularly on dynamics analysis and vocational education and training, including educational innovation. He has authored numerous books and journal articles (https://gtsite.xyz/1/). Since 2023, he has been paying particular attention to the development of generative artificial intelligence in education. Professor Tchibozo is also the Director of Analytrics and the Editor of *Education Thinking*.

Contributors

Benjamin Bewersdorf University College Groningen, University of Groningen, Groningen, The Netherlands

Clare Brett OISE, University of Toronto, Toronto, ON, Canada

Amy Burke Texas Woman's University, Denton, TX, USA

Heather Cato Texas Woman's University, Denton, TX, USA

Gayoung Choi University of Nebraska-Lincoln, Lincoln, NE, USA

Therese M. Cumming University of New South Wales, Sydney, NSW, Australia

Rutwa Engineer University of Toronto, Toronto, ON, Canada

Alejandro González Cerna Bethlehem University, Bethlehem, Palestine

Shelby Grosso State University of New York (SUNY) Oneonta, Oneonta, NY, USA

Tyler Harnish State University of New York (SUNY) Oneonta, Oneonta, NY, USA

Daniela Hau Ministry of Education, Luxembourg, Luxembourg

Stefanie A. Hillen Department of Education, University of Agder, Kristiansand, Norway

Jordana F. Hoenig University of New South Wales, Sydney, NSW, Australia

Claude Houssemand Department of Education, University of Luxembourg, Luxembourg, Luxembourg

Stephen Ip Southern Alberta Institute of Technology, Calgary, AB, Canada

Bérangère Laroudie IFSI, CHU Limoges, Limoges, France

Hee Min Lee University of New South Wales, Sydney, NSW, Australia

Xiǎo-Lí Lǐ Crown Institute of Higher Education, Sydney, NSW, Australia

O. Mariño Universidad de los Andes, Bogotá, Colombia

SungEun Min Kutztown University, Kutztown, PA, USA

Ibrahim Nantomah University for Development Studies, Tamale, Ghana

Hock Beng Tommy Ng National Institute of Education, Nanyang Technological University, Singapore, Singapore

Lìpíng Niú TESOL, Beijing, China

Esther Ntuli Idaho State University, Pocatello, ID, USA

Matthew Nyaaba University of Georgia, Athens, GA, USA

Heidi Partti Sibelius Academy, University of the Arts, Helsinki, Finland

Beverly B. Ray Idaho State University, Pocatello, ID, USA

Robert A. P. Reuter University of Luxembourg, Luxembourg, Luxembourg

Austin C. Ross University of Arizona, Tucson, AZ, USA

Michael Singh Western Sydney University, Sydney, NSW, Australia

Gina L. Solano State University of New York (SUNY) Oneonta, Oneonta, NY, USA

Domenica Spadoni State University of New York (SUNY) Oneonta, Oneonta, NY, USA

Athena Tassis University of Toronto, Toronto, ON, Canada

Guy Tchibozo LISEC UR2310, University of Strasbourg, Strasbourg, France

Ezechiel Thibaud Education University of Hong Kong, Hong Kong SAR, China

Lauri Väkevä University of Helsinki, Helsinki, Finland

Lesley Wilton OCT, University of Toronto, Toronto, ON, Canada

OISE, University of Toronto, Toronto, ON, Canada

Ryan Mitchell Wittingslow University College Groningen, University of Groningen, Groningen, The Netherlands

List of Figures

Fig. 3.1 Emotional stands towards AI (by subject groups) 27
Fig. 3.2 Model of the implementation gap of AI in education......................... 30

Fig. 4.1 UNESCO's recommendations on the values and principles of a human rights-centered approach to the Ethics of AI (Ramos, 2021).. 51
Fig. 4.2 Proposed Structure of Model Cards in Education 53
Fig. 4.3 Top 30 most relevant terms across all learner reflections 62
Fig. 4.4 Sentiment analysis heatmap.. 64

Fig. 5.1 Steps in the iterative teaching process 87

Fig. 7.1 Quantitative index for each student (left) and skills profile for the class as a whole (right) displayed on the teacher's iPad 118
Fig. 7.2 Anatomical locations of the skeleton-based prototype..................... 120
Fig. 7.3 Process flow of Human Pose Estimation 121
Fig. 7.4 Transformation of executed movement (left) to skeleton-based model in 3D space (right) 121

Fig. 8.1 Decodable Books Using AI-Generated Images 132
Fig. 8.2 Decodable Book Page Featuring the CVCe (Silent-E) Pattern, Created With DALL·E.. 134
Fig. 8.3 Decodable Book Page Featuring Digraphs, Created With DALL·E 134
Fig. 8.4 Sample Book Page From Tilly the Tiny Turtle, Featuring English-Korean Bilingual Text With Illustrations Generated by DALL·E 137
Fig. 8.5 Sample Book Page From The Day Luca Lost His Roar, Featuring English-Italian Bilingual Text With Illustrations Generated by DALL·E.. 138
Fig. 8.6 Sample Book Page From Henri the Hedgehog and the Eiffel Tower Adventure, Featuring English-French Bilingual Text With Illustrations Generated by DALL·E 138

Fig. 8.7 Image-Vocabulary Pairs ... 141
Fig. 8.8 Image-Vocabulary Pairs Incorporating English and Spanish... 142
Fig. 8.9 Henri the Hedgehog and the Eiffel Tower Adventure, featuring French voiceover with English captions... 144
Fig. 8.10 Tilly the Tiny Turtle, featuring English voiceover with Korean captions ... 144

Fig. 11.1 Continuum of authentic learning activities in teacher education... 190
Fig. 11.2 SimLab virtual classroom with student avatars ... 196
Fig. 12.1 The cascading effect of generative AI's role in transforming teacher education in the Global South ... 215

List of Tables

Table 3.1 Phases of thematic content analysis (Kuckartz & Rädiker, 2019) ... 24

Table 4.1 Administration tools ... 55
Table 4.2 Business tools ... 56
Table 4.3 General tools ... 57
Table 4.4 Health tools ... 58
Table 4.5 Imaging tools ... 58
Table 4.6 Language tools ... 59
Table 4.7 Math tools ... 61
Table 4.8 Music tools ... 62

Table 5.1 GenAI tools used during the learning process ... 87

Table 11.1 Descriptive statistics for NTSES domains ... 197

Table 14.1 Rubric results ... 253

Table 15.1 Research approaches, tools, learning groups, specifications, and notes ... 265
Table 15.2 Comparison between the teacher-assigned grades and those generated by GenAI ... 275
Table 15.3 Part II of the prompt: rubric with categories of student performance ... 278

Table 21.1 Acquiring know-how through using GenAI systems for professional learning ... 368
Table 21.2 Using 汉语 (Hànyǔ) and GenAI in automating teacher education ... 370
Table 21.3 GenAI systems replace aspects of teacher-researchers' work ... 372
Table 21.4 The governing power of GenAI in automating education ... 373

Part I
Introduction

Chapter 1
From Technology-Centric AI Conversations to Avenues in Educational GenAI

Guy Tchibozo

Abstract Artificial intelligence (AI) has gradually penetrated education over the last 30 years (Chan & Colloton, 2024; Du Boulay et al., 2023; Niemi et al., 2023; OECD, 2021). In this context, the bursting of generative AI (GenAI) since 2022 has led to several dramatic changes. While AI had long been confined to tech enthusiast discussion circles, GenAI has made AI a concrete reality for everyone in society. In education, GenAI has changed the game for learners and teachers. Renewed interest has emerged, and new opportunities and practices have flourished, bringing with them new perspectives, perceptions, needs, risks, and challenges; transforming teaching and learning; and questioning both what is at stake and ethics in education.

Artificial intelligence (AI) has gradually penetrated education over the last 30 years (Chan & Colloton, 2024; Du Boulay et al., 2023; Niemi et al., 2023; OECD, 2021). In this context, the bursting of generative AI (GenAI) since 2022 has led to several dramatic changes. While AI had long been confined to tech enthusiast discussion circles, GenAI has made AI a concrete reality for everyone in society. In education, GenAI has changed the game for learners and teachers. Renewed interest has emerged, and new opportunities and practices have flourished, bringing with them new perspectives, perceptions, needs, risks, and challenges; transforming teaching and learning; and questioning both what is at stake and ethics in education.

The aim of this book is to analyze AI in education in the wake of the generative artificial intelligence revolution. Going beyond the existing research literature on AI in education, the contributions place a specific emphasis on GenAI, analyzing its potential, effects, limits, risks, and challenges. This book also explores avenues for progress and suggests recommendations for practice, policy, and research.

The approach adopted in the book is to bring together perspectives from different contexts. AI and GenAI are confronting education systems around the world with

G. Tchibozo (✉)
LISEC UR2310, University of Strasbourg, Strasbourg, France
e-mail: editor@analytrics.org

G. Tchibozo (ed.), *International Perspectives of Generative AI in Education*, Advances in Artificial Intelligence in Education 3,
https://doi.org/10.1007/978-3-031-99804-1_1

similar questions. The answers may vary. This book aims to provide as comprehensive an exploration as possible of the potential value and limitations of GenAI for education. It offers a wide range of insights based on analyses conducted in different contexts, by authors from various countries, at all educational levels, questioning the complexities, potential, and challenges of educational GenAI in various fields, from different angles. The goal is to open up new perspectives and ideas. Behind the specificities, common threads emerge, enabling each player to interpret and evaluate the analyses and results in light of their own realities, and possibly to draw inspiration from them.

In November 2022, generative AI became a concrete reality for educational players worldwide. It took only a few months for everyone to become aware of this new reality, the prospects it opened up, and the challenges it posed. After 1 year of hindsight, we began writing the chapters of this book in November 2023. Therefore, the book presents the results of emerging research into a reality that is still evolving, but some main features of which can already be grasped and analyzed. Thus, this book is one of the very first to offer a panoramic range of research and results on the emergence of generative AI in education, including all levels of education, from a cross-border perspective that transcends the specificities of local educational contexts.

Exploring Educational GenAI

To address this challenge, we have adopted an exploratory epistemological stance. In the sense defined by Stebbins (2001, pp. 11–14), exploration is an organized approach aimed at discovering generalizations that make it possible to describe and understand an object of study in as many of its dimensions as possible, be they concepts, structures, processes, or beliefs. This discovery of generalizations across the board is the aim of the exploratory methodologies used in the studies presented in this book. Alongside theoretical articles, which establish general frameworks for analysis and reflection (for example, on the impact of GenAI on information literacy or student identity formation, or on the concept of 'critical GenAI literacy'), the research presented favors exploratory small-scale empirical qualitative studies. The reason for this approach is that the potential of generative AI in education, and the ways in which it can be used, are still largely to be identified, understood, and defined. We felt that exploratory approaches were best suited to account for this current state of knowledge on educational GenAI, and to better identify and understand potential benefits, limitations, risks, and challenges.

We also believe that small-scale empirical qualitative field studies are not only easier to grasp quickly by the widest possible audience, but also illustrative and inspiring for easy local replications and developments that can enable each stakeholder to swiftly identify, in their own field, avenues of interest that could be explored.

Finally, we believe that the exploratory approach we have adopted is essential to pave the way for more systematic and weighty research to be developed in the future, once the relevant avenues to be explored have been better mapped out.

Innovating in Education

This book renews approaches in the field of educational innovation. An illustration of this is Chap. 5, where Cato and Burke suggest how generative AI can help students master academic discourse across different media as part of an iterative process. These reflections are likely to inspire further research and methodological developments.

In Chap. 10, Laroudie and Tchibozo reveal an important distinction between GenAI-proof and GenAI-substitutable research tasks. The general concept of GenAI-proof research tasks is understudied. The idea advocated in Chap. 10 is to reserve a central role in knowledge assessment for GenAI-proof research tasks. Still, the analysis developed in Chap. 10 explicitly refers to the context of teaching through research. Therefore, the next question is: how does the distinction between GenAI-proof and GenAI-substitutable tasks play out in other teaching and learning contexts? A first case in point is the training of future researchers, which obviously, unlike the general framework of research-based teaching, requires that GenAI-substitutable research tasks be a major focus of knowledge assessment, because future researchers need to know GenAI as well as possible, how to use it, its limitations and pitfalls, its ethics, and be prepared to detect cases of inappropriate use of it. The other case in point is that of basic education up to the undergraduate level, which does not involve learners in the practice of research tasks because they do not yet have the necessary background. The useful distinction to be made before the graduate education stages is between GenAI-proof and GenAI-substitutable assessed activities (not research activities). Here, while learners should receive solid education in the ethics and best practices of GenAI use, knowledge assessment should be carried out exclusively through GenAI-proof learning activities. Chapter 10 is a step forward in thinking about these issues, which are of concern to most educators worldwide today.

A further example of pedagogical innovation proposed in this book is presented in Chap. 11, in which Cumming et al. draw on mixed reality learning environments. They show how mixed-reality simulations, leveraging artificial intelligence, adaptive learning, intelligent tutoring systems, and data analytics, create immersive, interactive, and adaptive educational experiences, and provide innovative and individualized learning experiences.

How Does GenAI Work?

This book focuses primarily on generative AI. Therefore, a brief introduction to GenAI may be useful. Chapter 2 in this introductory Part provides a brief overview of the origin and development of AI and GenAI.

Generative artificial intelligence systems are models that use algorithms to identify patterns from a data set and, based on the patterns observed, generate new outputs in the form of text, computer code, images, video, sound, and physical objects. Vafadar and Moradi Amani (2024) explained how it works. The keywords are Artificial intelligence (AI), Machine Learning (ML), Deep Learning (DL), and Artificial Neural Networks (ANNs). Artificial intelligence can be characterized as computer programs able to "carry out tasks that typically require human intelligence". Machine Learning (ML) is a type of AI that can extract patterns from data and learn from these patterns to make predictions. To improve the decision process that leads to these predictions, Deep Learning (DL), which is based on Artificial Neural Networks (ANNs) and can perform complex calculations on large volumes of data, is used. ANNs themselves are computer models designed to mimic the structures and functions of neural networks in the human brain. GenAI is a Machine Learning system that leverages multilayer ANNs to process complex patterns.

GenAI systems are trained on datasets to develop and improve their ability to identify patterns, make predictions based on these patterns, and generate outputs accordingly. Once ready, the GenAI systems are made available to users, who can then submit natural language queries to obtain a personalized output.

Vafadar and Moradi Amani (2024) highlight a series of techniques that underpin the generative AI process. Among these are the Transformer models, which are Deep Learning tools that support the processing of natural language by converting sentences into sequences, assessing the relative importance of words in each sequence, and prioritizing the most relevant words. Large Language Models (LLMs) are also important tools, as they learn statistical associations between words and phrases in order to infer relationships and generate new content based on the observed correlations. Generative Adversarial Networks (GANs) play an essential role in creating new content based on a user's input, as they combine output generation by a 'generator ANN' and generation refinement by a 'discriminator ANN', which leads to narrowing down the discrepancies between the baseline content and the generated output. Finally, autoencoders, which are neural networks capable of detecting and ignoring data noise and anomalies, are also useful for anomaly detection and image generation based on user-supplied inputs.

Understanding how GenAI works is of crucial importance for understanding how the output generated by GenAI systems should be used. Because GenAI tools are Machine Learning systems, their output is based on probabilistic inferences derived from correlations observed in the training datasets. This means that when they receive a query, GenAI systems do not 'understand' it in the human sense of the word. They 'simply' calculate the word sequence or, more generally, the result most likely to be associated with the query. However, the fact that A and B were strongly correlated in the training dataset does not mean that when a user's query is about A, the most relevant output to respond to that query is necessarily B. It may be otherwise. Therefore, it is of utmost importance that users take the results generated by GenAI for what they are, that is, suggestions to be considered, not answers to be imposed on them.

Content Overview

Overall, the harvest is substantial.

First, there appears to be strong demand from the education sector for a better understanding of artificial intelligence. **Part II** of the book investigates this issue. In Chap. 3, based on interviews with STEM, Language, Humanities, and Arts teachers in secondary education in Luxembourg, Hau and colleagues highlight teachers' perceptions and needs in relation to AI. The teachers surveyed recognize AI's potential for improving work efficiency and promoting critical thinking, and express their own needs for AI skills. However, they make no secret of their fears about the ethical and legal concerns that AI raises and the challenges it poses, particularly that of simultaneously acquiring AI knowledge and avoiding losing ground in core academic and disciplinary skills.

Not only teachers but also learners need to improve their AI knowledge. Wilton and her colleagues specifically address this need in Chap. 4. Based on their experience in teaching AI and AI Ethics in Education, these authors show that, due to the quick pace of technological innovation and change, and a lack of information about AI systems, learners find it difficult to form a critical understanding of AI. They highlight how model-card-type information could help improve AI literacy.

Better AI literacy among educators could help unleash AI's potential. **Part III** focuses on the potential and implications of AI and GenAI for pedagogy in a range of educational areas. Working on academic papers produced by master-level literacy education students, Cato and Burke (Chap. 5) analyze how the use of AI and GenAI tools can effectively contribute to improving students' academic writing skills. Bewersdorf and Wittingslow (Chap. 6) argue that GenAI changes the way we retrieve information and point out the implications in terms of updating information literacy curricula by introducing training in prompt engineering, reliability analysis, and education on the ethical and legal consequences of GenAI. In Chap. 7, Ng explores the potential of Human-Pose-Estimation algorithms to support the teaching and learning of physical education. In Chap. 8, Min and Choi suggest how GenAI-based still image and video generation can effectively support early and elementary literacy instruction.

Chapters 9 and 10 then focus on research education. In Chap. 9, Väkevä and Partti discuss the potential of GenAI to support the teaching of research writing—here in the particular case of Higher Art Education –, stressing the need to ensure, in parallel, the ethical awareness of learners and the GenAI competence of educators. In Chap. 10, Laroudie and Tchibozo, drawing implications, for research-based teaching, of the distinction between GenAI-proof and GenAI-substitutable research tasks, suggest ways to update pedagogy and assessment in this area.

Chapters 11 and 12 point to the potential benefits of AI and GenAI for teacher education and training. In Chap. 11, Cumming and her colleagues show that the use of Mixed-Reality Simulations, which combine real-world surroundings with virtual and augmented reality, may help reinforce pre-service teacher training and increase novice teachers' self-efficacy. In Chap. 12, which extends the scope to developing countries, Nyaaba uses the case of the Ghanaian education system to suggest how the potential of GenAI to support knowledge acquisition could help free up time for teacher educators to focus on improving pedagogical modeling, which in turn can have a positive impact on reducing resistance to change and improving student learning outcomes at the K-12 level.

AI and GenAI can support teachers' work and increase their productivity. **Part IV** begins by discussing the impacts of AI and GenAI on lesson planning (Chapters 13 and 14) and knowledge assessment (Chapters 15 and 16). In Chap. 13, Ray and Ntuli explore the views of a small sample of novice teachers on the use, benefits, challenges, and prospects of GenAI as a collaborative tool for lesson planning. Feedback from the study participants highlights the advantages of GenAI in terms of time-saving and creativity while insisting on the need for good preparation beforehand for the teachers to be able to evaluate and control the AI-generated input. In Chap. 14, Spadoni and Solano analyze the feedback of teachers after an experience of creating and implementing AI-generated lesson plans. The study participants' feedback indicated the high effectiveness of GenAI in the development of engaging and captivating lesson plans.

GenAI's potential support for knowledge assessment is then addressed. In Chap. 15, Hillen examines how GenAI applications can help teachers develop rubrics, criteria analysis, and written feedback reports to assess students' work. In Chap. 16, Harnish and Solano explore how GenAI can support the grading of written assignments. Based on an experience in an elementary school, they highlight the potential and limitations of the GenAI tools used, especially with regard to how they align with a human teacher's grading.

This fourth Part also highlights the benefits of AI and GenAI in terms of reducing teacher burnout and increasing productivity. AI and GenAI can save teachers time in the performance of their duties. In Chap. 17, which takes a closer look at an issue already raised in previous chapters, Ross reviews a range of AI and GenAI tools and indicates how these tools can help save educators' time, and consequently reduce their workload, stress, and burnout. In Chap. 18, Grosso and Solano report an experience of testing different AI tools on their ability to produce usable lesson plans, rubrics, and assessments. In this study, none of the tools clearly outperformed the others. However, one interesting point is that all participants acknowledged that the tools had saved them time and were beneficial in terms of productivity.

Students too are impacted by GenAI. **Part V** questions students' exposure to and views on it. In Chap. 19, Thibaud looks in depth at how GenAI may affect students' identity formation, in particular the formation of their "relational, dialectical, and agential identity". In Chap. 20, González-Cerna, drawing on a survey carried out at the Palestinian University of Bethlehem, shows how GenAI is perceived by the university's students, highlighting its potential to improve learning as well as their concerns in terms of ethics and dependence on technology.

The various chapters did not conceal the risks associated with AI. **Part VI** goes deeper, marking a strong critical step back. Its single chapter (Chap. 21) devotes exclusive attention to some of the major threats that GenAI poses to education. Singh and his colleagues offer a broad perspective, informed by their Australian experience as bilingual teacher-researchers proficient in Chinese (Hàn) and English. They first remind us that the use of GenAI, by prioritizing productivity over in-depth learning, and although it equips students with skills in high demand in the labor market, carries risks of unoriginality in student work, disregard for ethics, and a limited depth of learning and subject understanding. Then, they argue that the dominance of English in GenAI, a facet of hierarchical dominance in power relations between languages, jeopardizes the contribution of researchers from other languages to research and knowledge creation, and undermines the dissemination of research-based knowledge. Further, following in the footsteps of authors such as Feldstein (2019), Saltman (2020), and Schroeder (2020), Singh and his co-authors emphasize the risks that AI, through developments such as adaptive learning technologies, biometric pedagogy, and digital surveillance technologies, will lead to "digital unfreedom" and threaten critical thinking, democratic education, as well as democracy and freedoms more generally. To mitigate these risks, they strongly advocate that teacher-researchers develop a 'critical GenAI literacy', which involves not only systematically questioning GenAI's process, outputs, and outcomes, but also considering what human intelligence can do that GenAI cannot. Critical GenAI literacy would empower teacher-researchers to navigate the reconfiguration of their work.

This book revisits artificial intelligence in education, from the perspective of educators, specifically introducing novel insights in relation to generative AI. It addresses a wide range of educational fields at the primary, secondary, and tertiary levels, including adolescent development, the arts, language education, literacy, pedagogy, philosophy, policy, and teacher training. We hope that administrators, educators, policymakers, researchers, and technologists, will find this collection of analyses, experiences, and reflections, a rich and useful source of information and inspiration for taking stock and moving forward.

References

Chan, C. K. Y., & Colloton, T. (2024). *Generative AI in higher education. The ChatGPT effect*. Routledge.

Du Boulay, B., Mitrovic, A., & Yacef, K. (Eds.). (2023). *Handbook of artificial intelligence in education*. Edward Elgar Publishing.

Feldstein, S. (2019). The road to digital unfreedom: How artificial intelligence is reshaping repression. *Journal of Democracy, 30*(1), 40–52. https://doi.org/10.1787/589b283f-en

Niemi, H., Pea, R. D., & Lu, Y. (Eds.). (2023). *AI in learning: Designing the future*. Springer.

OECD. (2021). *OECD digital education outlook 2021: Pushing the frontiers with artificial intelligence, blockchain and robots*. OECD Publishing.

Saltman, K. (2020). Artificial intelligence and the technological turn of public education privatization: In defence of democratic education. *London Review of Education, 18*(2), 196–208.

Schroeder, J. (2020). Hannah Arendt's machines: Re-evaluating marketplace theory in the AI era. *First Amendment Studies, 54*(1), 28–51.

Stebbins, R. A. (2001). *Exploratory research in the social sciences*. SAGE Publications.

Vafadar, M., & Moradi Amani, A. (2024). Academic education in the era of generative artificial intelligence. *Journal of Electronics and Electrical Engineering, 3*(1), 117–133. https://doi.org/10.37256/jeee.3120244010

Chapter 2
A Brief Overview of Foundations and Advances in Programming with AI

Rutwa Engineer and Ibrahim Nantomah

Abstract AI and GenAI have revolutionized Computer Science in recent years. This short chapter briefly traces the origins of artificial intelligence and describes the impact of recent AI developments on programming today.

Keywords Programming · Software development

Programming as a primary instrument is used to design computer programs that mimic human intellectual processes, such as reasoning, learning and processing symbolic information contextually. Alan Turing's 1936 "Turing machine" concept showed that any clearly defined computational process could be mechanized. This served as the foundation for the original purpose of programming, which was to teach electronic computers to perform numerical calculations (Turing, 1950). It was later discovered that numbers and objects could be represented by strings of bits. Rules for connecting, producing or modifying symbols could be represented by operations on such symbols or features (Neumann, 2002). This led researchers, such as John McCarthy, to organize the Dartmouth workshop in the 1950s, coining the term "Artificial Intelligence" and suggesting that methods involving symbol manipulation could mimic human language comprehension and reasoning (McCarthy et al., 2006).

As the field matured, knowledge was encoded as logical statements or production rules. The early days of Artificial Intelligence (AI) relied on explicit, rule-based systems. These rule-based systems allowed reasoning to be traced and interpreted (Russell & Norvig, 2010). Later, in the 1980s the emphasis shifted to

R. Engineer
University of Toronto, Toronto, ON, Canada
e-mail: rutwa.engineer@utoronto.ca

I. Nantomah (✉)
University for Development Studies, Tamale, Ghana
e-mail: inantomah@uds.edu.gh

G. Tchibozo (ed.), *International Perspectives of Generative AI in Education*, Advances in Artificial Intelligence in Education 3,
https://doi.org/10.1007/978-3-031-99804-1_2

neuroscience-inspired artificial neural networks that learned patterns from data without the need for manually created rules. This paved the way for state-of-the-art performance in fields like Computer Vision, Natural Language Processing (NLP), and reinforcement learning (LeCun et al., 2015; Sutton & Barto, 2018), which has been fueled by advances in algorithms used to train artificial neural networks, known as backpropagation (Rumelhart et al., 1986). Additionally, deep learning architectures have enabled computers to make complex decisions through trial and error, significantly advancing reinforcement learning methods (Goodfellow et al., 2016; Sutton & Barto, 2018).

Artificial intelligence is an area in Computer Science that deals with the development of computer systems with human-like abilities such as reasoning, instruction, language understanding, language translation, and problem-solving, among others. AI has enabled computers to learn from their own experiences, adapt to specific conditions and perform activities that were previously only possible for humans. Natural language processing skills and deep learning are essential in many AI implementation scenarios. These technologies have made it possible for computers to be "taught" to carry out certain activities or jobs by analyzing large amounts of data they have been trained on (Asadbek, 2025).

Impact of AI in Programming

AI is now present at every stage of the software lifecycle, changing the tools developers use and the abilities they need to develop. Rapid prototyping is made possible in code generation and completion by Large Language Models (LLMs), like OpenAI Codex, which convert plain-English prompts into syntactically correct code snippets, complete functions, or even multi-file applications (Chen et al., 2021). AI offers tools that analyze the current code context and deliver intelligent suggestions by completing individual lines of code or automatically generating entire code blocks, which are tailored specifically to the project's structure coding conventions. Examples of these tools include GitHub Copilot and Amazon CodeWhisperer. These tools significantly reduce boilerplate and repetitive coding tasks (GitHub, 2023; Amazon Web Services, n.d.).

Beyond writing code, AI improves testing and debugging by using machine-learning models to detect security flaws and common coding errors more efficiently than traditional rule-based analyzers (Snyk, 2023) and by automatically creating unit tests (Fraser & Arcuri, 2011). At the same time, conversational assistants enable developers to engage with code through natural-language interfaces. By posing queries like "Why is this function failing?" or "Show me a binary search in Java," developers can get prompt answers or examples without ever leaving their editor. These features also support low-code and no-code platforms, which reduce the barrier to entry by enabling non-programmers to put together processes and basic apps (Cui, 2024). While AI-enhanced peer-review systems assess work against common criteria and provide consistent, actionable feedback, intelligent tutoring platforms in educational settings give students individualized guidance by providing hints and feedback that adjust to each student's progress (Holmes et al., 2019; Keuning et al., 2018).

Here is an overview of how AI has significantly impacted programming:

- **Code generation:** AI tools like ChatGPT can be used to generate lines of code. The programmer defines the parameters, and the code is automatically generated. These tools increase productivity since they reduce the amount of time a programmer would have used to write the lines of code.
- **Automation:** AI tools can be used to accomplish repetitive coding tasks such as auto completion and code suggestion, including code generation. This allows the developer more time to concentrate on more complex tasks.
- **Software testing:** AI tools are used to automatically test code and algorithms. They are able to detect errors that the human eye may find difficult to detect.
- **Natural Language Processing (NLP):** Software developers can write code using natural language commands or queries, thanks to the use of NLP modules. This makes it easier for non-programmers to interact with code by lowering the entrance barrier to coding.
- **Error detection:** AI-powered tools can be used to automatically detect and correct errors in programming codes, which reduces the time a developer would have spent in detecting bugs and also lowers the cost of hiring software developers.

Examples of AI tools and Their Roles in Programming

- **Codex (by OpenAI):** This tool allows users to express themselves in natural language which is then converted into code.
- **Amazon CodeWhisperer:** This AI tool helps developers write code faster and more securely by providing context-aware code suggestions.
- **GitHub Copilot:** This tool assists with generating entire functions from comments, auto-suggestions and real time code completion.
- **Tabnine:** This tool supports multiple programming languages and also provides AI-based code completion.
- **Snyk Code:** This utilizes AI to suggest ways to fix bugs and provides enhanced security.

Conclusion

The use of AI in programming has drastically transformed the way software is developed, tested and maintained. AI has made programming more efficient, effective, and accessible to those without strong programming background. This is made possible by automating route tasks, enabling natural language interactions, and enhancing code quality, among others. As AI tools continue to evolve, they are, among other things, redefining the software development industry, and are also redefining the role of programmers.

Competing Interests The authors have no conflicts of interest to declare that are relevant to the content of this chapter.

References

Amazon Web Services. (n.d.). What is CodeWhisperer? In *Amazon CodeWhisperer User Guide*. Retrieved May 11, 2025, from https://docs.aws.amazon.com/codewhisperer/latest/userguide/what-is-cwspr.html

Asadbek, A. (2025). Impact of artificial intelligence on the programming process and creating new opportunities. *Web of Teachers: Inderscience Research, 3*(2), 204–207.

Chen, M., Tworek, J., Heewoo, J., Yuan, Q., Ponde de Oliveira Pinto, H., Kaplan, J., Edwards, H., Burda, Y., Joseph, N., Brockman, G., Ray, A., Puri, R., Krueger, G., Petrov, M., Khlaaf, H., Sastry, G., Mishkin, P., Chan, B., Gray, S., …, & Zaremba, W. (2021). Evaluating large language models trained on code (arXiv:2107.03374). *arXiv*. Retrieved from https://arxiv.org/abs/2107.03374

Cui, J. (2024). The impact of low-code and no-code programming on software product delivery quality and development efficiency (SSRN scholarly paper ID 5010766). *SSRN*. https://doi.org/10.2139/ssrn.5010766.

Fraser, G., & Arcuri, A. (2011). EvoSuite: Automatic test suite generation for object-oriented software. In *Proceedings of the 19th ACM SIGSOFT Symposium on the Foundations of Software Engineering* (pp. 416–419).

GitHub. (2023). *Introducing GitHub copilot [blog post]*. GitHub. Retrieved from https://github.blog/2023-01-introducing-github-copilot/

Goodfellow, I., Bengio, Y., & Courville, A. (2016). *Deep learning*. MIT Press.

Holmes, W., Bialik, M., & Fadel, C. (2019). *Artificial intelligence in education: Promises and implications for teaching and learning*. Center for Curriculum Redesign.

Keuning, H., Jeuring, J., & Heeren, B. (2018). A systematic literature review of automated feedback generation for programming exercises. *ACM Transactions on Computing Education, 19*(1), 1–43. https://doi.org/10.1145/3231711

LeCun, Y., Bengio, Y., & Hinton, G. (2015). Deep learning. *Nature, 521*(7553), 436–444. https://doi.org/10.1038/nature14539

McCarthy, J., Minsky, M., Rochester, N., & Shannon, C. (2006). A proposal for the Dartmouth summer research project on artificial intelligence, 1956. *AI Magazine, 27*(4), 12–14.

Neumann, G. (2002). Programming languages in artificial intelligence. In *Encyclopedia of information systems* (Vol. 3, pp. 31–45). Academic.

Rumelhart, D. E., Hinton, G. E., & Williams, R. J. (1986). Learning representations by back-propagating errors. *Nature, 323*(6088), 533–536. https://doi.org/10.1038/323533a0

Russell, S., & Norvig, P. (2010). *Artificial intelligence: A modern approach* (3rd ed.). Prentice Hall.

Snyk. (2023). *Snyk Code AI-powered security testing* [Product documentation]. Retrieved May 08, 2025, from https://docs.snyk.io/products/snyk-code

Sutton, R. S., & Barto, A. G. (2018). *Reinforcement learning: An introduction* (2nd ed.). MIT Press.

Turing, A. M. (1950). Computing machinery and intelligence. *Mind, 59*(236), 433–460. https://doi.org/10.1093/mind/LIX.236.433

Rutwa Engineer is a computer science assistant professor at the Department of Mathematical and Computational Sciences at the University of Toronto Mississauga (UTM). She is also cross-appointed with the Institute for the Study of University Pedagogy (ISUP). Rutwa primarily teaches Introduction to computer programming and computer science, in addition to computer organization and systems programming. Her research invites new ways of thinking, dreaming, and coding in computing education and AI in education through epistemic diversity.

Ibrahim Nantomah is a lecturer at the University for Development Studies of Ghana and researcher specializing in Information Technology Education, Artificial Intelligence in Education and Educational Technology. He is a teacher trainer with a passion for transforming learning through digital innovation. Ibrahim Nantomah focuses on integrating emerging technologies into teaching and learning environments. His current works explores how AI can enhance pedagogical practices, improve student engagement, and support inclusive education. Ibrahim is committed to preparing future educators with the skills needed for the digital age and contributes to curriculum development and policy discourse in educational technology.

Part II
Caught Off Guard by GenAI: Teachers' and Learners' Needs, and Ways for Readiness

Chapter 3
Bridging the Gap: Exploring the Aspirations and Realities of AI Acceptance Among Secondary School Teachers in Luxembourg

Daniela Hau, Robert A. P. Reuter, O. Mariño, and Claude Houssemand

Abstract This study examines the gap between the aspirations and actual applications of artificial intelligence (AI) and generative AI (GenAI) in education, focusing on the multifaceted challenges to AI adoption among secondary school teachers in Luxembourg. Through 29 semi-structured interviews, the research reveals that educators often experience a perceived loss of control due to the opaque nature of AI systems, the rapid pace of technological change, and the sometimes superior digital literacy of students. This perceived loss hinders both psychological comfort and professional effectiveness, complicating AI integration. The study highlights the importance of fostering critical thinking skills in both teachers and students as well as the need for robust ethical and legal frameworks. Subject-specific factors also appear to play a critical role in shaping teachers' emotional and conceptual perceptions of AI. The findings advocate structured professional development and comprehensive organizational support as essential for effective AI implementation. By addressing barriers such as teacher resistance and ethical concerns, this study contributes to the growing discourse on AI acceptance, offers practical strategies for integrating AI into education, and suggests a multi-pronged approach to ensure that educators are well equipped for this transition.

Keywords AI acceptance · AI adoption · Technology acceptance

D. Hau (✉) · R. A. P. Reuter · C. Houssemand
University of Luxembourg, Luxembourg, Luxembourg
e-mail: daniela.hau@education.lu; robert.reuter@uni.lu; claude.houssemand@uni.lu

O. Mariño
Universidad de los Andes, Bogotá, Colombia
e-mail: olmarino@uniandes.edu.co

G. Tchibozo (ed.), *International Perspectives of Generative AI in Education*, Advances in Artificial Intelligence in Education 3,
https://doi.org/10.1007/978-3-031-99804-1_3

A distinctive feature of artificial intelligence (AI), including generative AI (GenAI), in education is that they are emerging, interfering, and disruptive, and not (yet) part f routine classroom practice. For the purposes of this study, we use AI as an umbrella term, deliberately including both "traditional" AI and more recent developments such as GenAI. This allows us to capture how educators conceptualize and respond to AI in all its forms, rather than pre-defining or restricting their understanding to specific types of AI.

Despite significant advances in AI and its potential to transform educational paradigms (Miao & Holmes, 2021; Zawacki-Richter et al., 2019), its integration into routine classroom practice remains uneven and context-dependent. The slow pace of educational change, systemic inertia, and reluctance to disrupt established teaching norms often inhibit the adoption of new technologies. Teachers, who are pivotal in embracing these innovations, face challenges such as threats to their pedagogical autonomy, insufficient training, and ethical concerns including privacy and the potential biases of AI (Chiu & Chai, 2020; Gupta & Bhaskar, 2020; Polak et al., 2022).

While theoretical models like the Technology Acceptance Model (TAM) (Davis, 1989) and the Unified Theory of Acceptance and Use of Technology (UTAUT) (Venkatesh et al., 2003) provide frameworks to understand technology adoption, they often fall short of addressing the dynamic and complex nature of AI in educational settings (Doroudi, 2022; Tlili et al., 2023).

This study aims to bridge the gap between the theoretical promise of AI or GenAI and their practical application. By employing an exploratory, qualitative approach focused on the perspectives of secondary school teachers in Luxembourg, the research explores a broad spectrum of AI (non)acceptance and (non)adoption.

By uncovering these complexities, the study not only enriches the discourse on AI and GenAI in education but also lays the groundwork for a new model of AI acceptance that is tailored to the intricacies of educational ecosystems.

Literature Review

AI in Education: From Aspirational Goals to Actual Implementation

Despite the significant potential of AI and GenAI to transform education, as demonstrated by extensive research (Holmes et al., 2019; Roll & Wylie, 2016), their implementation in classrooms remains limited (Johal et al., 2018). Choi et al. (2022, p.1) note that "teachers are hardly integrating educational AI tools (EAIT), and little is known about their perceptions of EAITs". This implementation gap is often linked to educators' limited understanding of AI's fundamental principles (Nazaretsky et al., 2022; Zawacki-Richter et al., 2019) as well as prevailing misconceptions and negative perceptions that hinder AI adoption (Cukurova et al., 2020). Schools often lack the technological infrastructure for AI integration (Zawacki-Richter et al., 2019), and unresolved ethical issues such as data privacy and algorithmic biases add to the complexity (Zhai et al., 2021). Furthermore, clear legal guidelines for the use of AI are lacking. In addition, some educators resist AI because they fear losing the personal interaction in teaching and losing their jobs (Buchanan et al., 2021; Chen et al., 2020).

However, teachers are crucial in driving technology adoption within educational settings (Polak et al., 2022). They are central to integrating AI tools into teaching, engaging students in discussions on AI, and adopting innovative AI-enabled pedagogical approaches (Aldosari, 2020; Mahligawati et al., 2023). Given the gap between the promising potential of AI and GenAI highlighted in research and their limited or uneven practical application in the classroom, it is essential to adopt a comprehensive approach to foster teachers' acceptance and integration of AI technologies.

Traditional Technology Acceptance Models

Teacher acceptance of technology is crucial for the successful adoption of devices, digital tools, and technologies. The understanding of this acceptance within educational settings has been shaped by models such as the Technology Acceptance Model (TAM) introduced by Davis (1989), and the Unified Theory of Acceptance and Use of Technology (UTAUT) developed by Venkatesh et al. (2003). These models, particularly TAM, which are widely adopted, focus on how individuals' perceptions of performance expectancy and effort expectancy drive their acceptance and adoption of technology (Granić & Marangunić, 2019; Scherer & Teo, 2019). UTAUT builds on TAM by adding social influence and facilitating conditions, highlighting the role of social and organizational factors in technology acceptance. This model also considers individual differences such as age, gender, and previous experience, which may influence intentions of technology use.

Empirical studies using technology acceptance models in educational settings commonly apply structural equation modelling to analyze survey data, exploring how various factors influence teachers' acceptance of technologies like learning management systems and mobile applications. Research in this area has typically focused on the general acceptance of information and communication technology (ICT) or AI-based products outside of educational contexts (Attuquayefio & Addo, 2014; Sohn & Kwon, 2020).

Recent AI Acceptance Models

Key dimensions such as transparency, trust and ethical use are often underemphasized in traditional adoption models, which are ill-equipped to address the pace and unpredictability of rapid AI developments. These models need updates to accommodate AI's continuous learning. (Cukurova et al., 2020; Sohn & Kwon, 2020).

In response, researchers have developed new models tailored to AI-adoption in education. For instance, the AI Device Use Acceptance model (AIDUA) by Gursoy et al. (2019) introduces a framework encompassing primary evaluation, secondary evaluation, and outcomes, recognizing the complex spectrum between acceptance and rejection. Other models, such as the General Attitudes towards AI Scale (GAAIS) by Schepman and Rodway (2022) and the enhanced UTAUT 2 (Gansser & Reich, 2021) address AI-specific challenges by emphasizing ethical considerations, personal sentiments, and individual fears.

These models acknowledge the importance of performance efficacy, hedonic motivation, and anthropomorphism in AI acceptance, highlighting the need for emotional and ethical considerations.

Towards a Common Understanding of Acceptance and Adoption

In the context of AI and GenAI acceptance or adoption, significant confusion often arises due to the interchangeable use of terms like behavioral intention, willingness to use, adoption intention, and attitude towards using. In this study, acceptance is defined as the readiness to embrace a technology, based on user attitudes, beliefs, and perceptions about its usefulness and ease of use, typically assessed through surveys, interviews, or observations. Adoption, on the other hand, refers to the actual uptake and utilization of a technology, focusing on how it is integrated into daily practices and its practical impact, monitored through usage metrics within an organization or user group.

Clear definitions of these terms are crucial for advancing research and enhancing decision-making in AI-integration in educational contexts. This study employs both terms to thoroughly investigate the complex dynamics between teachers and AI in education.

Study Purpose and Research Questions

The purpose of this study is to explore the integration of AI in educational settings, including both traditional AI and GenAI. This exploration recognizes that such integration entails significant changes in teaching, learning and assessment methodologies across technological, pedagogical, ethical and organizational dimensions (Jöhnk et al., 2021; Luan et al., 2020; Zawacki-Richter et al., 2019). While traditional technology acceptance models provide insights into conventional technology adoption, the unique characteristics of AI may require a re-evaluation or even a re-conceptualization of existing frameworks (Prieto et al., 2019). This study addresses these gaps through an exploratory, qualitative analysis of secondary school teachers' perspectives in Luxembourg.

This research is thus guided by four key questions:

1. What is the conceptual understanding of AI among secondary school teachers?
2. How do secondary school teachers perceive AI emotionally?
3. What is the perception of secondary school teachers about the role of AI in teaching and learning?
4. What are the perceived opportunities and challenges associated with the integration of AI in education?

Method

A qualitative approach using expert interviews was chosen to explore this under-researched phenomenon (Creswell & Creswell, 2018). Semi-structured interviews provided insights from experienced professionals, balancing structured themes with flexibility in responses (Helfferich, 2009). The interview guide was systematically developed by collecting, organizing and testing the relevance of potential questions. The interview guide covered teachers' understanding of AI, emotional perspectives, and the educational applications, opportunities, and challenges of AI (see Appendix 1).

Data Collection

Data collection involved conducting 29 semi-structured interviews with secondary school teachers in Luxembourg from August to October 2023. These interviews were conducted individually via the Teams online video conferencing platform, each lasting about 60 min. This method was chosen for its efficiency and ability to reach teachers across all Luxembourg regions, despite the challenges of building rapport in virtual settings (Saunders et al., 2016). Most of the interviews were conducted in German, but one was held in French and another in English, to meet the interviewees' language preferences and ensure their comfort and expressiveness. Informed consent was obtained before the interviews, addressing ethical concerns and data use.

Participants

The participants were carefully selected to reflect diverse backgrounds and perspectives on AI and GenAI in education (Tongco, 2007). The sample included 29 Luxembourg secondary school teachers from various disciplines (STEM, Languages, Humanities and Arts) and school types, exceeding the recommended sample size of 24 for thematic analysis (Ando et al., 2014). The selection of secondary school teachers was justified by their crucial role in integrating new technologies and shaping educational experiences (Nazaretsky et al., 2022). These teachers play a pivotal role during the critical transition stage, where students frequently engage with AI-driven tools (Chen & Zhu, 2023; Zhai et al., 2021). Efforts were made to balance gender, years of teaching experience, and the subjects taught (see Appendix 2).

Data Analysis

This study applied qualitative content-structuring content analysis (Kuckartz & Rädiker, 2019), which uses deductively and/or inductively formed categories. This approach allows for a detailed examination of the data and helps identify nuanced themes and patterns across the interviews.

The analysis process involved several key procedural tasks, outlined in Table 3.1.

Automated transcriptions from Teams were manually reviewed and translated into German as needed to ensure a consistent data corpus, adhering to established transcription rules and ensuring anonymity and accuracy (Dresing & Pehl, 2015).

After initial coding, a second rater independently reviewed 10% of the dataset to validate the coding system. Discrepancies were discussed and resolved before finalizing the codes for analysis (see Appendix 3).

MAXQDA, a qualitative data analysis tool, was used to extract meaningful insights, providing a range of analytical options and ensuring transparency

Table 3.1 Phases of thematic content analysis (Kuckartz & Rädiker, 2019)

Phase	Summary	Description
1	Initiatory case work	Transcribing data, (re)reading the data, noting down first memos and comments
2	Deductively developing main categories	Interview guideline as starting point for coding (deductive approach)
3	Coding data with main categories (1st coding process)	Assigning main categories to relevant text passages in the entire data set
4	Inductively forming subcategories	Reviewing comments and coded segments to refine and modify themes and subcategories, "try on" emerging themes through further coding of new or previously coded data (inductive approach)
5	Coding data with subcategories (second coding process)	Assigning main categories and subcodes to relevant text passages across the data set, continuously reviewing themes for internal consistency and external distinctiveness
6	Simple and complex analyses	Compiling and qualitatively analyzing text passages per (sub) category, determining frequencies, identifying patterns, visualizing data
7	Writing down results and documenting the procedure	Aggregating memos and comments into a report, documenting the category system, selecting exemplary text passages

throughout the process, including categories, notes, comments, analysis results, and interpretations.

Findings

What Is the Conceptual Understanding of AI Among Secondary School Teachers?

The interviewed teachers exhibit diverse understandings of AI and GenAI, ranging from viewing it as a basic data retrieval system to recognizing its wider implications for educational theory and practice.

- Simplistic perspective: Some teachers see AI as a simple data retrieval system, showing limited awareness of its capabilities. This view may restrict AI's integration as a transformative educational tool.

  ... *knowledge that comes from a computer*. (T21 [Teacher 21], Pos.9 [Note: Pos. stands for Position, which is the paragraph the citation is taken from])

- Utilitarian perspective: Many teachers see AI as a tool that improves instructional capabilities and administrative efficiency, valuing its potential to simplify tasks.

  AI simply makes the research process more efficient. (T19, Pos. 7)

- Reassurance perspective: Teachers emphasize human control over AI, expressing skepticism about its autonomous capabilities and reinforcing human authority in educational processes.

  In the end, it is not intelligence to me. (T28, Pos. 7)

- Emotional perspective: Concerns about AI's impact include fears of loss of control over learning processes and outcomes, with worries that reliance on AI could hinder student development.

  AI does all the work for students. This can hinder learning. (T10, Pos. 7)

- Technological perspective: Some teachers acknowledge AI's complex functionalities and its potential in education, seeing it as capable of autonomous actions and predictions.

  ... *all programs or algorithms that can perform actions independently*. (T8, Pos. 7).

Secondary school teachers' understanding of AI is reflected in their responses to a question about identifying different forms of AI, revealing a basic but limited comprehension of AI and GenAI applications in educational contexts. Teachers identified various forms of AI, such as GenAI exemplified by ChatGPT and DALL-E, but displaying limited engagement with broader functionalities. AI applications like Duolingo, Wolfram Alpha, Photomath, and plant recognition apps are noted for their direct applicability in teaching, while features in productivity software and automatic translation tools demonstrate an awareness of AI's utility in basic tasks.

In summary, the diverse perspectives underscore foundational AI comprehension and utilization, yet also reveal a gap in comprehensive knowledge and acceptance.

How Do Secondary School Teachers Perceive AI Emotionally?

The interviewees display a wide range of emotional responses to AI and GenAI in educational settings, revealing a complex interplay of anticipation, apprehension, and pragmatism.

- Neutral and balanced perspectives: Most teachers maintain a balanced view, recognizing AI's potential benefits and challenges. Some feel overwhelmed yet open to new technologies, while expressing concerns about data privacy and impacts on traditional educational practices.

  Today, unfortunately, AI is only used to cheat, but I am convinced that AI can be used sensibly in the future. (T27, Pos. 19)

- Negative emotions and concerns: A subset of educators expresses significant concerns about the disruptive potential and misuse of AI, often influenced by negative media portrayals. They fear loss of control and question the transparency of AI technologies.

  Without rules, we will be in total chaos in a few years, and nobody will be able to control the whole thing. (T24, Pos. 23)

- Positive emotions and enthusiasm: Conversely, some teachers show enthusiasm for AI's transformative potential, associating technological evolution with opportunities for educational advancements currently unachievable.

  I am very open and enthusiastic. I really look forward to all the radical changes it will bring. (T3, Pos. 21).

Emotional responses vary by subject, with arts and humanities teachers often more neutral or positive, while STEM teachers show a wider range of emotions. Language teachers generally show cautious or neutral feelings, probably due to concerns about the impact of AI on language authenticity. No differences were found in terms of gender or years of experience.

The bar graph below visualizes sentiment trends across teacher groups. The x-axis represents sentiment categories, ranging from positive to negative, while the y-axis represents sentiment frequencies, defined as the total number of times each sentiment was expressed across the interviews across different topics (e.g., current and future roles of AI). Within each sentiment category, grouped bars represent the

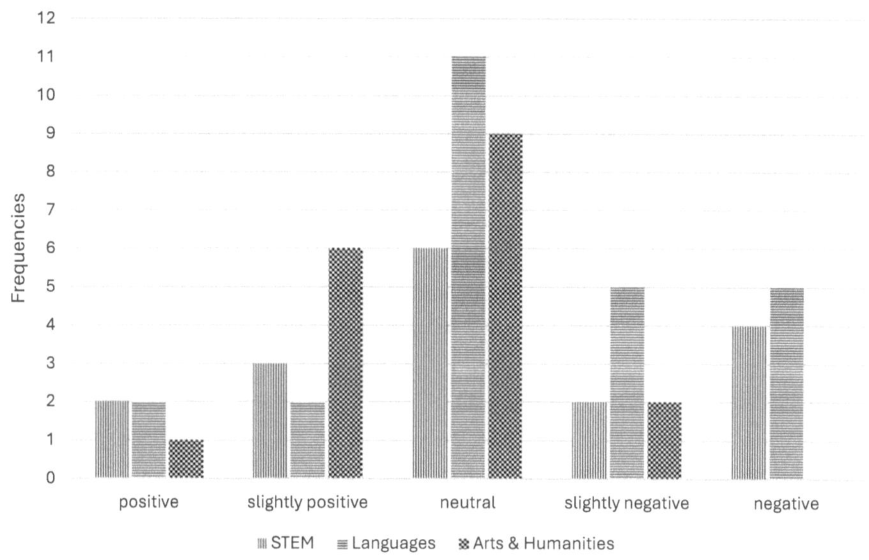

Fig. 3.1 Emotional stands towards AI (by subject groups)

three groups of teachers: STEM, Languages, and Arts and Humanities. The height of each bar indicates how often that sentiment was expressed by each group (Fig. 3.1).

In conclusion, the emotional landscape of AI and GenAI in education among the interviewed teachers ranges from cautious optimism to deep concern. The findings underscore the importance of customized approaches when implementing AI technologies in different academic disciplines.

What Is the Perception of Secondary School Teachers About the Role of AI in Teaching and Learning?

Interviewees expressed diverse perceptions of the current and future role of AI and GenAI in education, shaped by subject-specific expectations.

- Perceptions of AI's current role: Teachers' views of AI in education range from seeing it as transformative to seeing it as marginal. However, most consider AI's presence as minor but inevitable and recognize its evolving role.

  AI is a development that we cannot simply lock out in the sense of custodial pedagogy. (T19, Pos. 49)

- Predictions for AI's future role: Most teachers expect AI's influence to grow significantly within 5 years, with some comparing its impact to the Internet, while others remain skeptical, citing political constraints.

The Internet has changed schools, but AI will change schools more in 5 years than the Internet has changed it in the last 20 years. (T18, Pos. 21)

Perceptions of AI's current and future roles differ across subject areas. STEM and language teachers generally view AI's current role as limited, while arts and humanities teachers recognize a significant presence. Regarding future expectations, STEM teachers are more cautious, whereas arts, humanities, and language teachers are optimistic about AI's transformative potential. No disparities were detected based on gender or years of professional tenure.

In summary, teachers' views on AI's and GenAI's role in education vary widely, highlighting the gap between current perceptions and its anticipated transformative potential.

What Are the Perceived Opportunities and Challenges Associated with the Integration of AI in Education, According to Secondary School Teachers?

Perceived Challenges

The interviewed teachers have identified five primary challenges in integrating AI and GenAI into educational settings, ranging from ethical concerns to practical classroom impediments.

- Ethical and legal concerns: Teachers express concerns about data privacy and potential bias, underscoring the need for clear guidelines and responsible handling of student data.

  The integration of AI in education raises concerns about data protection and algorithms. (T5, Pos. 13)

- Demand for structural change: Educators call for updated curricula and evaluation formats, seeking direction from educational authorities. Opinions are divided on whether mandatory AI use would encourage or inhibit acceptance.

  The Ministry of Education must provide precise guidelines. What can you do, what are you allowed to do? (T27, Pos. 77)

- Skill-related concerns: There is a focus on avoiding deskilling while fostering digital literacy and critical thinking. Teachers worry that excessive reliance on AI might diminish student independent learning and fundamental academic skills.

  The habit of transferring everything to AI leads to less independent thinking and acting. (T8, Pos. 33)

- Teacher-related challenges: Resistance to change, fear of increased workload, and lack of digital skills are major concerns. Educators express concerns about maintaining control and competence in the digital realm.

The willingness to change is very low, tied to a traditional mindset. (T14, Pos. 48)

- Technological challenges: Inadequate infrastructure and the opaque nature of AI systems hinder integration, highlighting the need for user-friendly tools and robust support.

  Simple and intuitive use is important. (T16, Pos. 49)

Perceived Opportunities

The interviewees recognize several opportunities from integrating AI and GenAI in education, categorized into four distinct clusters.

- Fostering critical thinking: Using AI encourages students and teachers to critically engage with technology, improving their ability to examine and understand its functions and implications.

  Using AI consciously forces you to scrutinize things more critically, promoting critical thinking skills. (T13, Pos. 27)

- Efficiency and work simplification: AI is seen as a tool to streamline educational processes, automate routine tasks, and reduce workloads, allowing teachers and students to focus on more complex goals.

  It should improve my efficiency and that of my students. (T15, Pos. 31)

- Individualized learning: AI facilitates personalized learning experiences by offering tailored support and adaptive learning pathways that address various learning styles and paces.

  AI brings new possibilities for individualizing materials and differentiation that we did not have before. (T11, Pos. 47).

- Enhancing teaching and learning experiences: AI integration is expected to elevate teaching and learning, shifting focus towards more applied and practical lessons, and allowing teachers to better facilitate and interact with students.

  Teaching will change with AI, focusing much more on application and practice rather than pure theory. (T7, Pos. 17).

The perception of AI's opportunities in education remains consistent across different academic disciplines, with STEM teachers often showing greater enthusiasm for the advanced teaching and learning experiences AI can facilitate.

Teachers face multiple challenges in integrating AI and GenAI, including ethical concerns, resistance to change, and limited digital literacy, underscoring the need for clear guidance and institutional support. At the same time, they see opportunities for AI to enhance critical thinking, streamline tasks, and personalize learning, suggesting significant potential to transform educational practices.

Discussion

The present study reveals that secondary school teachers hold diverse perspectives on AI and GenAI, highlighting the need for a multi-dimensional approach to understanding their acceptance and adoption. Factors such as personal beliefs, digital literacy, pedagogical considerations, social influences, and institutional environments significantly shape teachers' attitudes toward AI, emphasizing the need for varied integration strategies (Wang et al., 2023).

There is a notable contrast between the current use of AI in education and its potential transformative impact, akin to changes brought by the internet. Bridging the gap requires addressing knowledge, perceptions, pedagogy, skills, organizational support, and ethical considerations through frameworks, training, awareness campaigns, and curriculum adjustments. Subject-specific variations further underscore the necessity for discipline-specific strategies to ensure effective AI integration.

The following graphic illustrates the key findings and structures the discussion section, providing a visual summary of the complex landscape of AI integration in education (Fig. 3.2).

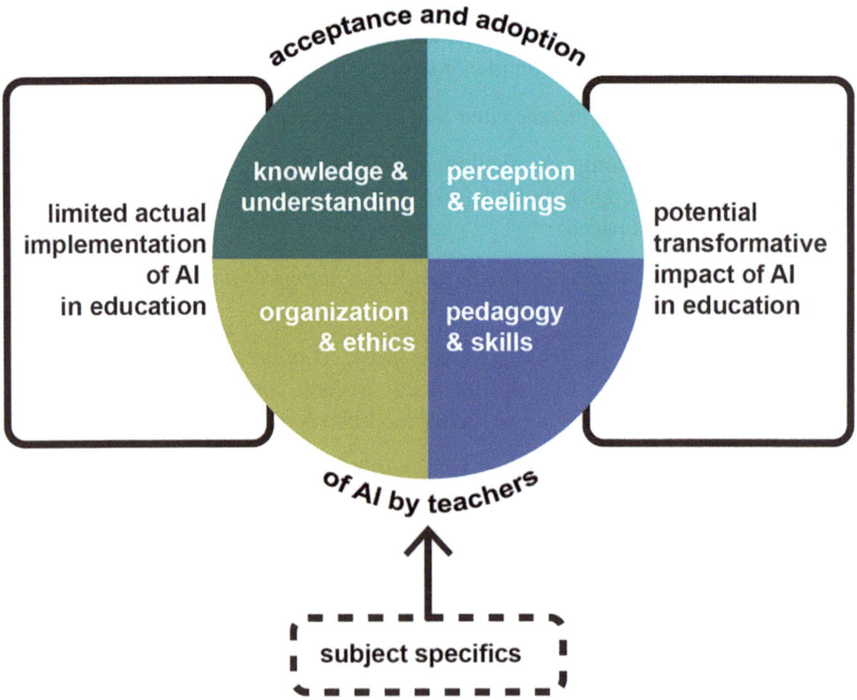

Fig. 3.2 Model of the implementation gap of AI in education

Limited Actual Implementation Versus Potential Transformative Impact

The present findings indicate that the integration of AI in educational settings is more aspirational than operational (Karan & Angadi, 2023). Educators are often reluctant due to a lack of organizational support and their mixed feelings about AI, including resistance to pedagogical transformations and a lack of understanding (Akgün & Greenhow, 2021).

In contrast, AI has great potential to bring about systemic change in education, from personalizing learning experiences to streamlining administrative tasks. It is anticipated to shift pedagogical roles towards facilitation, thus empowering students with tailored learning paths (Lameras & Arnab, 2021).

Addressing this gap requires thorough research into barriers that hinder AI acceptance and adoption (Schiff, 2020). Strategic planning and investment in professional development are crucial to prepare teachers for AI integration. In addition, collaborative efforts are needed to develop ethical and legal frameworks to guide the implementation process (Zawacki-Richter et al., 2019).

Teachers' Knowledge and Understanding of AI

The present study reveals that educators have a basic yet limited understanding of AI and GenAI, consistent with previous research (Ayanwale et al., 2022). Although they recognize AI's potential, educators struggle with its practical applications due to a shallow knowledge base. They often focus more on discussing AI's opportunities and challenges than on its definitions, emphasizing practical implications over theoretical foundations (Weidener & Fischer, 2023). The lack of consensus on AI's benefits and risks further complicates its integration into educational systems (Buchanan et al., 2021; Mello et al., 2023).

The findings highlight the need to improve teachers' understanding of AI for more informed discussions, given the careful consideration required for its use in education. Professional development should focus on both technical and ethical aspects, while roles such as AI ambassadors can facilitate integration. Future research should clarify AI applications and ethics.

Teachers' Feelings and Perception of AI

The study reveals educators' mixed feelings about AI and GenAI, ranging from optimism to apprehension. Concerns about loss of control—due to technological gaps, the opacity of AI, fears of plagiarism and threats to employment—are fueled by traditional attitudes (Piderit, 2000; Zimmerman, 2006). Yet teachers see their role as irreplaceable because of the relational and empathetic aspects of teaching (Karan & Angadi, 2023).

These emotional responses are not isolated, but symptomatic of deeper concerns that cut across pedagogical, ethical and institutional dimensions. One of the most significant—yet often underexplored—findings of this study is the nuanced emotional response associated with a perceived loss of pedagogical control. While previous research has acknowledged concerns around AI autonomy, student data, and role redefinition (e.g., Lawrence et al., 2023; Nazaretsky et al., 2022), this study adds new insights by unpacking how these concerns vary across disciplines and are intensified in a more centralized innovation environment. Rather than treating control as a binary variable of acceptance or rejection, the present findings show how it is experienced as a spectrum of emotional responses—from cautious optimism to professional vulnerability—shaped by both institutional pressures and discipline-specific epistemologies.

Future research should explore frameworks such as the Academic Resistance Model (ARM) to understand the dynamics of non-acceptance (Rienties, 2014) and support comprehensive AI training and national policies that promote balanced perceptions through awareness campaigns and sensitivity training (Buchanan et al., 2021; Popenici & Kerr, 2017).

Pedagogical and Skill-Related Implications of AI in Education

The present study underscores the essential relationship between learning with AI and about AI: A comprehensive understanding of AI is necessary to effectively utilize it in education (Holmes et al., 2021). Educators emphasize the importance of equipping students with robust critical thinking skills, fact-checking abilities, and foundational knowledge of AI technologies (Long & Magerko, 2020; Spector & Ma, 2019), as well as essential literacy skills (Leander & Burriss, 2020).

Critical thinking is essential in an AI-enhanced education, which presents both opportunities and challenges (Ciampa et al., 2023). Key issues include developing AI tools that encourage critical thinking without limiting creativity, and ensuring that teachers and students have the digital skills to use these tools effectively (Dergaa et al., 2023).

Research should investigate how AI can be effectively integrated into the curriculum, assessing its impact on learning outcomes and interaction with various pedagogical strategies (Mahligawati et al., 2023; Touretzky et al., 2019). Practically, structured professional development programs that emphasize critical thinking and ethical considerations are crucial (Aiken & Epstein, 2000).

Organizational Influence and Ethical Guidance

The interviewees emphasize the need for governmental and organizational guidance on AI and GenAI in education, highlighting a significant gap in current frameworks. Strategic policy initiatives are essential to leverage AI's benefits while mitigating its risks (Baker & Smith, 2019). Comprehensive policies should establish clear ethical guidelines, adjust curricula, and implement safeguards in evaluation processes to ensure a balanced introduction of AI into educational settings (Aiken & Epstein, 2000; Kaplan-Rakowski et al., 2023). These strategies must address educators' diverse needs, enhancing digital, AI, and data literacy, as well as ethical competence.

Opinions are divided on whether political measures, such as mandatory AI integration into curricula or specific legislative guidance, would promote or hinder AI acceptance among teachers (Çelik et al., 2022; Chounta et al., 2021).

The implementation of AI in education requires collaboration between researchers and practitioners. Academically, there is a need to assess the effectiveness of AI integration strategies and their impact on educational outcomes (Jöhnk et al., 2021; Luckin et al., 2022). Practically, it is crucial to develop clear, adaptable guidelines that support informed AI use and provide a reliable framework for educators as AI technologies evolve. These guidelines should be developed with educators' input to ensure they address real classroom needs (Chen et al., 2020).

Subject Specifics to Influence Teachers' AI Acceptance and Adoption

This study found that neither job experience nor gender significantly influenced teachers' attitudes or acceptance of AI, aligning with prior research showing inconsistent gender effects in pre-service teachers' technology acceptance (Teo et al., 2015). On the other hand, the subject area seems to significantly shape educators' perceptions and emotional responses to AI.

This disciplinary divergence is not only underexplored in current research, but also provides an innovative lens through which to understand AI acceptance. While most studies treat teachers as a homogeneous group, this study reveals how disciplinary epistemologies influence how educators engage emotionally and conceptually with AI. Humanities teachers, whose fields often value interpretation, creativity, and critical dialogue, tended to view GenAI as a productive addition. STEM teachers, on the other hand, expressed concerns rooted in technical complexity and a heightened awareness of ethical and epistemic limitations. Language teachers, situated between these poles, navigated both practical affordances and threats to authenticity.

Future research should explore effective AI integration across different teaching disciplines, aiming to understand the unique demands and opportunities within each field. This could lead to the development of more targeted AI tools and teaching strategies that align with discipline-specific educational goals.

Educational initiatives should prioritize developing subject-specific training programs and support mechanisms for AI integration. These programs should enhance teachers' confidence in AI in education while addressing the unique pedagogical needs and challenges in each field.

Contributions, Limitations and Future Directions

Taken together, the findings not only confirm known challenges, but also offer new angles for interpreting how GenAI is experienced and negotiated in real classrooms. While building on established models of technology acceptance, this study contributes several underexplored perspectives to the emerging field of GenAI in education. In particular, it foregrounds the psychological dimension of teachers' responses—particularly their perceived loss of control—as a barrier to meaningful adoption. In contrast to many existing studies that emphasize general attitudes or readiness, this research places particular emphasis on emotional responses and how they vary across subject areas. The nuanced differences observed—STEM teachers' apprehension, Language teachers' concern for authenticity, and Arts teachers' openness—suggest that disciplinary epistemologies significantly mediate how GenAI is perceived. This level of granularity is often lacking in broader survey research, which tends to treat teachers as a homogeneous group. Furthermore, by situating these findings within Luxembourg‘s centralized, multilingual education system, the study adds empirical depth to a field still largely dominated by Anglophone, decentralized contexts. Together, these features provide a distinctive lens on GenAI integration, extending current research with its emphasis on emotional responses, disciplinary identity, and the systemic conditions necessary for effective and ethical implementation.

While these contributions provide valuable insights into the emotional and contextual dimensions of GenAI integration, they must be interpreted in light of certain methodological limitations.

This study has two primary limitations that pave the way for future research endeavors. First, its focus on in-service secondary school teachers within a specific national context limits the generalizability of the findings (Venkatesh et al., 2016). The small sample size restricts the applicability of these conclusions to a broader population of teachers across different school types, grades, and national contexts, necessitating caution when extrapolating these results.

Second, the study's broad approach, covering the affective, cognitive, and perceptual aspects of teachers' interactions with AI and GenAI, may have limited the depth of analysis in each area. A more focused investigation of these facets could provide deeper insights into teachers' engagement with AI technologies (Granić & Marangunić, 2019; Scherer & Teo, 2019).

Future research should aim to include a larger and more diverse cohort of teachers to enhance the robustness and applicability of the findings. Exploring different educational levels and school contexts would offer a broader understanding of AI's perception and implementation across the educational spectrum. In addition, future research should employ structured methodologies—both quantitative and qualitative—to confirm or refine these findings. A clear distinction between constructs such as adoption, acceptance, perceptions, and attitudes toward AI will also improve conceptual precision and contribute to greater coherence in the field (Bawack & Desveaud, 2022).

The significant role of subject-specific variables observed suggests that further research could benefit from exploring how AI is integrated and perceived across various academic disciplines.

By addressing these limitations and exploring these suggested directions, subsequent studies can build on the foundational knowledge of this study.

Contextual Considerations in Relation to Transferability

This study was conducted in the Luxembourg secondary school system, a multilingual, centrally managed educational context characterized by significant technological investment and relatively high digital readiness. The trilingual environment (Luxembourgish, French and German) and the small but diverse school landscape shape how educators perceive and respond to the rapid emergence and spread of generative AI. The rather centralized nature of the educational landscape enables rapid top-down implementation of innovation, but may also concentrate the pressure to adapt, contributing to a widespread perception among teachers of a loss of pedagogical control. Compared to more decentralized systems, such as those of the United States or Germany, where regional differences in policy and infrastructure can buffer or fragment AI integration, the Luxembourg model seems to amplify both opportunities and fears. Subject-specific patterns observed here, such as the cautious pragmatism of STEM teachers versus the openness of humanities teachers, may also play out differently in contexts with different curricular cultures or levels of digital maturity. While the chapter's findings—especially the call for ethical guidance, development of critical thinking, and targeted professional support—are likely to resonate internationally, the transferability of findings related to emotional responses and perceived digital literacy gaps should be considered within the structural, cultural, and policy environments of each context. These dynamics highlight the importance of international comparative research to better understand how systemic, cultural and institutional differences mediate educators' engagement with GenAI.

Conclusion

This study reveals a profound gap between the aspirational goals of implementing AI and GenAI in education and current realities. This gap affects the acceptance of AI among educators and calls for a thorough re-evaluation of models, strategies, and policies to ensure more effective integration of AI in classrooms. While this paper focuses on the factors influencing its acceptance and adoption in educational settings, it is important to consider whether and to what extent the acceptance of AI is desirable. The rapid development of AI raises questions about its long-term impact on critical thinking, creativity, and the teacher-student relationship. As educators navigate these changes, careful consideration must be given to promoting AI in ways that enhance, rather than replace, essential pedagogical practices.

The findings highlight significant issues: teachers often feel a loss of control due to the opaque nature of AI systems, the rapid pace of technological change, and sometimes, their students' superior digital competencies. This perceived loss of control is both a technical and psychological challenge, affecting teachers' willingness and ability to integrate AI into their teaching. Addressing this requires training and support structures that boost teachers' confidence in using AI tools and discussing AI issues in class.

Critical thinking is emphasized as essential in an AI-driven educational landscape, vital for both students and teachers to navigate and critique AI's role and impact in the classroom. Integrating critical thinking into teacher training programs can empower educators to use AI judiciously, enhancing learning outcomes without compromising educational integrity.

Moreover, there is a clear need for ethical and legal guidance as AI technologies evolve. Developing clear ethical guidelines and robust legal frameworks is crucial to ensure responsible use of AI in education. These guidelines should address privacy, data security, and potential biases, ensuring fairness and transparency.

Teachers' acceptance of AI is also significantly influenced by its portrayal in the media, which shapes their emotional and conceptual understanding of technology. Furthermore, subject-specific needs play a crucial role in AI acceptance. Different disciplines may require customized approaches to AI integration, reflecting their unique pedagogical needs.

The complexities identified in this research underscore the need for structured teacher training and robust organizational support to facilitate seamless and ethical integration of AI in educational practices. Traditional technology acceptance models should be reviewed, and qualitative approaches must be encouraged to capture the nuanced factors at play in the acceptance and adoption of AI by teachers. Furthermore, this study advocates for a multi-pronged approach to address these challenges, aiming to equip teachers with the necessary confidence and ensuring that they actively participate in shaping AI integration in education.

Acknowledgements We would like to express our sincere gratitude to the teachers who generously contributed their time and insights to the interviews, enriching our understanding of AI and GenAI in education through their perspectives and experiences. Their voluntary participation was instrumental to this research.

Competing Interests The authors have no conflicts of interest to declare that are relevant to the content of this chapter.

Ethics Approval This study was conducted in accordance with the principles of the Declaration of Helsinki. Ethical approval for the qualitative research was granted by the Ethics Review Panel of the University of Luxembourg (10 July 2023/No. ERP 23-054). Informed consent was obtained from all participants prior to their involvement in the study to ensure their voluntary participation and consent for the use of their data.

Appendices

Appendix 1

Semi-structured interview guideline

Topics	Questions
Definition and understanding of AI	What is AI in education to you? How would you define AI in education?
Forms of AI in education	How would you organize, or structure AI used in education?
Actual role of AI in education	Which role does AI play in education these days? How would you rate AI's impact on education?
Future role of AI in education	Which role will AI play in education in the near future (5 years)? How would you rate AI's future impact on education?
Emotion	How do you feel about the use of AI in education?
Challenges and opportunities	Which are the reasons of (not) using AI in education in your eyes? Which opportunities (challenges) does AI present?
Accelerators and barriers	Which factors stimulate or foster (hinder) teachers' acceptance of AI in education?
Boundary conditions	What would prompt teachers to use AI in education?

Appendix 2

Interview participants

Code	Gender	Professional experience	Subject area	Type of school
T1	Male	23,00	Languages	ESC[a]
T2	Male	10,00	Arts and humanities	ESG[b]
T3	Male	15,00	Arts and humanities	ESG
T4	Male	12,00	STEM	ESC
T5	Male	2,00	STEM	ESG
T6	Female	6,00	Arts and humanities	ESC
T7	Male	7,00	STEM	ESG
T8	Female	15,00	Languages	ESC
T9	Male	16,00	Languages	ESC
T10	Female	19,00	Languages	International School
T11	Female	15,00	Languages	ESG
T12	Female	12,00	Languages	ESG
T13	Female	10,00	Arts and humanities	ESG
T14	Female	25,00	Languages	ESC
T15	Female	29,00	Arts and humanities	ESG
T16	Female	14,00	Languages	ESG
T17	Female	19,00	Languages	Adult Education
T18	Male	20,00	Languages	ESC
T19	Male	8,00	Arts and humanities	ESG
T20	Male	7,00	STEM	International School
T21	Male	31,00	Arts and humanities	ESC
T22	Female	7,00	Arts and humanities	ESG
T23	Female	13,00	STEM	ESG
T24	Male	8,00	STEM	ESG
T25	Male	8,00	Languages	ESG
T26	Female	4,00	STEM	ESG
T27	Female	22,00	STEM	ESC
T28	Female	12,00	Languages	ESC
T29	Female	22,00	STEM	ESC

[a]Enseignement secondaire classique [Classical secondary education]
[b]Enseignement secondaire général [General secondary education]

Appendix 3

Final code system

Code system
Boundary conditions
Technical infrastructure
Ministerial decision and structural support
Teacher professional development and support structure
Barriers of teachers' AI acceptance
Reactance of teachers
Lack of transparency
Lack of control
De-skilling and dependancy of AI
Ethical and legal concerns
Need for technical and support structure
Need for structural change
Accelerators of teachers' AI acceptance
Openness and innovative mindset
User-friendly technology
Work simplification
Information, sensibilization and training
Support structures and guidelines
Opportunities of AI in education
Sensibilization of students
Time saving and work simplification
Individualized support
New learning experiences
Motivation of pupils
Fast and easy access to knowledge
Inclusion and equal opportunities
Challenges of AI in education
Challenges of AI
Need for structural change and guidance
Ethical and legal concerns
De-skilling and dependency on AI
Need for technical infrastructure
Need for new skill sets
Reactance of teachers
Lack of control
Ensuring basic skills
Lack of technical skills of teachers
Negative image of AI in press and society
Lack of transparency
Loss of humanity
Societal divide

User-friendly AI
Replacement of teachers
Emotion towards AI in education
Emotion
Positive
Slightly positive
Neutral
Slightly negative
Negative
Role of AI in education
Future role of AI in education
No to little role
(Too) big or bigger role
Actual role of AI in education
(Too) big role
Can't ignore it
No to little role
Forms of AI in education
GenAI
GenAI text
GenAI music and music recognition
GenAI pictures
GenAI presentations and films
Specific AI-featured apps and software
Recognition apps
Language learning apps
Research
Green-screen app
Maths apps
Auto-correction and other assistive technologies
Automatic translation
Tools to learn about AI
Plagiarism checker
Definition and understanding of AI

References

Aiken, R. M., & Epstein, R. G. (2000). Ethical guidelines for AI in education: Starting a conversation. *International Journal of Artificial Intelligence in Education, 11*, 163–176.

Akgün, S., & Greenhow, C. (2021). Artificial intelligence in education: Addressing ethical challenges in K-12 settings. *AI and Ethics, 2*(3), 431–440. https://doi.org/10.1007/s43681-021-00096-7

Aldosari, S. A. M. (2020). The future of higher education in the light of artificial intelligence transformations. *International Journal of Higher Education, 9*(3), 145–151. https://doi.org/10.5430/ijhe.v9n3p145

Ando, H., Cousins, R., & Young, C. (2014). Achieving saturation in thematic analysis: Development and refinement of a codebook. *Comprehensive Psychology, 3*(4). https://doi.org/10.2466/03.cp.3.4

Attuquayefio, S. N., & Addo, H. (2014). Using the UTAUT model to analyse students' ICT adoption. *International Journal of Education and Development using Information and Communication Technology (IJEDICT), 10*(3), 75–86.

Ayanwale, M. A., Sanusi, I. T., Adelana, O. P., Aruleba, K., & Oyelere, S. S. (2022). Teachers' readiness and intention to teach artificial intelligence in schools. *Computers and Education: Artificial Intelligence, 3*, 100099. https://doi.org/10.1016/j.caeai.2022.100099

Baker, T., & Smith, L. (2019). *Educ-AI-tion rebooted? Exploring the future of artificial intelligence in schools and colleges*. Nesta. Retrieved from https://www.nesta.org.uk/report/education-rebooted/

Bawack, R., & Desveaud, K. (2022). Consumer adoption of artificial intelligence: A review of theories and antecedents. In *HICSS: Proceedings of the 55th Hawaii international conference on system sciences* (pp. 4306–4315). https://doi.org/10.24251/HICSS.2022.526

Buchanan, C., Howitt, M. L., Wilson, R., Booth, R., Risling, T., & Bamford, M. (2021). Predicted influences of artificial intelligence on nursing education: Scoping review. *JMIR Nursing, 4*(1), e23933. https://doi.org/10.2196/23933

Çelik, İ., Dindar, M., Muukkonen, H., & Järvelä, S. (2022). The promises and challenges of artificial intelligence for teachers: A systematic review of research. *TechTrends, 66*(4), 616–630. https://doi.org/10.1007/s11528-022-00715-y

Chen, B., & Zhu, X. (2023). Integrating generative AI in knowledge building. *Computers and education. Artificial Intelligence, 5*, 100184. https://doi.org/10.1016/j.caeai.2023.100184

Chen, L., Chen, P., & Lin, Z. (2020). Artificial intelligence in education: A review. *IEEE Access, 8*, 75264–75278. https://doi.org/10.1109/access.2020.2988510

Chiu, T. K. F., & Chai, C. S. (2020). Sustainable curriculum planning for artificial intelligence education: A self-determination theory perspective. *Sustainability, 12*(14), 5568. https://doi.org/10.3390/su12145568

Choi, S., Jang, Y., & Kim, H. (2022). Influence of pedagogical beliefs and perceived trust on teachers' acceptance of educational artificial intelligence tools. *International Journal of Human-Computer Interaction, 39*(4), 910–922. https://doi.org/10.1080/10447318.2022.2049145

Chounta, I., Bardone, E., Raudsep, A., & Pedaste, M. (2021). Exploring teachers' perceptions of artificial intelligence as a tool to support their practice in Estonian K-12 education. *International Journal of Artificial Intelligence in Education, 32*(3), 725–755. https://doi.org/10.1007/s40593-021-00243-5

Ciampa, K., Wolfe, Z. M., & Bronstein, B. (2023). ChatGPT in education: Transforming digital literacy practices. *Journal of Adolescent & Adult Literacy, 67*(3), 186–195. https://doi.org/10.1002/jaal.1310

Creswell, J. W., & Creswell, J. D. (2018). *Research design: Qualitative, quantitative, and mixed methods approaches*. SAGE Publications.

Cukurova, M., Giannakos, M. N., & Martínez-Maldonado, R. (2020). The promise and challenges of multimodal learning analytics. *British Journal of Educational Technology, 51*(5), 1441–1449. https://doi.org/10.1111/bjet.13015

Davis, F. D. (1989). Perceived usefulness, perceived ease of use, and user acceptance of information technology. *Management Information Systems Quarterly, 13*(3), 319–340. https://doi.org/10.2307/249008

Dergaa, I., Chamari, K., Żmijewski, P., & Saad, H. B. (2023). From human writing to artificial intelligence generated text: Examining the prospects and potential threats of ChatGPT in academic writing. *Biology of Sport, 40*(2), 615–622. https://doi.org/10.5114/biolsport.2023.125623

Doroudi, S. (2022). The intertwined histories of artificial intelligence and education. *International Journal of Artificial Intelligence in Education, 33*(4), 885–928. https://doi.org/10.1007/s40593-022-00313-2

Dresing, T., & Pehl, T. (2015). Praxisbuch nterview, Transkription & Analyse: Anleitungen und Regelsysteme für qualitativ Forschende. Retrieved from www.audiotranskription.de/praxisbuch

Gansser, O., & Reich, C. (2021). A new acceptance model for artificial intelligence with extensions to UTAUT2: An empirical study in three segments of application. *Technology in Society, 65*, 101535. https://doi.org/10.1016/j.techsoc.2021.101535

Granić, A., & Marangunić, N. (2019). Technology acceptance model in educational context: A systematic literature review. *British Journal of Educational Technology, 50*(5), 2572–2593. https://doi.org/10.1111/bjet.12864

Gupta, K. P., & Bhaskar, P. (2020). Inhibiting and motivating factors influencing teachers' adoption of ai-based teaching and learning solutions: Prioritization using analytic hierarchy process. *Journal of Information Technology Education, 19*, 693–723. https://doi.org/10.28945/4640

Gursoy, D., Hengxuan, O., Lu, L., & Nunkoo, R. (2019). Consumers acceptance of artificially intelligent (AI) device use in service delivery. *International Journal of Information Management, 49*, 157–169. https://doi.org/10.1016/j.ijinfomgt.2019.03.008

Helfferich, C. (2009). Interviewplanung und Intervieworganisation. In *Die Qualität qualitativer Daten* (pp. 167–193). VS Verlag für Sozialwissenschaften. https://doi.org/10.1007/978-3-531-91858-7_6

Holmes, W., Bialik, M., & Fadel, C. (2019). *Artificial intelligence in education: Promises and implications for teaching and learning*. Center for Curriculum Redesign.

Holmes, W., Porayska-Pomsta, K., Holstein, K., Sutherland, E., Baker, T. T., Shum, S. B., Santos, O. C., Rodrigo, M. M. T., Cukurova, M., Bittencourt, I. I., & Koedinger, K. R. (2021). Ethics of AI in education: Towards a community-wide framework. *International Journal of Artificial Intelligence in Education, 32*(3), 504–526. https://doi.org/10.1007/s40593-021-00239-1

Johal, W., Castellano, G., Tanaka, F., & Okita, S. Y. (2018). Robots for learning. *International Journal of Social Robotics, 10*(3), 293–294. https://doi.org/10.1007/s12369-018-0481-8

Jöhnk, J., Weißert, M., & Wyrtki, K. (2021). Ready or not, AI comes— An interview study of organizational AI readiness factors. *Business & Information Systems Engineering, 63*(1), 5–20. https://doi.org/10.1007/s12599-020-00676-7

Kaplan-Rakowski, R., Grotewold, K. S., Hartwick, P., & Papin, K. (2023). Generative AI and teachers' perspectives on its implementation in education. *Journal of Interactive Learning Research, 34*(2), 313–338. https://www.researchgate.net/publication/373821343

Karan, B., & Angadi, G. R. (2023). Potential risks of artificial intelligence integration into school education: A systematic review. *Bulletin of Science, Technology & Society, 43*(3–4), 67–85. https://doi.org/10.1177/02704676231224705

Kuckartz, U., & Rädiker, S. (2019). *Analyzing qualitative data with MAXQDA*. Springer. https://doi.org/10.1007/978-3-030-15671-8

Lameras, P., & Arnab, S. (2021). Power to the teachers: An exploratory review on artificial intelligence in education. *Information, 13*(1), 14. https://doi.org/10.3390/info13010014

Lawrence, L., Echeverria, V., Yang, K., Aleven, V., & Rummel, N. (2023). How teachers conceptualise shared control with an AI co-orchestration tool: A multiyear teacher-centred design process. *British Journal of Educational Technology, 54*(5), 1210–1228. https://doi.org/10.1111/bjet.13372

Leander, K. M., & Burriss, S. K. (2020). Critical literacy for a posthuman world: When people read, and become, with machines. *British Journal of Educational Technology, 51*(4), 1262–1276. https://doi.org/10.1111/bjet.12924

Long, D., & Magerko, B. (2020). What is AI literacy? Competencies and design considerations. In *Conference on Human Factors in Computing Systems—Proceedings*. https://doi.org/10.1145/3313831.3376727

Luan, H., Géczy, P., Lai, H., Gobert, J. D., Yang, S. J., Ogata, H., Baltes, J., Da Silva Guerra, R., Li, P., & Tsai, C. C. (2020). Challenges and future directions of big data and artificial intelligence in education. *Frontiers in Psychology, 11*, 580820. https://doi.org/10.3389/fpsyg.2020.580820

Luckin, R., Cukurova, M., Kent, C., & Du Boulay, B. (2022). Empowering educators to be AI-ready. *Computers and Education: Artificial Intelligence, 3*, 100076. https://doi.org/10.1016/j.caeai.2022.100076

Mahligawati, F., Allanas, E., Butar-Butar, M. H., & Nordin, N. A. (2023). Artificial intelligence in physics education: A comprehensive literature review. *Journal of Physics: Conference Series, 2596*, 012080. https://doi.org/10.1088/1742-6596/2596/1/012080

Mello, R. F., Freitas, E. L. S. X., Pereira, F. D., Cabral, L., Tedesco, P., & Ramalho, G. (2023). Education in the age of generative AI: Context and recent developments. *arXiv* (Cornell University). https://doi.org/10.48550/arxiv.2309.12332

Miao, F., & Holmes, W. (2021). *Artificial intelligence and education. Guidance for policy-makers*. United Nations Educational, Scientific and Cultural Organization (UNESCO).

Nazaretsky, T., Ariely, M., Cukurova, M., & Alexandron, G. (2022). Teachers' trust in AI-powered educational technology and a professional development program to improve it. *British Journal of Educational Technology, 53*(4), 914–931. https://doi.org/10.1111/bjet.13232

Piderit, S. K. (2000). Rethinking resistance and recognizing ambivalence: A multidimensional view of attitudes toward an organizational change. *The Academy of Management Review, 25*(4), 783–794. https://doi.org/10.5465/amr.2000.3707722

Polak, S., Schiavo, G., & Zancanaro, M. (2022). Teachers' perspective on artificial intelligence education: An initial investigation. In *CHI Conference on Human Factors in Computing Systems Extended Abstracts*. https://doi.org/10.1145/3491101.3519866

Popenici, S., & Kerr, S. (2017). Exploring the impact of artificial intelligence on teaching and learning in higher education. *Research and Practice in Technology Enhanced Learning, 12*, 22. https://doi.org/10.1186/s41039-017-0062-8

Prieto, J. C. S., Cruz-Benito, J., Therón, R., & García-Peñalvo, F. J. (2019). How to measure teachers' acceptance of AI-driven assessment in elearning. In *ACM International Conference Proceeding Series*. https://doi.org/10.1145/3362789.3362918

Rienties, B. (2014). Understanding academics' resistance towards (online) student evaluation. *Assessment and Evaluation in Higher Education, 39*(8), 987–1001. https://doi.org/10.1080/02602938.2014.880777

Roll, I., & Wylie, R. (2016). Evolution and revolution in artificial intelligence in education. *International Journal of Artificial Intelligence in Education, 26*(2), 582–599. https://doi.org/10.1007/s40593-016-0110-3

Saunders, M., Lewis, P., & Thornhill, A. (2016). *Research methods for business students* (7th ed.). Pearson.

Schepman, A., & Rodway, P. (2022). The general attitudes towards artificial intelligence scale (GAAIS): Confirmatory validation and associations with personality, corporate distrust, and general trust. *International Journal of Human-Computer Interaction, 39*(13), 2724–2741. https://doi.org/10.1080/10447318.2022.2085400

Scherer, R., & Teo, T. (2019). Editorial to the special section—Technology acceptance models: What we know and what we (still) do not know. *British Journal of Educational Technology, 50*(5), 2387–2393. https://doi.org/10.1111/bjet.12866

Schiff, D. (2020). Out of the laboratory and into the classroom: The future of artificial intelligence in education. *AI & Society, 36*(1), 331–348. https://doi.org/10.1007/s00146-020-01033-8

Sohn, K., & Kwon, O. (2020). Technology acceptance theories and factors influencing artificial intelligence-based intelligent products. *Telematics and Informatics, 47*, 101324. https://doi.org/10.1016/j.tele.2019.101324

Spector, J. M., & Ma, S. (2019). Inquiry and critical thinking skills for the next generation: From artificial intelligence back to human intelligence. *Smart Learning Environments, 6*, 8. https://doi.org/10.1186/s40561-019-0088-z

Tco, T., Fan, X., & Du, J. (2015). Technology acceptance among pre-service teachers: Does gender matter? *Australasian Journal of Educational Technology, 31*(3), 235. https://doi.org/10.14742/ajet.1672

Tlili, A., Shehata, B., Adarkwah, M. A., Bozkurt, A., Hickey, D. T., Huang, R., & Agyemang, B. (2023). What if the devil is my guardian angel: ChatGPT as a case study of using chatbots in education. *Smart Learning Environments, 10*, 15. https://doi.org/10.1186/s40561-023-00237-x
Tongco, M. D. C. (2007). Purposive sampling as a tool for informant selection. *Ethnobotany Research and Applications, 5*, 147–158. Retrieved from: https://ethnobotanyjournal.org/index.php/era/article/view/126
Touretzky, D. S., Martin, F., Seehorn, D., Breazeal, C., & Posner, T. (2019). Special session. In *Proceedings of the 50th ACM Technical Symposium on Computer Science Education*. https://doi.org/10.1145/3287324.3287525
Venkatesh, V., Morris, M., Davis, G. B., & Davis, F. D. (2003). User acceptance of information technology: Toward a unified view. *Management Information Systems Quarterly, 27*(3), 425–478. https://doi.org/10.2307/30036540
Venkatesh, V., Thong, J. Y., & Xu, X. (2016). Unified theory of acceptance and use of technology: A synthesis and the road ahead. *Journal of the Association for Information Systems, 17*(5), 328–376. https://doi.org/10.17705/1jais.00428
Wang, X., Li, L., Tan, S. C., Yang, L., & Lei, J. (2023). Preparing for AI-enhanced education: Conceptualizing and empirically examining teachers' AI readiness. *Computers in Human Behavior, 146*, 107798. https://doi.org/10.1016/j.chb.2023.107798
Weidener, L., & Fischer, M. (2023). Artificial intelligence teaching as part of medical education: Qualitative analysis of expert interviews. *JMIR Medical Education, 9*, e46428. https://doi.org/10.2196/46428
Zawacki-Richter, O., Marín, V. I., Bond, M., & Gouverneur, F. (2019). Systematic review of research on artificial intelligence applications in higher education—Where are the educators? *International Journal of Educational Technology in Higher Education Art, 16*, 39. https://doi.org/10.1186/s41239-019-0171-0
Zhai, X., Chu, X., Chai, C. S., Jong, M. S., Starčič, A. I., Spector, M., Liu, J., Jing, Y., & Li, Y. (2021). A review of artificial intelligence (AI) in education from 2010 to 2020. *Complexity, 2021*(6), 1–18. https://doi.org/10.1155/2021/8812542
Zimmerman, B. J. (2006). Development and adaptation of expertise: The role of self-regulatory processes and beliefs. In K. A. Ericsson, N. Charness, P. J. Feltovich, & R. R. Hoffman (Eds.), *The Cambridge Handbook of expertise and expert performance* (pp. 705–722). Cambridge University Press.

Daniela Hau is head of innovation at SCRIPT, part of Luxembourg's Ministry of Education. Her work focuses on AI and data literacy, media literacy, and digital game-based learning. She holds master's degrees, in economics and in game and media pedagogy, and brings 16 years of experience as a secondary school teacher. She is currently pursuing a Ph.D. in Psychology at the University of Luxembourg, where her research aims to bridge the gap between the limited actual implementation of AI in education and its potential transformative impact. Department of Education and Social Work, University of Luxembourg, Esch-Belval, Luxembourg, https://educ-ai-tion.eu

Robert A. P. Reuter is an Assistant-Professor in educational technology at the University of Luxembourg. He is interested in the strategic use of digital media and technologies in teaching activities and in the socio-cultural changes in learning brought about by the digital revolution. His work aims to improve our understanding of the complex interactions between technology, learning and society and to develop effective and meaningful use of digital media and technologies in education. Department of Education and Social Work, University of Luxembourg, Esch-Belval. Luxembourg, https://www.uni.lu/fhse-en/people/robert-a-p-reuter/.

O. Mariño is an Associate Professor at the Universidad de los Andes (Bogotá, Colombia), where she specializes in Artificial Intelligence, knowledge management, and e-learning. She holds a Ph.D. in Computer Science from the University Joseph Fourier (Grenoble, France) and has substantial expertise in AI-enhanced learning technologies. Dr. O. Mariño leads the Information Technology and Software Construction research group (TICSw) and is deeply engaged in advancing educational technology through research and practical application. Her work emphasizes the development of innovative AI applications for educational settings, striving to bridge the gap between technology and effective teaching methodologies. https://profesores.virtual.uniandes.edu.co/olmarino/es/inicio/.

Claude Houssemand, Ph.D., is a Professor of Differential Psychology and heads the Department of Education and Social Work at the University of Luxembourg. He directs the Master in Psychology: Evaluation and Assessment and the Master in Mediation Orientation Scolaire et Professionnelle. Professor Houssemand's expertise spans cognitive and differential psychology, scientific methodology, and statistics. His recent research focusses on mediation. He co-directs the journal "Mesure et Evaluation en Education", served as the European editor of "Adméé" and chaired the FREREF scientific committee. He is actively involved in the World Mediation Forum and the International Days of Differential Psychology. Department of Education and Social Work, University of Luxembourg, Esch-Belval, Luxembourg, https://www.uni.lu/fhse-en/people/claude-houssemand/.

Chapter 4
What Is AI? The Need for AI Literacy in Education

Lesley Wilton, Clare Brett, Stephen Ip, Rutwa Engineer, and Athena Tassis

Abstract This chapter describes a study investigating what AI is, what it does, and indicators of AI Literacy in Education (AILE) among graduate education students. Data was collected on the online activities of 133 learners and one instructor in six courses taking place over 5 years at a large urban university in Canada. Data covered multiple iterations of an Introduction to AI in Education (AIEd) course and an AI Ethics in Education course, and were processed in three sub-studies, i.e. (1) an "AI Applications Study", examining students' choices of AI tools; (2) an "AI Literacy Indicators Study"; and (3) an "AI Instructor's Reflections Study". The results suggest that, due to technological transience and a lack of information about AI systems, learners find it difficult to perform a critical analysis of AI. Model-card-type information appears crucial for enhancing AI literacy. Consideration of ethics is essential if AI is fully integrated into education. The "Instructor's Reflections" study acknowledges the challenge of designing courses with such rapidly evolving technology. Suggestions for addressing AI literacy in the future are discussed.

L. Wilton (✉)
OCT, University of Toronto, Toronto, ON, Canada

OISE, University of Toronto, Toronto, ON, Canada
e-mail: Lesley.Wilton@utoronto.ca

C. Brett
OISE, University of Toronto, Toronto, ON, Canada
e-mail: Clare.Brett@utoronto.ca

S. Ip
Southern Alberta Institute of Technology, Calgary, AB, Canada
e-mail: stephen.ip@sait.ca

R. Engineer
University of Toronto Mississauga, Mississauga, ON, Canada
e-mail: rutwa.engineer@utoronto.ca

A. Tassis
University of Toronto, Toronto, ON, Canada
e-mail: athena.tassis@mail.utoronto.ca

G. Tchibozo (ed.), *International Perspectives of Generative AI in Education*, Advances in Artificial Intelligence in Education 3,
https://doi.org/10.1007/978-3-031-99804-1_4

Keywords AI ethics · AI literacy · AI readiness · Model card

In recent years, technological advancements, changing societal needs, and a deeper understanding of pedagogical approaches have led to profound upheavals in the field of education. The rapid development of artificial intelligence (AI) systems has generated uncertainty (Bali & Mostafa, 2024; Correia et al., 2024; Muilenberg & Berge, 2015; Posner & Fei-Fei, 2020; Zawacki-Richter et al., 2019). Verdegem (2021) characterizes AI as a fuzzy concept that is difficult to define. Luckin's definition, that AI is a technology capable of actions and behaviors that require intelligence when done by humans (Luckin et al., 2022), remains broad. Additionally, the learning value and usefulness of generative AI (GenAI) systems in education is not always clear (Correia et al., 2024; Long & Magerko, 2020). Some researchers advocate for their use within higher education, citing increased equity for diverse learners and the fact that AI equips students with necessary future workforce skills (Carvalho et al., 2022; Luckin et al., 2022). Others (Selwyn, 2024; Verdegem, 2021) point to possible social harms from statistical frailties and algorithmic discrimination, the risk that GenAI hinders creativity and critical thinking, and concerns that learners will no longer need to think for themselves (Davenport & Mittal, 2022; Kartal, 2024). These uncertainties have led some (Blackie, 2024; Kramm & McKenna, 2023) to identify GenAI systems such as ChatGPT as leading to academic misconduct and teachers being replaced. Fowler (2023) and Klee (2023) note that action against generative AI has ensued, citing negative perceptions of educators taking a punitive view to catch and punish those using GenAI.

Such varied reactions to GenAI create a divide among educators and more confusion among students, who struggle to understand when and how they should use GenAI in academic work (Brevini, 2023; McMurtrie, 2023; Ng et al., 2021). Given the rapid and evolving innovation of GenAI systems, the great variation in beliefs may be due to lack of clarity about the nature of AI systems and AI literacy (Laupichler et al., 2022; Mills et al., 2024; Wilton et al., 2022). Further, educators wonder how to approach AI responsibly (Adams et al., 2021; Akgun & Greenhow, 2022; Borenstein & Howard, 2020; Dignum, 2021; OECD, 2019; Pedro et al., 2019; Vincent-Lancrin & Van der Viles, 2020).

Teaching with and about AI technologies is complex and multi-faceted. This current research looks at how graduate education students apprehend what AI is, and how they contextualize what it does in an educational setting. Critical examinations of the "AI" in AI-supported applications and the indicators for the need for AI literacy are identified through three studies, each with a data and thematic focus, but which are interconnected and together provide a rich picture of how aspects of these course experiences were enacted by the participants, providing an overall description of the current challenges and needed future developments for AIEd. The "AI Applications Study" examines free choices of AI applications by 111 learners from five 2020–2023 Introduction to AI in Education courses. The "AI Literacy Indicators Study" analyzes two sources of data on indicators of educators' AI literacy (AILE) needs, from one 2024 AI Ethics in Education course with 22 learners. The "AI Instructor's Reflections Study" is based on the instructor's reflective experience in teaching all six courses.

The research questions are as follows:

Research Question 1: What can be observed as graduate students build AI literacy skills in a course on AI in Education; particularly, how do student choices of AI tools for their educational context and their thoughts on understanding the complexities of AI technologies reflect their degree of AI readiness and their knowledge challenges in using AI systems?

Research Question 2: What is an instructor's experience in teaching these AI concepts in such a time of rapid evolution in AI tools?

Research Background, Main Drivers, and Key Concepts

In recent years, two major waves of change have affected the nature and scope of technology-enabled teaching and learning. On the one hand, the accelerating progress of AI with the widespread adoption of GenAI systems and, on the other, the lasting effects on education of the global move towards online learning environments and digital teaching tools, accelerated by the COVID-19 pandemic. Consequentially, the need for AI literacy is now more widely recognized, researched, and debated (Carolus et al., 2023).

These developments are infiltrating formal learning environments, sometimes without educators realizing it or necessarily understanding the implications in relation to data collection, privacy, and data security. While many in education may be able to identify the presence of AI in tools, their *implications* may be overlooked or unknown. According to Luckin et al. (2022), the current education and training sectors are unprepared to make effective decisions on how to leverage the benefits of AI to address learner needs. To provide better support, the concept of AI readiness through differentiation between human and AI intelligence, as well as the application of AI to specific educational tasks, can be introduced to educators to build understandings of AI and empower them to meet their needs (Luckin et al., 2022).

Despite the potential benefits of AI to support students' learning experiences and teachers' practices, the ethical drawbacks of these systems are complex to consider in educational contexts (Akgun & Greenhow, 2022). Research on how to develop instructional practices relating to AI and ethics, or AI pedagogy, is still emerging (Miao & Cukurova, 2024). According to UNESCO (2023a), AI is challenging educators to rethink the 'known-world' that we have been familiar with until now. Old assumptions and norms are unlikely to hold up alongside new AI systems.

Importantly, we recognize the environmental impact of AI as a significant cultural challenge to be addressed overall, as well as in the context of AI literacy. For example, building on her 2021 book, *Is AI Good for the Planet?*, Brevini (2023) reports that in 2018, researchers Belkhir and Elmeligi expected that "the tech industry's carbon footprint could increase to 14% by 2040" (p. 25) and that 45% of this could be attributed to data centers. AI can be better understood, according to Brevini, "as technologies, machines and infrastructures that demand amounts of energy to compute, analyze and categorize" (p. 26). Strubell et al. (2019) cautions that those using AI systems should understand the environmental impact.

To fully address the responsible use of AI, Dignum (2019) highlights the importance of deeper understandings of AI in context. Dignum (2021) asserts that "the current educational system is not generating enough experts, and everyday users are increasingly not able to understand the systems with which they are faced" (p. 1). Today, businesses and governments acknowledge the need for responsible, ethical, transparent, and safe use of AI-capable technologies (Long & Magerko, 2020; Ministry of Defence, 2022; UNESCO, 2021; Verdegem, 2021; Vincent-Lancrin & Van der Viles, 2020).

On the front line of education, we are seeing the problems that need to be tackled in order to achieve these necessary deeper understandings. Alternate learning methods, as proposed in learning sciences researcher Sawyer's (2008) key findings, provide potential guidance for developing a more systematic way to categorize and evaluate emerging AI systems. This involves aiming for deeper conceptual understanding, making contextual connections, and providing authentic and collaborative learning experiences (p. 9). A research review on AIEd (Chen et al., 2020) suggests several possible positive effects for learning. Other studies take a more critical view, identifying the need for a more transparent analysis of the educational AI landscape, particularly in relation to the importance of identifying ethical questions for the field, both at policy and classroom levels (Borenstein & Howard, 2020; Schiff, 2022). Schiff (2022) places emphasis on the importance of developers and policymakers, acknowledging in them a deeper awareness of the ethical implications of AI. Selwyn (2024) critically advocates avoiding hype about transformative opportunities and focusing on the complexities and nuances of AI's educational uses.

The second wave of changes involving an impact of technology on education was accelerated worldwide by the COVID-19 pandemic. During the pandemic, educational institutions across 190 countries were temporarily closed, affecting over 1.5 billion students (UNESCO, 2020). Transcending the spatial and temporal limitations of conventional classrooms, online platforms allowed students to learn at their convenient time and location (Crompton, 2013; Martin & Ertzberger, 2013; Oztok et al., 2014; Wilton, 2022; Wilton et al., 2020). Synchronous and asynchronous types of distance learning became the optimal solution for student learning while also providing flexibility to teachers (Hu, 2022). Online learning continues to play this bigger role in education.

Key Concepts and Definitions

The definition of AI is constantly shifting as new technologies emerge. A recent statement released by the United States government (The White House, 2024) calls for research from a range of individuals and institutions "who care about making AI safe, secure and trustworthy," noting that "AI is moving too fast, and is too complex" (p. 1).

UNESCO (2021) listed a set of values and principles as motivating ideals in shaping emerging policy measures and legal norms to inspire desirable behavior relating to the use of AI (see Fig. 4.1 below).

One of these principles, Awareness and Literacy, is the focus of the study being reported here. Much of the research to date in AIEd has taken place in the computer science discipline. In 2019, Zawacki-Richter et al. (2019) highlighted the lack of published research related to AIEd from those in the education discipline, including the lack of critical reflection on AIEd, weak theoretical pedagogical perspectives, and the need for ethical and educational AIEd. As educational researchers, we examine in this chapter issues of AI awareness and literacy in an educational context. Given the transdisciplinary nature of AI technology, it is essential for AIEd research to be more than just about the process of integrating various AI technologies (Dignum, 2019). Research highlights the importance of moving beyond simply implementing AI technologies to fully and thoughtfully integrating cultural, social, pedagogical, and ethical dimensions (Ouyang & Jiao, 2021; Pedro et al., 2019).

The challenges we address in this chapter are guided by the following interpretations derived from the literature:

- AI literacy for educators (AILE) involves basic competencies and fundamental skills. Appropriate technological and pedagogical strategies are needed to support AI literacy (Ng et al., 2021; Pedro et al., 2019). Detailed identification of competencies and assessment strategies are essential. UNESCO (as cited in Miao & Cukurova, 2024) identifies a set of competencies for teachers to effectively integrate AI pedagogy by identifying and critically assessing appropriate AI tools in an ethical manner.

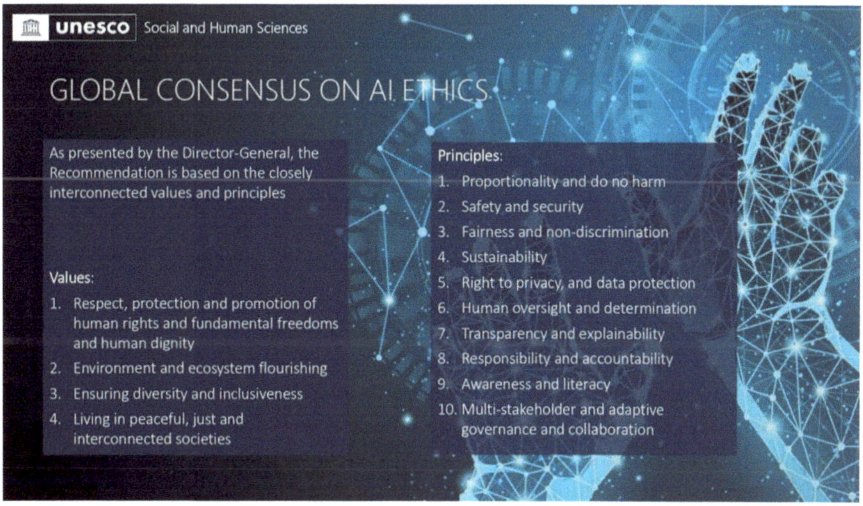

Fig. 4.1 UNESCO's recommendations on the values and principles of a human rights-centered approach to the Ethics of AI (Ramos, 2021)

- Continuous development of educators' AI knowledge is essential to approach the integration of constantly evolving technologies in a responsible and ethical manner (Ng et al., 2021).
- Societal needs, human-centered considerations, and AI contexts must be taken into account simultaneously (Ng et al., 2021; Vincent-Lancrin & Van der Viles, 2020).

GenAI systems are capable of producing different types of outputs such as text, code, images, videos and audio that can appear to be authentic and original (Trust et al., 2023). Assessing the credibility of these outputs can be difficult. Advocates of GenAI (Addy et al., 2023) argue that such systems facilitate more inclusive and equitable post-secondary learning. Personalized tutors facilitate access to support and resources often reserved for the financially well-off, or accessible only during restricted hours. Furthermore, GenAI systems have been praised for their anthropomorphic qualities of infinite patience and non-judgment. More introverted learners may benefit from these systems without fear of being judged or ridiculed. More research is needed to fully assess the benefits of AI systems.

Conceptually, it can be difficult for people without a computer science background to understand current AI tools such as Large Language Models (LLMs), which may have raised concerns in educators. Similarly, Selwyn (2024) highlighted that reorganizing education to be more "machine readable" and to produce data recognized and captured by AI technologies, has raised concerns about the needs of the technology taking precedence over educational processes, as this may usurp control over aspects of educational knowledge and values. Addressing such controversies, UNESCO (2023b) recommended the formulation of policies for the use of AI based on an explicitly human-centered approach, to ensure its ethical, safe, equitable and meaningful uses. This includes adopting AI to ensure inclusive access to learning programs, supporting personalized learning options, expanding access, alerting teachers to failure risks, and developing understanding and skills for the ethical and meaningful use of AI (Laupichler et al., 2022; Luckin et al., 2022).

The need to establish context and improve understanding of the complexities of AI systems led our research group to the idea of requiring access to developer information to inform the safe integration of AI systems into educational settings (Wilton et al., 2024). First proposed in 2018 (Mitchell et al., 2019; Tan & Subramonyam, 2024], model card reporting offers a means for developers and engineers to disclose parameters of AI systems in short documents that explain the context for intended use, details of performance evaluation procedures, potential biases, other training data concerns, data collection and privacy parameters, decision-making goals, explainability and/or interpretability and other relevant information. Stakeholders can benefit from the deployment of model cards in different ways. In the context of education, model cards can promote transparency and accountability when integrating AI systems for learning, help institutions better integrate the responsible use of AI, and promote collaboration and AI literacy among the community. To better support educators, we examine the concept of model cards as a potentially valuable way to help the development of AI literacy in context (see Fig. 4.2).

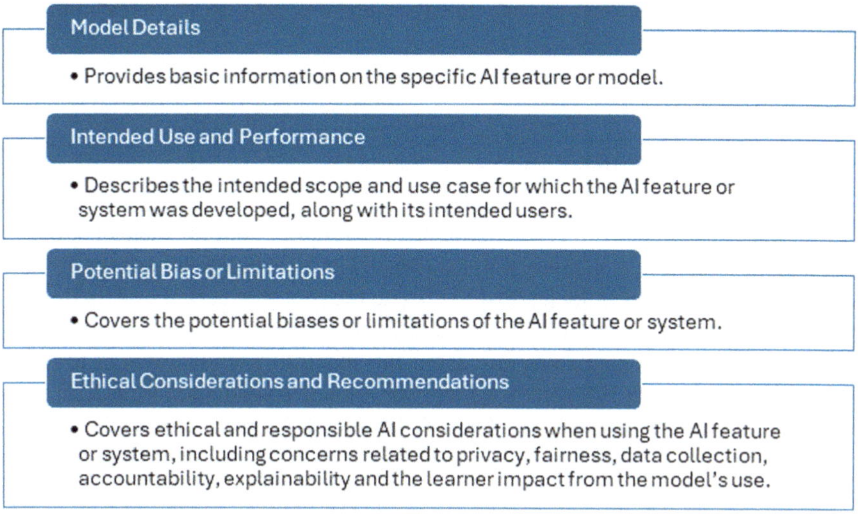

Fig. 4.2 Proposed Structure of Model Cards in Education

An earlier study (Wilton et al., 2022) of a Blended Learning course and an Introduction to AIEd course for educators had suggested a lack of AI readiness and the need for AI literacy to support students' greater confidence in discussing and learning about AIEd. The studies presented in this chapter are based on 5 years of teaching a variety of graduate learners, in (a) five Introduction to AIED courses, where learners critically examine AI tools that are applicable to their contexts, and (b) one AI Ethics in Education course where students, through coursework, deepen their understanding of AI literacy and explore the effectiveness of model cards to build AI literacy skills and assess the promise and risks of AI systems in education, guided by UNESCO's recommendations.

Method

The initial phase began with a comprehensive literature review in AIEd, identifying common interpretations of AI concepts for those with a limited technical background (Adams et al., 2021; Dignum, 2019; Long & Magerko, 2020). The data covered 133 learners and one instructor. The data were collected electronically through a collaborative learning management system featuring public and private discussion threads. Student activities were automatically tracked. The design of the courses was intentionally guided by the Community of Inquiry framework (Garrison et al., 2010) to encourage students to build community through online discussion and developing a sense of belonging. Most of the learners had not met and were globally located. Since these courses introduced very new and evolving AI concepts, it was important to create an environment of trust to support community learning.

AI Applications Study

In this study, the students had to choose an AI-supported tool for their final course assignments. Tables 4.1, 4.2, 4.3, 4.4, 4.5, 4.6, 4.7 and 4.8 below present the 73 tools available for selection. Students had to choose the tool that best aligned with their interests or context, based on information retrieved from relevant websites. The students and instructor critically discussed the specific functionalities of the tools and evaluated them for bias, privacy, inclusion, ethical considerations, accessibility, and explainability. Tables 4.1, 4.2, 4.3, 4.4, 4.5, 4.6, 4.7 and 4.8 specify the application types (namely Intelligent Tutoring Platform—ITP, or Intelligent Learning Systems—ILS) and the frequency with which each tool was chosen by a student or pair of students.

The data collected was analyzed inductively. This inductive process (Punch, 2009) guided the researchers in coding and identifying key elements (Miles & Huberman, 1994). The goal was to reduce researcher bias through thematic coding (Miles & Huberman, 1994; Yin, 2014).

AI Literacy Indicators Study

This study draws on data from an AI Ethics in Education course requiring graduate students to consider the implications of AI systems generally, and in their own educational context. Through online conversations, the learners shared their areas of interest in AIED, and their views on the application of UNESCO's four values and ten ethical principles of Ethics in AI (see Fig. 4.1). Journal entries captured their insights. Using model card type information, the learners critically analyzed AI systems and applied theoretical knowledge from the course, highlighting features such as bias, accountability, explainability, privacy, data collection, and transparency.

Together, student conversations, reflections and model cards effectively helped them both identify issues related to AI systems and address knowledge gaps in AI literacy and AI readiness. We reviewed the data from 22 learners' conversation notes (total of 19,297 words) and weekly journal reflections (total of 81,734 words). We examined the data in several ways to identify themes, sentiment trends, and frequencies of topics and terms relating to AI ethics and AI literacy.

Other measures to identify learners' understandings of AI systems and indicators of AI readiness and AI literacy, were the emotional tone and subjectivity of entries investigated by means of a sentiment analysis using a natural language processing API. Such analyses have been used with educational data to evaluate students' comments based on expressed sentiments and emotions. Shaik et al. (2023) argue that

Table 4.1 Administration tools

No.	Name of AI Tool	Available at	Type of AI Application	Categories	Frequency
1	BlippAR	www.blippar.com/	Augmented Reality Applications	Administration	1
2	Classcraft	www.classcraft.com/	Engagement Management System	Administration	1
3	Gradescope	https://www.gradescope.com/	AI grading tool	Administration	1
4	Microsoft Teams (Power Virtual Agents)	docs.microsoft.com/en-us/power-virtual-agents/teams/advanced-ai-features-teams	Microsoft AI Chatbot Builder	Administration	1
5	Moodle Analytics (API)	docs.moodle.org/311/en/Analytics	Learning Analytics Software	Administration	1
6	SnatchBot Chatbot	snatchbot.me/	AI Chatbot Builder	Administration	2
7	ALEKS	www.aleks.com/	Adaptive Learning Program	Administration/General	1
8	Ametros Learning	ametroslearning.com/	ILS	Administration/Business	1

Table 4.2 Business tools

No.	Name of AI tool	Available at	Type of AI Application	Categories	Frequency
9	Botsify Chatbot	botsify.com/	AI Chatbot Builder (for Business)	Business	2
10	Enskill	www.alelo.com/	ILS for virtual role play	Business	1

sentiment analysis can improve learning processes and assessment feedback, highlighting learner context. In particular, sentiment analysis provides insight on two metrics: polarity and subjectivity. Polarity measures the positivity, neutrality, or the negativity tones (Nikolić et al., 2020) in sentences, based on a scale from −1 (negative comments) to 1 (positive comments). The subjectivity metric focuses on whether the sentence is objective indicated by a 0, to subjective indicated by 1.

To identify underlying themes, topic modeling was performed using Latent Dirichlet Allocation (LDA), a probabilistic topic modeling technique used to identify the distribution of words over topics and the distribution of topics across entries (Blei et al., 2023). LDA is used to find a set of topics that best describe the prominent themes in the data. Yin and Yuan (2022) have used LDA to understand prominent trends in blended learning literature. Similarly, Kamatchi and Muthuraman (2022) have used an LDA model to analyze educational tweets. In our study, LDA is used to identify several main topics across students' reflections. Figure 4.3 shows the 30 most relevant terms across all learner reflections. LDA helped with identifying themes students discussed in their learner's reflections by identifying clusters of words that frequently occur together. Each student's writing can then be represented as a mixture of these topics, showing, for instance, that a reflection is 70% about "AI" and 30% about "students." In our case, the topics that were identified included "AI," "students," "learning," and "ethics."

Instructor's Reflections Study

A self-study methodology for inquiry-guided research was used to examine the instructor's observations and learnings. Tidwell et al. (2009) define self-study as "the improvement of practice by reflecting on oneself and one's practices as a teacher educator" (p. 57). The instructor's observations were collected throughout all courses and served to guide further iterations of the courses. Reflections on course themes were collected and were compared to student feedback to guide updates for the next iteration. The instructor's feedback on assignments was also collected in a separate Microsoft Word document for review and planning. This was particularly necessary as AI systems and relevant resources are constantly evolving. Therefore, these courses require significant redevelopment to remain current and relevant.

Table 4.3 General tools

No.	Name of AI tool	Available at	Type of AI application	Categories	Frequency
11	Brainly	brainly.com/	Adaptive Intelligent Tutoring	General	1
12	CallAnnie	https://callannie.ai/	AI Chatbot	General	2
13	ChatGPT	https://chat.openai.com/	Generative AI	General	11
14	Microsoft Power Apps	https://www.microsoft.com/en-us/power-platform/products/power-apps	Collection of AI apps	General	1
15	Plaito AI	https://chatgate.ai/store/plaito/	Adaptive Intelligent Tutor	General	2
16	Talk To Books	books.google.com/talktobooks/	AI Search Engine for Books	General	1
17	Socratic by Google	socratic.org/	ITP—Homework Help Chatbot	General/Administration	1
18	Century	www.century.tech/	ILS - English, Math & Science Learning	General/Administration	1
19	Feedback Fruits	https://feedbackfruits.com/	Learning Management System	General/administration	1
20	Nolej AI	https://nolej.io/	AI Content generator	General/administration	2
21	Pepper	www.pepperproject.ca	ILS - Chatbot	General/Administration	1
22	Watson Enlight for Educators	https://www.ibm.com/watson/education/pearson	ITP—Chatbot for all Subjects	General/Administration	1

Table 4.4 Health tools

No.	Name of AI tool	Available at	Type of AI application	Categories	Frequency
23	The USC Standardized Patient	https://www.standardpatient.org/	ILS - Medical environment simulation	Health	1
24	Headspace	https://www.headspace.com/	ITP—Mental Health	Health & Wellness	1
25	Navi	https://prod.virtualagent.utoronto.ca/	Mental Health Chatbot	Health & Wellness	1
26	NewT	www.newtfit.com/	ITP—Digital Nutrition Chatbot	Health & Wellness	1
27	Woebot Health	woebothealth.com/	ITP—Mental Health Chatbot	Health & Wellness	1
28	Wysa	https://www.wysa.com/	Mental Health Chatbot	Health & Wellness	1

Table 4.5 Imaging tools

No.	Name of AI tool	Available at	Type of AI application	Categories	Frequency
29	Autodraw	www.autodraw.com/	Google AI Drawing Experiment	Imaging tool	1
30	Canva Text to Image	https://www.canva.com/ai-image-generator/	AI Image builder	Imaging tool	1
31	DALL-E2	https://openai.com/dall-e-2	Generative AI	Imaging tool	2
32	Eduic	lens.google	Image Search Engine with AI	Imaging tool	1
33	Midjourney	https://www.imagine.art/	AI Image builder	Imaging tool	1
34	NightCafe	https://nightcafe.studio/	AI art generator	Imaging tool	1
35	Transformer by Hugging Face	huggingface.co/docs/transformers/index	Machine Learning for PyTorch, TensorFlow and JAX	Imaging tool	1

The Instructor's Reflections self-study data was thematically analyzed. The instructor reflected on possible improvements of practice from the perspective of a teacher educator teaching about a complex subject in times of rapidly evolving innovation. Themes from these data were then compared to the interconnected themes identified from the AI Literacy Indicators data.

Table 4.6 Language tools

No.	Name of AI tool	Available at	Type of AI application	Categories	Frequency
36	Otter.ai	otter.ai/	AI Transcription & Note-Taking Tool	General/Language	1
37	Acciolbis	https://www.accioibis.com/	ITP—French Language Learning	Language	1
38	Baidu AI Translate	https://fanyi.baidu.com	AI supported translation application	Language	1
39	Charisma AI	https://charisma.ai/	ILS—Natural Language Processing	Language	1
40	Convai	https://www.convai.com/	ILS—Natural Language Processing	Language	1
41	DingDong Class	ddkt365.com/	ILS - English Language Learning	Language	1
42	Duolingo	www.duolingo.com/	Former AI Chatbot - Discontinued	Language	4
43	ELSA Speak	elsaspeak.com/en/	ITP—English Language Learning	Language	2
44	ETS's e-rater	www.ets.org/erater/	AI Essay Grading Tool	Language	1
45	Grammarly	www.grammarly.com/	AI Grammar Assistance Tool	Language	3
46	Knowji	www.knowji.com/	ILS—English Vocabulary Learning	Language	1
47	Konwji AI	https://www.knowji.com/	ITL - English Vocabulary Learning	Language	1
48	Lingvist	lingvist.com/	ITP—Language Learning Chatbot	Language	2
49	Microsoft Translator	translator.microsoft.com/	ITP—Language Translation Chatbot	Language	1
50	Mondly	www.mondly.com/	ITP—Language Learning Chatbot	Language	1
51	Moonbeam	https://www.gomoonbeam.com/	AI writing tool	Language	1
52	Packback	https://www.packback.co/	AI Essay Grading Tool	Language	1
53	QuillBot	https://quillbot.com/	AI Grammar Assistance Tool	Language	1
54	ShanBay	www.shanbay.com/	AI Driven Word Learning	Language	1
55	Speak AI	speakai.co/	ILS—Natural Language Processing	Language	1

(continued)

Table 4.6 (continued)

No.	Name of AI tool	Available at	Type of AI application	Categories	Frequency
56	The Readability Tutor	www.readabilitytutor.com/	ILS—Reading & Comprehension Learning Application	Language	1
57	Thing Translator	https://families.google/external/ai-experiments-thing-translator/	Language learning	Language	1
58	Trinka	https://www.trinka.ai/	AI Grammar Assistance Tool	Language	1
59	Zaplingo	https://zaplingo.com/	ILS - English Language Learning	Language	1
60	Seeing AI	www.microsoft.com/en-us/ai/seeing-ai	Intelligent Camera Application—Description of Surroundings	Language/Imaging tool	1
61	iTalk2Learn	www.italk2learn.com/	ITP Chatbot	Language/Administration	1
62	Interplay	experiments.withgoogle.com/interplay-mode/view/	Interactive Video with AI	Language/Imaging tool	1

Table 4.7 Math tools

No.	Name of AI tool	Available at	Type of AI application	Categories	Frequency
63	Knowledgehook	https://www.knowledgehook.com/	ILS - Math	Math	1
64	MATHia	www.carnegielearning.com/solutions/math/mathia/	ITP—Math Chatbot	Math	1
65	MathWhizz	www.whizz.com/	ITP—Math Chatbot	Math	1
66	Querium	https://www.querium.com/	ITP - Math learning	Math	1
67	Thinkster Math	hellothinkster.com/	ITP—Math Chatbot	Math	1
68	Thirdspace Learning Chatbot	thirdspacelearning.com/	ITP—Math Chatbot	Math	1

Table 4.8 Music tools

No.	Name of AI tool	Available at	Type of AI application	Categories	Frequency
69	MuseNet	openai.com/blog/musenet/	GPT-2, Neural Network for Musical Compositions	Music	1
70	Music Transformer	https://magenta.tensorflow.org/music-transformer	Neural Network for Musical Compositions	Music	1
71	Simply Piano	www.joytunes.com/simply-piano	ILS - Instrument Learning Applications for Piano	Music	1
72	Trala	www.trala.com/	ILS - Instrument Learning Applications for Violin	Music	1
73	Homework Gang	N/A	Application Not Found	N/A	1

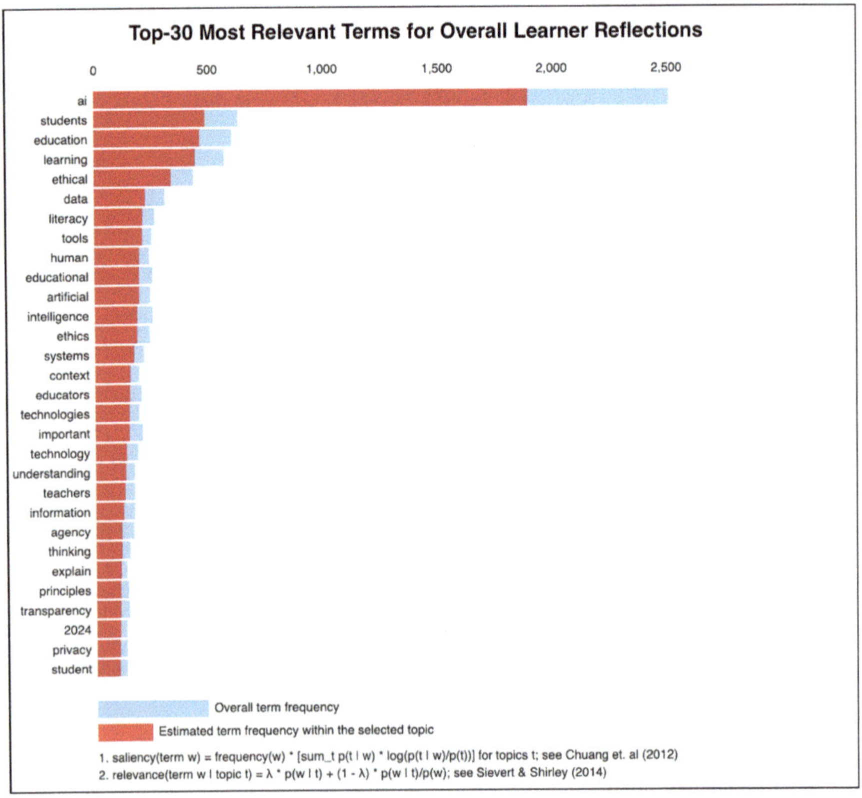

Fig. 4.3 Top 30 most relevant terms across all learner reflections

Results

AI Applications Study

The analyzed AI tools often proved quite hard to categorize. First, because many of them are proprietary and the AI functionality is not well-explained, making it difficult for students to describe risks and learning potential of these tools. Secondly, because the extraordinary speed at which GenAI technologies are evolving creates challenges in user understanding. This affects purpose and perception. For example, AI systems can be seen as plagiarism tools by both teachers and administrators, and the lack of transparency and clarity in their descriptions made it very challenging for those in educational contexts to investigate their reliability and ethical use.

AI Literacy Indicators Study

The sentiment analysis results showed that the majority of student entries were positive, with a significant level of subjectivity, indicating that students felt comfortable expressing personal opinions on AI Ethics in Education topics (see Fig. 4.4). This is important to confirm the authenticity and value of the learners' discussion notes and the meaningfulness of their reflections on such a complex topic.

Frequency analysis across conversation notes and journal entries revealed the core ideas of students' focus in the entries. The word "ethical" appeared 486 times, "transparency" 211 times, "model cards" 143 times, "fairness" 125 times, "responsible" 101 times, and "accountability" 98 times. These results show a sustained attention to those ethical dimensions reviewed in the literature during the course.

LDA analysis revealed student focus on topics such as AI, education, learning, students, and ethics. The LDA analysis complements the thematic analysis. Some common themes include discussions on strategies to embed AI literacy into the existing curriculum or professional development, the need to use age-appropriate language when explaining what the AI system is and what it does, and the importance of fostering critical thinking skills when using an AI system. As well, the challenges and barriers related to bias, fairness, privacy, access, and equity were identified and discussed.

The thematic analysis highlighted the following areas of importance: AI Literacy, Ethical AI conversations and Model Cards conversations.

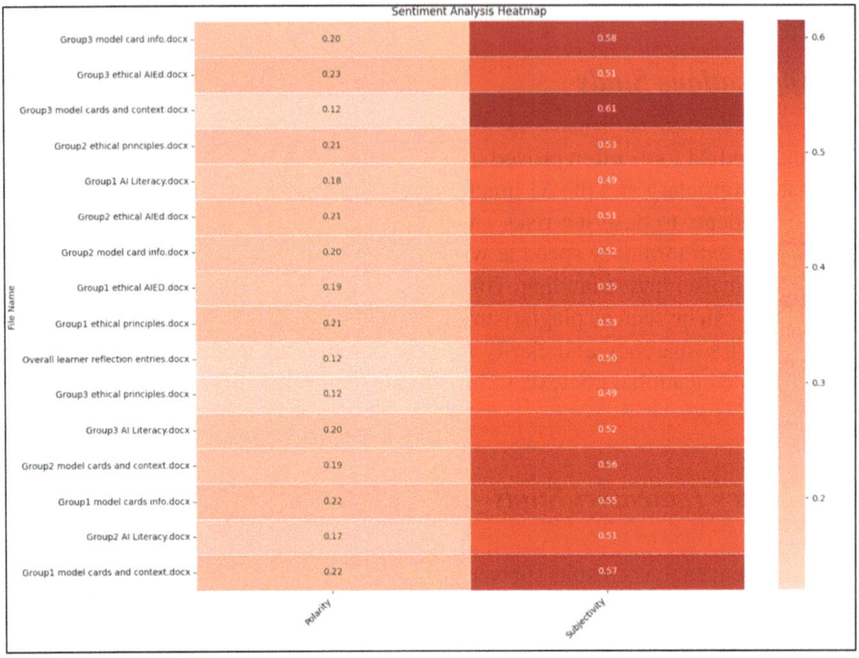

Fig. 4.4 Sentiment analysis heatmap. *Note:* A heatmap of the sentiment analysis detecting subjectivity in the posts indicated by scores above 0.5 as well as positive tone in the documents as indicated by polarity scores superior to zero

AI Literacy

Gradual and Scaffolded Exposure to Learning

Learners pointed out in their own analyses that AI literacy should be introduced with clear steps, starting with easy-to-understand sections from primary education and sophisticated parts about ethics from secondary and higher education. A student stated that "by allowing students to engage with AI tools early in their education career, they build AI literacy skills and are better equipped to engage responsibly with the tools later in their personal and professional lives."

Ethics and Critical Thinking

Learners in this course suggested that considerable teacher effort should be extended in training students to analyze AI-generated content, identify different types of biases, and decide whether AI usage is truly justified. A learner provided specific examples of the need for critical thinking by explaining that:

> the way that LLMs work, they often create work that looks original and authentic each time (not a direct copy of any previous work). The focus needs to be building that critical AI literacy so that students are viewing the AI outputs and examining them for bias, accuracy and relevancy.

That learner further shared the view that "calling inaccurate AI outputs hallucinations is very ableist language. At work, we have adopted the term fabrications instead." Another learner expressed concern that learners may think "AI is magic" and may begin to trust what is produced or recommended without question. A third one expressed concern for anthropomorphizing AI systems, where learners begin to relate to the AI system as if it were capable of human actions, such as thinking or empathy. Learners noted this may become common practice where an AI assistant or chatbot, to whom a user assigns pronouns, could then be assumed human capable.

Interdisciplinary Integration

Learners raised the issues of integrating AI literacy into all disciplines through a variety of teaching and learning strategies. These included solving application problems and talking about use cases, and thereby linking the topic of AI to other stakeholders and disciplines. Learners agreed that to be able to use AI tools as an educator, it was fundamental to be an actor in the ethical deployment of AI in education and to monitor it. Being open to the integration of AI technologies in the educational system and creating protocols that safeguard its appropriate application within the classroom was very important.

Ethical AI Conversations

Accountability

Many of the learners noted that AI technologies must be used ethically, regardless of the opportunities. Promoting learner benefits and countering any negative consequences was discussed by many. A learner stated:

> I would implement feedback mechanisms so that students and even parents can share their thoughts and feelings about AI tools and their impacts. I would try to monitor how AI tools are being used so that they are providing more benefit than harm to student learning.

Fairness

More focus on bias in AI systems and equitable use of AI technology was seen as important but complex.

Privacy

There was confusion about how to address privacy without enough understanding of the AI systems. A learner stated that "there's not enough knowledge and support regarding AI in education." Student confidentiality and full consent was considered most important.

Explainability

Learners grappled with understanding the AI systems they were critically examining. Many noted that providing access to practical apps could help students and teachers understand and properly critique the AI systems.

Balance and Dependence

Concerns were raised about dependence on AI tools, along with a clear awareness that training in these tools prepares students for the future.

Model Cards Conversations

The combination of the reflections and the creation of model cards effectively addressed perceptions and gaps in AI literacy and AI readiness.

Bias Reduction

Overall, learners agreed that model cards are needed to promote transparency in educational AI systems.

Ethical Issues

Learners highlighted the importance of model cards addressing ethical issues, including abuse of privacy, issues with data encryption, and irresponsible use of the AI systems.

Instructor's Reflections Study

The Instructor's Reflections Study identified that AI applications in education, despite marketing claims, sometimes feature AI elements that are challenging to identify or understand. The proprietary nature of these AIEd systems can hinder their transparency and explainability. This observation continued over time, particularly once learners began to explore ChatGPT and similar tools. Furthermore, it was identified that conceptions of AI greatly influence assumptions of responsible use. From an instructor's perspective, it is often difficult to get information about AI applications and to stay up to date given the rapid pace of change. It is also challenging to identify AIEd systems that quietly collect student information. This is highly problematic because student data is highly protected by local laws, education ministry policies, or school board regulations (Paludi, 2023; Zimmerle, 2021).

Furthermore, the instructor, in the spirit of inquiry-based learning pedagogies, found it necessary to verify learner observations about their AI system choice, and agreed that it was, indeed, difficult to identify key information, such as that within the categories provided by the model cards. Some elements were proprietary, some were unexplained, and some were so complicated that an explanation was challenging to find and apply to the context. Many applications include a disclaimer where the often difficult to understand terms of service may change at any time without notice. Additionally, the handling of privacy was often unclear.

Discussion and Suggestions

In this section, we link our findings back to our two research questions, i.e.: (1) how do student choices of AI tools reflect AI readiness and knowledge challenges as they build AI literacy skills? And (2) What are an instructor's perceptions of teaching this content at a time of rapid evolution of AI tools.

Building on earlier research, results from the studies presented in this chapter support the following key findings.

AI Applications Study

AI technology can be difficult to identify and understand from the material created by the developers. Some use the term AI as a marketing term only, some AI elements are proprietary or not explained and many AI systems are rapidly evolving.

Product explanations of AI tools can be complex, limited or even difficult to find. Model-card-type information in understandable language is needed from developers.

While free AI applications are practical for educators, they may rapidly change or disappear, or may be collecting data without explicitly stating so, making them unsuitable choices for many educational contexts.

Institutions or employers must approve AI systems in a timely manner for use in an educational context, before educators are asked to provide students' access to these systems. Systems that are inappropriate in terms of privacy, data collection and other ethical considerations should not be approved.

AI Literacy Indicators Study

AI literacy support is essential in an educational context and must be thoughtfully introduced with a scaffolded approach. Context is essential and must be considered when addressing the development of AI literacy.

Ethical and critical perspectives are integral to incorporating AI systems within an educational context. Identifying factors that affect issues such as data collection, privacy, bias, ethics, explainability, can be difficult. Many AI systems' terms of use state that they can change at any time. At this time, most information provided by the developers of AI products appears inadequate for understanding ethical issues. The UNESCO (2023c) Recommendations on the ethics of AI were consistently appreciated as helpful by learners and served as a useful guide for the instructor.

Learners need to develop a certain level of AI Literacy in order to understand that AI is not magic. The underlying explanation of fabrications should be well understood. Educators and learners must understand the differences between machine capabilities and human capabilities. Anthropomorphizing is a serious challenge in this AI age.

AI is all around us and therefore does not sit within one discipline. Interdisciplinary integration supports understandings of issues involving other stakeholders such as those related to the climate or energy conservation. Protocols to safeguard appropriate use of AI is also key.

Balance, dependence on AI systems and accountability were viewed by our learners as important issues that could involve parents and others. Educational institutions must be responsible for the AI systems they are providing.

Inclusion was seen as highly related to fairness with examples of equitable access to AI technologies.

The concerns about privacy highlighted confusion about how to best address this issue. Responsibility for data collection that potentially compromises student privacy is often unclear (Wilton et al., 2022). There was heightened concern about this issue particularly because of the regulations and laws protecting student data.

Explainability should be addressed through model-card-type information. As AI systems continue to be more and more complex, critical examinations of these systems become more difficult.

Model-card-type information should address understandings of bias, privacy, data collection and more, and issues of irresponsible usage of AI.

Instructor's Reflections Study

An AI Literacy and Ethics Framework must be developed or adopted and validated like the TPACK framework (Mishra & Koehler, 2006) currently used by educators. An effective framework must include detection of the AI dimension and understanding of the AI tool. The AI Competency Framework for teachers (Miao & Cukurova, 2024) holds promise and should be introduced in further courses.

Teaching courses about rapidly evolving AI systems is challenging because the course materials need constant updating. Instructor's understandings of how the technologies work can be difficult without ongoing and scaffolded educational supports and model-card-type information.

Student privacy must be protected. This represents a major challenge for instructors if they do not have clear guidelines from their institutions regarding safety in the context of an artificial intelligence system.

Discussions with other learners about these complex topics appeared to contribute to confidence in understanding and the development of AI literacy. AI literacy takes time to develop and is complicated and contextual. Many countries and states are adopting AI literacy integration into K-12 curricula or for their general population (Kim & Kwon, 2023; Scottish AI Alliance, 2022). It is important to critically review the implications of these plans to help us develop ours, in our contexts.

Conclusion

Drawing on emerging AIEd literature, common concepts of AI Literacy were identified and gathered from learners and an instructor's reflections about 73 AI applications. These data substantiate the need for AI literacy support for educators. In particular, the reliable and fair use of AI needs to be addressed by broadening common understandings of fairness, accountability, explainability, transparency and ethics, not only for those from within the various technical AI fields, but also for educators. As already noted by Ng et al. (2021), enhancing common understanding to support the identification of safe and responsible use of AI tools is necessary. It is also important in course design to support those with a range of technology experiences to foster foundational knowledge and common understanding of AI concepts so that learners can confidently discuss their thinking with each other.

Competencies and measurement instruments are evolving. There are no agreed-upon standards. It is strongly recommended that educators be "at the table" when educational technologies and standards are developed, particularly with those AI systems that could be explained through model-card-type information. Teachers are responsible for preparing future citizens and life-long learners but they need support to understand AI systems without necessarily having a technical background. Learning about AI systems is complex and requires more than a few Professional Development sessions—it takes time to understand rapidly evolving technologies such as these. Guides such as UNESCO's Recommendations on the Ethics of AI (Ramos, 2021) are helpful—more guides specifically written for those in education are needed.

Advances in AI have led to a proliferation of AI tools in everyday life, yet teachers and students require scaffolded and continuous support to thoroughly explore the educational value of those underlying technologies—work that will require time, in an era where AI development is moving faster than any preceding generation of information technology.

More research is needed on the ethical aspects of AIEd to ensure that robust and safe AI products can be available for all educators. Educating future generations in the ethical use and development of AI, including its environmental footprint, will require the building of collaborative interdisciplinary relationships where those working in education can share their critical experiences with AI developers and suggest resources and strategies.

As AI technologies evolve, it is necessary to address additional ways of deepening educators' understandings of AIEd and the development of AILE. The results of this overall set of studies suggests that a well-designed AILE course would provide educators with opportunities to build their knowledge of AI. Finally, the data highlights the need for the broader culture of AI development that specifically considers educator perspectives.

Competing Interests The authors have no conflicts of interest to declare that are relevant to the content of this chapter.

Ethics Approval This study was performed in line with the principles of the Declaration of Helsinki. Approval was granted by the Ethics Committee of the University of Toronto (Date April 8, 2024/No. 38253).

References

Adams, C., Pente, P., Lemermeyer, G., & Rockwell, G. (2021). Artificial intelligence ethics guidelines for K-12 education: A review of the global landscape. In I. Roll, D. McNamara, S. Sosnovsky, R. Luckin, & V. Dimitrova (Eds.), *Artificial Intelligence in Education. AIED 2021. Lecture Notes in Computer Science* (pp. 24–28). Springer. https://doi.org/10.1007/978-3-030-78270-2_4

Addy, T., Kang, T., Laquintano, T., & Dietrich, V. (2023). Who benefits and who is excluded?: Transformative learning, equity, and generative artificial intelligence. *Journal of Transformative Learning, 10*(2), 92–103.

Akgun, S., & Greenhow, C. (2022). Artificial intelligence in education: Addressing ethical challenges in K-12 settings. *AI and Ethics (Online), 2*(3), 431–440. 10.1007%2Fs43681-021-00096-7

Bali, M., & Mostafa, H. (2024). *How AUC faculty are addressing AI in their teaching spring 2023*. The American University in Cairo. Retrieved from https://learnhub.aucegypt.edu/cltnewsletter/?p=1083

Blackie, M. A. L. (2024). ChatGPT is a game changer: Detection and eradication is not the way forward. *Teaching in Higher Education, 29*(4), 1109–1116. https://doi.org/10.1080/13562517.2023.2300951

Blei, D., Ng, A., & Jordan, M. (2023). Latent Dirichlet Allocation. *Journal of Machine Learning Research, 3*, 993–1022. Retrieved from https://www.jmlr.org/papers/volume3/blei03a/blei03a.pdf

Borenstein, J., & Howard, A. (2020). Emerging challenges in AI and the need for AI ethics education. *AI and Ethics (Online), 1*(1), 61–65. https://doi.org/10.1007/s43681-020-00002-7

Brevini, B. (2023). Chapter 3: Artificial intelligence, artificial solutions. In H. S. Saetra (Ed.), *Technology and sustainable development* (pp. 23–33). Routledge.

Carolus, A., Koch, M. J., Straka, S., Latoschik, M. E., & Weinrich, C. (2023). MAILS—Meta AI Literacy scale: Development and testing of an AI literacy questionnaire based on well-founded competency models and psychological change- and meta-competencies. *Computers in Human Behavior: Artificial Humans, 1*(2), 100014. https://doi.org/10.1016/j.chbah.2023.100014

Carvalho, C., Martinez-Maldonado, R., Tsai, Y., Markauskaite, L., & De Laat, M. (2022). How can we design for learning in an AI world? *Computers and Education: Artificial Intelligence, 3*, 100053. https://doi.org/10.1016/j.caeai.2022.100053

Chen, L., Chen, P., & Lin, Z. (2020). Artificial intelligence in education: A review. *IEEE Access, 8*, 75264–75278. https://doi.org/10.1109/ACCESS.2020.2988510

Correia, A. P., Hickey, M. S., & Xu, F. (2024). Beyond the virtual classroom: Integrating artificial intelligence in online learning. *Distance Education, 45*(3), 481–491. https://doi.org/10.1080/01587919.2024.2338706

Crompton, H. (2013). Mobile learning: New approach, new theory. In Z. L. Berge & L. Y. Muilenburg (Eds.), *Handbook of mobile learning* (pp. 47–57). Routledge. https://doi.org/10.4324/9780203118764-12

Davenport, T. H., & Mittal, N. (2022). How generative AI is changing creative work. *Harvard Business Review*. Retrieved from https://hbr.org/2022/11/how-generative-ai-is-changing-creative-work

Dignum, V. (2019). *Responsible Artificial Intelligence—How to develop and use AI in a responsible way* (1st ed.). Springer. https://doi.org/10.1007/978-3-030-30371-6

Dignum, V. (2021). The role and challenges of education for responsible AI. *London Review of Education, 19*(1), 1–11. https://doi.org/10.14324/LRE.19.1.01

Fowler, G. A. (2023). We tested a new ChatGPT-detector for teachers. It flagged an innocent student. *The Washington Post*. Retrieved from https://www.washingtonpost.com/technology/2023/04/01/chatgpt-cheating-detection-turnitin/

Garrison, D. R., Anderson, T., & Archer, W. (2010). The first decade of the community of inquiry framework: A retrospective. *The Internet and Higher Education, 13*(1–2), 5–9.

Hu, Y. H. (2022). Effects of the COVID-19 pandemic on the online learning behaviors of university students in Taiwan. *Education and Information Technologies, 27*(1), 469–491. https://doi.org/10.1007/s10639-021-10677-y

Kamatchi, S., & Muthuraman, T. (2022). Analyzing educational tweets using LDA model. *International Journal of Intelligent Systems and Applications in Engineering, 10*(4), 100–104. Retrieved from https://ijisae.org/index.php/IJISAE/article/view/2202

Kartal, G. (2024). The influence of ChatGPT on thinking skills and creativity of EFL student teachers: a narrative inquiry. *Journal of Education for Teaching, 50*(4), 627–642. https://doi.org/10.1080/02607476.2024.2326502

Kim, K., & Kwon, K. (2023). Exploring the AI competencies of elementary school teachers in South Korea. *Computers and Education: Artificial Intelligence, 4*, 100137. https://doi.org/10.1016/j.caeai.2023.100137

Klee, M. (2023). *She was falsely accused of cheating with AI—And she won't be the last.* RollingStone. Retrieved from https://www.rollingstone.com/culture/culture-features/student-accused-ai-cheating-turnitin-1234747351/

Kramm, N., & McKenna, S. (2023). AI amplifies the tough question: What is higher education really for? *Teaching in Higher Education, 28*(8), 2173–2178. https://doi.org/10.1080/13562517.2023.2263839

Laupichler, M. C., Aster, A., Schirch, J., & Raupach, T. (2022). Artificial Intelligence literacy in higher and adult education: A scoping literature review. *Computers and Education: Artificial Intelligence, 3*, 100101. https://doi.org/10.1016/j.caeai.2022.100101

Long, D., & Magerko, B. (2020). What is AI Literacy? Competencies and design considerations. In *CHI '20: Proceedings of the 2020 CHI Conference on Human Factors in Computing Systems* (pp. 1–16). Association for Computing Machinery. https://doi.org/10.1145/3313831.3376727

Luckin, R., Cukurova, M., Kent, C., & du Boulay, B. (2022). Empowering educators to be AI-ready. *Computers and Education. Artificial Intelligence, 3*, 100076. https://doi.org/10.1016/j.caeai.2022.100076

Martin, F., & Ertzberger, J. (2013). Here and now mobile learning: An experimental study on the use of mobile technology. *Computers & Education, 68*, 76–85. https://doi.org/10.1016/j.compedu.2013.04.021

McMurtrie, B. (2023). ChatGPT Is everywhere: Love it or hate it, academics can't ignore the already pervasive technology. *The Chronicle of Higher Education, 69*(15), 32–38. Retrieved from https://link.gale.com/apps/doc/A757640057/AONE

Miao, F., & Cukurova, M. (2024). *AI competency framework for teachers*. UNESCO. https://doi.org/10.54675/ZJTE2084

Miles, M. B., & Huberman, A. M. (1994). *Qualitative data analysis: an expanded sourcebook* (2nd ed.). Sage Publications.

Mills, K., Ruiz, P., & Lee, K. (2024). *Revealing an AI literacy framework for learners and educators*. Digital Promise. Retrieved from https://digitalpromise.org/2024/02/21/revealing-an-ai-literacy-framework-for-learners-and-educators/

Ministry of Defence. (2022). *Ambitious, safe, responsible: our approach to the delivery of AI-enabled capability in Defence*. Government of UK. Retrieved from https://www.gov.uk/government/publications/ambitious-safe-responsible-our-approach-to-the-delivery-of-ai-enabled-capability-in-defence/ambitious-safe-responsible-our-approach-to-the-delivery-of-ai-enabled-capability-in-defence#using-ai-ethically

Mishra, P., & Koehler, M. J. (2006). Technological pedagogical content knowledge: A framework for teacher knowledge. *Teachers College Record, 108*(6), 1017–1054. https://doi.org/10.1111/j.1467-9620.2006.00684.x

Mitchell, M., Wu, S., Zaldivar, A., Barnes, P., Vasserman, L., Hutchinson, B., Spitzer, E., Raji, I. D., & Gebru, T. (2019). Model cards for model reporting. In *FAT* '19: Proceedings of the Conference on Fairness, Accountability, and Transparency* (pp. 220–229). Association for Computing Machinery. https://doi.org/10.1145/3287560.3287596

Muilenberg, L. Y., & Berge, Z. L. (2015). Revisiting teacher preparation: Responding to technology transience in the educational setting. *The Quarterly Review of Distance Education, 16*(2), 93–105.

Ng, D. T. K., Leung, J. K. L., Chu, K. W. S., & Qiao, M. S. (2021). AI literacy: Definition, teaching, evaluation and ethical issues. *Asis&t, 58*(1), 504–509. https://doi.org/10.1002/pra2.487

Nikolić, N., Grljević, O., & Kovačević, A. (2020). Aspect-based sentiment analysis of reviews in the domain of higher education. *The Electronic Library, 38*(1), 44–64. https://doi.org/10.1108/EL-06-2019-0140

OECD. (2019). *OECD AI principles overview*. OECD, AI Policy Observatory. Retrieved from https://oecd.ai/en/ai-principles

Ouyang, F., & Jiao, P. (2021). Artificial intelligence in education: The three paradigms. *Computers and Education: Artificial Intelligence, 2*, 100020. https://doi.org/10.1016/j.caeai.2021.100020

Oztok, M., Wilton, L., Lee, K., Zingaro, D., MacKinnon, K., Makos, A., Phirangee, K., Brett, C., & Hewitt, J. (2014). Polysynchronous: dialogic construction of time in online learning. *E-Learning and Digital Media, 11*(2), 154–161. https://doi.org/10.2304/elea.2014.11.2.154

Paludi, M. (2023). *The right to privacy and data protection for high school students in the context of digital learning models and learning analytics*. LASI Europe DC. Retrieved from https://api.semanticscholar.org/CorpusID:271916840

Pedro, F., Subosa, M., Rivas, A., & Valverde, P. (2019). Artificial intelligence in education: Challenges and opportunities for sustainable development. In *Working papers on education policy*. Retrieved from https://unesdoc.unesco.org/ark:/48223/pf0000366994

Posner, T., & Fei-Fei, L. (2020). AI will change the world, so it's time to change AI. *Nature, 588*, S118. https://doi.org/10.1038/d41586-020-03412-z

Punch, K. F. (2009). *Introduction to research methods in education*. Sage Publications.

Ramos, G. I. (2021). *Press conference: Global consensus on AI ethics*. Retrieved from https://gabrielailianramos.wordpress.com/2021/11/29/press-conference-global-consensus-on-ai-ethics/

Sawyer, K. S. (2008). Optimizing learning: Implications of learning sciences research. In *Innovating to Learn, Learning to Innovate* (pp. 45–65). OECD Publishing. https://doi.org/10.1787/9789264047983-4-en
Schiff, D. (2022). Education for AI, not AI for Education: the role of education and ethics in national AI policy strategies. *International Journal of Artificial Intelligence in Education, 32*(3), 527–563. https://doi.org/10.1007/s40593-021-00270-2
Scottish AI Alliance. (2022). *The Scottish AI Playbook: Open and practical guidance on doing AI in Scotland.* Retrieved from https://www.scottishaiplaybook.com/resources-database/the-scottish-ai-playbook
Selwyn, N. (2024). On the limits of Artificial Intelligence (AI) in education. *Nordisk tidsskrift for pedagogikk og kritikk, 10*(1), 3–14. https://doi.org/10.23865/ntpk.v10.6062
Shaik, T., Tao, X., Dann, C., Xie, H., Li, Y., & Galligan, L. (2023). Sentiment analysis and opinion mining on educational data: A survey. *Natural Language Processing Journal, 2*, 100003. https://doi.org/10.1016/j.nlp.2022.100003
Strubell, E., Ganesh, A., & McCallum, A. (2019). *Energy and policy considerations for deep learning in NLP. arXiv* (Vol. 1906, p. 02243). Cornell University.
Tan, M., & Subramonyam, H. (2024). More than model documentation: Uncovering teachers' bespoke information needs for informed classroom integration of ChatGPT. In F. F. Mueller (Ed.), *CHI '24: Proceedings of the CHI Conference on Human Factors in Computing Systems* (pp. 1–19). Association for Computing Machinery. https://doi.org/10.1145/3613904.3642592
The White House. (2024). *Fact sheet: Biden-Harris administration outlines coordinated approach to harness power of AI for U.S. national security.* The White House. Retrieved from https://www.whitehouse.gov/briefing-room/statements-releases/2024/10/24/fact-sheet-biden-harris-administration-outlines-coordinated-approach-to-harness-power-of-ai-for-u-s-national-security/
Tidwell, D., Heston, M., & Fitzgerald, L. (2009). Introduction. In L. Fitzgerald, M. Heston, & D. Tidwell (Eds.), *Research methods for the self-study of practice* (Vol. 9). Springer.
Trust, T., Whalen, J., & Mouza, C. (2023). Editorial: ChatGPT: Challenges, opportunities, and implications for teacher education. *Contemporary Issues in Technology and Teacher Education, 23*(1) Retrieved from https://citejournal.org/volume-23/issue-1-23/editorial/editorial-chatgpt-challenges-opportunities-and-implications-for-teacher-education/
UNESCO. (2020). *Education: From COVID-19 school closures to recovery.* Retrieved from https://en.unesco.org/covid19/educationresponse
UNESCO. (2021). *Recommendation on the Ethics of Artificial Intelligence.* Retrieved from https://unesdoc.unesco.org/ark:/48223/pf0000381137/PDF/381137eng.pdf.multi
UNESCO. (2023a). *Generative AI and the future of education.* https://doi.org/10.54675/HOXG8740
UNESCO. (2023b). *Guidance for generative AI in education and research.* https://doi.org/10.54675/EWZM9535
UNESCO. (2023c). *UNESCO's Recommendation on the Ethics of Artificial Intelligence: Key facts.* Retrieved from https://unesdoc.unesco.org/ark:/48223/pf0000385082
Verdegem, P. (2021). *AI for Everyone?: Critical Perspectives.* University of Westminster Press.
Vincent-Lancrin, S., & Van der Viles, R. (2020). Trustworthy Artificial Intelligence (AI) in education: Promises and challenges. In *OECD Education Working Papers, No. 218.* OECD Publishing. https://doi.org/10.1787/a6c90fa9-en
Wilton, L. (2022). *Not Busy Work! The benefits of new literacies and social practices in online discussion.* Retrieved from https://ecampusontario.pressbooks.pub/designingforonlinediscussion/chapter/chapter-2/
Wilton, L., Khan, R., Brett, C., & Alexander, P. (2020). Private interactions in online learning discussions: Instructor perspectives. In L. Wilton & C. Brett (Eds.), *Handbook of research on online discussion-based teaching methods.* IGI Global. https://doi.org/10.4018/978-1-7998-3292-8
Wilton, L., Ip, S., Sharma, M., & Fan, F. (2022). Where is the AI? AI literacy for educators. In M. M. Rodrigo, N. Matsuda, A. I. Cristea, & V. Dimitrova (Eds.), *Artificial Intelligence*

in Education. Posters and Late Breaking Results, Workshops and Tutorials, Industry and Innovation Tracks, Practitioners' and Doctoral Consortium. AIED 2022. Lecture Notes in Computer Science (Vol. 13356). Springer. https://doi.org/10.1007/978-3-031-11647-6_31

Wilton, L., Brett, C., & Ip, S. (2024). From TPACK to Model Cards in AIED—Supporting AI readiness and AI literacy in education. In *EDULEARN24 Proceedings* (pp. 7941–7947). IATED. https://doi.org/10.21125/edulearn.2024.1869

Yin, R. K. (2014). *Case study research: Design and methods* (5th ed.). Sage Publications.

Yin, B., & Yuan, C. H. (2022). Detecting latent topics and trends in blended learning using LDA topic modeling. *Education and Information Technologies, 27*, 12689–12712. https://doi.org/10.1007/s10639-022-11118-0

Zawacki-Richter, O., Marín, V. I., Bond, M., & Gouverneur, F. (2019). Systematic review of research on artificial intelligence applications in higher education—Where are the educators? *International Journal of Educational Technology in Higher Education, 16*(1), 1–27. https://doi.org/10.1186/s41239-019-0171-0

Zimmerle, J. C. (2021). Safe, sound, and private: Promoting data protection for students. *Computers in the Schools, 38*(1), 1–18.

Lesley Wilton, PhD, OCT, moving from a career in technology to one researching technology in teaching, digital literacy and online learning, has been teaching and researching in AIEd at York University and the University of Toronto for more than a decade. She leads the AI in Education research cluster of multidisciplinary scholars studying the social implications of disruptive digital technologies at the Digital Life Institute. She has published widely and presented at many conferences. Lesley is the Vice-Chair of the IEEE SA P7015, working on the Draft Standard for Data and AI Literacy, Skills and Readiness.

Emerita Clare Brett from OISE, University of Toronto, is a former Department Chair of Curriculum, Teaching and Learning. She has been involved in research in the design of blended and online learning environments for the last 30+ years. Professor Brett's research interests have focused on investigating technical and social supports for collaborative online learning, issues of diversity and inclusion in online spaces, and more recently, understanding the role of AI in Education. With her colleague Professor Jim Hewitt, she leads the PeppeR Project (https://pepperproject.ca), that was awarded an SSHRC grant on "What does online interaction really contribute to the online learning experience?"

Stephen Ip is a program development coordinator and educational researcher at the Southern Alberta Institute of Technology (SAIT). He is currently involved in a number of cross-faculty research initiatives, including collaboration with the Digital Learning Exchange Group at SAIT to explore applicable tools, pedagogical approaches, and technology solutions required to support course designs that align with the institution's emphasis on applied education. Stephen's research interests lie in the field of Applied Learning and Educational Technology, particularly educational tools that can make learning more practical and engaging for distance learners.

Rutwa Engineer is a Computer Science assistant professor at the Department of Mathematical and Computational Sciences at the University of Toronto Mississauga (UTM). She is also cross-appointed with the Institute for the Study of University Pedagogy (ISUP) at UTM and is a faculty affiliate at the Schwartz Reisman Institute for Technology and Society (SRI) at the University of Toronto. Rutwa primarily teaches Introduction to Computer Programming and Computer Science, in addition to Computer Prganization and Systems Programming. Her research invites new ways of thinking, dreaming, and coding in computing education and AI in education through epistemic diversity.

Athena Tassis is a PhD student in Curriculum and Pedagogy, with an emphasis on Digital Technologies, at OISE, University of Toronto. She holds a Master of Education from Harvard University, where she specialized in Learning Design, Innovation, and Technology. Her research explores the role of AI in education, focusing on how students and educators interact with AI systems, the development of AI literacy, and the implications of human–AI collaboration in learning environments. Athena has worked across sectors to support the development of AI-integrated learning solutions and to advance best practices in adult learning. She is committed to fostering thoughtful and responsible uses of AI in education.

Part III
Improving Pedagogy and Instruction: Potential and Issues

Chapter 5
Development of Academic Discourse Through Generative Artificial Intelligence-Enabled Transmediation

Heather Cato and Amy Burke

Abstract This chapter examines the use of generative artificial intelligence (GenAI) as an innovative teaching tool in literacy education, focusing on its potential to scaffold students' development of academic discourse. The pedagogy was developed in response to an analysis of academic papers from three cohorts in a master's-level literacy program, which revealed that students struggled to translate informal insights into formal academic discourse. A series of GenAI-enhanced assignments moving across different modes were designed to help students deepen their thinking and articulate their learning via formal academic discourse. The findings suggest that iterative GenAI use not only supports academic discourse articulation but also deepens conceptual understanding and organizational skills. The study highlights GenAI's scholarly significance in enhancing communicative competence and academic writing within literacy education. This approach demonstrates how GenAI can be leveraged more broadly to address specific challenges in higher education, particularly in developing students' ability to express complex ideas in academic contexts.

Keywords Academic discourse · Multimodal learning · Technology-enhanced learning · Transmediation

This chapter explores the integration of generative artificial intelligence (GenAI) as an educational tool within a master's-level literacy education course. We take a conceptual approach, describing the integration of artificial intelligence through an exploratory lens. Our work is informed by reflective practice, offering insights not through a structured experiment but through the natural evolution of teaching strategies based on real classroom experiences. We describe how the use of GenAI tools

---

H. Cato (✉) · A. Burke
Texas Woman's University, Denton, TX, USA
e-mail: hcato@twu.edu

G. Tchibozo (ed.), *International Perspectives of Generative AI in Education*, Advances in Artificial Intelligence in Education 3,
https://doi.org/10.1007/978-3-031-99804-1_5

across modes scaffolded students in deepening their thinking and their ability to communicate their learning across settings and audiences.

As part of their capstone project, students in a master's-level literacy education course were asked to synthesize their learning from across their coursework, articulating their beliefs about literacy learning, supported by research and theory, in a traditional academic paper. These papers are expected to adhere to a structured format that presents well-researched arguments and insights, conforming rigorously to scholarly conventions and citation practices. In analyzing papers across three cohorts of students, the course instructor, Heather (Author 1), noted that students' use of academic discourse was not fully developed and did not reflect the learning they had been able to articulate informally. This suggested that students were encountering challenges in translating their thoughts for an academic audience. In response, Heather designed a series of connected assignments that each utilized a GenAI tool and that asked students to translate their thinking into a different modality, scaffolding students in the development of their final paper. The transmediation of students' thinking across mode and genre, leveraging Open GenAI's language models as a tool to help students reflect on their own work, facilitated and strengthened students' ability to communicate to academic audiences via academic discourse. The use of GenAI language models did not entail the generation of entirely novel content; rather, it served as a tool to support students in refining their own language, conceptual understanding, and organization of ideas, thereby allowing students to more deeply consider what they know, what they mean, and how to best communicate it to various audiences.

Drawing on the constructs of semiotic mediation (Vygotsky, 1981) and transmediation (Batchelor, 2015; McCormick, 1995; Siegel, 1995; Suhor, 1984), the authors argue for the transformative potential of machine learning to scaffold the learning process. These theories illuminate GenAI's role in fostering a nuanced exchange across different modalities and genres, assisting students in refining their academic discourse from informal insights to structured, formal expression. This process underscores GenAI's potential to aid teachers in facilitating enriching educational experiences.

Definitions of Terms

Semiotic mediation: The process by which social and cultural signs and tools (like language) mediate and shape cognitive development (Vygotsky, 1981).

Modality: A specific channel or resource for meaning-making (e.g., visual, auditory, tactile). Each mode has its own potential for meaning and its own limitations (Jewitt, 2014; Kress & van Leeuwen, 2001).

Mode: Related to communicative purpose, the specific way a modality is used (Bezemer & Kress, 2008; Kress & van Leeuwen, 2001; O'Halloran, 2011).

Multimodality: The use of several semiotic modes in the design of a semiotic product or event, together with the particular way in which these modes are combined (Kress, 2010).

Transmediation: The process of transforming or adapting content from one medium to another while preserving the core message (Suhor, 1984).

Theoretical Framework

Our theoretical framework is rooted in Vygotsky's concept of semiotic mediation, which we further extend by incorporating the principle of transmediation. These interrelated ideas form the core foundation of the work presented in this chapter. Together, they help illuminate how meaning-making processes evolve across different sign systems and modes of communication.

Semiotic Mediation

Our perspective on learning is grounded in Vygotsky's (1981) sociocultural theory with a strong emphasis on the role of semiotic mediation, which refers to the use of culturally constructed and situated signs and symbols as tools to mediate and make sense of our interactions with the world, in the development of higher mental functions and the construction of complex learning. Semiotic mediation plays a crucial role in Vygotsky's theory, as he believed that these symbolic tools (e.g., language, writing systems, number systems, diagrams, maps) serve as the means through which we interact with and make sense of our environment. These semiotic mediators not only aid in communication but are also instrumental in shaping our cognitive processes. Vygotsky emphasized the importance of language as the primary semiotic mediator, as it allows us to internalize social interactions and construct meaning. Through language, we can engage in self-regulation, planning, and abstract thinking, which are essential for cognitive development. In the work described here, we also draw on Vygotsky's concept of the "zone of proximal development" (ZPD), which refers to the distance between a learner's actual developmental level and this learner's potential level of development with the guidance of a more knowledgeable other or by way of semiotic mediators. These semiotic tools can serve as scaffolds that support the learner in achieving higher levels of understanding and cognitive functioning.

Transmediation

Extending the ways in which semiotic mediation functions in the learning process, this work also suggests how transmediation, which refers to the process of translating meanings from one sign system or representational mode into another, can serve to deepen learning, as students must refine, redesign, and/or extend their thinking as the modality changes (e.g., from academic writing to oral interviews). Suhor (1984) coined the term transmediation to describe the act of translating content from one sign system (e.g., writing, speech, graphics) into another. He argued that transmediation can deepen students' understanding of the subject matter by requiring them to represent it in multiple ways. Siegel (1995) examined the role of transmediation in fostering critical thinking and literacy skills. She suggested that transmediation encourages students to analyze and synthesize information across different modes of representation, which can enhance their comprehension and critical thinking abilities. McCormick (1995) explored the use of transmediation in science education. She argued that transmediation can help students better understand scientific concepts by representing them through various modes, such as diagrams, models, equations, and written explanations. Batchelor (2015) investigated transmediation in the context of multimodal literacy education. She proposed that transmediation can help students develop multimodal literacy skills by requiring them to navigate and translate meanings across different semiotic modes (e.g., text, images, sounds, gestures).

Related Literature

Academic discourse plays a critical role in literacy learning, shaping how knowledge is communicated and understood across different disciplines. It requires students to engage with complex language structures and abstract ideas, often posing significant challenges, especially for those from diverse linguistic and cultural backgrounds. Mastery of academic discourse is not only essential for success in education but also serves as a gatekeeper to academic achievement. Researchers have examined how GenAI can assist and support students' learning in academic settings.

Challenges of Academic Discourse

Researchers have identified several challenges associated with academic discourse in literacy learning. Because academic discourse employs specialized vocabulary, complex sentence structures, and discipline-specific genres, it can pose challenges for students, particularly those from diverse linguistic and cultural backgrounds, as they may struggle to comprehend and produce academic texts (Snow & Uccelli, 2009; Zwiers, 2008). In addition, academic discourse tends to be abstract and decontextualized, focused on generalizations and principles rather than concrete personal experiences. This level of abstraction can make it difficult for students to grasp and engage with academic concepts and texts (Gee, 2004; Schleppegrell, 2004). Furthermore, each academic discipline has its own discourse conventions, rhetorical patterns, and ways of constructing knowledge, so students may struggle to adapt to these varying discourse practices across different subject areas (Moje, 2007; Shanahan & Shanahan, 2008). Academic discourse is often perceived as a gatekeeper to academic success, and students may feel disempowered or disconnected from this discourse, especially if it conflicts with their cultural or linguistic identities (Delpit, 1988; Gee, 1989). Many educators may not explicitly teach the conventions and practices of academic discourse, assuming that students will acquire them implicitly. However, research suggests that explicit instruction and scaffolding are often necessary for students to develop proficiency in academic language and discourse (Fang & Schleppegrell, 2010; Zwiers, 2008). Assessments and evaluations in academic settings often prioritize and privilege certain forms of academic discourse, which can disadvantage students who are still developing proficiency in these discourse practices (Abedi & Herman, 2010; Bunch, 2014).

To address these challenges, researchers recommend adopting a more inclusive and explicit approach to academic discourse instruction, valuing and bridging diverse linguistic and cultural resources, and fostering critical awareness of the power dynamics inherent in academic discourse practices (Bunch, 2014; Delpit, 1988; Gee, 2004).

Use of GenAI Applications in Educational Settings

Several studies examining the use of GenAI applications in educational settings suggest that GenAI tools have the potential to positively impact learning, motivation, and engagement. However, it is important to note that the effectiveness of GenAI applications in education depends on several factors, such as the quality of the GenAI system, the specific learning domain, what is being measured and how it is measured, its integration with pedagogical strategies and, we emphasize, the expertise and support of human instructors.

Intelligent Tutoring Systems (ITS)

Intelligent tutoring systems (ITSs) are GenAI-powered systems designed to provide personalized instruction and feedback to students. These systems leverage machine learning algorithms and cognitive models to adapt their teaching strategies to individual student needs and learning styles. Studies have shown that well-designed ITSs can be as effective as human tutors in improving student learning and performance, particularly in domains such as mathematics, physics, and computer science (Koedinger et al., 1997; VanLehn, 2011).

Conversational GenAI Agents

Researchers have explored the use of conversational GenAI agents as virtual teaching assistants or peer learning companions. These GenAI agents utilize natural language processing and machine learning algorithms to understand and respond to student queries in real time, simulating human-like conversations. Research findings suggest that these agents can engage students in productive dialogues, provide feedback, and foster motivation and engagement (Kerly et al., 2008; Winkler & Söllner, 2018).

Automated Writing Feedback Systems

GenAI systems have also been developed to analyze and provide feedback on students' writing assignments. These GenAI-powered writing assessment tools typically employ natural language processing techniques to evaluate various aspects of writing, including grammar, style, organization, and content, offering students detailed and timely feedback on their compositions. Studies have shown that these systems can provide feedback that is comparable to that of human graders and can help improve students' writing skills (Correnti et al., 2022; Dong, 2023; Shermis & Burstein, 2003; Wilson & Czik, 2016).

Adaptive Learning Systems

GenAI-powered adaptive learning systems can personalize the learning experience by adjusting the content, pace, and difficulty level based on individual student needs and progress. These adaptive systems utilize sophisticated algorithms to analyze student performance data in real time, creating dynamic learning paths that optimize the educational experience for each individual learner. Studies have shown that these systems can improve student learning outcomes, engagement, and motivation (e.g., Essa & Ayad, 2012; Walkington, 2013).

Learning Analytics Tools

GenAI techniques, including machine learning and natural language processing, have been applied to analyze student data (e.g., performance, engagement, behavior) to provide insights and recommendations for instructors and students. Research suggests that these learning analytics tools can help identify at-risk students, predict performance, and inform instructional strategies (Ahmed, 2024; Issah et al., 2023; Sandra et al., 2021). These tools often allow the leveraging of large datasets and complex algorithms, potentially uncovering patterns and trends that might be difficult for human observers to detect.

Methodology: An Iterative Pedagogical Process

Our method reflects an iterative, reflective practice, suggesting the potential of GenAI in enhancing literacy practices and academic discourse. This work took place within the capstone course of a master's-level literacy education program. The program is situated at a mid-sized regional comprehensive university in the southwestern part of the United States. The program is respected throughout the area and is known for its focus on literacy and literacy leadership.

Heather, a white cisgender woman and faculty member, has 5 years of teaching experience in higher education at the undergraduate and master's levels. She directs the department's master's program and brings extensive leadership experience from her time in the K-12 public school system. Amy, also a faculty member in the department, is a white cisgender woman who has taught in higher education for over 15 years and who previously taught in K-12 public schools for 6 years. She served as a reflective thought partner and peer debriefer for Heather and greatly contributed to the theoretical framing that situates the reflective iterative process within larger bodies of theory and research.

The department's partnership with a local school district, which has allocated federal Title I funds (i.e., federal funds for supporting schools with high-need student populations), specifically for professional development, highlights a strategic effort to empower educators from these schools to complete an advanced degree focused on literacy education. Educators who participate in this partnership take master's-level courses at the university. These courses count as continuing professional development credit with the district and toward a master's degree from the university.

In the master's-level literacy education course, the major assignment involves creating a digital professional learning portfolio, which serves as the culminating project for the program. This comprehensive assignment begins with students writing three reflexive professional narratives that document their literacy knowledge and expertise in alignment with the International Literacy Association's Standards for the Preparation of Literacy Professionals (International Literacy Association, 2017). These narratives are crucial, as they demonstrate the students' ability to evaluate their educational experiences and growth within the field. Subsequently, students develop a digital professional presence through a personal website that showcases these reflections and their competencies in effective literacy instruction. The assessment of both the narratives and the website is rigorously conducted via rubrics that evaluate content mastery and digital presentation skills, ensuring a holistic approach to measuring student learning outcomes.

The students in the course highlighted in this chapter represented a variety of roles within the educational system, including classroom teachers across different grade levels and subjects, literacy coaches, principals, and other specialist roles. With teaching experience ranging from 3 to 25 years, these educators brought their unique literacy teaching background to the program, sharing a collective goal to enhance their instructional practices and leadership in literacy.

Analysis of Previous Students' Writing

Reflecting on the previous year's course (Year 1), Heather recognized the significant strides students made in developing their instructional confidence and professionalism through our program. Despite meeting the course expectations, she felt that there was an emerging need for students to articulate their educational beliefs more robustly, especially in an increasingly politicized school environment where clear and well-supported arguments are crucial for supporting or defending instructional decision making.

In response to the challenges observed during Years 1 and 2, when students could articulate important literacy concepts but struggled to back them with substantial evidence or were unable to articulate them in formal academic discourse, the Year 3 approach focused on creating micro-opportunities for students to develop and express their beliefs. This pedagogical shift was designed to provide smaller, more manageable steps that would ultimately lead to the creation of comprehensive and well-supported professional portfolios accessible to a global audience on the web. These changes aimed mainly to aid students' ability to articulate, support, and situate their literacy beliefs and practices in a way that was not only reflective of their personal educational journey but also grounded in rigorous academic discourse.

Overview of the Iterative Teaching/Learning Process

The iterative process (see Fig. 5.1) consisted of several interconnected steps, each leveraging GenAI tools to facilitate different aspects of student learning (see Table 5.1). Students were first asked to create social media posts that represented the overarching themes of what would become their paper. Next, Heather interviewed students about the ideas in their posts in a podcast-style format, asking a series of questions designed to further elicit students' beliefs and understandings about literacy learning. Each discussion was recorded using Zoom Video Conferencing and then uploaded to an Open GenAI-powered app, which then transcribed the interview. Next, with a programmed command, the app utilized the transcription to render the interview into a blog post. Students then critically reflected on and revised their blog posts and then used the revised posts to draft their formal academic paper. The students' final papers showed evidence of a greater ability to engage in academic discourse, arguably as a result of the iterative reflection and revision process, which was partially supported by the use of GenAI.

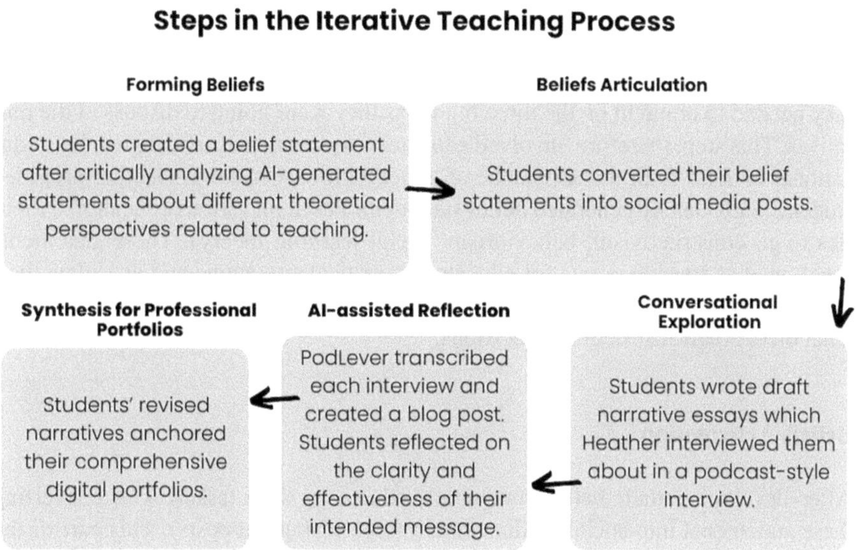

Fig. 5.1 Steps in the iterative teaching process

Table 5.1 GenAI tools used during the learning process

Tool	Description	Purpose
ChatGPT	A GenAI-driven language model designed to understand and generate human-like text based on the input it receives	Used to generate initial prompts and responses that helped scaffold students to articulate their preliminary ideas and beliefs about literacy in a structured way
Zoom Video Conferencing Transcription Software	Captures the dialogue in meetings and discussions	Utilized during podcast-style interviews to accurately capture verbal discussions and convert them into text for further analysis and refinement
PodLever	A specialized GenAI tool that transforms audio recordings or transcripts into coherent blog posts by interpreting the text to maintain the essence of the original discussions while structuring them in a more polished and readable format (https://www.podlever.com/)	This tool helped students see an external interpretation of their thoughts

Forming Beliefs

Before students began drafting their reflexive professional narratives for the course, they needed to home in on the three big ideas they were going to discuss in the narratives. This step, therefore, involved educators exploring and articulating their educational beliefs. With the assistance of a GenAI tool, ChatGPT, Heather provided students with GenAI-generated belief statements based on various educational theories (e.g., constructivism, behaviorism, social learning theory). These statements functioned as starting points for educators to critically examine and articulate their own pedagogical positions, beginning students' process of consciously defining what drives their instructional decisions.

Beliefs Articulation

After developing their belief statements, educators were tasked with converting these statements into social media content (e.g., Instagram posts). This part of the process involved the first transmediation, as students layered their increasingly complex ideas into more succinct, engaging language suitable for broader public engagement while also integrating visual elements to clarify and enhance their messages. This transition between initial belief formation and public articulation was crucial for educators to refine and clarify their pedagogical perspectives because they had a clear and real audience in mind, for whom they wrote their messages and to whom they addressed them.

Conversational Exploration

Using their refined belief statements, educators then crafted draft narrative essays (second transmediation) linking their beliefs to their working theoretical frameworks and personal teaching practices. As a part of this process, the students used these drafts as the basis of a podcast-style interview with their professor, Heather. At a time of their choice, the students scheduled a web-based virtual call with Heather. During the interview, she asked a series of questions that required students to state, define, and explain their beliefs. These interviews served as a platform for them to articulate and expand upon their beliefs in a conversational (verbal) manner (transmediation 3).

GenAI-Assisted Reflection

Utilizing the GenAI tool PodLever, transcripts from the podcasts were used to generate blog posts about the students' beliefs. The blog posts allowed educators to see their spoken words in a written format (transmediation four) through the application of GenAI tools. This step provided an opportunity for students to critically assess the clarity and effectiveness of their intended message. This approach made it easier for the students to recognize and address any gaps or inconsistencies in the articulation of their beliefs. The students then used this information to revise and edit their original narrative drafts (transmediation five). The goal was to ensure that their ideas were coherently and effectively expressed in written form and that they were ready for a wider academic audience.

Synthesis for Professional Portfolios

As the final assignment in the course, educators were required to synthesize their articulated beliefs into comprehensive digital professional portfolios. This task involved the thoughtful and detailed compilation and organization of their contributions, demonstrating their developmental progress throughout the program and anchoring it in research. The portfolios were not simply collections of assignments but were curated to represent each educator's professional growth and insights. Designed for peer and professional review, these portfolios provided a platform for educators to showcase their abilities in academic discourse and to effectively present their perspectives on literacy education. This step was essential for educators to display their professional evolution and establish themselves as literacy leaders within the educational community. Heather saw a marked difference in these students' ability to communicate their thinking in formal academic discourse compared with that of students in the previous year.

Reflective Insights

The integration of GenAI tools into a master's-level literacy education course unfolded throughout the semester, guided by responsive adjustments based on faculty observations and emerging student needs. In prior iterations of this capstone course, the instructors observed notable advances in student confidence and understanding of literacy instruction across their graduate coursework. However, challenges remained: while students could identify their literacy beliefs, their ability to articulate, exemplify, and substantiate these beliefs with research was inconsistent. Some students relied on limited sources, whereas others struggled to synthesize research to support their positions. This observation highlights the need for ongoing, adaptive support in developing robust academic discourse skills. Recognizing this, the instructor dynamically incorporated GenAI-mediated activities to scaffold students' abilities to strengthen and express their pedagogical positions more effectively.

The GenAI-facilitated framework comprises several stages, each designed to incrementally develop students' abilities to engage with complex literacy theories and articulate them effectively across different platforms. Reflecting on the stages of the process described above and shown in Fig. 5.1 in retrospect, we believe that each stage afforded students specific learning opportunities through the transmediation that occurred from stage to stage:

Forming Beliefs → Identification of Core Beliefs
Beliefs Articulation → Crafting Core Beliefs for a Specific Audience
Conversational Exploration → Articulating Core Beliefs Verbally
GenAI-assisted Reflection → Shift into Written Academic Discourse
Synthesis for Professional Portfolio → Refinement of Academic Discourse

Identification of Core Beliefs

The initial stage in the GenAI-enabled educational framework involved students identifying and articulating three core beliefs about literacy education. In previous years of teaching the course, students typically crafted widely broad statements disconnected from theory, such as "Literacy requires practice from students to master their skills" or "All students can learn to read at high levels when their needs are met." To scaffold this critical process, the instructor decided to utilize ChatGPT to generate sample literacy belief statements to be used as a scaffold for students. The tool was prompted to produce statements about a variety of educational theories to produce a diverse array of belief statements that students could use as a starting point to develop their own belief statements.

These GenAI-generated samples served multiple purposes for the students. First, they provided concrete examples that modeled for students how to crystallize their abstract understandings into articulated statements. Second, by including belief statements from a variety of pedagogical stances, the exercise challenged the students' own views and encouraged critical thinking and debate. In class, the students discussed the statements with each other. The comments from the students ranged from "this is a truly great way to word this belief," to "yikes! I do not agree with this one at all." This approach not only pushed students to engage more deeply with the material but also fostered a more thoughtful and reflective process of their beliefs, preventing them from merely adopting prepared statements. This was essential for moving from initial belief formation to expressing these beliefs in a structured and meaningful way, developing well-articulated beliefs that aligned with their educational philosophies and were actionable in real-world teaching scenarios.

By starting with this foundational activity, students were better prepared to engage in the subsequent stages of the capstone project, which included translating these beliefs into various formats, such as social media posts, podcasts, and academic papers. This first step ensured that the core ideas driving their educational practices were solidly in place, thus enhancing the coherence and impact of their further academic and professional communications.

Crafting Core Beliefs for a Specific Audience

The progression through GenAI-enabled modalities in the course led students to a pivotal activity: crafting and sharing their core beliefs on social media, specifically through Instagram. In this stage, students began transitioning abstract pedagogical ideas and theoretical beliefs into concrete, communicative expressions designed to engage a broader audience. Initially, the students took the three core beliefs they had identified and articulated with the help of GenAI tools and transformed them into visually appealing social media posts. Owing to its visual nature and broad reach, Instagram encouraged engagement and dissemination beyond academic circles, allowing students to freely express and mold their ideas in a familiar and less formal environment. In this way, Instagram served as an entry point for students' academic thinking.

The transition from a purely academic exercise to creating public-facing social media posts marked a significant shift for students, requiring them to refine their language and presentation skills to ensure clarity and accessibility. This transmediation process involved not only adapting their academic content to diverse audiences potentially unfamiliar with academic jargon but also critically considering the aesthetics of their posts—how visuals and colors could effectively represent their beliefs and attract attention on Instagram, a visually driven platform. Students were encouraged to use ChatGPT as a means to play with language and word choice, further enhancing the communicative effectiveness of their posts. The creation of these posts was not merely about dissemination but also about reflection and iteration. As students prepared their content for social media, they engaged in revising their statements, focusing on clarity and impact. Knowing that their work would be viewed by peers, educators, and potentially a broader public audience instilled a sense of responsibility and urgency to articulate their beliefs authentically and persuasively.

The informal yet public nature of social media encouraged more open and creative engagement with content, allowing students to experiment and evolve their academic expressions in real time. Reflecting on the social media posts created by students, it became evident that there was a broad spectrum of understanding and engagement. Some posts stuck closely to basic definitions or included personal anecdotes about literacy, whereas others bridged connections to broader educational frameworks or societal implications. This variation not only highlights the diverse starting points of the students but also underscores the potential for significant growth through guided, reflective practice in a public setting.

This stage not only facilitated the initial expression of student beliefs in an accessible format but also set the stage for more sophisticated academic interactions. By engaging with a familiar platform in an academic context, students began to see the value of their ideas and gained confidence in their ability to communicate these ideas effectively, setting a solid foundation for the subsequent, more formal stages of their academic and professional discourse development.

Articulating Core Beliefs Verbally

After the students crafted their belief statements and shared them via Instagram carousels, the course design called for an integration of their personal experiences and research to further substantiate these beliefs. This phase involved using a graphic organizer to collate experiences from the master's program and compile relevant research, setting the stage for writing narrative essays for each belief statement. These essays were intended to develop academic arguments backed by personal insights and evidence. However, during the iterative process of drafting and revising these narrative essays, a critical challenge emerged. Students struggled to effectively incorporate feedback that suggested that they better align their experiences with research findings. For example, a student might describe how they fostered student engagement through project-based learning but had difficulty connecting this practice to research on active learning strategies. To address this, the instructor introduced podcast-style interviews to enable students to view their writing from a new perspective and critically evaluate their own narratives as if they were conversing with an unfamiliar audience.

The podcast-style interviews served multiple pedagogical purposes, enhancing the course's reflective nature. Conducting the interviews via Zoom allowed the students to engage in dialogues about their beliefs, supporting research, and how their experiences reinforced these beliefs. This dialogic form encouraged more natural and reflexive expression than did the written form. The interviews required students to articulate the academic discourse behind their beliefs, exposing challenges in citing research, constructing compelling arguments, or articulating the significance of their beliefs beyond classroom confines. The real-time nature of the interviews also meant that students had to transmediate their thoughts from the written essays to oral conversation during the interviews, which required students to think on their feet, a skill crucial for educators in any setting. This setup was designed to simulate real-world thought leadership experiences, preparing students for professional educational leadership roles.

During the interviews, the students faced questions designed to draw out and support the articulation of their beliefs. This method illuminated the core issue with their essays: a lack of compelling arguments that were both research-backed and articulated with conviction. Initially, the nervousness of the podcast format, which demanded on-the-spot articulation, provided an authentic impetus for preparation, compelling students to internalize and thus better express their beliefs. These podcast-style interviews became a transformative course component, offering a platform for deeper exploration and clarification of beliefs and bridging the gap between written and spoken word. This bridging was crucial in preparing students for more formal academic writing that would follow, enabling them to engage in academic discourse that was both authentic and research informed.

Shift into Written Academic Discourse

After the podcast-style interviews, the course moved into a critical juncture: the transformation of spoken insights into written form through GenAI-assisted transcriptions to blog posts. This transition was crucial not only for the students' development in academic communication but also for fostering deeper introspection into the substance of their expressed beliefs. The use of GenAI to transcribe the podcast interviews served as a pivotal tool for students to see their spoken words laid out in text. The transcriptions acted as an unvarnished reflection of their oral discourse, capturing the nuances of conversational language. This raw, textual mirror allowed students to observe their communicative strengths and weaknesses from a new vantage point, highlighting areas that required further explanation or clarification.

Using PodLever, a specialized GenAI tool, the transcripts of the podcast-style interviews were transformed into blog posts. This stage highlights the predictive capabilities of artificial intelligence. The students witnessed firsthand how GenAI interpreted and presented their spoken words. Some were pleasantly surprised by how well they "sounded," while others were disappointed that PodLever missed nuances they believed were clear in their interviews. This experience revealed that their explanations might not have been as straightforward as they thought. As the GenAI constructed narratives around their discussions, students engaged with these texts to critically evaluate and refine their own writing. This process of revision was crucial in enhancing their academic writing skills and deepening their understanding of literacy education. In addition to just converting speech to text, the GenAI-assisted blog posts served as a vital reflective tool, empowering students to critically assess and improve their expression of beliefs with greater precision, clarity, and academic rigor and preparing them for future scholarly and professional challenges.

This stage focused on guiding students through a reflective process. The GenAI-assisted transcriptions and blog posts were an essential reflective tool that empowered students to critically evaluate their own articulation of their beliefs and experiences. Engaging with GenAI-drafted content, students developed a keen eye for detail and a deeper understanding of academic discourse demands. This interaction allowed them to critically evaluate their writing, highlighting discrepancies between their intended meanings and the GenAI interpretations, which provided a concrete starting point for refining their expressions.

Refinement of Academic Discourse

The GenAI-generated blog posts initially acted as a scaffold, converting spoken language from interviews into structured, coherent written content. This transition provided students with their first insight into how oral discussions could evolve into compelling written material. The next crucial step involved students returning to revise their initial drafts. Students utilized the discrepancies identified between their intended messages and the GenAI-interpreted text as a springboard for refinement. By methodically aligning their informal expressions with the stringent demands of academic writing, the iterative nature of this stage transformed into a profound learning experience. It not only enhanced students' engagement with their text but also deepened their grasp of the underlying subject matter, preparing them for more rigorous academic challenges.

As students used what they learned from the GenAI-generated drafts, they engaged in a critical and deliberate revision process of their narrative essays, focusing on how their expressions aligned with academic rigor and where they diverged. This phase allowed the students to delve deeply into the core of their content, scrutinizing the depth, clarity, and relevance of their arguments. Students also realized that the GenAI's predictive capabilities were limited by the quality of the input, which underscored the need for clarity and thoroughness in their own communication. This insight led to a deeper understanding of the revisions needed, enabling students to refine their initial narrative essays about their literacy beliefs for academic discourse. Through peer review and collaboration, students enhanced their ability to critically evaluate and elevate their academic writing through a scaffolded iterative process that transformed informal expressions into formal academic articulations.

By the end of this stage, students had not only revised their initial essays to better reflect their beliefs and academic standards but also positioned themselves as emerging thought leaders in the field of literacy. The engagement with GenAI-generated content had, in essence, become a practice arena, equipping students with the critical skills necessary to navigate and contribute to the scholarly discourse within their field. The iterative revision process thus served as a critical bridge, carrying students from the initial stages of expression to a place where their academic voice could emerge with confidence and clarity.

From Articulation to Advocacy

The transmediation journey culminated with students constructing their professional portfolios, a process that synthesized all the learning and refinement they had engaged in. These portfolios encapsulated not only the students' academic growth but also their evolution from simple articulations to sophisticated, critically engaged discourse. Throughout the portfolio construction process, students critically evaluated and selected pieces that best represented their beliefs, skills, and pedagogical stances. This reflective selection process was underpinned by their earlier work, which included nuanced content from blog posts and social media interactions. By revisiting and curating these pieces, the students engaged in a rigorous refinement process, ensuring that each element of the portfolio articulated their educational philosophies with clarity and was supported by robust research. This iterative process not only enhanced their understanding and expression of complex academic concepts, such as literacy development theories, differentiated instruction, and formative assessment practices but also prepared them to present themselves as professionals ready to lead and innovate in literacy education.

The completion of these digital professional portfolios marked a significant milestone in the students' journey from articulation to advocacy. The portfolios enabled the students to make informed arguments for instructional practices and policies, effectively moving them from discussing theoretical concepts to advocating for practical applications. As a result, students emerged as confident leaders equipped to influence and guide literacy discourse at a professional level, advocating for practices that enhance literacy education across diverse contexts. This final transmediation step ensured that the students were not only ready to share their coherent vision of literacy but also prepared to engage in professional discourse with authority and insight.

This reflective narrative on the use of GenAI tools in literacy education underscores a significant transformation in student engagement and mastery of academic discourse. The faculty's responsive and iterative approach to incorporating GenAI effectively supported students' immediate needs and catalyzed their development in articulating complex literacy concepts. This adaptive exploration highlighted GenAI's potential as a scaffold, enhancing students' academic communication and critical thinking. Observations revealed substantial progress in students' engagement with academic discourse, from initial social media interactions evolving into sophisticated analyses. The transmediation process enabled a profound shift in students' ability to refine and express their educational philosophies. The journey from personal belief articulation to professional advocacy is emblematic of the transformative power of GenAI integration in educational practices, reflecting innovative pedagogical strategies that can shape the future of literacy instruction and leadership.

Pedagogical Implications

The integration of GenAI in literacy education represents a significant evolution from traditional teaching methods to a more technologically enhanced learning environment. The capacity of AI to provide personalized feedback and adapt learning materials to individual student needs is a powerful tool that can dramatically broaden educational possibilities and innovate teaching strategies. By facilitating more tailored and responsive educational experiences, GenAI can effectively support both educators and students in achieving higher levels of academic engagement and understanding. This strategic use of GenAI harnesses its strengths as a teaching aid, emphasizing its role in augmenting the educational process while allowing for the maintenance of the essential human elements of teaching.

The exploratory findings suggest that GenAI tools can significantly increase students' confidence and authority in academic contexts. For example, students reported that using GenAI-based writing assistants such as Grammarly and ChatGPT helped them refine their arguments and structure their essays more coherently, which led to increased self-assurance when presenting their work. Additionally, students who used GenAI to generate preliminary outlines or brainstorming ideas indicated that the process made them feel more prepared and knowledgeable when engaging in class discussions. By enhancing the development of complex argumentation skills and encouraging more thorough engagement with academic content, GenAI tools serve as vital support for empowering students. This support enables them to articulate their viewpoints more clearly and effectively, thus bolstering their presence and impact within academic discussions.

Future Research Directions

Future research should explore a variety of educational settings and student demographics to better understand the adaptability and effectiveness of GenAI tools. Comparative studies are especially crucial, as they can offer insights into how GenAI-enhanced teaching methods perform against traditional pedagogical approaches. Additionally, methodological studies could assess GenAI's role in various instructional contexts, helping to identify the conditions under which GenAI tools are most beneficial. Such research would provide a more comprehensive understanding of how GenAI can be integrated effectively into educational practices, ensuring that it meets the diverse needs of learners and educators.

The potential of GenAI to revolutionize literacy education is highlighted through this conceptual exploration, which suggests that GenAI can scaffold learning processes, enhance student engagement, and support the development of sophisticated academic skills. As educational practices continue to integrate technological advancements, GenAI holds promise for enriching the educational landscape, fostering a more engaged and effective learning environment.

Conclusion

This chapter explores the innovative intersection of generative artificial intelligence and literacy education, emphasizing the roles of semiotic mediation and transmediation. It presents GenAI not only as a facilitative tool but also as a pedagogical ally that can significantly increase the learning experience. Through various stages of GenAI-mediated activities, GenAI can effectively scaffold and support students as they navigate and articulate complex literacy concepts across diverse communicative modalities. The implications of integrating GenAI in education go beyond enhancing traditional pedagogical outcomes; they introduce novel, multimodal learning strategies that are adaptive and responsive to students' nuanced needs. The potential of AI to craft educational experiences that are engaging, reflective, and conducive to developing competent and versatile learners is clearly demonstrated.

In synthesizing the insights from this exploratory practice, we are led to a conclusion filled with possibility and anticipation. While the narrative presented remains conceptual, it highlights GenAI's transformative potential when applied through the lenses of semiotic and transmediation theories. The pathway forward necessitates rigorous research to transform these theoretical constructs into actionable pedagogical frameworks and to assess GenAI's impact on educational processes and outcomes thoroughly.

As we continue to integrate GenAI into the educational landscape, a critical and thoughtful approach is essential—not only acknowledging its capabilities but also scrutinizing its limitations and potential drawbacks. While GenAI has the potential to enhance educational practices and enrich learning experiences, it can also introduce challenges, such as overreliance on automated feedback or reduced opportunities for authentic human interaction. To navigate these complexities, educators must evaluate the ethical implications of GenAI use, ensure equitable access, and remain vigilant about its role in shaping students' critical thinking and engagement. The aim is for GenAI to serve as a thoughtful complement to human instruction, fostering a generation of learners who are not only literate but also capable of critically analyzing the tools they use and the information they encounter.

Competing Interests The authors have no conflicts of interest to declare that are relevant to the content of this chapter.

Ethics Statement This manuscript is a conceptual paper that does not involve primary research or studies with human participants. As such, no ethical approval or informed consent was required for its preparation. The paper aligns with the guidelines outlined for conceptual and theoretical contributions and adheres to the ethical standards of academic publishing.

References

Abedi, J., & Herman, J. (2010). Assessing English language learners' opportunity to learn mathematics: Issues and limitations. *Teachers College Record, 112*(3), 723–746. https://doi.org/10.1177/016146811011200301

Ahmed, E. (2024). Student performance predictions using machine learning algorithms. *Applied Computational Intelligence and Soft Computing, 2024*(1). https://doi.org/10.1016/j.dajour.2023.100204

Batchelor, K. E. (2015). Digital transmediation and revision. *Voices from the Middle, 23*(2), 69–73.

Bezemer, J., & Kress, G. (2008). Writing in multimodal texts: A social semiotic account of designs for learning. *Written Communication, 25*(2), 166–195. https://doi.org/10.1177/0741088307313177

Bunch, G. C. (2014). The language of ideas and the language of display: Reconceptualizing "academic language" in linguistically diverse classrooms. *International Multilingual Research Journal, 8*(1), 70–86. https://doi.org/10.1080/19313152.2014.852431

Correnti, R., Matsumura, L. C., Wang, E. L., Litman, D., & Zhang, H. (2022). Building a validity argument for an automated writing evaluation system (eRevise) as a formative assessment. *Computers and Education Open, 3*, 100084. https://doi.org/10.1016/j.caeo.2022.100084

Delpit, L. D. (1988). The silenced dialogue: Power and pedagogy in educating other people's children. *Harvard Educational Review, 58*(3), 280–299.

Dong, Y. (2023). Revolutionizing academic English writing through GenAI-powered pedagogy: Practical exploration of the teaching process and assessment. *Journal of Higher Education Research, 4*(2), 52–57.

Essa, A., & Ayad, H. (2012). Student success system: Risk analytics and data visualization using ensembles of predictive models. In *Proceedings of the 2nd international conference on learning analytics and knowledge* (pp. 158–161). https://doi.org/10.1145/2330601.2330641
Fang, Z., & Schleppegrell, M. J. (2010). Disciplinary literacies across content areas: Supporting secondary reading through functional language analysis. *Journal of Adolescent & Adult Literacy, 53*(7), 587–597. https://doi.org/10.1598/JAAL.53.7.6
Gee, J. P. (1989). Literacy, discourse, and linguistics: Introduction. *Journal of Education, 171*(1), 5–17. https://doi.org/10.1177/002205748917100101
Gee, J. P. (2004). Language in the science classroom: Academic social languages as the heart of school-based literacy. In E. W. Saul (Ed.), *Crossing borders in literacy and science instruction: Perspectives on theory and practice* (pp. 13–32). International Reading Association.
International Literacy Association. (2017). *Standards for the preparation of literacy professionals*. ILA. Retrieved from https://www.literacyworldwide.org/get-resources/standards/standards-2017
Issah, I., Appiah, O., Appiahene, P., & Inusah, F. (2023). A systematic review of the literature on machine learning application of determining the attributes influencing academic performance. *Decision Analytics Journal, 7*, 100204. https://doi.org/10.1016/j.dajour.2023.100204
Jewitt, C. (Ed.). (2014). *The Routledge handbook of multimodal analysis* (2nd ed.). Routledge.
Kerly, A., Hall, P., & Bull, S. (2008). Bringing chatbots into education: Towards natural language negotiation of open learner models. *Knowledge-Based Systems, 20*(2), 177–185.
Koedinger, K. R., Anderson, J. R., Hadley, W. H., & Mark, M. A. (1997). Intelligent tutoring goes to school in the big city. *International Journal of Artificial Intelligence in Education, 8*(1), 30–43.
Kress, G. (2010). *Multimodality—A social semiotic approach to contemporary communication*. Routledge.
Kress, G., & Van Leeuwen, T. (2001). *Multimodal discourse: The modes and media of contemporary communication*. Bloomsbury Academic.
McCormick, R. (1995). Conceptual and procedural knowledge. *International Journal of Technology and Design Education, 5*(2), 141–159.
Moje, E. B. (2007). Developing socially just subject-matter instruction: A review of the literature on disciplinary literacy teaching. *Review of Research in Education, 31*(1), 1–44.
O'Halloran, K. L. (2011). Multimodal discourse analysis. In K. Hyland & B. Paltridge (Eds.), *Companion to discourse* (pp. 120–137). Continuum.
Sandra, L., Lumbangaol, F., & Matsuo, T. (2021). Machine learning algorithm to predict student's performance: A systematic literature review. *TEM Journal, 10*, 1919–1927. https://doi.org/10.18421/TEM104-56
Schleppegrell, M. J. (2004). *The language of schooling: A functional linguistics perspective*. Lawrence Erlbaum Associates.
Shanahan, T., & Shanahan, C. (2008). Teaching disciplinary literacy to adolescents: Rethinking content-area literacy. *Harvard Educational Review, 78*(1), 40–59.
Shermis, M. D., & Burstein, J. (Eds.). (2003). *Automated essay scoring: A cross-disciplinary perspective*. Routledge.
Siegel, M. (1995). More than words: The generative power of transmediation for learning. *Canadian Journal of Education/Revue Canadienne de l'éducation, 20*(4), 455–475.
Snow, C. E., & Uccelli, P. (2009). The challenge of academic language. In D. R. Olson & N. Torrance (Eds.), *The Cambridge handbook of literacy* (pp. 112–133). Cambridge University Press.
Suhor, C. (1984). Towards a semiotics-based curriculum. *Journal of Curriculum Studies, 16*(3), 247–257.
VanLehn, K. (2011). The relative effectiveness of human tutoring, intelligent tutoring systems, and other tutoring systems. *Educational Psychologist, 46*(4), 197–221. https://doi.org/10.1080/00461520.2011.611369
Vygotsky, L. S. (1981). The genesis of higher mental functions. In J. V. Wertsch (Ed.), *The concept of activity in soviet psychology* (pp. 144–188). M.E. Sharpe.

Walkington, C. (2013). Using adaptive learning technologies to personalize instruction to student interests: The impact of relevant contexts on performance and learning outcomes. *Journal of Educational Psychology, 105*(4), 932–945. https://doi.org/10.1037/a0031882

Wilson, J., & Czik, A. (2016). Automated essay evaluation software in English language arts classrooms: Effects on teacher feedback, student motivation, and writing quality. *Computers & Education, 100*(1), 94–109.

Winkler, R., & Söllner, M. (2018). Unleashing the potential of chatbots in education: A state-of-the-art analysis. *Academy of Management Annual Meeting Proceedings, 2018*(1), 15903.

Zwiers, J. (2008). *Building academic language: Essential practices for content classrooms, grades 5–12*. International Reading Association.

Heather Cato is an assistant clinical professor in the Department of Literacy and Learning at Texas Woman's University, where she teaches courses in the literacy education master's program. Her research and teaching interests include writing instruction, writing assessment, and the uses of technology for instructional practice. Her work has been published in peer-reviewed journals such as *English in Texas* and *National Journal of Middle Grades Reform.*

Amy Burke is an associate professor in the Department of Literacy and Learning at Texas Woman's University, where she teaches undergraduate literacy courses for preservice teachers, as well as in the literacy education master's program and the literacy, language, and culture Ph.D. program. Her research and teaching interests include the social-cultural-historic-political contexts of language and literacy teaching/learning; children's and young adult literature; multimodal composing; critical literacy; and the role of talk in literacy learning. Her work has been published in peer-reviewed journals such as *Journal of Children's Literature*, *Language Arts*, *Literacy Research and Instruction*, and *English in Texas*.

Chapter 6
Information Literacy in the Age of Large Language Models

Benjamin Bewersdorf and Ryan Mitchell Wittingslow

Abstract Large language models (LLMs) drastically change the way we produce and search for information and thereby create new challenges to how we evaluate information as well. After briefly reviewing the history of information literacy, we argue that the developments of LLMs require us to update our information literacy curricula to meet the goals of the now conventional framework of information literacy introduced by the American Library Association (2015).

Keywords Information literacy · Large language models · Pedagogy

When ChatGPT was publicly released in November 2022, it became immediately clear that it would pose a huge threat to how we assess students' work (Marche, 2022). Other, more optimistic, commentators offered accounts of how artificial intelligence (AI) can create new opportunities for our educational practice. These two approaches have thus dominated public and professional discourse on the role of AI in education. In this chapter, we would like to discuss a third, equally important question: How do the developments in AI impact the content of our curricula?

In particular, we would like to explore how the developments of large language models (LLMs) impact how we provide information literacy training. As such, the discussions in the following can not only serve as an exemplary exploration for how to think about adjusting curricula in response to these developments, but also more concretely, start a discussion on adjusting information literacy training in particular, a topic which is at least to some extent present in most educational programs. What

B. Bewersdorf (✉) · R. M. Wittingslow
University College Groningen, University of Groningen, Groningen, The Netherlands
e-mail: g.b.bewersdorf@rug.nl; r.m.wittingslow@rug.nl

G. Tchibozo (ed.), *International Perspectives of Generative AI in Education*, Advances in Artificial Intelligence in Education 3,
https://doi.org/10.1007/978-3-031-99804-1_6

we hope to show in the following is that the developments in AI not only require us to rethink how we think of information literacy, but also on how we teach it.

This chapter is divided into the following parts. First, we offer a brief history of the term 'information literacy', providing a representative survey of how information literacy has been conceptualized by educators. Second, we introduce what we consider the now-conventional definition of informational literacy, as defined by the American Library Association (ALA). Third, we diagnose the challenges that LLMs pose to the proper realization of information literacy as outlined by the ALA. As part of this diagnosis, we offer an analysis of two use cases for LLMs: direct 'first-order' use of LLMs and mediated 'second-order' use of LLMs. We also offer a tentative account of what it would take for a student to be information literate in an age of large language models. Finally, we offer some general comments on some of the ethical and legal problems posed by LLMs, as well as how these problems should be integrated into the information literacy curricula.

A Brief History

According to Shirley Behrens (1994), the first printed record of 'information literacy' dates back to 1974, in a proposal written by Paul Zurkowski, the then-president of the Information Industry Association (IIA). In that proposal, Zurkowski writes that people who are information literate "have learned techniques and skills for utilizing the wide range of information tools as well as primary sources in molding information-solutions to their problems" (Zurkowski, 1974, quoted in Behrens, 1994).

It did not take long for other writers to expand this account. Writing 2 years later, librarian and future US congressman Major R. Owens was among the first people to link information literacy to active citizenship. He agrees with Zurkowski that to be information literate is to know and understand techniques about how to appropriately find, engage with, and use information. However, he goes a step further, arguing that this skill is necessary for effective and intelligent civic engagement, and thus necessary for properly engaging in public life:

> Beyond information literacy for greater work effectiveness and efficiency, information literacy is needed to guarantee the survival of democratic institutions. All men are created equal but voters with information resources are in a position to make more intelligent decisions than citizens who are information illiterates. The application of information resources to the process of decision-making to fulfill civic responsibilities is a vital necessity. (Owens, 1976, quoted in Behrens, 1994)

This basic insight—that information literacy is one of the cornerstones of civic engagement—returns throughout the literature. As David Bawden points out in his survey article, when scholars talk about 'literacy' in the context of 'information literacy', we mean much more than the capacity to read and write. Instead, 'literacy' refers to a person's ability to *understand* different kinds of texts, with this capacity to understand contributing to a person's general capacity to function and act in broader society.

As he writes, quoting from various sources: "Literacy can be defined as having the skills one needs to make the connection to the information necessary to survive in society"; "the goal is an active literacy which allows people to use language to enhance their capacity to think, create and question, in order to participate effectively in society"; to be literate is "to compute and solve problems at levels of proficiency necessary to function on the job and in society, to achieve one's goals, and develop one's knowledge and potential"; information literacy "now embodies the general ability to understand and perform functions successfully" (cf. Campbell, 1990; Dupuis, 1997; National Literacy Act, 1991; Olsen & Coons, 1989; all quoted in Bawden, 2001,[1] pp. 221–222). Or, as Jeremy J. Shapiro and Shelley K. Hughes forcefully claim in their "Information Literacy as a Liberal Art: Enlightenment Proposals for a New Curriculum":

> An extended notion of information literacy is essential to the future of democracy, if citizens are to be intelligent shapers of the information society rather than its pawns, and to humanistic culture, if information is to be part of a meaningful existence rather than a routine of production and consumption. (Shapiro & Hughes, 1996)

These information literacy definitions are primarily concerned with how readers or consumers engage with many different kinds of texts. However, this is not the only feature of these definitions. Instead, they also ask that informationally literate people be aware of both the *provenance* of the texts with which they're engaging and the intentions that underwrite the creation of those texts: they need to know who is writing, their level of epistemic authority and the grounds upon which that authority is granted, the different kinds of information value at play, the institutions that might be influencing information production, and so on. This is how information literacy contributes to our fulfillment of our civic responsibilities.

The sensitivity to information production in these definitions is, as best we can tell, a product of the ongoing association between information literacy and what scholars call 'critical thinking'. Information literacy and critical thinking emerge from different intellectual traditions—with the former coming from library and information sciences, and the latter from philosophy and psychology. Nonetheless, they also share several qualities and convictions—among them the idea that knowing how to properly make sense of, contextualize, and appropriately employ novel information is an important intellectual virtue.

Information literacy and critical thinking are often considered complementary domains, with information literacy being nothing more than the applied end of critical thinking: "Critical thinking and information literacy skills need to be consciously merged. They must become part of the assessment criteria for American students. While critical thinking skills provide the theoretical basis for the process, information literacy provides the skills for practical, real world application" (Doyle, 1994, p. 9). Still others go even further, arguing that information literacy and critical

[1] Bawden also identifies several subordinate skill-based literacies, including library literacy, media literacy, computer literacy, and so on, all of which contribute to information literacy *in toto*.

thinking are simply discipline-specific terms for the same set of norms (Hollis, 2019; Weiner, 2011).

Critical thinking literature shares with information literacy a concern with the provenance of texts. In order to think critically, a person must also know how to accommodate for and correct biases in the information being considered. This emphasis on provenance has been a feature of the critical thinking literature from the beginning. As Lamont (2020) argues in his paper "The Construction of 'Critical Thinking'", much of what we now think of as critical thinking and its related concepts has its origins in the American anti-propaganda research of the 1930s and 1940s. American psychologists—among them Edward Glaser, author of the volume that catapulted critical thinking into the public consciousness (Glaser, 1941)—were keen to counteract the effects of war propaganda, and sought methods by which to inoculate American voters against the influence of foreign powers. These counteracting measures are what we now call 'critical thinking'.

Although it would not be quite exact to state that information literacy definitions are motivated by the same fear of propaganda, it is fair to say that these definitions appear to rest on the critical thinking assumption that to be information literate is to be cognizant of the reasons, attitudes, and intentions that motivate why texts are created.

The Definition

These sentiments have, *in toto*, contributed to what now seems to be considered the conventional definition of 'information literacy', as furnished by the American Library Association (2015).

In its *Framework for Information Literacy for Higher Education*, the ALA provides the following definition: "Information literacy is the set of integrated abilities encompassing the reflective discovery of information, the understanding of how information is produced and valued, and the use of information in creating new knowledge and participating ethically in communities of learning" (, 2015, p. 8). Students' development of this set of competences and dispositions is anchored in six equally weighted 'frames', with each frame referring to a constitutive concept within information literacy.

In alphabetical order, these six frames are as follows:

1. *Authority Is Constructed and Contextual.* Students competent in this frame understand that the epistemic authority of information sources is neither absolute nor universal. They understand both that epistemic authority is constructed and contextual, and the conditions under which that authority is conferred. This frame thus encourages students to critically evaluate the authority of information sources by considering factors such as the expertise, credibility, and biases of the authors or creators, as well as the cultural, social, and historical contexts in which the information was produced (2015, pp. 12–13).

2. *Information Creation as a Process.* Students competent in this frame understand that information creation is the consequence of an iterative process. They also understand that there exist multiple and sometimes non-overlapping processes by which information can be created. This framework thus encourages students to recognize that different information formats are produced through different processes and may vary in terms of reliability, authority, and purpose. It also underscores the importance of understanding these processes to critically evaluate and effectively use information in academic or real-world contexts (2015, pp. 14–15).
3. *Information Has Value.* Students competent in this frame understand not only that information has value, but that value can be assessed and evaluated according to different metrics, including economic, social, and research value. Because information has value, external interests can and do influence the production and dissemination of information. This framework thus underscores the importance of critically evaluating information sources to ensure their credibility and reliability, thereby maximizing their value (of whatever kind or kinds) in academic or professional contexts (2015, pp. 16–17).
4. *Research as Inquiry.* Students competent in this frame understand that research is fundamentally driven by processes of inquiry within or between different disciplinary frameworks, with these processes underwritten by a battery of investigative methods. These processes of inquiry can be motivated by any combination of personal, professional, or societal needs. Furthermore, students competent in this frame understand that new lines of inquiry can emerge because of research processes (2015, pp. 18–19).
5. *Scholarship as Conversation.* Students competent in this frame understand that science is a collaborative enterprise. They appreciate that research is a dialogue among scholars who engage in critical analysis, interpretation, and synthesis of existing information. This framework thus encourages individuals to recognize their role as contributors to this ongoing conversation by engaging with scholarly literature, evaluating diverse perspectives, and constructively adding their own insights and interpretations (2015, pp. 20–21).
6. *Searching as Strategic Exploration.* Students competent in this frame understand that information production is often both non-linear and recursive. They understand that they must actively engage with different search tools and techniques to locate relevant information effectively. This framework encourages students to develop critical thinking skills, such as analyzing information needs, selecting appropriate search strategies, and evaluating search results for relevance, credibility, and reliability. This frame thus underscores the fact that students should be prepared to continually refine research strategies based on feedback and new discoveries (2015, pp. 22–23).

A New Curriculum

When Shapiro and Hughes called for a new information literacy curriculum in 1996, their call was motivated by the rise of the early internet. For those who were not around during the mid-1990s, it is difficult to capture the sense of raw, utopian possibility that the early internet offered. It seemed a new frontier: a public forum where ideas and values could be discussed and contested in a truly open and democratic fashion. This new frontier, Shapiro and Hughes thought, required new curricular approaches to information literacy.

While the present-day internet is a very different creature—it is difficult to preserve a feeling of frothy optimism in an age of misinformation and computer barons—we nonetheless believe that LLMs and other generative AIs pose another (and maybe more dramatic) turning point that demands another renewal of information literacy curricula. To substantiate this claim it is helpful to distinguish between two use cases of LLMs: *first-order* and *second-order* uses of LLMs. As we will discuss below, both kinds of use pose questions regarding:

1. how we find information (frame 6),
2. how we produce information (frames 1, 2, and 3), and
3. how we evaluate information (frames 1, 3, 4, and 5).

Addressing these problems will require that we revisit how we teach information literacy in order to help students best meet the standards as outlined by the ALA.

First-Order Use

By 'first-order' use, we refer to interactions that take place directly between a user and an LLMs. In the case of first-order interactions, the human role in the production of information is limited to direct interactions with the technology.

First-order use of LLMs offers people new methods to find information. Before the public release of ChatGPT, students tasked with finding and analyzing information were required to submit search queries through search engines, whether general (Google, Bing, and so on), or academic (Google Scholar, SmartCAT, JSTOR, and so forth). Students would then—at least ideally—assess the relevance and reliability of these sources per the six frames summarized above.

LLMs, however, offer new strategies. In a first-order interaction with an LLM, the user is directly responsible for the design and input of the prompt that produces the text. Instead of searching for prewritten text which fits the information needed, students can ask LLMs to generate information on demand on the subject they are interested in. Through follow-up prompts, this information can be tailored towards the specific information needs of the student. For example, a student in a classroom might ask an LLM a question related to course content: "What factors contributed to Napoleon's defeat at Waterloo?"; "What techniques can be used to precipitate gold ions out of aqua regia?", and so on.

LLMs, used in this way, constitute an undeniably useful resource—and particularly for people who might otherwise lack the institutional, educational, or cognitive resources to answer these questions via more traditional means (library databases and journal subscriptions, for example). However, using this resource effectively requires significant practice and/or instruction.

In some respects, this might make acquiring the desired information easier, given that LLMs seem to be less sensitive to requiring specific keywords to produce the desired information. That being said, it does require skillful prompt engineering for students to get the information they want. Prompt engineering requires practice. Formal training on optimal prompt engineering might have to become a staple in an information literacy curriculum. As a consequence, we should expect to invest significant resources in ensuring that students can engineer LLM prompts appropriately.

Other similar first-order strategies include using the LLM to produce new texts. Producing certain types of new texts will involve similar competences to searching for information with LLMs.

The student searching for information on "What factors contributed to Napoleon's defeat at Waterloo?" and asking follow-up questions based upon the answers received might then submit a prompt requesting the production of a new text: "Write a 2,000-word essay on Napoleon's defeat at Waterloo, emphasizing the relationship between [factor 1], [factor 2], and [factor 3]". While the desired outcome is different, students require similar competences when it comes to prompt engineering in order to fully take advantage of the affordances furnished by LLMs. Given the importance of prompt engineering in the production of information, a thorough understanding of this process will also be essential for meeting the conditions of the ALA definition of information literacy, and in particular the requirements discussed in frame 2.

The most significant challenge is posed by the evaluation of information. When we evaluate information, part of what we are doing is evaluating the epistemic authority of the speaker. That speaker has certain features (such as institutional affiliations, apparent competences, opinions or degrees of expertise) that all contribute to our understanding of whether an interlocutor should take them seriously. These contextual metadata give us grounds upon which to evaluate a speaker's outputs. These are the factors that underwrite whether readers bestow epistemic authority to the texts that writers produce. However, it is much more difficult to evaluate the outputs of LLMs because these outputs are decontextualized from the data upon which they are trained. When reading the output, whether the training data which caused the LLM to produce a particular piece of information is written by someone with the relevant authority is not obvious (even when the output contains links to existing information).

This disconnect between the persons fundamentally responsible for the training data and those who consume it via the first-order use of LLMs poses serious problems for our understanding of the provenance and reliability of that information, for two reasons. The first is that LLM outputs are not unbiased. LLMs themselves inherit biases from their training data—not only because of biases present in the texts themselves, but also in (a) the selection of those texts that comprise the training data and (b) how that data is then used and manipulated by the neural networks. For example, choices with regards to the training material (as well as choices with regards to how strongly to regulate the answers of LLMs) can result in differences with respect to biases as well as political orientation of LLMs (Feng et al., 2023).

Second, and this has been well documented (Ji et al., 2023), LLMs readily hallucinate, providing incorrect but plausible-sounding responses (Frankfurt, 1986) in the event that the data used to train the LLM is incomplete or compromised, or the prompt itself was flawed. Unfortunately, it is extraordinarily difficult to discern a correct if decontextualized response from an incorrect and hallucinated response, unless a student is already in possession of the information that they seek.

Of course, we know that there is no magic bullet here. Even a relatively informed user of LLMs—someone with at least a basic understanding of how neural networks are trained on large tranches of textual data—will still face unavoidable knowledge gaps when it comes to the composition of that training data and/or the underlying information architecture that develops in response to that training data. Users are not protected against the risk of being convinced by bad or false information produced by an LLM. Nonetheless, possessing some theoretical understanding of how LLMs come about is important for properly evaluating whether a given piece of text should be taken seriously as an epistemic authority. Ideally, this theoretical understanding could also help more advanced students reconstruct the hidden context that underwrites LLM-produced texts.

Moreover, there might even be good reason to be optimistic about what happens when users acquire this understanding. Following the cue of Friederich and Symons (2023), we think it likely that a proficient first-order user should be able to use LLMs as "partners" in research and information creation—but only under the condition that this user is appropriately informed and trained. As a consequence, part of information literacy training will have to acknowledge how LLMs can (or cannot) be used productively in different academic domains.

Second-Order Use

'Second-order' uses of LLMs are an extension of the first-order case, but pose different challenges. Second-order use is typified by the presence of first-order human intermediaries that stand between LLM-generated content and the second-order consumer.

Like first-order use, second-order processes begin when first-order users prompt LLMs to generate texts. What differs, however, is the next step: the first-order user then functions as an intermediary, disseminating those texts to an audience. The intermediary is responsible for curating the content generated by LLMs, as well as for any editing or other tasks. Examples of second-order interactions include website or journal articles with procedurally generated contents: whether because the authors are trying to seek some market advantage, or because they are using the software as a drafting and summarizing tool, or for any other reason. While this case is in some ways similar to how information was produced before widespread accessibility to LLMs, it still requires adjustments to the information literacy curriculum.

Speaking optimistically, one might think that the presence of human intermediaries between LLM-produced content and a second-order user helps to address our concerns about the provenance of information. However, we should not be too bullish about whether the mere presence of intermediaries will make for higher quality content. Indeed, there might be reason to think that widespread use of LLMs will do the opposite, making the evaluation of the reliability of information more challenging, as we will discuss in the next paragraphs.

LLMs make it easier for bad faith actors to produce plausible-sounding texts. This makes the evaluation of individual texts harder and requires special attention to already existing elements of information literacy training. Many superficial markers for reliable texts (academic English, argumentative writing, mentioning of sources) can easily be generated through LLMs, so checking the reliability of text requires more careful attention to other factors (author reputation, content and quality of the sources). Of course, being able to properly make these assessments often requires more prior knowledge of the topic in question. This is clearly a chicken-and-egg problem: how can a person gain the relevant knowledge to judge the reliability of a source if they cannot judge the reliability of the sources providing that knowledge?

This problem is compounded by the nature of the internet itself. With the rise of the internet and social media in particular, the way we share information has drastically changed. In the relatively near past, large media companies had a monopoly on the ability to share information (Herman & Chomsky, 1988/2002). Sharing information in the social media age became much easier. Indeed, until the introduction of LLMs, the only real throttle to how quickly information could be disseminated was the speed at which human agents could produce it. This was still a barrier to sharing information since not everyone had the necessary skills (such as the ability to write in an inviting and convincing manner) and resources (such as time) to produce information. Because of the low cost of production, LLMs have, to a large extent, removed this barrier. This means that it is easier than ever for a bad faith actor to spread plausible-sounding falsehoods if they were so inclined.

Without exaggeration, we think that this phenomenon poses a potential threat to the future of democracy. As the early information literacy scholars well knew, fulsome and proper engagement with liberal democratic systems relies upon being able to tell good information from bad. One of the things that is often argued to make democratic systems successful is a phenomenon known as 'the wisdom of the crowd': the fact that when you put enough people together under the right conditions, they tend to make better choices than individuals (Lyon & Pacuit, 2013). However, for crowds to produce wisdom, their constituent individuals need to be at least minimally competent, as formally shown in Condorcet's (1785) jury theorem.

It is our concern that, because of the ease in which enormous amounts of plausible-sounding but false texts can be generated, LLMs will undermine the minimal competence of individuals, and thereby the wisdom of crowds. We should expect this influence to have deleterious effects: compromising the wisdom of crowds also compromises the proper functioning of the shared decision-making processes upon which liberal democratic processes rest. It is thus enormously important that we update information literacy syllabi in order to address this problem. Students enrolled in information literacy programmes will need to understand the roles (both positive and negative) that humans play in the curation and dissemination of LLM-generated texts.

Given this flood of information, it is obvious we will need better pedagogical techniques. This should involve not only the evaluation of whether a text contains nonsense, but also involve the training of students in search techniques to actively avoid encountering misleading information. Moreover, a substantial chunk of that training should emphasize identifying the provenance of information. Because there exists a human intermediary in second-order interactions, it could be the case that at least some of the concerns voiced here about the dangers of first-order use are blunted: while the first-order user may not have written the text themselves, a second-order user can, at least in principle, determine the reliability of the content on the basis of the epistemic authority of the generating first-order user. It is in this capacity for discernment that we need to train students.

The Value of Information

As rightly stressed in the ALA framework, the value of information can be measured on multiple scales. When evaluating the reliability of information, we evaluate the epistemic value of the information. Next to this, information can also have monetary and ethical value, the assessment of which requires awareness of ethical and legal consequences of LLMs. We would like to close with some brief remarks on these topics which equally apply to first- and second-order uses.

On the ethical side, we might want to discuss with students the ethical implications of LLM training and usage. These include the working conditions of human trainers, the environmental effects (energy consumption) of LLM training and operation, and the fair attribution and remuneration of the (often anonymous) people responsible for generating training data. In addition, there are concerns about LLMs contributing to suppressing already marginalized perspectives: since LLMs base their output on probability, they are unlikely to reproduce underrepresented views.

The ethical considerations regarding fair attribution and remuneration of original authors have a legal side as well, most importantly concerning intellectual property rights. Which material should be legal to use by tech companies to train their LLMs and how should authors be compensated when their work is used for LLM training? Who holds the intellectual property rights of texts produced by LLMs given that they so heavily rely on the texts they are trained upon?

LLMs might also force us to reconsider our definitions of authorship and our practice of crediting sources. Part of information literacy training involves teaching students how to give credits not only to novel insights produced by researchers, but also to particular ways to present information. We tell our students that they cannot reproduce the formulations of other authors without citing them. This practice made sense in an age when a limited number of texts on particular topics were published. But how well does this fit with the rapid production of texts through LLMs, given that there is a finite number of reasonable ways to present the same information?

Conclusion and Next Steps

LLMs drastically change the way we produce and search for information and thereby create new challenges to the evaluation of information as well. While the general framework of information literacy introduced by the ALA remains relevant, LLMs do force us to update our information literacy curriculum to meet the goals of the ALA framework. While the considerations of this chapter are to some extent speculative, it still seems clear to us that we need to update information literacy curricula in light of the new challenges posed by LLMs.

We will close with some initial suggestions on how we might update our information literacy curriculum based on the considerations above, understanding that these suggestions should be interpreted considering both the specific needs of educators and the capacities and resources available to students.

With all that in mind, information literacy training should help students:

1. understand how LLMs work, are built, trained, and tested, including why LLMs are predisposed to produce biased content as a consequence of that training. This is essential for students to grasp the process of information creation in the age of LLMs (frame 2: Information Creation as a Process) as well as to be in a position to critically evaluate information (frame 1: Authority Is Constructed and Contextual) stemming from both first and second order uses of LLMs;
2. understand the ethical and legal implications surrounding the development, deployment, and impact of LLMs. As we argue above, the value of information is not restricted to what can be done with it; it is at least partly determined by how it is generated as well. Information produced by LLMs creates new ethical challenges of which students need to be aware (frame 3: Information Has Value);
3. understand how LLMs can be used legitimately for scientific, creative, and professional writing, thereby improving the quality of research, collaboration, and innovation. When used appropriately, LLMs can be used both by students and working scientists to streamline and democratize aspects of the knowledge production process via second-order use (frame 5: Scholarship as Conversation). As an obvious example, while LLMs might produce text that is uninspired and unlistenable, they grant scholars who work in non-majority languages a real opportunity to increase the visibility and accessibility of their work, as well as the opportunity to engage with scholarship to which they otherwise might not have had access;

4. understand how LLMs can challenge and/or complement the role of scientific experts, including how LLMs can be used to fill knowledge gaps. Being an expert in a given domain is not simply about having mastery of that domain; it is also about knowing how and where to look to fill gaps in one's knowledge (frame 4: Research as Inquiry). LLMs, used carefully and adroitly by a person with the appropriate sensitivity, training, and expertise, can help fill these gaps via first-order use (frame 5: Scholarship as Conversation and frame 6: Searching as Strategic Exploration);
5. understand how LLMs can be used by bad-faith actors across different domains and identify the resulting ethical and societal implications; as well as use different strategies to identify, evaluate, and counteract malicious uses of LLM-generated content. When determining whether a given piece of information has been produced by a bad-faith actor (and thereafter determining how that information is to be used, if at all) students should be trained to be cognizant of the fact that epistemic authority is something earned (frame 1: Authority Is Constructed and Contextual). They must realize that knowledge creation is a rigorous process that takes place within communities of scholars and other experts: while it may be necessarily contingent and value-laden, it is also non-arbitrary and epistemically robust (frame 3: Information Has Value and frame 5: Scholarship as Conversation). Keeping these epistemic norms in mind will aid students in their ability to discriminate between sense and (harmful) nonsense (frame 6: Searching as Strategic Exploration). This involves both the first- and second-order use of LLMs.

Competing Interests The authors have no conflicts of interest to declare that are relevant to the content of this chapter.

References

American Library Association. (2015). *Ferameworkfor Information Literacy for Higher Education*. Retrieved October 4, 2023, from http://www.ala.org/acrl/standards/ilframework

Bawden, D. (2001). Information and digital literacies: A review of concepts. *Journal of Documentation, 57*(2), 218–259.

Behrens, S. J. (1994). A conceptual analysis and historical overview of information literacy. *College & Research Libraries, 55*(4), 309–322.

Campbell, B. (1990). What is literacy? Acquiring and using literacy skills. *Australasian Public Libraries and Information Services, 3*, 149–152.

Condorcet, M. (1785). *Essai sur l'application de l'analyse à la probabilité des décisions rendues à la pluralité des voix*. Imprimerie Royale.

Doyle, C. S. (1994). *Information literacy in an information society: A concept for the information age*. ERIC Clearinghouse on Information & Technology.

Dupuis, E. A. (1997). The information literacy challenge: Addressing the changing needs of our students through our programs. *Internet Reference Services Quarterly, 2*(2–3), 93–111.

Feng, S., Park, C. Y., Liu, Y., & Tsvetkov, Y. (2023). From pretraining data to language models to downstream tasks: Tracking the trails of political biases leading to unfair NLP models. In

Proceedings of the 61st annual meeting of the Association for Computational Linguistics (volume 1: Long papers) (pp. 11737–11762). Association for Computational Linguistics.
Frankfurt, H. (1986). On bullshit. *Raritan Quarterly Review, 6*(2), 81–100.
Friederich, S., & Symons, J. (2023). Norms for academic writing in the era of advanced artificial intelligence. *DISO, 2*(48).
Glaser, E. (1941). *An experiment in the development of critical thinking*. Teachers College, Columbia University.
Herman, E. S., & Chomsky, N. (2002). *Manufacturing consent: The political economy of the mass media*. Pantheon. (Original work published 1988).
Hollis, H. (2019). Information literacy and critical thinking: Different concepts, shared conceptions. In *Proceedings of the Tenth International Conference on Conceptions of Library and Information Science* (Vol. 24).
Ji, Z., Lee, N., Frieske, R., Yu, T., Su, D., Xu, Y., Ishii, E., Bang, Y. J., Madotto, A., & Fung, P. (2023, March). Survey of hallucination in natural language generation. *ACM Computing Surveys, 55*(12), 1–38.
Lamont, P. (2020). The construction of "critical thinking": Between how we think and what we believe. *History of Psychology, 23*(3), 232–251.
Lyon, A., & Pacuit, E. (2013). The wisdom of crowds: Methods of human judgement aggregation. In P. Michelucci (Ed.), *Handbook of human computation*. Springer.
Marche, S. (2022). The college essay is dead. *The Atlantic*. Retrieved from https://www.theatlantic.com/technology/archive/2022/12/chatgpt-ai-writing-college-student-essays/672371/
National Literacy Act. (1991). United States of America. *National Literacy Act*, § 3.
Olsen, J. K., & Coons, B. (1989). Cornell University's information literacy program. In G. E. Mensching & T. B. Mensching (Eds.), *Coping with information illiteracy: Bibliographic instruction for the information age* (pp. 7–20). Pierian Press.
Owens, M. R. (1976). State government and libraries. *Library Journal, 101*.
Shapiro, J. J., & Hughes, S. K. (1996). Information literacy as a liberal art: Enlightenment proposals for a new curriculum. *Educom Review, 31*(2).
Weiner, J. M. (2011). Is there a difference between critical thinking and information literacy? A systematic review 2000-2009. *The Journal of Information Literacy, 5*(2).
Zurkowski, P. G. (1974). *The information service environment relationships and priorities*. National Commission on Libraries and Information Science.

Benjamin Bewersdorf completed his Ph.D. in formal epistemology with distinction at the University of Konstanz, Germany in 2012. His postgraduate studies included 1 year visits at the University of Massachusetts and at the Massachusetts Institute of Technology. He has held positions at the University of Konstanz and the University of Groningen and has been working as Academic Director of Education for the University College Groningen since 2023. Dr. Bewersdorf is interested in innovative teaching methods and interdisciplinary research on critical thinking and decision making.

Ryan Mitchell Wittingslow is an associate professor at the University of Groningen and a research affiliate of the University of Sydney. From September 2022 to February 2024, he was a Humboldt research fellow at TU Darmstadt. He is the author of the monograph *What Art Does* (Rowman & Littlefield 2023) and the editor-in-chief of the *Philosophy of the City Journal*. Most of his research sits at the fertile delta connecting aesthetics, philosophy of design, philosophy of technology, and political philosophy. He writes a lot about cities. He also has devastating opinions about art. www.ryanwittingslow.com.

Chapter 7
Can AI Enhance Teaching and Learning in Physical Education?

Hock Beng Tommy Ng

Abstract Several enduring challenges persist in physical education (PE), such as inadequate demonstration, 'eyeballing' assessment of motor performance, and subjective feedback. These issues could potentially be addressed through the integration of technology employing artificial intelligence (AI) to enhance learning. This approach involves embedding a predefined (*criterion*) motor action into a human pose estimation (HPE) algorithm. Learners can observe this motor action on an iPad and utilize its kinematic characteristics to guide practice of the motor skill. The learner's (*executed*) movements are then captured by the device, and the recorded motor action is analyzed by the HPE algorithm to assess movement proficiency. The algorithmic computation generates a quantitative measure of movement quality, providing learners with prompt and objective feedback. Additionally, a separate device utilized by the PE teacher compiles quantitative data from other students in the class. This collective information aids the teacher in selecting appropriate instructional strategies.

Keywords AI-assisted assessment · Movement demonstration · Objective feedback · Technology-enhanced learning

This chapter describes a proof-of-concept study. It proposes a novel technology-based approach for addressing challenges encountered by teachers and students in PE. The implementation of the solution is ongoing; thus, no results will be presented here.

H. B. T. Ng (✉)
National Institute of Education, Nanyang Technological University, Singapore, Singapore
e-mail: hockbeng.ng@nie.edu.sg

G. Tchibozo (ed.), *International Perspectives of Generative AI in Education*, Advances in Artificial Intelligence in Education 3,
https://doi.org/10.1007/978-3-031-99804-1_7

Challenges in Physical Education

Over the past decades, research in education has converged on four key pedagogical dimensions that collectively influence the quality of teaching practices. These encompass conceptualization of content, enactment of content, classroom management, and assessment of students' performance (Ball & Forzani, 2007; Enright et al., 2014; Reynolds, 1992; Rovegno, 2003). Teacher's skillful execution of these dimensions has the propensity to enhance students' learning (Lampert & Graziani, 2009; Shulman & Wilson, 2004).

In terms of content conceptualization, subject knowledge is important, and it is possible that teachers can deepen their understanding through structured professional training (Darling-Hammond et al., 2017). However, when it comes to enactment of the conceptualized content, there is a consensus that not all PE teachers possess the ability to effectively demonstrate the motor skills they are teaching. According to Van Holst (1997), proficient demonstration is crucial because many of the motor skills taught require specific movement patterns that are best communicated visually. It is theorized that when an accurate model of a motor skill is executed by the PE teacher, key features of the movement containing salient visual information enable the learners to emulate the optimal technique, timing, and execution (Blandin & Proteau, 2000). While movements generated by individual learners may differ due to differences in physique, strength, and fitness level, the fundamental mechanics of the movement must be accurately modelled by the students to attain proficiency (Ferrari, 1996; Gibson, 1988; Haibach-Beach et al., 2023; Soderstrom & Bjork, 2015). Therefore, demonstration plays a central role in the development of movement characteristics, and through practice, facilitates the acquisition of motor skills. Therefore, when a PE teacher incorrectly demonstrates a motor skill, the resulting inaccurate visual information can lead learners to develop sub-optimal movement patterns (Van Holst, 1997).

A separate problem concerns the obstruction of learners' field of vision due to large class sizes. Class sizes vary significantly across Western and Asian countries, reflecting a divergence in educational philosophies, resource allocation, and socio-cultural priorities (Lai et al., 2016). In many Western countries, smaller class sizes are prioritized to facilitate individualized instruction and cognitive engagement. Data from the TALIS 2013 survey illustrated this trend with countries like Belgium (17.3), Croatia (20.0), and England (23.9) maintaining class size averages below 25 (Strizek et al., 2014). In contrast, many Asian countries face systemic pressures such as high population density, resource constraints, and competitive academic cultures, leading to markedly larger classes. Japan (31.2), Malaysia (32.1), and South Korea (32.4) exemplify this trend, with classes accommodating up to 40 students. In Singapore, the average class size is around 35. Such classroom environments create logistical challenges, as overcrowded spaces hinder visibility during skill demonstrations and limit opportunities for personalized corrections. These geographical contrasts underscore a global tension between educational efficiency and quality, with Western models investing in lower ratios to optimize engagement and Asian systems navigating the demands of scale (Zhou et al., 2025).

Several studies have implicated the effects of large class sizes on learning behaviors in PE. Hastie and Saunders (1991) observed that students in a large class setting ($n = 44$) spent significantly more time in nonacademic tasks and scrimmage activities, whereas more time in smaller class setups ($n = 12$; $n = 24$) was spent in skill practice. In the smaller classes, students' involvement was notably more related to motor-appropriate behaviors and cognitive engagement. There was also a concomitant decrease in organizational activity. In a separate study, Adeyanju et al. (2017) evaluated the effects of class size on learning a novel motor skill and found that motor proficiency in a medium size ($n = 16$) class significantly ($t = 2.81$, $p < 0.05$) exceeded those in a large size ($n = 32$) class. In a large-scale ($n = 295$) intervention study, Cheung and Zhang (2020) found that the development of fundamental motor skills was more robust ($p < 0.001$) in small compared to large class sizes. A number of other studies have also highlighted the challenges of delivering quality PE in large classes (Blatchford & Russell, 2019; Burson et al., 2021; Ehrenberg et al., 2001; Gross & Buchanan, 2014). While the class size in Singapore primary schools is unlikely to decrease in the near future, the issue of obstructed vision could potentially benefit from a technology-based solution, in which pre-recorded proficient motor skills (criterion) stored in digital devices could offer unobstructed and reliable visual guidance for motor learning in PE.

After the demonstrations, students would start practicing the skill. During practice, PE teachers often find it difficult to effectively monitor motor performance. It is common for teachers to either focus on some students having difficulty or through subjective 'eyeballing', estimate overall class performance. This form of informal assessment is ubiquitous in PE (López-Pastor et al., 2013; MacPhail & Halbert, 2010; Piotrowski & Capel, 2013). Given the limited active movement time in PE classes, these assessments provide quick, actionable feedback to help teachers allocate practice time or determine when to progress to the next activity in the lesson plan. Up until now, there is no efficient way of assessing motor performance in large class settings. The technology-based solution discussed in this chapter can be applied here. By getting students to work in pairs, while a student practices the skill, his/her partner uses a digital device to record the movement. The executed movement is compared with the criterion motor action stored in the digital device. The result of the comparison yields a quantitative index that represents the student's motor competence. The digital device also generates three video playbacks of the most prominent movement deviations. In this way, the student would receive timely and objective feedback for improving subsequent motor performance.

To facilitate monitoring of motor performance at the teacher's end, quantitative data in the student's device (20 devices for 40 students) are wirelessly transmitted to a separate device held by the PE teacher. On that device, a series of quantitative index is displayed. These indices are then analyzed to generate a skill proficiency profile for the class (Fig. 7.1).

Student Name	Similarity Score	View Video
Student 01	70	▶
Student 02	20	▶
Student 03	55	▶
Student 04	-	-
Student 05	-	-
Student 06	90	▶
Student 07	60	▶
Student 08	45	▶

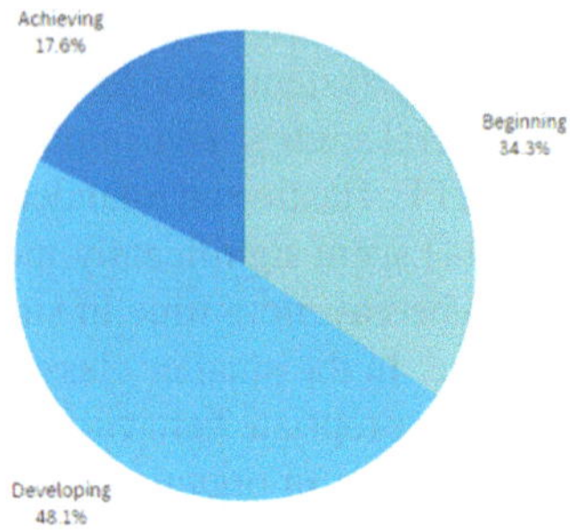

Fig. 7.1 Quantitative index for each student (left) and skills profile for the class as a whole (right) displayed on the teacher's iPad

Brief History of Technology in PE

The turn of the century saw a concerted push for the infusion of technology in PE (Koehler & Mishra, 2008; Liang et al., 2006; Settlage et al., 2004). PE teachers were introduced to the use of electronic devices such as heart rate monitors, bioelectrical impedance devices, and pedometers to assess health-related physical fitness. More recently, PE teachers have had access to software applications such as Calorie Counter and Google Fit to track students' dietary trends and physical activity levels. In some parts of the world, applications such as PE Manager have been used to alleviate arduous processes in PE assessment (Franklin & Smith, 2015; Woods et al., 2008). Albeit advantageous, it may be argued that the benefits afforded by technology have thus far been teacher-centric rather than student-centric. Therefore, a crucial question is whether technology can be strategically implemented in PE to enhance both teaching and learning experiences.

A Technology-Based Solution

The proposed technology-based solution utilizes a method called Human Pose Estimation (HPE). For decades, HPE has been an active area of computer vision research but it is only recently that significant advancements are made due to the availability of large datasets, powerful computational resources, and innovation in computing techniques (Massaoudi et al., 2021; Pouyanfar et al., 2018; Wang et al., 2020). The applications of HPE are diverse. Notably, it has been used in security and surveillance for detecting human behaviors, in human-computer interaction for recognizing human gestures, and in autonomous driving (Du et al., 2019; Kim et al., 2019; Lamas et al., 2022; Liu et al., 2021). In sports training and analysis, HPE has been used for tracking athletes' movements, analyzing performance, and providing feedback for improvement (Chae et al., 2023; Gajbhiye et al., 2022; Hülsmann et al., 2018; Ji et al., 2023; Scott et al., 2017; Zecha et al., 2018). Hitherto, no published studies have demonstrated the successful implementation of HPE in large PE classes.

Human Pose Estimation

HPE in 2D and 3D spaces represent two distinct paradigms with unique challenges and applications. In 2D-pose-estimation, the goal is to localize key points of the human body within a two-dimensional image or frame, typically derived from a single camera view. This method primarily focuses on determining the position of body joints such as elbows, knees, and wrists, without considering depth information. While 2D-pose-estimation algorithms can achieve real-time performance and are computationally efficient, they often struggle with occlusions and ambiguous poses due to the lack of depth perception. The inherent ambiguity of depth in 2D space can lead to inaccuracies, especially in cases where body parts overlap or when the subject is viewed from non-frontal angles (Gamra & Akhloufi, 2021; Sigal, 2021; Tsai et al., 2020).

In contrast, 3D-pose-estimation records three-dimensional coordinates of human body joints in physical space. By incorporating depth data, 3D-pose-estimation methods provide a more comprehensive understanding of human motion, enabling applications such as motion capture, augmented reality, and biomechanical analysis. One of the key differences between 2D and 3D pose-estimation lies in their respective representations of human motion. While 2D-pose-estimation focuses solely on the spatial arrangement of body joints within the image plane, 3D-pose-estimation provides deeper coverage of motion dynamics by capturing the depth, orientation, and scale of body movements (Hwang et al., 2017). This additional depth information enables more accurate motion tracking and analysis, making 3D-pose-estimation particularly valuable in applications such as sports performance analysis, healthcare, and human-computer interaction (Chiang et al., 2022; Liu et al., 2021; Wang et al., 2021). Furthermore, given that 3D-pose-estimation algorithms operate in 3D space, they are less susceptible to ambiguities caused by overlapping body parts or variations in camera perspectives.

At the core of HPE lies the process of modeling the human body. The current study utilized a 3D-pose-estimation system leveraging on MMPOSE, a PyTorch-based open-source toolkit of the OpenMMLab Project. Renowned for its versatility and high performance, MMPOSE integrates state-of-the-art algorithms and methodologies, empowering complex computations of human-centric data inherent in the detection and recognition of human actions. While several models of the human body can be used for pose estimation, a skeleton-based prototype consisting of anatomical landmarks including the ankles, knees, shoulders, and other prominent joints was employed in the current study (Fig. 7.2).

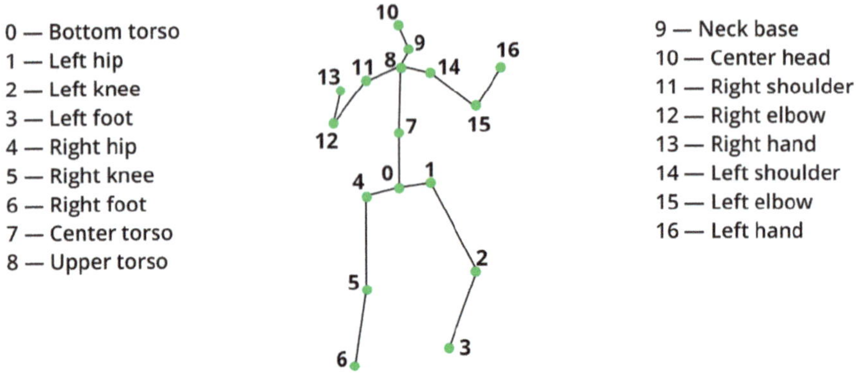

Fig. 7.2 Anatomical locations of the skeleton-based prototype

Application of 3D HPE in PE

The aim of the current study was to develop a technology-based solution to specifically address the problems of inadequate demonstrations, obstructed field of vision, and subjective assessment in PE. Here, we applied 3D HPE to inspect errors in students' (executed) movements benchmarked to a criterion originating from a teacher or an expert.

The first process in HPE was the determination of the criterion movement. To this end, motor actions of overarm throws performed by PE student-teachers were video-recorded and analyzed offline. Movements that met the criteria outlined in Colvin et al.'s (2000) checklist were designated as criterion movements. A mean of the criterion movements was generated and the resulting video was embedded in iPads (n = 10). Based on the input, MMPOSE algorithms detected anatomical key points of the human body and created a skeleton-based model of the criterion movement. The video in the iPads served as a supplementary aid for PE teachers who are not proficient at demonstrating the skill. It was expected that PE teachers, regardless of their proficiency, would make their best effort at demonstrating the skill. After the demonstration, students could watch the criterion video to further enhance their understanding of the motor action. A benefit of viewing the movement digitally was that it afforded slow-motion playback and repeated viewings. In this way, the proposed solution addressed the problem of inadequate demonstrations in PE. Subsequent processes of HPE entailed the recording of executed movement, inspecting the correctness of movement, and indexing the movement quality (Fig. 7.3).

During practice, overarm throw movements executed by a student were recorded by his/her partner. The video entered the MMPOSE algorithms for the detection of anatomical key points in 3D space, contributing to the formation of the *executed* skeleton-based model (Fig. 7.4). Subsequent steps in MMPOSE followed a systematic iteration of (a) matching the frame speed of the *executed* and *criterion* videos,

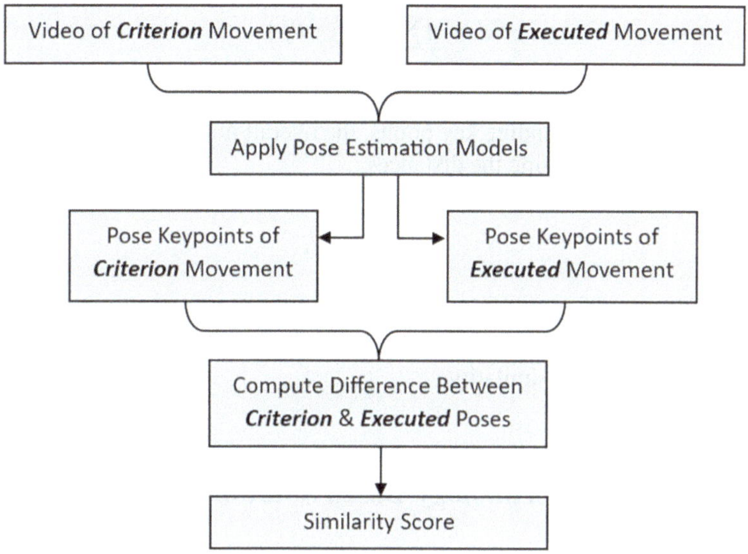

Fig. 7.3 Process flow of Human Pose Estimation

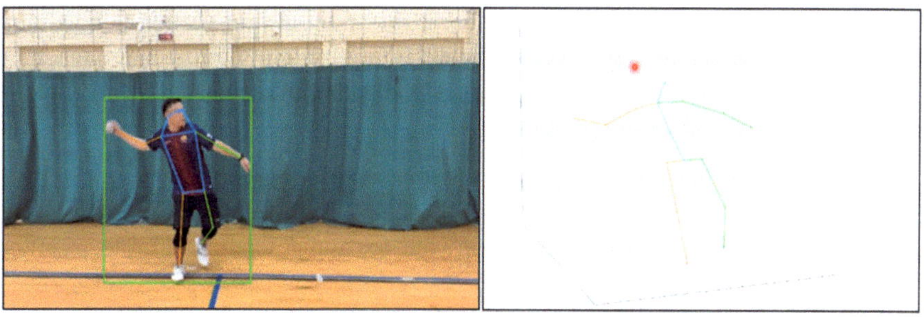

Fig. 7.4 Transformation of executed movement (left) to skeleton-based model in 3D space (right)

(b) aligning and normalizing the *executed* and *criterion* skeleton models, (c) image-by-image comparison of joint angles subtended by key points of the two models to inspect motion consistency, and lastly (d) repeating the process for different groups of joints.

In the current study, Euclidean distance between corresponding key points in the *executed* and *criterion* skeleton models were computed to determine movement consistency. In essence, each pose of the movement was represented as a set of key points in 3D space. For instance, key points of the first pose were denoted as P_i^1 and key points of the second pose as P_i^2, where *i* ranged over the number of key points. Mathematically, the Euclidean distance d_i between corresponding key points P_i^1 and P_i^2 was computed as:

$$d_i = \sqrt{\sum_{j=1}^{n} \left(P_{ij}^1 - P_{ij}^2\right)^2}$$

where n is the dimensionality of the key points. After calculating the Euclidean distances for all corresponding key points, the overall movement consistency score S was obtained by averaging the distances:

$$S = \frac{1}{N} \sum_{i=1}^{N} d_i$$

where N is the total number of key points. The score provided a quantitative measure of how similar the human poses were between the two movements, with lower values indicating higher similarity.

Evaluation of the Technology-Based Solution

The impact of the proposed solution will be evaluated through interviews and questionnaires. PE Teacher Education (PETE) instructors and students enrolled in PETE courses will be invited to participate in the surveys. At the start of the semester, instructors will provide a brief description of the study, its aims, and intended outcomes. iPads housing the HPE program will be intermittently utilized as a teaching tool throughout the duration of the course. At the end of the semester, the instructors will be interviewed. An outline of the interview questions is provided below:

1. What are the benefits of using the program as a teaching tool?
2. Did you face any challenges using the device?
3. What impact did the program have on your teaching? Comment on instruction, assessment, and feedback.
4. What are the implications of the program on pedagogical development?

A questionnaire survey will also be conducted at the end of the course to gather students' feedback on the program. An outline of the questionnaire is provided below.

1. Did you encounter any technical issues while using the software? Yes / No
2. Did you find the criterion movement videos useful? Yes / No
3. Was the slow-motion playback of the demonstration useful? Yes / No
4. Did the software enhance your learning experience? Yes / No
5. To what extent did the teaching tool facilitate collaborative and experiential learning?
6. Comment on your experience regarding this type of pedagogical approach for teaching and learning in PE.

Two separate questionnaires will also be conducted to assess students' engagement and ease of use of the teaching tool. Specifically, the Student Engagement Inventory

(SEI) will be used to assess the former and the System Usability Scale (SUS) for the latter.

The SEI is a comprehensive tool designed to assess various dimensions of student engagement in educational settings. This inventory evaluates student's level of involvement, motivation, and overall learning experiences (Esposito et al., 2022; Sinval et al., 2021). It consists of a series of questions or statements that students respond to, providing insights into their levels of engagement in the behavioral, emotional, and cognitive domains. The questionnaire is designed to capture students' perceptions of their learning environment, including aspects like interest in the subject matter, sense of belonging, interaction with peers and teachers, and the degree of challenge and support experienced (Appleton et al., 2006; Assunção et al., 2020). By analyzing the responses to the SEI, educators can identify areas of strength and areas for improvement in their teaching practices, fostering a more engaging and effective learning environment. Ten questions will be asked, each with five response options, namely "Strongly Disagree", "Disagree", "Neutral", "Agree", and "Strongly Agree. " The questions are as follows:

1. I find the subject interesting and relevant to my life.
2. I feel connected to my classmates and enjoy working with them.
3. I feel supported by my teachers when I encounter challenges.
4. I am motivated to participate actively in class discussions and activities.
5. I understand the goals and expectations of this course.
6. I feel that my opinions and contributions are valued by my teachers.
7. I feel challenged in this class, but I also feel capable of meeting those challenges.
8. I am able to apply what I've learned in this class to real-world situations.
9. I feel a sense of belonging and inclusion in this learning community.
10. Overall, I am engaged and invested in my learning experience in this class.

The System Usability Scale (SUS) evaluates the user-friendliness of the teaching tool. The SUS is a widely used tool for evaluating the usability of a wide range of systems, including software, websites, mobile apps, and hardware devices (Bangor et al., 2008; Lewis, 2018). Created by John Brooke in 1986, the scale has since become one of the most popular methods for assessing usability due to its simplicity and effectiveness (Brooke, 2013). The SUS consists of a 10-item questionnaire, each item rated on a 5-point Likert scale ranging from "Strongly Disagree" to "Strongly Agree." The items are designed to capture different aspects of usability, including ease of use, learnability, efficiency, and user satisfaction. The SUS does not focus on specific usability attributes but provides a general assessment of the overall usability of a system. An outline of the SUS questionnaire is provided below:

1. I think that I would like to use this system frequently.
2. I found the system unnecessarily complex.
3. I thought the system was easy to use.
4. I think that I would need the support of a technical person to be able to use this system.
5. I found the various functions in this system were well integrated.

6. I thought there was too much inconsistency in this system.
7. I would imagine that most people would learn to use this system very quickly.
8. I found the system very cumbersome to use.
9. I felt very confident using the system.
10. I needed to learn a lot of things before I could get going with this system.

To calculate the SUS score, the scores for items 1, 3, 5, 7, and 9 are reversed (i.e., 1 becomes 5, 2 becomes 4, etc.) Then, for each item, subtract 1 from the selected score. The sum of these scores is then multiplied by 2.5 to obtain the final SUS score, which ranges from 0 to 100. A score above 68 is generally considered above average usability, while a score above 80 is considered excellent.

Summary and Conclusion

This chapter introduces a technology-based approach to overcome challenges commonly faced in PE. The proposed solution addresses three core issues: suboptimal demonstration of motor skills, visual obstructions in crowded classrooms, and subjective assessment of student performance. First, in the proposed solution, students can consult the criterion movement within the digital device to improve their learning. Second, visual obstructions can be effectively minimized when students pair up to analyze the criterion movement. Third, the HPE-generated similarity score provides an objective measure of motor competence. This approach not only tackles immediate barriers but also creates a framework for tenable pedagogy in PE. As the study continues, its anticipated findings are expected to impact instructional methods and student engagement, aligning technological novelty with pedagogical advancement.

Competing Interests The author has no conflicts of interest to declare that are relevant to the content of this chapter.

References

Adeyanju, S. A., Mamudu, M. M., & Danıa, E. T. (2017). Effect of class size on the learning of motor skill among selected secondary school students in Ife central local government area of Osun state, Nigeria. *European Journal of Physical Education and Sport Science, 3*(1), 52–60. https://doi.org/10.5281/zeodo.290301

Appleton, J. J., Christenson, S. L., Kim, D., & Reschly, A. L. (2006). Measuring cognitive and psychological engagement: Validation of the student engagement instrument. *Journal of School Psychology, 44*(5), 427–445.

Assunção, H., Lin, S. W., Sit, P. S., Cheung, K. C., Harju-Luukkainen, H., Smith, T., Maloa, B., Duarte Bonini Campos, J. A., Ilic, I. S., Esposito, G., Francesca, F. M., & Marôco, J. (2020). University student engagement inventory (USEI): Transcultural validity evidence across four continents. *Frontiers in Psychology, 10*, 489785.

Ball, D. L., & Forzani, F. M. (2007). 2007 Wallace Foundation distinguished lecture—What makes education research "educational"? *Educational Researcher, 36*(9), 529–540.

Bangor, A., Kortum, P. T., & Miller, J. T. (2008). An empirical evaluation of the system usability scale. *International Journal of Human Computer Interaction, 24*(6), 574–594.

Blandin, Y., & Proteau, L. (2000). On the cognitive basis of observational learning: Development of mechanisms for the detection and correction of errors. *The Quarterly Journal of Experimental Psychology: Section A, 53*(3), 846–867.

Blatchford, P., & Russell, A. (2019). Class size, grouping practices and classroom management. *International Journal of Educational Research, 96*, 154–163.

Brooke, J. (2013). SUS: A retrospective. *Journal of Usability Studies, 8*(2), 29–40. Retrieved from https://uxpajournal.org/sus-a-retrospective/

Burson, S. L., Mulhearn, S. C., Castelli, D. M., & van der Mars, H. (2021). Essential components of physical education: Policy and environment. *Research Quarterly for Exercise and Sport, 92*(2), 209–221.

Chae, H. J., Kim, J. B., Park, G., O'Sullivan, D. M., Seo, J., & Park, J. J. (2023). An artificial intelligence exercise coaching mobile app: Development and randomized controlled trial to verify its effectiveness in posture correction. *Interactive Journal of Medical Research, 12*(1), e37604.

Cheung, P., & Zhang, L. (2020). Environment for preschool children to learn fundamental motor skills: The role of teaching venue and class size. *Sustainability, 12*(22), 9774. https://doi.org/10.3390/su12229774

Chiang, J. C., Lie, W. N., Huang, H. C., Chen, K. T., Liang, J. Y., Lo, Y. C., & Huang, W. H. (2022). Posture monitoring for health care of bedridden elderly patients using 3d human skeleton analysis via machine learning approach. *Applied Sciences, 12*(6), 3087. https://doi.org/10.3390/app12063087

Colvin, A. V., Egner Markos, N. J., & Walker, P. J. (2000). *Teaching the nuts and bolts of physical education: Building basic movement skills*. Human Kinetics.

Darling-Hammond, L., Hyler, M. E., & Gardner, M. (2017). *Effective teacher professional development*. Learning Policy Institute.

Du, X., Vasudevan, R., & Johnson-Roberson, M. (2019). Bio-lstm: A biomechanically inspired recurrent neural network for 3-d pedestrian pose and gait prediction. *IEEE Robotics and Automation Letters, 4*(2), 1501–1508.

Ehrenberg, R. G., Brewer, D. J., Gamoran, A., & Willms, J. D. (2001). Class size and student achievement. *Psychological Science in the Public Interest, 2*(1), 1–30.

Enright, E., Hill, J., Sandford, R., & Gard, M. (2014). Looking beyond what's broken: Towards an appreciative research agenda for physical education and sport pedagogy. *Sport, Education and Society, 19*(7), 912–926.

Esposito, G., Marôco, J., Passeggia, R., Pepicelli, G., & Freda, M. F. (2022). The Italian validation of the university student engagement inventory. *European Journal of Higher Education, 12*(1), 35–55.

Ferrari, M. (1996). Observing the observer: Self-regulation in the observational learning of motor skills. *Developmental Review, 16*(2), 203–240.

Franklin, R. M., & Smith, J. (2015). Practical assessment on the run—Ipads as an effective mobile and paperless tool in physical education and teaching. *Research in Learning Technology, 23*(1), 27986. https://doi.org/10.3402/rlt.v23.27986

Gajbhiye, R., Jarag, S., Gaikwad, P., & Koparde, S. (2022). AI human-pose-estimation: Yoga pose detection and correction. *International Journal of Innovative Science and Research Technology, 7*(5), 1649–1658.

Gamra, M. B., & Akhloufi, M. A. (2021). A review of deep learning techniques for 2D and 3D human-pose-estimation. *Image and Vision Computing, 114*, 104282. https://doi.org/10.1016/j.imavis.2021.104282

Gibson, E. J. (1988). Exploratory behavior in the development of perceiving, acting, and the acquiring of knowledge. *Annual Review of Psychology, 39*(1), 1–41.

Gross, M. K., & Buchanan, A. M. (2014). Perspectives of physical education specialists who teach in large class settings. *Journal of Physical Education and Sports Management, 1*(2), 67–90. https://doi.org/10.15640/jpesm.v1n2a5

Haibach-Beach, P. S., Perreault, M. E., Brian, A. S., & Collier, D. H. (2023). *Motor learning and development*. Human Kinetics.

Hastie, P. A., & Saunders, J. E. (1991). Effects of class size and equipment availability on student involvement in physical education. *The Journal of Experimental Education, 59*(3), 212–224. https://doi.org/10.1080/00220973.1991.10806561

Hülsmann, F., Göpfert, J. P., Hammer, B., Kopp, S., & Botsch, M. (2018). Classification of motor errors to provide real-time feedback for sports coaching in virtual reality—A case study in squats and tai chi pushes. *Computers & Graphics, 76*, 47–59. https://doi.org/10.1016/j.cag.2018.08.003

Hwang, J., Park, S., & Kwak, N. (2017). Athlete pose estimation by a global-local network. In *Proceedings of the IEEE Conference on Computer Vision and Pattern Recognition* (pp. 58–65).

Ji, H. R., Githinji, K. S., & Kenji, T. (2023). AI fitness coach at home using image recognition. *International Journal of Human Movement and Sports Sciences, 11*(4), 850–857. https://doi.org/10.13189/saj.2023.110419

Kim, W., Ramanagopal, M. S., Barto, C., Yu, M. Y., Rosaen, K., Goumas, N., Vasudevan, R., & Johnson-Roberson, M. (2019). Pedx: Benchmark dataset for metric 3-D pose estimation of pedestrians in complex urban intersections. *IEEE Robotics and Automation Letters, 4*(2), 1940–1947. https://doi.org/10.1109/LRA.2019.2896705

Koehler, M. J., & Mishra, P. (2008). Introducing TPCK. In AACTE Committee on Innovation and Technology (Ed.), *The handbook of technological pedagogical content knowledge (TPCK) for educators*. American Association of Colleges of Teacher Education & Routledge.

Lai, K. C., Blatchford, P., & Dong, B. (2016). Eastern and western perspectives: Educational and policy contexts and how they have shaped approaches to class size. In P. Blatchford, K. W. Chan, M. Galton, K. C. Lai, & J. C.-K. Lee (Eds.), *Class size—Eastern and western perspectives* (pp. 21–39). Routledge.

Lamas, A., Tabik, S., Montes, A. C., Pérez-Hernández, F., García, J., Olmos, R., & Herrera, F. (2022). Human-pose-estimation for mitigating false negatives in weapon detection in video-surveillance. *Neurocomputing, 489*, 488–503.

Lampert, M., & Graziani, F. (2009). Instructional activities as a tool for teachers' and teacher educators' learning. *The Elementary School Journal, 109*(5), 491–509.

Lewis, J. R. (2018). The system usability scale: Past, present, and future. *International Journal of Human Computer Interaction, 34*(7), 577–590.

Liang, G., Walls, R. T., Hicks, V. L., Clayton, L. B., & Yang, L. (2006). Will tomorrow's physical educators be prepared to teach in the digital age? *Contemporary Issues in Technology and Teacher Education, 6*(1), 143–156.

Liu, H., Nie, H., Zhang, Z., & Li, Y. F. (2021). Anisotropic angle distribution learning for head pose estimation and attention understanding in human-computer interaction. *Neurocomputing, 433*, 310–322.

López-Pastor, V. M., Kirk, D., Lorente-Catalán, E., MacPhail, A., & Macdonald, D. (2013). Alternative assessment in physical education: A review of international literature. *Sport, Education and Society, 18*(1), 57–76.

MacPhail, A., & Halbert, J. (2010). 'We had to do intelligent thinking during recent PE': Students' and teachers' experiences of assessment for learning in post-primary physical education. *Assessment in Education: Principles, Policy & Practice, 17*(1), 23–39. https://doi.org/10.1080/09695940903565412

Massaoudi, M., Abu-Rub, H., Refaat, S. S., Chihi, I., & Oueslati, F. S. (2021). Deep learning in smart grid technology: A review of recent advancements and future prospects. *IEEE Access, 9*, 54558–54578.

Piotrowski, S., & Capel, S. (2013). Formal and informal modes of assessment in physical education. In *Issues in physical education* (pp. 99–114). Routledge.

Pouyanfar, S., Sadiq, S., Yan, Y., Tian, H., Tao, Y., Reyes, M. P., Shyu, M. L., Chen, S. C., & Iyengar, S. S. (2018). A survey on deep learning: Algorithms, techniques, and applications. *ACM Computing Surveys (CSUR), 51*(5), 1–36.

Reynolds, A. (1992). What is competent beginning teaching? A review of the literature. *Review of Educational Research, 62*(1), 1–35.

Rovegno, I. (2003). Teachers' knowledge construction. In *Student learning in physical education: Applying Research to Enhance Instruction* (Vol. 2, pp. 295–310).

Scott, J., Collins, R., Funk, C., & Liu, Y. (2017). 4D model-based spatiotemporal alignment of scripted Taiji Quan sequences. In *Proceedings of the IEEE international conference on computer vision* (pp. 795–804).

Settlage, J., Odom, A. L., & Pedersen, J. E. (2004). Uses of technology by science education professors: Comparisons with teachers: Uses and the current versus desired technology knowledge gap. *Contemporary Issues in Technology and Teacher Education, 4*(3), 299–312.

Shulman, L. S., & Wilson, S. M. (2004). *The wisdom of practice: Essays on teaching, learning, and learning to teach.* Jossey-Bass.

Sigal, L. (2021). Human-pose-estimation. In *Computer vision: A reference guide* (pp. 573–592). Springer International Publishing.

Sinval, J., Casanova, J. R., Marôco, J., & Almeida, L. S. (2021). University student engagement inventory (USEI): Psychometric properties. *Current Psychology, 40*, 1608–1620.

Soderstrom, N. C., & Bjork, R. A. (2015). Learning versus performance: An integrative review. *Perspectives on Psychological Science, 10*(2), 176–199.

Strizek, G. A., Tourkin, S., & Erberber, E. (2014). *Teaching and Learning International Survey (TALIS) 2013: US technical report. NCES 2015–010.* National Center for Education Statistics.

Tsai, Y. S., Hsu, L. H., Hsieh, Y. Z., & Lin, S. S. (2020). The real-time depth estimation for an occluded person based on a single image and OpenPose method. *Mathematics, 8*(8), 1333. https://doi.org/10.3390/math8081333

Van Holst, A. (1997). The use of demonstration in teaching physical education. *Journal Canadian Association for Health, Physical Education Recreation and Dance, 63*(2), 20–22.

Wang, X., Zhao, Y., & Pourpanah, F. (2020). Recent advances in deep learning. *International Journal of Machine Learning and Cybernetics, 11*, 747–750.

Wang, J., Tan, S., Zhen, X., Xu, S., Zheng, F., He, Z., & Shao, L. (2021). Deep 3D human-pose-estimation: A review. *Computer Vision and Image Understanding, 210*, 103225. https://doi.org/10.1016/j.cviu.2021.103225

Woods, M. L., Karp, G., Miao, H., & Perlman, D. (2008). Physical educators' technology competencies and usage. *The Physical Educator, 65*(2), 82–99.

Zecha, D., Einfalt, M., Eggert, C., & Lienhart, R. (2018). Kinematic pose rectification for performance analysis and retrieval in sports. In *Proceedings of the IEEE Conference on Computer Vision and Pattern Recognition* (pp. 1791–1799).

Zhou, Y., Wang, L., Chen, R., & Wang, B. (2025). Associations between class-level factors and student physical activity during physical education lessons in China. *International Journal of Behavioral Nutrition and Physical Activity, 22*(1), 1.

Hock Beng Tommy Ng is a faculty member of the Physical Education and Sports Science academic group at the National Institute of Education, Nanyang Technological University, Singapore. His research interests lie in the use of technology and machine learning in education and the application of neuroscience to pedagogical practices in education. He teaches courses in human growth and development, motor control, and motor learning. https://dr.ntu.edu.sg/cris/rp/rp01576.

Chapter 8
AI-Generated Images for Linguistically Responsive and Multimodal Elementary Literacy Curriculum and Instruction

Gayoung Choi and SungEun Min

Abstract This chapter explores how generative AI—including image and video generation tools—can be meaningfully integrated into early and elementary literacy curriculum and instruction. Grounded in teacher education programs, we identify four areas of pedagogical application through which AI can support the development of multimodal, culturally and linguistically responsive, and technology-integrated phonics and literacy instruction. First, AI image tools can be used to create decodable books aligned with phonics patterns, enabling preservice teachers to design attractive visual aids. Second, the creation of bilingual books promotes the inclusion of students' home languages, fostering biliteracy and cultural relevance through the use of generative AI image tools, read-aloud applications, and translation technologies. Third, AI-generated image–vocabulary pairs offer differentiated scaffolding to support diverse learners in vocabulary acquisition. Lastly, text-to-video tools provide accessible read-aloud support, particularly for emerging bilinguals and students with learning differences. Through concrete examples, project procedures, and classroom applications, this chapter highlights the potential of AI as a pedagogically embedded resource—rather than a standalone tool—for enhancing equity, creativity, and inclusivity in literacy education. By showcasing practices in teacher preparation, we demonstrate how thoughtful AI integration can expand instructional possibilities and equip educators to navigate the future of literacy teaching in digitally mediated, multilingual classrooms.

Keywords Culturally responsive teaching · Elementary literacy · Multimodal instruction

---

G. Choi
University of Nebraska-Lincoln, Lincoln, NE, USA

S. Min (✉)
Kutztown University, Kutztown, PA, USA
e-mail: min@kutztown.edu

G. Tchibozo (ed.), *International Perspectives of Generative AI in Education*, Advances in Artificial Intelligence in Education 3,
https://doi.org/10.1007/978-3-031-99804-1_8

This chapter introduces how educational AI tools for image generation can serve as powerful supports for linguistically responsive, multimodal, and technology-integrated literacy curriculum and instruction. Drawing on the authors' experiences in both elementary education and teacher education programs in South Korea and the United States, we explore the implications of AI-generated visuals in early childhood and elementary settings, with a particular focus on literacy and English as a Second Language (ESL)/sheltered instruction for English Language Learners (ELLs).

AI Tools for Image Generation

Today, we live in an age dominated by visuals, where people regularly produce and consume both still and moving images in their daily lives. Generative AI tools such as Sora and Canva exemplify the advancement of image generation technologies that now extend into video production. Additionally, text-to-video GenAI platforms like Veed and CapCut enable users to create videos that incorporate moving images, avatars, and multilingual voice-overs and captions with increasing ease and accessibility.

These AI tools for image and video generation blur the boundary between the real and the artificial—what Baudrillard (1981) referred to as simulacra—raising critical questions about authenticity, representation, and plagiarism (Anthology, 2023). Despite these challenges, such technologies hold significant potential for education, especially in supporting multimodal and multilingual learning experiences.

In this chapter, based on our teaching experiences in U.S. teacher education programs, we introduce potential areas in early and elementary literacy curriculum and instruction where the incorporation of generative AI—for both still and video image generation—can effectively support the development of multimodal, culturally and linguistically responsive, and technology-integrated phonics and literacy instruction.

Envisioning AI-Generated Image Incorporation in Early and Elementary Literacy Instruction

This section introduces four areas in early and elementary literacy curriculum and instruction where the incorporation of generative AI can support educators in designing multimodal, culturally and linguistically relevant, and technology-integrated phonics and literacy instruction: (a) decodable book creation, (b) multimodal and linguistically responsive children's book creation, (c) image-vocabulary pair creation, and (d) read-aloud video creation. Based on our teaching experience in early and elementary literacy instruction courses, as well as the projects and assignments conducted with preservice teachers, we present the rationale, purpose, and implementation procedures of these class activities. The detailed descriptions of our processes aim to help readers envision how they might incorporate AI tools into their own future literacy instruction.

Decodable Book Creation Using AI Image Tools

One area in early and elementary literacy curriculum and instruction where the incorporation of generative AIs can support educators is creating decodable books. As part of a literacy methods course, preservice teachers engaged in a decodable book-making project that combined phonics instruction with digital innovation. Using AI-based image generation tools, the teachers created phonics-based images accompanied by custom visuals. This project served as a bridge between structured literacy approaches and creative technology integration in the early literacy classroom.

Rationale

This project was grounded in the Science of Reading, particularly the word recognition strand of Scarborough's Reading Rope (Scarborough, 2001). In this framework, preservice teachers apply structured literacy principles to the design of decodable texts. Many preservice teachers are familiar with the concept of decodable books, but few have had hands-on experience creating visually engaging, phonics-aligned materials for classroom use (Spear-Swerling, 2019). While systematic and explicit phonics instruction is widely recognized as essential for early literacy, there is often a gap between theoretical knowledge and the ability to design customized instructional texts (Moats, 2020). By integrating AI image generation tools into the book-making process, this project offers preservice teachers the opportunity to apply their phonics knowledge in creative and practical ways. The use of AI also empowers them to produce personalized visuals that enhance readability and support beginning readers.

Purpose

This project aimed to help preservice teachers design and produce their own decodable books that aligned with specific phonics patterns (Fig. 8.1). By writing phonics-based stories and creating visual materials using AI image generation tools, the preservice teachers gained practical experience in developing instructional resources that support early literacy. The project also fostered creativity, technological literacy, and a deeper understanding of how to make phonics instruction engaging, developmentally appropriate, and visually supportive for beginning readers. The

Fig. 8.1 Decodable Books Using AI-Generated Images

project also encouraged preservice teachers to reflect critically on the pedagogical use of AI as a purposeful tool that can support, reshape, and ethically inform their instructional practices in early literacy.

Procedures

This project followed a structured instructional sequence designed to integrate phonics instruction and AI-supported visual composition. The entire process was completed within a 60-minute session, allowing preservice teachers to focus on instructional design without being overwhelmed by technical complexity.

Step One: Choose a Phonics Focus

Each preservice teacher selected a target phonics pattern such as CVC (consonant-vowel-consonant) words, digraphs (sh, ch, th, wh, ck), consonant blends (bl, cr, sp., st, tr, pl), silent e, or r-controlled vowels based on early literacy instructional goals. To simulate real classroom decision-making, preservice teachers were provided with a sample spelling inventory for a hypothetical small group of learners. They used this data to determine which phonics pattern would be most instructionally appropriate for their target group.

Step Two: Draft a Decodable Story

Preservice teachers composed original decodable texts using words aligned with the selected phonics pattern. They first brainstormed key vocabulary and then wrote a coherent short story with simple sentences appropriate for beginning readers.

Step Three: Generate Illustrations With AI

Using tools like DALL-E, Sora, and Canva, the teachers generated custom images to represent the content of their texts. The images were selected not only for visual appeal but also for their ability to support comprehension and reinforce phonics-based vocabulary.

Step Four: Compile the Book

Preservice teachers used the app Book Creator to assemble the story and illustrations into a digital book. This step emphasized coherence between text and images and allowed for basic layout design.

Step Five: Revising and Editing

Next, preservice teachers reviewed both the text and visuals, revising for clarity, consistency, and alignment with the phonics focus. They also evaluated whether the images accurately supported the intended meaning and were developmentally appropriate for young readers.

Step Six: Presentation (Reading Aloud)

Preservice teachers shared their books through read-alouds and reflected on how the materials could be integrated into phonics instruction, for example, guided reading, small-group phonics, or independent practice, and how the visual elements could scaffold learners' decoding and comprehension.

Below are examples of the preservice teachers' work (Figs. 8.2 and 8.3).

Reflection on the Project

Importantly, because the focus of this project was on phonics content and instructional purpose rather than design complexity, student teachers did not feel pressured by the visual design aspect. The intuitive tools allowed them to complete the project including story writing, illustration, and publishing within a 60-minute session. This accessibility helped the preservice teachers concentrate on instructional clarity, student engagement, and phonics alignment, rather than technical hurdles.

Fig. 8.2 Decodable Book Page Featuring the CVCe (Silent-E) Pattern, Created With DALL·E

Fig. 8.3 Decodable Book Page Featuring Digraphs, Created With DALL·E

Multimodal and Linguistically Responsive Children's Book Creation

Another area in early and elementary literacy curriculum and instruction where the incorporation of generative AI can support educators is creating multimodal and linguistically responsive children's books.

As a culminating activity of the semester, preservice teachers created digital children's books that reflected their understanding of narrative structure, character development, theme, and vocabulary, which they had studied through novels and mentor texts. This project served as an opportunity to move from analysis to creation, inviting preservice teachers to compose and illustrate original stories that incorporated multimodal and multilingual features. In doing so, they applied both their literary knowledge and pedagogical insights to story-based instruction.

Rationale

Children's literature is a powerful tool for developing language, imagination, and cultural awareness (Galda et al., 2017; Norton & Norton, 2009; Sipe, 2008). In increasingly diverse classrooms, books that combine multimodal features with linguistic responsiveness help create more equitable and engaging literacy learning experiences. Drawing on the Linguistically Responsive Teaching (LRT) framework (Lucas & Villegas, 2011), the project also emphasized the value of story-based instruction that affirms students' identities by incorporating ELLs' home languages as assets and funds of knowledge, differentiating instruction, and expanding access to literacy for all. Lucas and Villegas (2011) emphasized that teachers must understand how language and culture shape student learning and intentionally plan instruction that builds on ELLs' linguistic resources. In their linguistically responsive instruction, they advocated for scaffolding academic language development while affirming students' home languages and experiences as valuable assets to the classroom. Through the integration of multiple languages by incorporating AI tools—including English and ELLs' home languages—educators can design mentor texts that are both developmentally appropriate and linguistically responsive.

Purpose

The purpose of this project was to promote cultural and linguistic inclusion through bilingual storytelling while fostering creative expression through digital multimodal tools. By designing 10–15 page bilingual digital books in English and one additional language of their choice through platforms such as BookCreator, ChatGPT, Canva, Adobe AI Image Generator, or Sora, preservice teachers modeled inclusive literacy instruction grounded in principles of equity and accessibility. As part of this process, they translated or adapted texts into another language, using both their knowledge and AI-generated suggestions, while learning to evaluate the accuracy, tone, and cultural appropriateness of those translations. This project also introduced AI tools as intentional collaborators in literacy design, encouraging future educators to engage critically with AI-generated visuals and translations. This process helped them practice critical engagement with AI tools, treating them not as a shortcut but as a collaborative design partner in intentional literacy design.

Procedures

Step One: Choose a Theme and Plan the Story

Preservice teachers selected a central theme or moral like kindness, friendship, responsibility, or perseverance, that would guide their children's book. They then outlined the story with key narrative elements, including characters, setting, plot, and resolution.

To support this process, preservice teachers used AI as a brainstorming partner, generating and refining ideas collaboratively.

AI Prompt Examples:

- Suggest 3 story ideas for a children's book that teaches a lesson about kindness.
- Suggest 5 names for a friendly rabbit character.
- Give me a story outline with Beginning, Middle, and End for a story about friendship.

Step Two: Draft the Story

The preservice teachers wrote short, simple sentences under 10 words each, using child-friendly vocabulary. They were encouraged to use ChatGPT for support but required to revise its output to maintain clarity, age appropriateness, and pedagogical intent.

Step Three: Translate the Story (Multilingual Integration)

Each page included both English and one additional language (e.g., Spanish, Korean, or German). Preservice teachers used BookCreator's built-in translation tool and then revised outputs using ChatGPT, Gemini, or another tool for clarity and natural phrasing. The instructor, a native Korean speaker, shared her experience of testing BookCreator's Korean translation feature, which, while contextually correct, sounded awkward and unnatural. This example highlighted the importance of double-checking AI-generated translations using at least two tools and applying human judgment to ensure readability, tone, and appropriateness for child readers. Preservice teachers were encouraged to think critically about not just accuracy, but language fluidity, cultural nuances, and developmental suitability in both languages.

AI Prompt Examples:

- Translate this sentence into smooth Korean for a child reader.
- Make this sound playful in Spanish.
- Is this German translation natural and easy to understand for a 7-year-old?

Preservice teachers used two separate text boxes per page, applied color coding (e.g., English in black, second language in blue), and evaluated whether translations matched the intended tone and audience.

Step Four: Create Illustrations (Multimodal Composition)

The preservice teachers created or sourced custom illustrations using DALL·E, Canva, Sora, or Adobe AI Image Generator. They matched visuals to events, emotions, and settings described in the text. Layout guidelines included placing illustrations at the top or left and text at the bottom or right. AI-generated images were critically evaluated for accuracy, tone, and cultural relevance.

Step Five: Compile, Revise, and Edit the Book

Preservice teachers assembled their text and images in BookCreator. Using a checklist, they revised for narrative flow, visual-text alignment, grammar, and translation quality.

Checklist Highlights

- Book cover with title, author, and date
- 10–15 pages with full-color illustrations
- English and second-language text on each page
- Natural-sounding translations
- Developmentally appropriate language.

Step Six: Create a Book Trailer

As a multimodal extension, preservice teachers produced 30–60 second book trailers using Veed.io, CapCut, or Invideo. Trailers featured 3–5 key scenes and included either English voiceover and captions in the second language or second-language voiceover and English captions. This task allowed preservice teachers to explore pacing, voice, and audience engagement in audiovisual storytelling.

Below are examples of the preservice teachers' work (Figs. 8.4, 8.5 and 8.6).

Fig. 8.4 Sample Book Page From *Tilly the Tiny Turtle*, Featuring English-Korean Bilingual Text With Illustrations Generated by DALL·E

Fig. 8.5 Sample Book Page From *The Day Luca Lost His Roar*, Featuring English-Italian Bilingual Text With Illustrations Generated by DALL·E

Fig. 8.6 Sample Book Page From *Henri the Hedgehog and the Eiffel Tower Adventure*, Featuring English-French Bilingual Text With Illustrations Generated by DALL·E

Reflection on the Project

The project concluded with a classroom showcase where preservice teachers presented their digital children's books and trailers in a celebratory, low-stakes setting. This public sharing served as both a reflection and celebration of student learning, allowing teacher candidates to articulate their creative choices and recognize the instructional value of multilingual, multimodal storytelling.

Many preservice teachers reported that the project helped them better understand how to support young learners through the use of visual scaffolds, accessible language, and culturally responsive content. The integration of text, images, and linguistic diversity deepened their understanding of how children's literature can reflect and affirm a wide range of identities and experiences.

By working across visual, textual, and linguistic modes, preservice teachers moved beyond traditional notions of literacy and embraced inclusive practices that reflected the realities of today's multilingual classrooms. In doing so, they strengthened their capacity to design instruction that is culturally responsive, developmentally appropriate, and pedagogically intentional, which are core principles aligned with the LRT framework.

While preservice teachers acknowledged the limitations of translation, particularly the challenge of verifying AI-generated output in languages they did not speak, they also recognized that these tools provided a valuable entry point for inclusive material design. Despite their initial uncertainty, most came to see AI as a supportive resource that, when used critically and ethically, can meaningfully expand access and representation in early literacy instruction.

Creating Image-Vocabulary Pairs as Differentiated Visual Scaffolding

A third area in early and elementary literacy curriculum and instruction where the incorporation of generative AI can support educators is in creating image-vocabulary pairs as differentiated visual scaffolding for vocabulary development.

Rationale

Visual scaffolding can be a powerful tool for younger learners and ELLs' vocabulary growth. Visual scaffolding is a strategy that enhances comprehension by pairing spoken English with drawings or photographs, helping students link the language they hear to corresponding visual representations (Echevarria et al., 2010; Herrell & Jordan, 2015). Images play an essential role in supporting vocabulary development and phonemic awareness, particularly for young learners and ELLs. Visuals offer tangible representations of otherwise abstract concepts, helping young learners and ELLs make connections between written words and their associated sounds and meanings. By pairing images with vocabulary, learners are more likely to remember new words and decode unfamiliar ones through visual cues (Wright, 2015). This multisensory approach accommodates a range of learning styles and reinforces the link between print and meaning. In particular, incorporating students' home languages along with corresponding images further promotes vocabulary development.

The created image-vocabulary pairs can be used as flashcards or word wall displays in the classroom to support vocabulary building and phonemic awareness practice.

Purpose

The purpose of the project was to create a set of images that corresponded to vocabulary words relevant to learners' grade levels or language development stages. The project had two main goals. First, it helped preservice teachers understand and analyze areas where their students needed to grow in vocabulary. This could be achieved in two ways: (1) by identifying sight words or high-frequency words appropriate for the students' grade level, and (2) by assessing individual students' English proficiency in listening, speaking, reading, and writing to determine specific vocabulary needs. The next step involved having preservice teachers create image-vocabulary pairs tailored to these identified needs.

Procedures

Step One: Analyze the Areas of Strengths and Need for Vocabulary Growth

Preservice teachers analyzed areas of strength and need for growth by exploring ELL profiles provided by Purdue University. The website offers background information on various ELLs, along with oral language, reading, and writing samples, to help assess their English proficiency across different domains (https://education.purdue.edu/elllps/elementary-school).

Step Two: Create the Image-Vocabulary Pairs by Prompting AI Tools

Based on their understanding of ELLs' language needs—particularly vocabulary—preservice teachers created image-vocabulary pairs by prompting AI tools such as Sora. They were also asked to incorporate ELLs' home languages when generating the images. The following prompt was used for this task:

AI Prompt Example:

- Create a visual scaffold to help an English language learner understand the meaning of the word "run" by integrating English and Spanish translation.

Step Three: Incorporate the Image-Vocabulary Pairs into Lesson Planning

The image-vocabulary pairs were to be incorporated into the preservice teachers' lesson plans, particularly in SIOP (Sheltered Instruction Observation Protocol) lesson planning for ELLs.

Below are examples of preservice teachers' work (Figs. 8.7 and 8.8).

Fig. 8.7 Image-Vocabulary Pairs

Reflection on the Project

Through this assignment, preservice teachers explored practical visual scaffolding strategies to support differentiated vocabulary development for students. By analyzing ELL profiles, they learned to interpret student data in order to plan targeted instruction that addresses both areas of weakness and essential vocabulary such as sight words and high-frequency words.

While preservice teachers recognized the effectiveness of AI tools in creating differentiated visual scaffolds for their future classrooms, they also acknowledged challenges—such as inaccurate translations or images that were only loosely connected to the intended concepts. These reflections led to deeper discussions about the ethical and critical use of AI tools in educational settings.

Fig. 8.8 Image-Vocabulary Pairs Incorporating English and Spanish

Leveraging Text-to-Video AI for Read-Aloud Support

The final area in early and elementary literacy where the incorporation of generative AI can support educators is the use of AI-generated videos to provide read-aloud support for early learners and ELLs. Preservice teachers created short book trailers to accompany their multilingual children's books. These trailers extended the written and illustrated texts into audiovisual formats, offering an engaging, multimodal entry point for young readers, particularly ELLs. Using tools like Veed.io, CapCut, and Invideo, preservice teachers explored how AI can support listening comprehension, oral language development, and bilingual access through digital storytelling.

Rationale

For emergent bilinguals, audiovisual storytelling provides multiple entry points to meaning-making through visuals, sound, and language. This approach is supported by multimodal learning theory and universal design for learning (UDL) principles, which emphasize the importance of offering content through various modalities to accommodate diverse learners.

Purpose

The purpose of this project was to explore how text-to-video AI tools can be leveraged to support read-aloud instruction for emerging bilinguals and early readers. By transforming written texts into animated, narrated videos, preservice teachers designed accessible, engaging literacy content that modeled fluent reading, supported listening comprehension, and provided visual scaffolding for word recognition. Projects included videos with multilingual subtitles and English voiceovers, or English captions paired with second language voiceovers, allowing for flexible and culturally responsive language support. This project also encouraged critical reflection on the pedagogical value and limitations of generative AI in early literacy contexts.

Procedures

Step One: Storyboard and Scriptwriting

Preservice teachers identified 3–5 key scenes from their books that best illustrated the plot or theme. Using these scenes, they drafted short scripts that would serve as the voiceover or caption content in their videos. This step emphasized narrative focus, language clarity, and oral fluency appropriate for early readers and emergent bilinguals.

Step Two: Create The Video

Using AI-powered video platforms such as Veed.io, Invideo, or CapCut, students transformed their scripts into animated or narrated read-aloud videos. They incorporated English voiceovers with multilingual subtitles, or second language voiceovers with English captions, depending on their linguistic goals. Visuals were selected or generated to support word recognition, comprehension, and cultural relevance.

Step Three: Peer Review and Final Touches

After an initial draft, students engaged in peer feedback sessions focused on clarity, pacing, and accessibility. When possible, they also sought feedback from peers who spoke the target language to ensure the appropriateness of translations, captions, or voiceovers. Based on this input, students revised their videos to enhance visual coherence, timing, and alignment with UDL principles. Final videos were shared with classmates or uploaded as part of a digital literacy showcase.

Below are examples of preservice teachers' work (Figs. 8.9 and 8.10).

Fig. 8.9 *Henri the Hedgehog and the Eiffel Tower Adventure*, featuring French voiceover with English captions

Fig. 8.10 *Tilly the Tiny Turtle*, featuring English voiceover with Korean captions

Reflection on the Project

As they worked on their projects, preservice teachers not only applied design and literacy principles but also engaged in practices aligned with the LRT framework. By incorporating students' home languages, critically evaluating translation choices, and creating materials that centered multilingual learners, they enacted key orientations of LRT such as valuing linguistic diversity, recognizing the sociocultural dimensions of language use, and advocating for equitable literacy access. In doing so, they demonstrated growing awareness of how instructional decisions can either affirm or marginalize students' identities, and how pedagogical tools like AI can support more inclusive, linguistically responsive classrooms.

While the integration of AI in education often raises concerns, particularly in elementary contexts where teachers may fear screen overexposure or loss of human connection (Selwyn, 2016; Zhao, 2017), this project approaches AI not as a standalone technology but as a pedagogically embedded tool. The use of AI image generation is not the goal of the activity but rather a supporting strategy to enhance literacy instruction that is already grounded in evidence-based practice such as phonics, writer's workshop, or multimodal learning.

Conclusion

This chapter introduced key areas in early and elementary literacy where AI-generated images can be integrated to support students' multimodal, culturally and linguistically relevant, and technology-enhanced phonics and literacy learning. These areas include: (a) decodable book creation, (b) multimodal and linguistically responsive children's book creation, (c) image-vocabulary pair creation, and (d) read-aloud video creation.

To extend the learning beyond this project itself, teachers should be invited to reflect on the potential of AI in their future classrooms. This reflective component will encourage them to consider AI not just as a convenience but as a pedagogical responsibility. The following questions can guide individual and group discussion:

- How might you use AI tools to support student writing or storytelling?
- In what ways can image generation support language learners or emergent readers?
- How can you ensure AI is used ethically and developmentally appropriately in early literacy instruction?
- What guidelines would you set for students when using AI tools in the classroom?
- How might AI tools help differentiate instruction or increase engagement?

Through this dialogue, educators can pose critical questions around authorship, access, equity, and creativity, acknowledging both the possibilities and limitations of generative AI. Many of the preservice teachers in our study initially expressed hesitation or skepticism, particularly regarding the accuracy and authenticity of AI-generated content, but they ultimately learned to see AI as an adaptable tool that must be guided by thoughtful, inclusive pedagogy.

Acknowledgments We would like to thank the preservice teachers enrolled in the literacy methods courses at the University of Nebraska–Lincoln, who generously allowed their instructional materials and digital books to be included as examples in this chapter. Their creativity, dedication, and critical engagement with educational AI tools made this work possible.

Competing Interests This study was supported by internal funding from the University of Nebraska–Lincoln through the project titled Future-Ready Literacy: Equipping Preservice Teachers with Instructional Tech Tools. Programs such as Book Creator and Veed were purchased using this funding. The authors declare no conflicts of interest relevant to the content of this chapter.

Ethics Approval This study was approved by the Institutional Review Board (IRB) at the University of Nebraska-Lincoln. Informed consent was obtained from participating students whose projects are included or referenced in this work.

References

Anthology. (2023). *AI, academic integrity, and authentic assessment: An ethical path forward for education (White Paper).* Retrieved from https://www.anthology.com/sites/default/files/2023-09/White%20Paper-AI%20Academic%20Integrity%20and%20Authentic%20Assessment-An%20Ethical%20Path%20Forward%20for%20Education-v2_09-23.pdf

Baudrillard, J. (1981). *Simulacra and Simulation*. The University of Michigan Press.

Echevarria, J., Vogt, M., & Short, D. (2010). *Making content comprehensible for elementary English learners: The SIOP model*. Allyn & Bacon.

Galda, L., Liang, L. A., & Cullinan, B. E. (2017). *Literature and the child* (9th ed.). Cengage Learning.

Herrell, A. L., & Jordan, M. L. (2015). *50 strategies for teaching English language learners* (5th ed.). Pearson.

Lucas, T., & Villegas, A. M. (2011). A framework for preparing linguistically responsive teachers. In T. Lucas (Ed.), *Teacher preparation for linguistically diverse classrooms: A resource for teacher educators* (pp. 55–72). Routledge.

Moats, L. C. (2020). *Teaching reading is rocket science: What expert teachers of reading should know and be able to do* (2nd ed.). American Federation of Teachers. Retrieved from https://www.aft.org/sites/default/files/moats.pdf

Norton, D. E., & Norton, S. E. (2009). *Through the eyes of a child: An introduction to children's literature* (8th ed.). Pearson.

Scarborough, H. S. (2001). Connecting early language and literacy to later reading (dis)abilities: Evidence, theory and practice. In S. B. Neuman & D. K. Dickinson (Eds.), *Handbook of early literacy research* (Vol. 1, pp. 97–110). Guilford Press.

Selwyn, N. (2016). *Education and technology: Key issues and debates* (2nd ed.). Zed Books. https://doi.org/10.5040/9781474235952

Sipe, L. R. (2008). *Storytime: Young children's literary understanding in the classroom*. Teachers College Press.

Spear-Swerling, L. (2019). Structured Literacy and Typical Literacy Practices: Understanding Differences to Create Instructional Opportunities. *Teaching Exceptional Children, 51*(3), 201–211. https://doi.org/10.1177/0040059917750160

Wright, W. E. (2015). *Foundations for teaching English language learners: Research, theory, policy, and practice* (2nd ed.).

Zhao, Y. (2017). What works may hurt: Side effects in education. *Journal of Educational Change, 18*(1), 1–19. https://doi.org/10.1007/s10833-016-9294-4

Gayoung Choi is a Ph.D. candidate in the Department of Teaching, Learning, and Teacher Education at the University of Nebraska-Lincoln. She has taught courses in elementary education, including Teaching Reading in the Elementary School, Teaching Language Arts, and Instructional

Technology. Prior to her doctoral studies, she was a tenured elementary school teacher in South Korea for five years, where she served as a homeroom teacher, English teacher, English department coordinator, and head of technology. In these roles, she led curriculum planning, supervised instructors, and managed digital infrastructure and instructional technology integration.

SungEun Min is an assistant professor in the Department of Elementary and Middle Level, Library, and Technologies Education at Kutztown University. He earned his Ph.D. in Elementary Education and Teacher Education from the University of Georgia. At Kutztown, he has taught courses such as Culturally Responsive Teaching for English Language Learners. Prior to moving to the United States, Dr. Min was a tenured elementary school teacher in South Korea, where he served as both a homeroom and English teacher for eight years. He also holds a TESOL certificate from California State University, Long Beach.

Chapter 9
Towards AI Didactics: Call for Teachers to Train Large Language Models for Research Writing in Higher Arts Education

Lauri Väkevä and Heidi Partti

Abstract Large Language Models (LLMs) have the potential to significantly enhance teaching and learning in higher arts education (HAE). However, HAE institutions have been slow to embrace LLMs' pedagogical potential. These institutions must provide their staff with guidance, resources, and training on effectively utilizing LLMs in educational contexts while upholding ethical principles. In this chapter, we explore theoretically the implementation of LLMs in supporting research writing in HAE. We argue that LLMs could significantly bolster pedagogical frameworks in HAE-based research education. However, user-end prompting is needed to refine LLMs' contextual capabilities to support the iterative research writing process. Our exploration envisages a pragmatic pathway for training LLMs as part of AI pedagogy (i.e., applying AI tactfully for educational purposes) and invites a scholarly dialogue towards responsibly harnessing the potential of LLMs in refining the pedagogical approaches in research education.

Keywords Art education · Research education · Research writing

A recent survey conducted by *Nature*, involving more than 1600 researchers worldwide, indicates that AI tools might soon play a pivotal role in research practices (Van Noorden & Perkel, 2023). This has implications for research writing and raises concerns about research integrity, data protection, ecological sustainability, and the future of research. There is still much work to be done in terms of developing

L. Väkevä (✉)
University of Helsinki, Helsinki, Finland
e-mail: lauri.vakeva@helsinki.fi

H. Partti
Sibelius Academy, University of the Arts, Helsinki, Finland
e-mail: heidi.partti@uniarts.fi

G. Tchibozo (ed.), *International Perspectives of Generative AI in Education*, Advances in Artificial Intelligence in Education 3,
https://doi.org/10.1007/978-3-031-99804-1_9

consistent standards regarding guidelines and regulations, as well as learning about AI technologies (Bouhouita-Guermech et al., 2023).

In this chapter, we address the supervision of research writing in the context of research education, that is, a systematic effort to advance the skills and competencies needed for making and understanding research.[1] Research education encompasses various components, including theoretical, methodological, and communication skills. We believe that all of these components converge in research writing, which serves as a practical foundation for fostering the development of research skills.

A growing number of research organizations (e.g., University of Helsinki, 2024), publishing houses (e.g., Elsevier, 2023), and other stakeholders (e.g., European Commission, 2024; McAdoo, 2024) have begun to publish normative guidelines, policies, and recommendations for the use of Generative AI (GenAI) in research. However, there is as yet no unitary rationale for how LLMs can or should be used in research education. Instead, there have been various suggestions on how these tools could be implemented in academic workflows, often presented on non-academic platforms.[2] Thus, there is a need to exchange ideas and compare experiences of the pedagogical use of LLMs within the wider research education community, as well as in specific fields, including higher arts education (HAE).[3]

In what follows, we will address these perspectives from a theoretical standpoint, beginning with a general discussion of how LLMs can be used to support research education and continuing with how they can support research writing supervision within HAE. We claim that the study programs of HAE institutions introduce new potential for the creative use of LLMs in the academic context but also pose specific ethical challenges that need to be acknowledged by research educators. The present discussion hopefully serves as a catalyst for further studies on effective strategies for AI integration in academic contexts within and outside HAE.

Possibilities and Limitations of LLM-Based GenAI Tools in Research Education

It is characteristic of LLMs that they are capable of "flexible generation of content … that can readily accommodate a wide range of distinctive tasks" (Future of Life Institute, 2024). While LLMs have been lately expanded to manage data in

[1] We agree with Boud and Lee (2005) that research education requires creating a supportive and enriching environment for research studies beyond mere supervision and provision of resources.

[2] See, e.g., Andy Stapleton's YouTube channel at https://www.youtube.com/@DrAndyStapleton. Bhat et al. (2023) have developed a framework for the interaction design of intelligent writing assistants. They discuss several aspects of how LLMs can support writing projects but not in the specific context of research writing.

[3] HAE encompasses all higher education in the arts subjects, including education that mediates artistic disciplines (Treacy & Gaunt, 2021; Väkevä, 2023).

different forms, in this chapter, we focus on models that primarily operate with written or spoken language. However, we also acknowledge that the rapid development of Multimodal Large Language Models (MLLMs) introduces creative possibilities as they "seamlessly integrate visual and textual modalities" (see Caffagni et al., 2024).

LLMs can be used in various ways to support research (Ivanov, 2023; OECD, 2023; Rahman & Watanobe, 2023; Rohwer, 2023). For instance, they can be applied in brainstorming, making literature surveys, analyzing data, and supporting the writing process. The adaptability and flexibility of LLMs also mean that they can be assigned to different research support roles; for instance, they can mimic supervisors, tutors, mentors, or writing coaches. However, assigning LLMs to professional roles is challenging, considering their principle of operation. The underlying operational logic of these models is based on their ability to make statistical guesses about how linguistic tokens should be ordered in a given context. Hence, instead of judging LLMs based on how accurate information they convey, they are better understood as *linguistic prediction mechanisms*, viz., systems capable of generating human-like language by anticipating what kind of linguistic output is needed (Lee & Trott, 2023).[4]

Without delving deeper into the technical details of LLMs (for that, see e.g., Zhao et al., 2023), it is worth noting that much of their usefulness depends on their pre-training. While such general-purpose models as GPT-4 have been pre-trained with hundreds, even thousands of millions of linguistic tokens (the smallest unit into which text data is broken down), an extensive amount of their pre-training data represents major languages.[5] Since research writing adheres to specific established standards and rules widely accepted in the academic world, and much research is reported in the major languages anyway, there is no reason why LLMs could not be used in supporting the writing of research texts in their present state. Indeed, for some time, there have been AI-based products on the market that support academic writing in English (e.g. Grammarly). Some of these tools can also be integrated into popular writing platforms (e.g. MS Word), helping with the use of LLMs in projects developed on less common linguistic platforms.[6] In addition, user-based fine-tuning of LLMs has become more accessible due to personalized chatbots such as OpenAI's Custom GPTs, which can be locally guided to generate content in particular styles and idioms. The contextualization of AI assistants no doubt provides future directions for enhancing users' experience of LLM-based systems and, thus, holds potential for research education, as well (Gates, 2023; Roose, 2023).

---

[4] This predictive approach to language generation may not be that alien to human intelligence (see Clark (2023).

[5] The linguistic bias of LLMs is evident when one asks them to produce content in less commonly used languages, such as our native Finnish. Hopefully, differences between the language-specific abilities of LLMs diminish when their pre-training data diversifies.

[6] Small language specific LLMs are also currently developed, e.g., in the project *Deep Generative Language Modeling for Finnish* (Luukkonen et al., 2023).

One challenge in utilizing LLMs in research education is their episodic tendency to generate nonsensical content generally referred to as "hallucinations" (Rawte et al., 2023). This inclination, coupled with the statistical operational logic of these models, has prompted some commentators to label them "stochastic parrots" (Bender et al., 2021; Henrique et al., 2023), while others attribute to them a creative, even artistic, agency (Cappaletti, 2023). Whatever the case, the tendency of LLMs to fabricate content means that the end-users should not consider them as knowledge providers but, instead, as *information generators* capable of generating content in different domains when adequately guided. It also implies that whatever information LLMs generate, a control system, preferably a human agent, is needed to warrant it as knowledge. In the context of studying research writing, it falls to the supervisors to advise the students on using these technologies for the full epistemic benefit. Thus, it could be argued that employing GenAI as a supervisor in research education necessitates the presence of a human supervisor to supervise the AI supervisor. This means that human tutors are essential for facilitating the relationship between LLMs and students, extending the classical didactic triangle between teacher, student, and subject matter (see also Bieger et al., 2017).

Despite occasionally producing nonsensical content and requiring epistemic supervision, LLMs excel in managing large amounts of textual data and finding connections between linguistic tokens. Because research supervision involves teaching a lot of technicalities related e.g., to formatting and finding links between parts of the text, using LLM-based tools could liberate the students' and academic supervisors' time for higher-level tasks, such as focusing on how the research project bridges theoretical and empirical realms, what is its relevance for the real-world problems, and how it advances the academic disciplines in question. Capitalizing on this potential would mean that more resources can be allocated to knowledge creation and acquisition without being inhibited by routine information tasks.

Overall, LLMs seem to hold the potential to support academic workflows by optimizing the distribution of tasks between human and machine agents and automating everyday chores. However, taking advantage of this potential in research supervision requires that the supervisors familiarize themselves with the possibilities and challenges of using LLMs, keeping an eye on their propensity to confabulate. This requires a pedagogically tactful approach to their use.[7]

The Academic Uses of LLMs: Research Writing in Focus

As discussed above, LLMs can support research writing in several ways. We will focus here on brainstorming, constructing a theoretical background, summarizing and defining concepts, personal knowledge management, writing, and editing.

[7] Here we lean on van Manen's (1991) idea that tactful teachers act creatively, caringly, and appropriately in pedagogical situations for the benefit of the student.

Brainstorming

LLMs can be helpful when students need support developing their preliminary ideas into coherent research questions and designs. In such situations, LLMs can act as critical friends, providing feedback on the students' ideas and encouraging them to develop their ideas further. In this way, these models can provide conversational partners for idea generation (see also Pérez-Marín, 2021).

One benefit of working with GenAI models in a conversational manner is their perseverance: They are up to discuss the topic as long as their context window allows.[8] However, the process of using GenAI in this role has to be iterative: the model needs to learn from the context of use and the user's expectations, and its instruction often takes time and effort.

The user-end instruction of LLMs takes place by providing textual cues to the model so that they can perform in a particular manner. LLMs must be constantly prompted for optimal results, and the users need to be alert to what prompts work best in given situations and contexts (Liu et al., 2023; White et al., 2023). Acquiring prompt engineering skills can help immensely in this adjustment: learning how to design prompts, students, teachers, and supervisors will be able to guide LLMs in a structured and systematic manner (Chen et al., 2023). Thus, assisting the students in prompting LLMs should be considered an essential part of AI pedagogy, namely applying AI tactfully for educational purposes.[9]

Significantly, as discussed above, the capabilities of LLMs are not entirely preconditioned by pre-training. This is not just because of the propensity of these models to hallucinate but also because they manifest a certain degree of adaptability. Thus, LLMs have emergent qualities, meaning they possess a degree of self-directness in generating their responses (Chang & Bergen, 2023; Wei et al., 2022). This adaptiveness potentially increases the appeal of LLMs as conversational partners in research education but may also produce anomalies, which the students and supervisors have to correct by further prompting.

---

[8] The context window defines how many tokens an LLM can manage when processing input. As of this writing (October 2024), the most popular LLM-based chatbot, ChatGPT, can manage up to 128,000 tokens in one context window. The size of the context window will increase substantially in the upcoming models. For instance, in June 2024 Google promised that its Gemini 1.5 Pro model will be available for the developers with a two million token context window (Kilpatrick et al., 2024).

[9] For an earlier attempt to argue for AI pedagogy, see Bieger et al. (2017). In line with what has been discussed above, we suggest that AI pedagogy involves teaching both the students and the AI models.

Constructing a Theoretical Background

LLMs can also be used at various stages of constructing a theoretical background, such as searching for references, generating ideas from sources, and relating theoretical concepts to each other.

For instance, LLMs can aid in finding, organizing, and categorizing academic sources, either with the help of integrated access to research databases or within specialized research platforms (e.g., Consensus, Elicit, SciSpace, and Research Rabbit). LLMs can also be used with popular reference management platforms (e.g., Zotero), and they can be merged with other third-party tools that support academic workflow, e.g., by managing notes-taking (see the subsection below). In addition to using LLMs to select the most relevant sources, users can harness GenAI-based research tools to identify widely cited literature, e.g., with the help of reference maps that show citation links between key publications.

With the help of appropriate prompting, LLMs can aid in generating ideas from sources, helping the students to identify themes relevant to their research questions and the disciplines they are working in. By conversing with LLMs about the relevance of their sources to their study projects, students can also pinpoint research gaps or areas that require further investigation. This helps them to narrow their theoretical focus, devise ideas more relevant to their study project, and avoid excess literature.

In addition to using LLMs to search sources and generate ideas, the students can use them to relate theoretical concepts to each other. For instance, they can ask GenAI models to generate mind maps that connect key concepts, thus providing a skeleton structure for the theoretical discussion, or use them to compare ideas and to aid in selecting the most appropriate ones.

Summarizing, Defining, and Personal Knowledge Management

LLMs can also help students explore academic literature more thoroughly. For instance, these models can summarize the key takeaways of individual texts or even collections of documents. This allows students to understand complex ideas across disciplines, enabling them to engage with scholarly work at a more advanced level.

In addition to facilitating a deeper understanding of academic literature, LLMs can help define concepts. For instance, these models can aid the students in formulating definitions for technical terms, adding to conceptual clarity within and between linguistic idioms. This enhances the students' academic writing skills and enables effective communication within their respective fields of study. Again, supervisors are needed to check the viability of the definitions against the discipline in question. However, LLM-based tools can also be locally trained to remember definitions and use them systematically in further conversations, which increases their trustworthiness.

Finally, LLMs can support personal knowledge management (PKM) by aiding in organizing information to make it easier to access and use in the future.[10] By developing efficient procedures for PKM, e.g., systematizing individual note-taking workflows, student researchers can save time and effort and improve the quality of their work in the long run. LLMs can be directly integrated or linked with PKM platforms to make searches from users' notes databases and suggest links between new and existing notes. By organizing their notes into logical frameworks properly tagged or linked, students can learn to better understand the relationships between their key concepts and build a more comprehensive theoretical understanding of their study topic.

Writing and Editing

LLMs can potentially guide the students' actual writing process in various ways. To begin with, they can assist students in overcoming the fear of the blank page. Many students experience anxiety when starting a writing assignment, unsure of how to begin or organize their thoughts (Castello, 2022). LLMs can also provide cues for initial writing ideas. As discussed above, because the pre-training of these models is based on immense amounts of textual data, they excel in providing suggestions for text composition, especially in major languages. However, as also discussed above, when working in non-dominant languages, the LLMs need supervision to keep their compositions in line with the domain-specific requirements. A tactful strategy for applying these models in research writing would be to balance using them for initial impetus with supervisors' quality control, following the rationale of the expanded didactic triangle.

Despite being biased towards popular languages, LLMs can, to a degree, help work between linguistic idioms. Language barriers can be significant obstacles for students who are not native speakers or have to study in a foreign language. LLMs can aid in translation, providing alternative phrasings and synonyms and helping the students clarify technical terms with no corresponding terms in their native languages. Lately, there have been reports that LLMs surpass dedicated third-party translation tools in performance (Wang et al., 2023). When the pre-training data of these models expands, it can be presumed that their translation capabilities will be even more impressive.

LLMs can also offer stylistic guidance when efficiently prompted, e.g., with the help of style templates provided by the supervisors. Writing with a cohesive and

[10] Personal knowledge management (PKM) can be defined as both a system of collecting information and a methodological approach that helps develop information towards knowledge (Grundspenkis, 2007; Wright, 2005). When writing this, popular PKM platforms include Obsidian, Research Roam, and Notion, but new tools constantly appear in the market. One of the most popular current approaches in PKM is Zettelkasten, based on Niklas Luhmann's notes-taking and linking system (see Zettelkasten.de, 2024).

engaging style is often challenging for research students, especially at the beginning of their studies. LLMs can suggest improvements in sentence structure, word choice, and overall flow of the texts, helping students to communicate their ideas more efficiently.

LLMs can also serve as proofreading tools, at least when writing in major languages. Students may struggle to identify grammatical errors, spelling mistakes, typos, or inconsistencies such as changing tenses. LLMs can quickly and accurately detect such errors, providing students with feedback and suggestions for improvement. Again, this capacity can be extended with prompting that guides the models to pay attention to different details according to the student's needs and the linguistic idiom. However, such use requires careful attention on the part of the supervisors as the pre-training material of LLMs might also contain errors.

Above, we have presented some ways in which LLMs can support supervising research writing projects in general. In what follows, we will discuss challenges more specific to HAE-based research writing supervision.

HAE as the Context of LLM-Assisted Research Writing Supervision

Higher arts education (HAE) can be seen as a particular mode of tertiary education because higher arts education institutions (HAEIs) customarily integrate research into artistic disciplines (Buekers & Nugteren, 2012). This integration is reflected in the variety of research approaches that can be found among HAEI departments. Quantitative research often plays a minor role in these institutions compared to qualitative and post-qualitative approaches.[11] Many HAEIs are also interested in artistic research, namely "research through means of … artistic practice and reflection" (Culture Action Europe, 2020), which has different varieties based on how central the role the artistic process plays in the research practice (Arlander, 2013; Barone & Eisner, 2012; Biggs & Karlsson, 2010).[12]

As regards research writing, HAEIs train students in various textual approaches, some of which adopt artistic composition for research writing.[13] Consequently, research writing pedagogies in higher arts education must be tailored to fit these

[11] Post-qualitative research here refers to approaches that criticize traditional humanist points of departure of the qualitative methodologies while still collecting and analyzing qualitative data (St. Pierre, 2021).

[12] When discussing HAEI-based research more generally, we use the term "art-related research." The latter encompasses all research in which art plays a significant part.

[13] For instance, University of the Arts Helsinki has its own writing study program that understands writing "as versatile textual skills that can be applied in different environments" (University of the Arts Helsinki, 2024b).

approaches while keeping an eye on academic rigor.[14] This is particularly crucial in cases where the students' previous training has not included research courses.

Having worked as supervisors in the HAE context for several years, we recognize that academic rigor requirements must be adapted to diverse research writing styles and idioms in these institutions. However, we also believe that despite this variety, supervision of research writing should aim at clarity and transparency, aided by the conventions developed in scientific academic domains, even if different academic conventions might lead to different technical solutions in different departments and study programs.[15] Furthermore, we acknowledge that there are pedagogical challenges common to writing supervision in HAE and that these challenges have implications for implementing GenAI in writing supervision in the HAEIs.

One challenge is that in HAE-based research studies, researchers often become part of what they study, working as artists or other art-related professionals. This adds complexity to the research process and requires careful consideration of the ethical implications of the artist/researcher's decisions. While the student-researchers invest themselves in artistic studies, they also need to recognize the difference between their artistic engagement and the more reflective stance required by the researcher's position. Introducing LLMs to art-related research writing processes demands extra effort from the supervisors to guide them in recognizing situations where the students work in multiple roles: the models must be trained by the users to recognize the idiosyncratic requirements of art-related research.

Art-related research also has unique characteristics and idiosyncrasies that must be considered in writing supervision. Due to the central role of artistic practice in HAE research environments, the data collection, analyzing methods, and ways of reporting may differ from the traditional research approaches where art is considered merely as a study object. For instance, a report of artistic research might have such creative writing as poems or prose overlapping with theoretical discussion and presentation of the research results, requiring that the reader can identify different text types and roles that they play in the whole project. This might present challenges to the traditional approaches of supervising research writing that are not adjusted to deal with artistic content. LLMs need to be trained to recognize different kinds of content and be able to guide the students in different styles of composing texts.

---

[14] Following Draeger et al. (2013, p. 268), we argue that promoting academic rigor "requires attending to a number of overlapping elements, including active learning, meaningful content, higher-order thinking, and appropriate expectations."

[15] For instance, humanist writing styles seem to be often favored in musicology-based study programs, whereas research writing in music education seems to follow more the conventions of the behavioral sciences. Here we define "scientific academic domains" extensively, encompassing social and humanist disciplines.

Ethical Points of Departure for AI Pedagogy in HAE

Based on the above discussion, we argue that implementing LLMs in research education, and specifically in research writing supervision, brings about multiple possibilities but also introduces challenges for students, supervisors, and research organizations within HAE. It is, therefore, essential to determine how utilizing LLMs can be done in a critical manner, which we consider an essential aspect of tactful AI pedagogy. The focus should not solely be on the tools themselves but also on how they are used, for what purposes, by whom, and under what conditions.

Despite the potential benefits of utilizing LLMs in writing studies, specific concerns and pitfalls raised by art-related research require careful attention from the writing supervisors. These concerns and pitfalls revolve around the use of AI technology in responsible ways. As underscored by UNESCO (2022), the significance of ethical considerations must be highlighted in the field of AI—especially as there remains a lack of global standards and guidelines to frame and support its responsible use in research (Bouhouita-Guermech et al., 2023). It is crucial for writing supervisors to identify ethical questions and challenges specific to art-related research and consider how they may differ from those of artistic practices. Even in cases where artmaking is an integral part of the research process, seemingly allowing liberties from the scientific norms, common standards need to be respected in the ethical evaluation of the research projects provided that it is accepted that all research should adhere to the good practices of research ethics as recognized by national and international research agencies. This would seem to present a challenge for using GenAI tools, as they are incapable of ethical deliberation, even if they may be trained to spot legal risks given the proper contextual information.

We would like to argue that in the realm of research education, issues related to AI extend to broader ethical questions such as transparency, standards for fair representation and diversity, as well as strategies to prevent "reproducing real world biases and discrimination, fueling divisions and threatening fundamental human rights and freedoms" (UNESCO, 2022, p. 4). Students should develop a critical understanding of the conditions and implications of applying these technologies, which might also lead to decisions not to use them. For instance, the widely reported ethical challenges related to pre-training and maintaining GenAI can hardly be avoided in critical AI pedagogy, and they may alienate students from using LLMs (Bacciarelli & Aufiero, 2023; Perrigo, 2023). Also, issues such as research integrity, data privacy, bias, social justice, student equity, ecological sustainability, and the ownership of the learning process need to be acknowledged when developing pedagogically tactful approaches to GenAI use.

Research Integrity

An essential aspect of all research education is to acquaint students with the questions, guidelines, and regulations regarding research integrity (RI). While the fundamental principles of the RI guidelines (ALLEA, 2023)—reliability, honesty, respect, and accountability—are to be applied in all research settings, it may not always be evident how to guarantee adherence to good research practices when using GenAI systems, especially as LLMs may offer tempting shortcuts, both intentionally and unintentionally. For example, unintended plagiarism may occur as the LLMs' pre-training data sources are not openly disclosed. It can also be exceedingly challenging for supervisors to identify AI-generated texts or determine whether students have obtained their materials responsibly and utilized LLMs in a manner that respects the work of others.[16]

The responsibility of research organizations to ensure that students and researchers are well-versed in the RI guidelines is increasingly central in the age of AI. Furthermore, upholding an ongoing ethical discussion is crucial: the continuously expanding and swiftly evolving opportunities presented by GenAI require not only the awareness of regulations and ethical guidelines but also an understanding of the rationale behind key decisions—ranging from research design and methodological choices to the selection of publication platforms—that ensure the ethical integrity of research (Björk & Juntunen, 2019). This may be particularly important in the intricate contexts of artistic research.

Data Privacy

Data privacy concerns here include compliance with data protection regulations (e.g., European GDPR), security and accessibility of the data uploaded to AI systems, as well as the lack of transparency in its possible further use by the private sector (Bouhouita-Guermech et al., 2023; Mazurek & Karolina, 2019). Also, due to the black-box nature of GenAI pre-training, it is close to impossible to know whether the data is gathered from consenting users (Bouhouita-Guermech et al., 2023). Therefore, it is crucial for student researchers to adhere to privacy guidelines and determine which types of data can be safely uploaded in GenAI models—if any. Additionally, the use of GenAI in research education emphasizes the importance of safeguarding one's unpublished work and considering whether it is advisable to

[16] There are at least two intertwined problems involved with identifying AI-based plagiarism: the current AI detectors are not trustworthy and the universities' regulations and ethical codes may make it difficult for the teachers and supervisors to make their case against plagiarism (see e.g., Elali & Rachid, 2023; Elkhatat et al., 2023).

upload it to platforms that may share the material with third parties or utilize it for training future versions of LLMs.[17]

While the principles of open science may provide substantial freedom to utilize the work of other scholars, in the context of artistic research, the question of using the work of others may be legally and ethically more complicated. For instance, the output of GenAI-based image generators may contain copyrighted material (Aalto University, 2024). Thus, HAEIs need to specifically consider their role in securing the responsible and safe use of GenAI in artistic and art-related research. This may involve developing robust protocols and frameworks that prioritize protecting the creator's rights. HAEIs should also provide training in ethical data handling practices and copyright legislation for the students and the staff. By actively engaging in discussions on copyright laws, authorship, and ownership, these institutions can develop transparent practices in utilizing AI tools and help minimize data privacy risks.

Biases

The biases in the data on which GenAI tools are trained are also an important issue worth exploring and discussing in research education. There may be a heightened need for a critical understanding of how GenAI model algorithms work, beyond a limited focus on issues of data privacy and governance (Samuel et al., 2021). It is likely that the data on which GenAI systems are trained does not always adhere to the standards of fair representation and diversity, despite the ongoing efforts to detect and remove its bias (Müller, 2021). The knowledge base employed to pretrain GenAI systems usually originates from "well-funded institutions in high-income, English-speaking countries", reflecting dominant values of these contexts (Li et al., 2023a), making GenAI systems "less capable of producing outputs that accurately represent the cultural values, beliefs and practices of users from diverse geographies" (United Nations, 2023, 16). As AI-generated content heavily reflects its pre-training data, the biases present in this data can significantly impact the output by, for example, replicating the underrepresentation or disadvantage of certain demographic groups. In research education, it is therefore crucial to investigate how biases pertaining to race, gender, language, and culture, among others, seep into AI-generated content. Furthermore, it is essential to determine whether users have the ability to influence or mitigate these biases by prompting, ensuring more equitable outcomes.

[17] To alleviate these concerns, universities and other research organizations have adopted local implementations of LLMs where one can feed project-specific data while ensuring complete data protection (see, e.g., Aalto University, 2024; University of Helsinki, 2023).

Social Justice

Using LLMs in research education also raises critical ethical questions that extend beyond the immediate situations of supervising research writing. Among these concerns are issues related to social justice. Reports have highlighted individuals' exposure to disturbing and traumatizing material when reviewing and curating the pre-training data of these models (e.g., Perrigo, 2023). Some interest groups, such as Human Rights Watch, have suggested that this dependency not only increases the potential for (re)establishing human biases and discriminatory ideas but also violates the rights of those performing this work (Bacciarelli & Aufiero, 2023). Data labeling is often outsourced by technology companies to workforces located in the Global South, often involving minors who work "in grueling conditions, some paid less than $2 an hour for sifting through toxic and biased data" (ibid.). If these reports are accurate, the implications of subjecting individuals to such distressing content need to be openly discussed and challenged by GenAI users, within and outside the academia. This discussion could involve users actively demanding that companies and institutions take responsibility for ensuring the dignity, safety, and fair wages of workers who contribute to the development of AI.

Student Equity

Using LLMs in research education within higher education institutions can have implications for equity among students. While some may actively engage with these tools in their academic and personal pursuits, others may be reluctant or even fearful of their use. GenAI platforms often demand paid subscriptions for access to all functionalities, the installments of which can be expensive. GenAI also requires operational internet connections and a reliable electricity supply, which is not equally available to everyone worldwide. Thus, it is crucial to consider how the use of these tools may impact on the equity between students, ensuring that those who are less familiar or comfortable with them or who have restricted access to online resources are not disadvantaged. Pedagogically tactful strategies that promote inclusivity and provide necessary support and resources for all students should be implemented to bridge potential equity gaps.

Ecological Sustainability

The alignment of GenAI tools with the ecological sustainability goals in HAEIs is another area of concern. The carbon footprint of these technologies, particularly in terms of their energy consumption, needs to be evaluated. Sustainability principles in many HAEIs (see, e.g., University of the Arts Helsinki, 2024a) emphasize minimizing environmental impact, and it is crucial to assess whether the use of GenAI tools aligns with these objectives. The potential exploitation of valuable resources, such as clean water, in the operation of the server halls required by these systems raises further sustainability concerns that require attention (Li et al., 2023b).

Ownership of the Learning Process

Finally, when addressing AI-related ethical questions and striving for responsible practices in HAE, it is crucial to ensure that the learning process remains students' responsibility. Using LLMs in research writing supervision requires a human supervisor to guide the student's decisions, especially at the early stage of the studies. Such interventions may be provided on the pedagogical principle of scaffolding, first providing hands-on support and diminishing guidance as the student's skills advance.[18] However, supervisors are also required to work in another role, helping the students form informed judgments about the relevance of the LLMs' suggestions and guiding the models to generate more relevant content. As discussed throughout this chapter, a significant goal of AI pedagogy in HAE is to equip students with the necessary skills and knowledge to actively promote a culture of ethical reflection within their communities. Students must be encouraged to take ownership of their learning by actively engaging with the feedback provided by LLMs, critically evaluating their suggestions, and making informed decisions about what revisions and changes are needed. It is, therefore, essential to advise students to systematically reflect on their own actions and critically examine and discuss the potential and drawbacks of LLM tools.

Conclusion

Acknowledging the potential of LLMs in supervising research writing does not necessarily require expert technical knowledge. Instead, it requires pedagogical know-how about how these models can be used in a tactful manner. One aspect of this know-how is recognizing the need to supervise both the students and the models to work together better, which requires expanding the pedagogical competencies of the supervisors. To ensure that supervisors thoroughly understand how LLMs can be used in educational settings while upholding ethical principles, it is necessary to incorporate GenAI into in-service training. This training should be anchored in the practical situations of university pedagogy and tailored to the specific use cases of the students' research projects.

[18] Scaffolding has previously been studied in technological learning environments by, for example, Sharma and Hannafin (2007).

There are at least two challenges related to this pedagogical approach in HAEIs. Firstly, these institutions may not primarily operate on a scientific basis but instead lean on artistic working cultures, which might mean that implementing GenAI solutions in their research activities may face skepticism or even resistance. This challenge should be met by developing appropriate approaches to using these models in specific cases of art-related research. Secondly, individuals within these institutions may primarily use AI for artistic work rather than research, which might mean their workflows must be readjusted to the research context. These challenges highlight the need for building HAE-based communities of practice (Wenger, 1998) around GenAI use, viz., groups in which colleagues and students can exchange ideas, learn with and from each other, and foster ethical reflection related to GenAI daily. By forming such communities, HAEs can promote critical agency in constructing technological knowledge rather than just technical knowledge.[19]

Building such communities of practice requires resources, not just in terms of purchasing or licensing hardware or software but also in terms of fostering collaboration and knowledge-sharing. By investing in human resources, HAEIs can empower their teachers better to navigate the ethical complexities of using LLMs and other GenAI solutions. This proactive approach also ensures that ethical considerations will be integrated into the educational processes and that teachers, supervisors, and students are equipped to make informed decisions regarding the tactful use of GenAI.

In this chapter, we have discussed the viability of developing tactful AI pedagogy in HAE, especially in relation to the supervision of research writing. The challenges we have presented are not restricted to this specific context but touch on all uses of GenAI in higher arts education. Yet we also suggest that in the present stage of the development of GenAI tools, their application in research writing supervision provides specific use cases through which more general concerns can be addressed. At the time of writing this, LLMs provide restricted possibilities to work on less-dominant languages and disciplinary idioms. This means that the supervisors need to develop capabilities to localize these models, paying attention both to how the students use them and how the models themselves can be guided by user-end prompting. The future will most probably introduce new possibilities for such localization within and outside HAE.

Competing Interests The authors have no conflicts of interest to declare that are relevant to the content of this chapter.

References

Aalto University. (2024). *Responsible use of artificial intelligence in the research process*. retrieved from https://www.aalto.fi/en/services/responsible-use-of-artificial-intelligence-in-the-research-process

[19] Here we lean on an extensive reading of technology as a discipline that encompasses both epistemic and normative aspects (see e.g., Herschbach, 1995).

ALLEA. (2023). *The European code of conduct for research integrity*. Retrieved from https://allea.org/code-of-conduct/
Arlander, A. (2013). Artistic research in a Nordic context. In R. Nelson (Ed.), *Practice as research in the arts* (pp. 152–162). Palgrave Macmillan. https://doi.org/10.1057/9781137282910_9
Bacciarelli, A., & Aufiero, P. (2023). Pandora's box: Generative AI companies, ChatGPT, and human rights. What's at stake in tech's newest race? [interview]. *Human Rights Watch*. Retrieved from https://www.hrw.org/news/2023/05/03/pandoras-box-generative-ai-companies-chatgpt-and-human-rights
Barone, T., & Eisner, E. W. (2012). *Arts based research*. SAGE. https://doi.org/10.4135/9781452230627
Bender, E. M., Gebru, T., McMillan-Major, A., & Shmitchell, S. (2021). On the dangers of stochastic parrots: Can language models be too big? In *Proceedings of the 2021 ACM conference on fairness, accountability, and transparency* (pp. 610–623). Association for Computing Machinery. https://doi.org/10.1145/3442188.3445922
Bhat, A., Shrivastava, D., & Guo, J. L. C. (2023). *Approach intelligent writing assistants usability with seven stages of action*. arXiv. https://doi.org/10.48550/ARXIV.2304.02822
Bieger, J., Thórisson, K. R., & Steunebrink, B. R. (2017). The pedagogical pentagon: A conceptual framework for artificial pedagogy. In T. Everitt, B. Goertzel, & A. Potapov (Eds.), *Artificial General Intelligence* (Vol. 10414, pp. 212–222). Springer. https://doi.org/10.1007/978-3-319-63703-7_20
Biggs, M., & Karlsson, H. (Eds.). (2010). *The Routledge companion to research in the arts*. Routledge. https://doi.org/10.4324/9780203841327
Björk, C., & Juntunen, M.-L. (2019). Ethical considerations on conducting research about music teaching in primary schools: A virtue ethics approach. *European Journal of Philosophy in Arts Education, 2*(4), 61–110. https://doi.org/10.5281/zenodo.3674130
Boud, D., & Lee, A. (2005). 'Peer learning' as pedagogic discourse for research education. *Studies in Higher Education, 30*(5), 501–516. https://doi.org/10.1080/03075070500249138
Bouhouita-Guermech, S., Gogognon, P., & Bélisle-Pipon, J.-C. (2023). Specific challenges posed by artificial intelligence in research ethics. *Frontiers in Artificial Intelligence, 6*. https://doi.org/10.3389/frai.2023.1149082
Buekers, M., & Nugteren, B. (2012). Creative arts and research-intensive universities: A crucial partnership. In *Briefing paper no. 2*. League of European Research Universities. Retrieved from https://www.leru.org/files/Creative-Arts-and-Research-Intensive-Universities-A-Crucial-Partnership-Full-paper.pdf
Caffagni, D., Cocchi, F., Barsellotti, L., Moratelli, N., Sarto, S., Baraldi, L., Baraldi, L., Cornia, M., & Cucchiara, R. (2024). *The (R)evolution of multimodal large language models: A survey*. arXiv. https://doi.org/10.48550/ARXIV.2402.12451
Cappaletti, G. M. (2023). Unveiling AI hallucinations: Exploring the enigmatic art of 20 visionary AI creators. *Red Eye*. Retrieved from https://www.red-eye.world/c/unveiling-ai-hallucinations-exploring-the-enigmatic-art-of-20-visionary-ai-creators
Castello, M. (2022). Research writing, what do we know and how to move forward. In M. Gustafsson & A. Eriksson (Eds.), *Negotiating the intersections of writing and writing instruction* (pp. 89–122). The WAC Clearinghouse & Louisville: University Press of Colorado. https://doi.org/10.37514/INT-B.2022.1466.2.04
Chang, T. A., & Bergen, B. K. (2023). *Language model behavior: A comprehensive survey*. arXiv. Retrieved from http://arxiv.org/abs/2303.11504
Chen, B., Zhang, Z., Langrené, N., & Zhu, S. (2023). *Unleashing the potential of prompt engineering in large language Models: A comprehensive review*. arXiv. https://doi.org/10.48550/ARXIV.2310.14735.
Clark, A. (2023). *The experience machine: How our minds predict and shape reality*. Pantheon Books.

Culture Action Europe. (2020). *The Vienna declaration on artistic research.* Retrieved from https://cultureactioneurope.org/wp-content/uploads/2020/06/Vienna-Declaration-on-AR_corrected-version_24-June-20-1.pdf

Draeger, J., Del Prado Hill, P., Hunter, L. R., & Mahler, R. (2013). The anatomy of academic rigor: The story of one institutional journey. *Innovative Higher Education, 38*(4), 267–279. https://doi.org/10.1007/s10755-012-9246-8

Elali, F. R., & Rachid, L. N. (2023). AI-generated research paper fabrication and plagiarism in the scientific community. *Patterns, 4*(3), 100706. https://doi.org/10.1016/j.patter.2023.100706

Elkhatat, A. M., Elsaid, K., & Almeer, S. (2023). Evaluating the efficacy of AI content detection tools in differentiating between human and AI-generated text. *International Journal for Educational Integrity, 19*(17). https://doi.org/10.1007/s40979-023-00140-5

Elsevier. (2023). *The use of generative AI and AI-assisted technologies in writing for Elsevier [Elsevier Policies].* Retrieved from https://www.elsevier.com/about/policies-and-standards/the-use-of-generative-ai-and-ai-assisted-technologies-in-writing-for-elsevier

European Commission. (2024). *Living guidelines on the responsible use of generative AI in research.* ERA Forum Stakeholders' document. Retrievd from https://research-and-innovation.ec.europa.eu/document/download/2b6cf7e5-36ac-41cb-aab5-0d32050143dc_en?filename=ec_rtd_ai-guidelines.pdf

Future of Life Institute. (2024). *Recital 60c of EU Artificial Intelligence Act.* Retrieved from https://artificialintelligenceact.eu/recital/60c/

Gates, B. (2023). The age of AI has begun. *GatesNotes.* Retrieved from https://www.gatesnotes.com/The-Age-of-AI-Has-Begun

Grundspenkis, J. (2007). Agent based approach for organization and personal knowledge modelling: Knowledge management perspective. *Journal of Intelligent Manufacturing, 18*(4), 451–457. https://doi.org/10.1007/s10845-007-0052-6

Henrique, D. S. G., Kucharavy, A., & Guerraoui, R. (2023). *Stochastic parrots looking for stochastic parrots: LLMs are easy to fine-tune and hard to detect with other LLMs.* arXiv. Retrieved from http://arxiv.org/abs/2304.08968

Herschbach, D. R. (1995). Technology as knowledge: Implications for instruction. *Journal of Technology Education, 7*(1). https://doi.org/10.21061/jte.v7i1.a.3

Ivanov, S. (2023). The dark side of artificial intelligence in higher education. *The Service Industries Journal, 43*(15–16), 1055–1082. https://doi.org/10.1080/02642069.2023.2258799

Kilpatrick, L., Basu Mallick, S., & Kofman, R. (2024). *Gemini 1.5 pro 2M context window, code execution capabilities, and Gemma 2 are available today.* Retrieved from https://developers.googleblog.com/en/new-features-for-the-gemini-api-and-google-ai-studio/

Lee, T., & Trott, S. (2023). *Large language models, explained with a minimum of math and jargon.* Retrieved from https://www.understandingai.org/p/large-language-models-explained-with

Li, H., Moon, J. T., Purkayastha, S., Celi, L. A., Trivedi, H., & Gichoya, J. W. (2023a). Ethics of large language models in medicine and medical research. *The Lancet Digital Health, 5*(6), E333–E335. https://doi.org/10.1016/S2589-7500(23)00083-3

Li, P., Yang, J., Islam, M. A., & Ren, S. (2023b). *Making AI less "thirsty": Uncovering and addressing the secret water footprint of AI models.* arXiv. https://doi.org/10.48550/ARXIV.2304.03271

Liu, P., Yuan, W., Fu, J., Jiang, Z., Hayashi, H., & Neubig, G. (2023). Pre-train, prompt, and predict: A systematic survey of prompting methods in natural language processing. *ACM Computing Surveys, 55*(9), 1–35. https://doi.org/10.1145/3560815

Luukkonen, R., Komulainen, V., Luoma, J., Eskelinen, A., Kanerva, J., Kupari, H.-M., Ginter, F., Laippala, V., Muennighoff, N., Piktus, A., Wang, T., Tazi, N., Scao, T. L., Wolf, T., Suominen, O., Sairanen, S., Merioksa, M., Heinonen, J., Vahtola, A., Antao, S., & Pyysalo, S. (2023). *FinGPT: Large generative models for a small language.* arXiv. https://doi.org/10.48550/ARXIV.2311.05640

Mazurek, G., & Karolina, M. (2019). Perception of privacy and data protection in the context of the development of artificial intelligence. *Journal of Management Analytics, 6*, 344–364. https://doi.org/10.1080/23270012.2019.1671243

McAdoo, T. (2024). *How to cite ChatGPT.* APA Style. https://apastyle.apa.org/blog/how-to-cite-chatgpt.

Müller, V. C. (2021). Ethics of artificial intelligence and robotics. In E. N. Zalta (Ed.), *The Stanford Encyclopedia of Philosophy (Summer 2021 Edition)*. Retrieved from https://plato.stanford.edu/archives/sum2021/entries/ethics-ai/

OECD. (2023). *Artificial intelligence in science: Challenges, opportunities and the future of research.* https://doi.org/10.1787/a8d820bd-en

Pérez-Marín, D. (2021). A review of the practical applications of pedagogic conversational agents to be used in school and university classrooms. *Digital, 1*(1), 18–33. https://doi.org/10.3390/digital1010002

Perrigo, B. (2023). Exclusive: OpenAI used Kenyan workers on less than $2 per hour to make ChatGPT less toxic. *TIME*. Retrieved from https://time.com/6247678/openai-chatgpt-kenya-workers/

Rahman, Md. M., & Watanobe, Y. (2023). *ChatGPT for education and research: Opportunities, threats, and strategies*. https://doi.org/10.20944/preprints202303.0473.v1.

Rawte, V., Sheth, A., & Das, A. (2023). *A survey of hallucination in large foundation models.* arXiv. https://doi.org/10.48550/ARXIV.2309.05922

Rohwer, D. (2023). Research-to-resource: ChatGPT as a tool in music education research. *Update: Applications of Research in Music Education, 42*(3), 4–7. https://doi.org/10.1177/87551233231210875

Roose, K. (2023). Personalized A.I. Agents are here. Is the world ready for them? *The New York Times*. Retrieved from https://www.nytimes.com/2023/11/10/technology/personalized-ai-agents.html

Samuel, G., Chubb, J., & Derrick, G. (2021). Boundaries between research ethics and ethical research use in artificial intelligence health research. *Journal of Empirical Research on Human Research Ethics, 16*(3), 325–337. https://doi.org/10.1177/15562646211002744

Sharma, P., & Hannafin, M. J. (2007). Scaffolding in technology-enhanced learning environments. *Interactive Learning Environments, 15*(1), 27–46. https://doi.org/10.1080/10494820600996972

St. Pierre, E. A. (2021). Why post qualitative inquiry? *Qualitative Inquiry, 27*(2), 163–166. https://doi.org/10.1177/1077800420931142

Treacy, D., & Gaunt, H. (2021). Promoting interconnections between reflective practice and collective creativity in higher arts education: The potential of engaging with a reflective matrix. *Reflective Practice, 22*(4), 488–500. https://doi.org/10.1080/14623943.2021.1923471

UNESCO. (2022). *Recommendation on the ethics of artificial intelligence.* Retrieved from https://unesdoc.unesco.org/ark:/48223/pf0000381137

United Nations. (2023). *Taxonomy of human rights risks connected to generative AI.* Retrieved from https://www.ohchr.org/sites/default/files/documents/issues/business/b-tech/taxonomy-GenAI-Human-Rights-Harms.pdf

University of Helsinki. (2023). *Guidelines for the use of AI in teaching at the University of Helsinki.* Retrieved from https://teaching.helsinki.fi/system/files/inline-files/Tekoaly_linjaukset_HYn_opetuksessa-ONE-pa%CC%88ivitys_0.pdf

University of Helsinki. (2024). *Using AI to support learning*. Retrieved from https://studies.helsinki.fi/instructions/article/using-ai-support-learning

University of the Arts Helsinki. (2024a). *Uniarts Helsinki's environmental programme*. Retrieved from https://www.uniarts.fi/en/general-info/uniarts-helsinkis-environmental-programme/

University of the Arts Helsinki. (2024b). *Writing, bachelor*. Retrieved from https://www.uniarts.fi/en/study-programmes/writing-bachelor/

Väkevä, L. (2023). *Considering Deweyan cultural naturalism as a philosophy of art(s) education: Restoring continuity*. Springer. https://doi.org/10.1007/978-3-031-38817-0

Van Manen, M. (1991). *The tact of teaching: The meaning of pedagogical thoughtfulness*. State University of New York Press.

Van Noorden, R., & Perkel, J. M. (2023). AI and science: What 1,600 researchers think. *Nature, 621*(7980), 672–675. https://doi.org/10.1038/d41586-023-02980-0

Wang, L., Lyu, C., Ji, T., Zhang, Z., Yu, D., Shi, S., & Tu, Z. (2023). *Document-level machine translation with large language models*. arXiv. https://doi.org/10.48550/ARXIV.2304.02210

Wei, J., Tay, Y., Bommasani, R., Raffel, C., Zoph, B., Borgeaud, S., Yogatama, D., Bosma, M., Zhou, D., Metzler, D., Chi, E. H., Hashimoto, T., Vinyals, O., Liang, P., Dean, J., & Fedus, W. (2022). *Emergent abilities of large language models*. arXiv. Retrieved from http://arxiv.org/abs/2206.07682

Wenger, E. (1998). *Communities of practice: Learning, meaning, and identity*. Cambridge University Press.

White, J., Fu, Q., Hays, S., Sandborn, M., Olea, C., Gilbert, H., Elnashar, A., Spencer-Smith, J., & Schmidt, D. C. (2023). *A prompt pattern catalog to enhance prompt engineering with ChatGPT*. arXiv. Retrieved from http://arxiv.org/abs/2302.11382

Wright, K. (2005). Personal knowledge management: Supporting individual knowledge worker performance. *Knowledge Management Research and Practice, 3*(3), 156–165. https://doi.org/10.1057/palgrave.kmrp.8500061

Zettelkasten.de. (2024). *Zettelkasten*. Retrieved from https://zettelkasten.de/

Zhao, W. X., Zhou, K., Li, J., Tang, T., Wang, X., Hou, Y., Min, Y., Zhang, B., Zhang, J., Dong, Z., Du, Y., Yang, C., Chen, Y., Chen, Z., Jiang, J., Ren, R., Li, Y., Tang, X., Liu, Z., & Wen, J.-R. (2023). *A survey of large language models*. arXiv. Retrieved from http://arxiv.org/abs/2303.18223

Lauri Väkevä is currently working as a Professor of Didactics of Crafts and Arts at the University of Helsinki, Finland. He has previously worked as a Lecturer, Professor, and Vice-Rector at the University of the Arts Helsinki and as a researcher at the University of Oulu. His research interests cover crafts and arts education and didactics with a special focus on music education, popular culture, educational philosophy, instructional technology, and the sociology of education. He has published and lectured widely in these fields.

Heidi Partti works as Professor of Music Education at the Sibelius Academy of the University of the Arts Helsinki in Finland. Her research aims at a deeper understanding of the surrounding world in order to help the music education profession in adapting to rapid changes and global challenges. Her articles address topics such as music-related learning communities, digital technology, composition pedagogy, and the development of intercultural competencies in music teacher education. Professor Partti serves as the Research Integrity Adviser and Chair of the Research Ethics Committee at the University of the Arts Helsinki.

Chapter 10
Updating the Research-Teaching Nexus Framework in the Age of Generative AI: Prioritizing GenAI-Proof Research Tasks

Bérangère Laroudie and Guy Tchibozo

Abstract The advent of generative artificial intelligence (GenAI) is transforming the concept of the research-teaching nexus, and specifically its "research-based teaching" version, i.e. teaching through research, where teaching is carried out through involving students in doing research. Taking as its starting point the literature on the research-teaching nexus, this chapter shows that the democratization of generative AI requires a distinction to be drawn between GenAI-substitutable and GenAI-proof research tasks. The chapter examines the implications of this distinction for pedagogy and uses an example drawn from the field to illustrate the point. The results suggest directions for teaching delivery and knowledge assessment in research-based teaching built on GenAI-proof tasks. Further research is called for into reference principles for pedagogy in this field.

Keywords GenAI-proofness · GenAI-substitutability · Research-based teaching · Teaching through research

Artificial intelligence (AI) is a computer system that is capable of autonomously and reactively replacing human intelligence. The specific function of generative AI (GenAI) is to generate text, computer code, images, videos, sound, and physical objects (Vafadar & Moradi Amani, 2024). Communication between humans and generative AI to produce outputs occurs via computer programs. Computer programs that use natural human language are known as chatbots.

The popularization of chatbots since November 2022 is affecting the way we think of research as a vehicle for teaching. According to Zhang et al. (2020), the academic community has been questioning the existence of a link between teaching

B. Laroudie
IFSI, CHU Limoges, Limoges, France

G. Tchibozo (✉)
LISEC UR2310, University of Strasbourg, Strasbourg, France
e-mail: editor@analytrics.org

G. Tchibozo (ed.), *International Perspectives of Generative AI in Education*, Advances in Artificial Intelligence in Education 3,
https://doi.org/10.1007/978-3-031-99804-1_10

and research since the nineteenth century. However, it was above all as of the 1990s that the literature on the research-teaching nexus developed (Arimoto, 2020; Boyd et al., 2010; Boyer Commission, 1998; Gretton et al., 2022; Griffiths, 2004; Healey, 2005; Healey & Jenkins, 2009; Jenkins et al., 2007; Roberts et al., 2012; Slapcoff & Harris, 2014; Wagner et al., 2011; Woolf, 2017).

The literature on the research-teaching nexus considers that, although it can be problematic and complex to craft (Nhem, 2023; Tadesse & Khalid, 2023; Weenink et al., 2023), integrating research into teaching has a positive effect on student learning in higher education. Authors (Griffiths, 2004; Healey, 2005; Healey & Jenkins, 2009; Slapcoff & Harris, 2014; Woolf, 2017) distinguished four forms of research-teaching integration: the presentation of scientific advances as part of the content taught ('*research-led approach*'); the teaching of research methods and a research culture ('*research-oriented approach*'); the critical discussion of research articles as part of seminars ('*research-tutored approach*'); and student participation in research work ('*research-based approach*', also referred to as '*research-apprenticed approach*' by Gretton et al., 2022). The participation required from the learner is passive in the first two forms, and active in the next two. The last form, the *research-based approach*, that is, teaching through research, where teaching is carried out by involving students in doing research, represents the most complete form of integration.

This literature credits research-teaching integration with a long list of positive effects for the learner, notably in terms of personal and professional development, self-efficacy as a researcher, development of critical thinking, and communication skills (Seymour et al., 2004). It also suggests that integrating research and teaching fosters a deeper understanding of the subjects studied (Healey, 2005), leads to a better understanding of the links between theory and practice and between the curriculum and the reality of professional practice (Roberts et al., 2012), enables more mature reflection on career choices (Seymour et al., 2004), enhances students' interest and motivation to pursue their studies further (Lopatto, 2007), and enables them to better grasp the complexity of problems (Cantor et al., 2015). Gilmore et al. (2015) indicated that it is indeed to the combination of research and teaching (and not to one or the other in isolation) that students attribute their progress in terms of deepening knowledge, ability to communicate about their disciplinary specialty, capacity to adopt new or multiple perspectives, and ability to conduct systematic observations. Various studies have also shown that students who have experienced research-integrated teaching often have a positive perception of such teaching, judging in particular that it increases their employability (Gretton et al., 2022; Healey et al., 2010). Of course, students' perceptions of the benefits may vary, depending on the type of institution they attend (Macheridis et al., 2024).

However, the literature on the research-teaching nexus does not discriminate between types of research activities that should or should not be integrated into research-based teaching. Yet, such discrimination now seems necessary. Indeed, the emergence of generative AI creates a distortion between research tasks. In some research tasks (let us call them 'GenAI-substitutable'), human intervention can be replaced by generative AI, but not in others, which we will then label as 'GenAI-proof'.

This chapter examines the implications of generative AI for pedagogy in research-based teaching–that is, the most advanced form of integration between teaching and research, to which we are particularly interested. In the following sections, we begin by reviewing the tasks involved in an academic research process, distinguishing these tasks according to whether they are GenAI-substitutable, and we show the implications of this distinction. Next, we review the literature and derive guidelines for teaching delivery and knowledge assessment in research-based teaching. We then illustrate the proposed perspective using, as an example, the field implementation of a research-based teaching built on a GenAI-proof research task. Finally, we discuss the implications and the generalizability of this analysis, and conclude the chapter.

GenAI-Substitutability of Research Tasks

Academic research is defined as a methodical process of knowledge creation. The methodical nature of research implies an explicit approach that articulates a succession of clearly identified steps in line with the general practices of the research community. Deviations from these steps must be duly justified. The approach is set within a theoretical and conceptual framework, within which the researcher's words take on their full meaning, and the research results can be interpreted. Making the approach explicit enables replication for verification and validation by the research community. The process must lead to the *creation* of knowledge, i.e., *new* knowledge that was previously unknown or not yet formally validated. These criteria have implications. A non-methodically constructed or theoretically or conceptually unfounded discourse is an opinion, not research. Neither is the compilation, repetition, paraphrase, commentary or exegesis of existing works.

Against this backdrop, academic research takes a variety of forms. Yazdani et al. (2021) have surveyed research forms in the behavioral sciences, social sciences, educational sciences, and medicine. They distinguished 11 forms, differentiated by their links between epistemological posture, methodological options, and objectives in terms of knowledge creation. Yazdani et al. (2021) distinguish between research that is descriptive, psychometric, or exploratory, or that aims to synthesize the results of primary research (literature reviews and meta-analyses), identify factors or causalities, formulate theories, convert general results into operational solutions, compare competing options in a decision-making process, implement programs or decisions in the field, or carry out evaluations.

Whatever the form, most research tasks today can be performed using generative AI. Provided that it has been properly trained on a sufficiently rich specialized corpus, GenAI can produce problem statements, research questions, definitions, concepts, theories, literature reviews, and data presentation and analysis (see, for example, the chapter by Väkevä and Partti in this book). GenAI can also write analyses, syntheses, and discussions of the results. It can establish the implications of the results and their scope. GenAI can even formulate recommendations for practice, policy, and research, and make suggestions for future research. Simply prompting, no matter how "engineered" and sophisticated the prompt crafting, can generate each of these types of outputs. The performance of GenAI on these types of tasks can be comparable to that of a standard researcher.

GenAI is also capable of building physical prototypes such as solids, liquids, or gases. Designing, building, and testing prototypes are essential steps in several scientific research fields. This has long been the case in the fields of physics, computer science, chemistry, pharmacy, and health sciences. More recently, the construction of prototypes has been extended to the field of educational sciences, particularly through research on the development of educational technology tools. For this type of task too, GenAI can replace human researchers.

However, generative AI is not necessarily capable of collecting field data on its own.

The data used for research can be drawn from the real world or, on the contrary, artificially created (e.g., simulated, synthetic, dummy). What it is about in this chapter is real data, as observed in the field.

On one hand, given that the objective of research is to create *new* knowledge, research most often addresses issues about which too little is known, and the field data of which, in particular, are poorly documented. Consequently, field data of interest to research tend to be too scarce to constitute sufficient material in which generative AI can be trained or which it can tap into. Therefore, because the ability of generative AI to produce results depends on the documentation with which it has been fed, generative AI is not well placed for generating useful and truthful field data. Of course, GenAI can invent data, but in that case, it is still possible (although, let's admit, not guaranteed) that a sufficiently informed and critical expert or researcher will detect the cases of 'hallucinations'.

On the other hand, data collection involves operations that are not limited to conversation, but instead require human intervention that cannot be replaced by GenAI.

Field data can be factual or perceptual, and in either case textual or numerical. Numerical data can be qualitative or quantitative. However, whatever the nature of the data, collecting data requires surveys to be carried out by observation, interviews, questionnaires, requests to institutions, or database queries.

In the current state of technology, while GenAI tools are capable of autonomously extracting data from databases on a simple prompt, human intervention is irreplaceable for some other types of surveys. The nature of these other types of surveys and the conditions required to implement them explain the need for human agency. In general, these types of data collection surveys require more than simply prompting.

Collecting data from different institutions requires contacting these institutions and adapting to the diversity of reactions, approaches, channels (telephone, e-mail, and physical appointment), and operating methods of each of these institutions, not to mention the need to discuss with them to refine the search and select the relevant data. An important keyword here is "adapting", because the researcher is in the position of a requester and, therefore, cannot impose on institutions to conform to some standard AI-led procedure.

Observation can be participant or non-participant. Participant observation requires the researcher to immerse oneself in the daily life of a community under study, participate in the activities of the community members, interact with them, and collect data through these interactions. These human activities and interactions go beyond the mere production of textual, oral, audio, visual, and physical artifacts. As a result, generative AI cannot replace a human being in all the activities and interactions carried out by the community members and, consequently, cannot replace human agency in data collection based on participant observation.

On the contrary, non-participant observation is a type of data collection survey that GenAI could conduct autonomously. Conducting non-participant observations using audio and/or video recordings existed well before generative AI. The introduction of GenAI strengthens the possibilities of replacing the human researcher with technology in this type of data collection survey.

Unstructured interviews take the form of fluid conversations in which the researcher asks open-ended questions and flexibly adapts to the directions taken by the interviewee. Still, even if unstructured, research interviews are nonetheless intentional, which requires the researcher to react in real time to readjust throughout the conversation and keep it in line with the research objectives. The same applies to semi-structured interviews with open-ended questions, in which the interviewer has some leeway in terms of the questions to be asked, and their order and wording. Open-ended questions, by their very nature, give the respondent latitude in the terms used, which may prove insufficiently clear or precise in relation to the research objective. The answers may also be superficial, partial, incomplete, or off topic. The researcher must then be able to insist on, ask for clarification, rephrase, and ask for developments and details, which requires being able to evaluate in real time the adequacy of the response to the research objectives. This assessment is obviously delicate, and the researcher's follow-up must be skillful to avoid disturbing or irritating the respondent, putting him or her on the defensive, and hindering the success of the data collection. Generative AI cannot replace humans in this role because it does not possess the relevant subject knowledge and interviewing skills in a sufficiently fine-grained manner across all domains. Only if it has been trained on a specific research project can GenAI replace the human researcher for unstructured or semi-structured interviews as part of that project.

Finally, fully structured interviews and questionnaires, with only closed-ended questions, do not require substantial interaction with the respondent or responsiveness on the part of the interviewer. Therefore, these are types of data-collection surveys in which generative AI can replace the human interviewer.

This scrutiny shows that, while generative AI can replace human researchers in data-collection surveys based on database extraction, non-participant observation, and structured interviews and questionnaires, it is clear that researchers cannot have generative AI replace them to collect field data by means of participant observations, unstructured and semi-structured interviews, or requests to institutions.

Consequently, in the research process, research tasks the completion of which essentially consists in producing and presenting written, oral, audio, visual, or physical outputs, including field data collected by means of database extraction, non-participant observation, and structured interviews and questionnaires, can be considered GenAI-substitutable. In contrast, field data collection through participant observation, unstructured and semi-structured interviews, and requests to institutions can be considered GenAI-proof.

Therefore, not all research tasks have an equal status when it comes to implementing research-based teaching in the age of generative AI. Making room in teaching for GenAI-substitutable activities could prove to be rather ineffective and a source of deception. Indeed, unless learners carry out their assignments in controlled environments, we can expect at least some learners to limit themselves to having such exercises carried out by GenAI (Topaz et al., 2024), with little risk of being discovered (Scarfe et al., 2024). The possibility of this happening is even greater when learners are not destined for an academic career (Wagner et al., 2011; Woolf, 2017).

As a result, the democratization of access to chatbots and generative AI means that we now need to refocus research-based teaching primarily on GenAI-proof research tasks.

This has implications for teaching delivery and knowledge assessment.

Teaching Delivery and Knowledge Assessment in Research-Based Teaching Built on GenAI-Proof Research Tasks

In the early 2010s, Wagner et al. (2011) highlighted the extreme paucity of literature on the pedagogy of teaching research methods in social sciences. This observation also applies to teaching through research, more generally. Today, there is still no general theory of the pedagogy of research-based teaching, and this observation is even truer for research-based teaching built on GenAI-proof tasks. Nevertheless, a number of studies have gone some way to fill the gap meanwhile, providing some interesting starting points for framing teaching delivery and knowledge assessment in this area.

Framing Delivery Phases in Research-Based Teaching

The literature on research-based teaching pedagogy published since the 2010s has consistently supported active learning methods. Reporting on an experience involving Childhood Studies students in field data collection, Sambell (2010) emphasized that students appreciated playing an active role, attempting to elaborate theories, and being able to co-construct and appropriate their knowledge. Focusing on problem-based learning, Kaeedi et al. (2023) showed that this pedagogical approach outperforms lecture-based learning in that it enables learners to acquire broader knowledge, learn more deeply and enjoyably, be more active in their learning, make more sense of it, and become more autonomous. Reviewing the literature, Ekmekci et al. (2012) identified that case-based learning is popular as well, although surpassed by problem-based learning when it comes to cultivating problem-solving skills.

Problem-based learning itself is just one of the essential components of a more comprehensive pedagogical approach, team-based learning, which also involves peer collaboration and learning by doing (Peachey & Baller, 2015).

Collaboration between learners is a decisive determinant of the effectiveness of problem-based learning, and team-based learning more generally. Mandel (2017) showed how the Jigsaw approach (Slavin, 1978; Slavin & Karweit, 1979) can be used to structure peer collaboration in research-based teaching built on data-collection activities. The Jigsaw approach requires each peer to specialize in one aspect of the problem, so that each depends on the others and must interact with them for the problem to be solved. In her case study of enquiry-based learning, Sambell (2010) showed that students enjoyed interacting with each other and receiving active, direct formative and developmental communication and feedback in real time from their peers. They were able to "internalise meaning and make connections with what individuals already knew" (p. 57), and enjoyed this enriched classroom dialogue. Sambell concluded that students perceived peer collaboration in research-based teaching as a gas pedal for conceptual understanding.

The literature points to the crucial role of group size in collaboration effectiveness. For peer-to-peer interactions within groups to be systematic and sustained, it is important that the groups are small. From a terminological point of view, Willett et al. (2011) distinguished between team-based learning and small-group learning, reserving the former term for large groups in which active learning methods are nonetheless implemented when the educational institution cannot afford to practice small-group learning. These authors showed that learning in small groups in a strict sense (eight to ten participants) generated greater satisfaction among learners. The importance of small-group collaboration was also highlighted by Guetterman et al. (2019) and Kaeedi et al. (2023). In the article by Mandel (2017), which followed the same line of thought, group sizes ranged from three to five participants, while whole classes had 15 and 21 students, respectively. Barraket's (2005) experience suggests that small groups, while suitable for a variety of activities (discussion, role-playing, and problem-based learning), can also be articulated in other formats, such as individual exercises and large-group discussions, to target differentiated learning objectives.

The literature also stresses the importance of learning-by-doing. However, exercises must not only have a strong practical dimension but must also be realistic. According to various authors (Kaeedi et al., 2023; Paufler, 2023; Peachey & Baller, 2015), authenticity of learning exercises plays a crucial role. Authenticity is a prerequisite for stimulating the interest and motivation of learners, enabling them to make sense of their learning, and ultimately maximizing their ability to effectively apply the skills they have acquired. Along with problem-based learning and learning by doing, realism is at the heart of the fundamental principles of pedagogy identified by Merrill (2006).

Paufler's (2023) experience of teaching research methods to doctoral students in the educational sciences also highlighted the importance of familiarizing learners with the use of technological tools (including for survey administration, data management, data analysis, and online collaboration). Paufler insisted on the need to ensure that these tools are accessible to learners and that learners have effective guides for using them. She emphasized the potential of these tools to foster collaboration between learners, in "e.g., analyzing data in small groups using statistical software" (p. 13).

In addition, Ekmekci et al. (2012) considered that the learning environment and learning process should respect various principles derived from adult learning theory. The learning setting should enable the learner to feel comfortable, free to concentrate on learning, and not be distracted, intimidated, or oppressed by the perception of obstacles and threats. The learning content should draw on learners' experiences and be relevant to their professional goals. The learning process should enable the learner to become aware of the link between research and practice. It should also commit the learner to his or her learning, so that he or she takes ownership of it, and becomes responsible for it and a major player in it. Moreover, the learning process should enable the learner to understand the crucial importance of critical reflection.

These principles can be considered as providing a preliminary framework for research-based teaching in general, and teaching through GenAI-proof research tasks in particular. In the absence of comprehensive research into the pedagogy of teaching through research, it is possible that this framework is incomplete. It is also possible that certain elements of this framework could be optional. For example, we do not know whether teaching is less relevant or less effective if any of the framework components is absent. Therefore, while this general framework is useful, it is also merely indicative at this stage. In other words, given the current state of knowledge on the subject, there is no reason to require every research-based teaching course to include all the components of this general framework, and on the other hand, there may be room for including other additional components. Further research in this area is certainly needed.

However, at this stage, this analysis already provides us with some clear directions.

Prioritizing GenAI-proof tasks when teaching through research implies that teaching delivery should be based on the collection of field data through participant observation, unstructured or semi-structured interviews, or requests to institutions. For learners to be able to carry out such activities, they must first acquire an in-depth understanding of the research project for which field data will be collected. Therefore, the teaching delivery phases should cover all aspects that enable learners to understand the subject of the research; the research questions and background; the state of knowledge; and the research objectives, strategy, methods, and expected outcomes. Involving learners as deeply as possible in the design of the research project can only enhance their understanding of it. This also includes involving the learners in the preparatory phases of the data collection operations, such as, for example, sampling interviewees, drawing up the interview guide questionnaire, and checking its thematic coverage, reliability, internal consistency, and readability.

Thus, taking into account both the implications of GenAI democratization and the lessons learned from the pedagogical literature, delivery in research-based teaching built on GenAI-proof tasks should be implemented through activities that immerse the learners in the research project, prepare them to collect field data (including training them in the technological tools that enable data collection), and have them operate by themselves the collection of data, all in ways that allow as much as possible for learning by doing, authenticity of learning activities, and collaboration among learners within small groups, while respecting the principles of adult learning theory.

Framing Assessment Phases

Black and Wiliam (2018, p. 1) observed that "the scholarly literature in the area of pedagogy says little or nothing about assessment". This is even truer of the literature on the pedagogy of teaching through research. The few studies in this field (Leary & Ness, 2021; Robertson & Kingsley, 2015) do, however, illustrate some common assessment practices in such teaching. These include written examinations with open-ended questions designed to assess the understanding of research articles or the ability to establish a plan of analysis, open-ended or multiple-choice questions designed to assess the understanding of concepts, and written and oral presentations of article evaluation reports. In the experiment reported by Robertson and Kingsley (2015), the share of formative assessment was reinforced at the expense of summative assessment, so as to bring learners to better perceive and understand how assessments can contribute to their progress.

In their undertaking to theorize formative assessment, Black and Wiliam (2009, 2018) identified several elements, two of which in particular could provide an interesting starting point for establishing a frame of reference for assessing learners' achievements in research-based teaching.

The first element is the objectification of assessment. Black and Wiliam's (2009, 2018) approach suggests that assessment should be purged of any subjective dimension and be based on explicit principles and criteria, of which the learner should have clear and precise knowledge. This knowledge is necessary to enable the learner to analyze his or her own performance with clarity and precision, to understand the teacher's assessment, to discuss it in a context of mutual understanding, to accept it, to define a progression plan, and to measure his or her own progress as would the teacher or any outside observer.

The second element, complementary to the first one, is that the assessment should be constructive. The teacher should provide the learner with feedback (individual or group) that is well-argued and indicates to the learner (a) that there is room for progress, (b) that progress is within reach, and (c) the ways and means to achieve it.

Clearly, however, further research is needed into an operational approach to knowledge assessment as part of research-based teaching prioritizing GenAI-proof tasks. A few considerations will be essential. For the sake of consistency, the assessment should—like the teaching delivery—exclude any possibility for the student to use generative AI. To this end, the assessment should take full account of the distinctive features of the "GenAI-proof-task-focused research-based teaching" model. These features mean that the summative assessment criteria should exclusively take into account (a) the student's active contribution and collaboration during live small-group discussions (which rules out benefitting from chatbot assistance), throughout the pre-data collection period; (b) the student's contribution to the data collection operations; and (c) how the student has made the most of the learning framework provided to progress in terms of the course objectives.

The following example will illustrate the point.

An Experience of Research-Based Teaching Built on a GenAI-Proof Research Task

In 2022, the same year that ChatGPT came to the attention of the general public, a team of teachers at the Institut de Formation en Soins Infirmiers (IFSI) [Nursing Training Institute] in Limoges (France) organized an action for final-year students to collect field data. This undertaking had no connection with the concomitant emergence of generative AI, which the general public was unaware of at the time. The data-collection operation was part of a research project designed and implemented by the teacher team. The operation was aimed at actively preparing students for the work they would carry out as part of their final dissertation. The research project itself, which was part of the teachers' regular research commitments, consisted of identifying the perceptions of paramedical staff (nurses and care assistants) regarding undernutrition as a health problem, its prevalence, and its related patient management. The data collection operation is presented here as an example of how research-based teaching can be implemented by drawing on a GenAI-proof research task, in line with the perspective adopted in this chapter.

Experience Description

A preliminary step for the teacher team was to have the research project validated by the Institute's scientific and administrative authorities. Then, at the start of the academic year, the preparatory phase was launched, involving students for the first time. Third-year students (n = 123) attended a nutrition course. Next, divided into small groups of eight or nine, these students drew up questionnaire proposals (structured questionnaires only, for the sake of simplification), which were then discussed and amended in full class sessions. These discussions led to the adoption of a common version of the questionnaire. The questionnaire was then tested and validated as part of a pilot survey with a dozen caregivers.

Next came the actual data collection phase. Seventy-nine students were tasked with administering the questionnaire to a sample of 768 paramedics. The sample included 14 medical establishments (hospitals and care centers) and medico-social establishments (accommodation facilities for dependent elderly people) in the Limoges region. Each student operated alone, collecting responses using pen and paper. The staff of the medical and medico-social establishments had been informed of the operation in advance by their respective administrations. The students arranged appointments with respondents to meet them at the Institute. Two teachers were on hand throughout the survey to assist the students in case of difficulty. The completed questionnaires were then returned to the teacher team for analysis. The initiative did not include an assessment of student learning outcomes.

Throughout the process, the teacher team took care of creating a climate conducive to active, collaborative, and serene learning. Several guiding principles were followed all along the project. The teacher team set the framework and guided the students step by step, while allowing them autonomy; it encouraged collaboration, respectful relationships, listening, and mutual trust; it mediated exchanges; and it fostered benevolent supervision. The approach was inspired in part by the concept of the "pedagogical alliance", referred to by Côté et al. (2018, p. 88). According to these authors, a "quality pedagogical alliance" leads teachers and students to work together to achieve common goals in a climate of mutual trust. Teacher and learner ensure "a respectful relationship that, although hierarchical in pedagogical terms, remains egalitarian in human terms, with listening and openness to the other's point of view deemed essential". Pedagogical alliance implies that "supervisor and student speak to each other with clarity and honesty, and listen to each other with respect, even when their points of view diverge".

Experience Evaluation

A student satisfaction survey was also conducted. The results of the survey are positive. Students said that they felt better prepared for their final dissertation work, having been able to familiarize themselves with questionnaire construction, conducting pilot survey, validity issues (analysis of consistency between the questionnaire questions and the research objectives), administering questionnaires, and managing respondent reminders. A number of students found the experience "motivating", not least because of its practical nature and transferability to their future professional practice. They also appreciated the supervision and support they received, particularly the feedback and readjustment phases, as well as the supervisors' availability, attention, responsiveness, commitment, and competence, which enabled them to overcome difficulties as they arose. Students reported that they felt the autonomy they had been given was a sign of trust, and that the whole scheme had given them a sense of "well-being".

However, the students also expressed reservations regarding the size of the groups. They felt that the size of the small groups (eight or nine people per group) was too large to enable satisfactory collaboration, and that the size of the team (the entire class of 123 students) was inappropriate to allow each individual to speak sufficiently.

From the teaching team's perspective, the experience confirmed the value of using active teaching methods. The teacher team felt that the students were able to give meaning to the theoretical teaching they had received (the nutrition course) by applying it in the field under realistic conditions. They were also able to project themselves into their future practices. Their motivation and commitment were boosted. In retrospect, student satisfaction reinforced the choices made by the teaching team regarding supervision and support.

However, this experience also sounded two major alarms. First, it highlighted that exercises focusing on data collection alone would not suffice to provide students with a comprehensive overview of all the stages of academic research. This is a reminder that the aim of integrating research into teaching is to harness research to enhance learning. The training of future professional researchers is quite a different story. Second, even when the activities on which teaching is built are limited to data collection tasks, getting the most out of these tasks does not occur by itself. In this case, providing students with access to technological tools proved out of reach, not only from a financial and technical point of view, but also because students and teachers should have been trained in these tools beforehand.

Implications

Prioritizing GenAI-proof tasks in research-based teaching has potential implications for the nature of teaching and assessment activities, the enhancement of disciplinary knowledge, and the strengthening of research skills.

On the one hand, except for students performing their assignments in controlled environments, research-based teaching should in future considerably reduce the emphasis hitherto placed on assignments that consist solely of written, oral, audio, or visual productions of problem statements, research questions, definitions, concepts, theories, literature reviews, data presentation, and data analysis. Assignments aimed to the production of results analyses, syntheses, and discussions, the description of results implications and scope, recommendations for practice, policy, or research, as well as the production of physical prototypes and the collection of data by means of database extraction, non-participant observation, and structured interviews and questionnaires, should also be reduced. This does not mean that these types of tasks should be excluded from the teaching. They could remain a part of research-based teaching and formative assessment but should not play any role in the summative assessment of student learning outcomes.

On the other hand, research-based teaching courses should, in the future, rely much more on GenAI-proof research tasks, such as the collection of field data through participant observation, unstructured interviews, semi-structured interviews, and requests for data from institutions. These types of GenAI-proof research tasks should be the only ones used in summative assessment.

Prioritizing GenAI-proof tasks would have the advantage of reducing the risk of GenAI-fueled academic misconduct among students while reinforcing both subject learning and research education. Field data collection has great potential to enhance both subject knowledge and research skills when integrating research into teaching. Collecting data means adapting to circumstances without losing sight of what is essential in terms of both subject matter and research conduct, and making choices that do not compromise the coherence and solidity of research. For example, the researcher-investigator must select the most appropriate data from among the range of proxies held by an institution, or reformulate a question appropriately during an interview, or select the most appropriate sequence to follow from several simultaneous events during an immersive observation process. To operate in an informed and relevant way, the researcher-investigator must have fully assimilated the research question, its meaning, the problem it addresses, its issues, its conceptual and theoretical universe, the risks of misinterpretation and false sense it conveys, the traps and pitfalls to avoid, as well as the methodological treatment planned for the data collected. For example, data that are heuristic but outside the theoretical universe of the research, or data that are informative but qualitative and cannot be processed by the planned quantitative methods, will have to be kept away. Consequently, prioritizing data collection in research-based teaching actually means presenting the learner in advance with a series of essential aspects linked to both the subject being taught and the research process and method. Therefore, data collection appears to be a powerful potential vehicle for acquiring in-depth knowledge and skills on the subject, and on research processes and methods in research-based teaching.

Transferability and Generalizability

The approach presented here to capture the implications of generative AI on pedagogy and assessment in research-based teaching is conceptual and, as such, applies to any teaching context in which learning is fundamentally driven by the involvement of learners in doing research. However, research-based teaching is only one of the possible teaching contexts. When it comes to positioning research in relation to teaching, two other contexts need to be distinguished.

The first, the most general, is characterized by the absence of any particular link with involving learners in research. It encompasses primary, secondary, and higher undergraduate education, in which students are still acquiring the foundations of knowledge and are not ready to become involved in research. The other teaching context is the more specific one of training future researchers.

Addressing the implications of GenAI for pedagogy and assessment is a challenge for these other two contexts too. Faced with this challenge, each of them has a specific mission that implies specificity in the response.

In primary education up to undergraduate level, the aim is to prepare learners for their future roles in society. When it comes to generative AI, this means knowing how best to use it from a practical and ethical point of view, and being prepared to deal with its pitfalls, for example, in terms of misinformation (see Chap. 6 of the present book). Consequently, schools from primary to undergraduate level should train students to become familiar with GenAI (see for example the framework proposed by Firth et al., 2024). The approach to assessment is more nuanced. Some authors, such as Werse and Smith (2025), recommend supplementing assignments with oral discussions to check students' ability to demonstrate their learning. Others are more along the lines of excluding GenAI-substitutable learning activities from the summative assessment process. Gonsalves (2025) suggests a greater emphasis on contextualizing assessments, arguing that GenAI tools may not be very useful to students when assignments need to take account of practical real-world contexts, personal real-life experience and interdisciplinarity. Furze et al. (2024) and Page et al. (2024) have shown how GenAI can be integrated in formative assessment, but Page et al. (2024) emphasize that:

> it is likely preferable for summative assessments to primarily, if not entirely, represent original work of the student rather than the output of generative AI to uphold institutional integrity. If a vast majority of assessments completed by students are predominately facilitated by generative AI, internal and external stakeholders may question the aptitudes of program graduates. Program leaders, faculty, and course designers need to make deliberate decisions about the incorporation of generative AI in assessments, as well as when they may choose to disallow it. (Page et al., 2024, p. 119)

On the other hand, in the context of training future researchers, not only should learners be taught about GenAI, but they should also be assessed in terms of mastering the appropriate practical and ethical use of GenAI in research, as well as how to detect and manage the misuse of GenAI in research.

Conclusion

Considering the breakthrough of generative artificial intelligence, this chapter has revisited the concept of research-based teaching, stemmed from the literature on the research-teaching nexus. The chapter introduced the notions of GenAI-proof and

GenAI-substitutable research tasks and showed that, except in cases where learners perform their assignments in controlled environments, the GenAI revolution requires research-based teachings to be refocused on GenAI-proof research tasks. This implies that summative assessment should prioritize field data collection activities in which GenAI cannot replace the human researcher.

In the absence of a general theory of pedagogy in research-based teaching built on GenAI-proof tasks, the chapter has identified from the literature various reference principles that are likely to guide teaching delivery and knowledge assessment practices. Active pedagogy, peer collaboration, small groups, learning-by-doing, authenticity of learning activities, linking research and practice, learner empowerment, critical thinking, objective assessment, and constructive feedback appeared to be keywords. A reported field experience illustrates the perspective, also echoing Willett et al.'s (2011) observations on learner frustration with overly large groups, and Barraket's (2005) conclusions on the importance of small groups in fostering learner involvement and collaboration as well as learning effectiveness. The reported experience also alerts us to the need to train teachers and students in technological tools well in advance of data-collection sessions.

The experience reported in this chapter also enriches the literature by highlighting the crucial role of student supervision and support models. The satisfaction survey showed that students were enthusiastic about the model put in place, which was based on the principles of framed autonomy, step-by-step guidance, pedagogical alliance in a collaborative climate (mutually respectful relationships, listening, shared trust, and mediation), and benevolent support. This feedback from students suggests that particular attention should be paid to models of supervision and support when considering the pedagogy of research-based teaching giving priority to GenAI-proof tasks.

More thorough research into these supervision and support models is called for. More generally, further research is needed to identify a more comprehensive and elaborate frame of reference for pedagogy in research-based teaching in this new era of generative AI.

Competing Interests The authors have no conflicts of interest to declare that are relevant to the content of this chapter.

Ethics Approval This study was conducted in accordance with the principles of the Declaration of Helsinki. Ethical approval for the research was granted by the Ethics Committee of Limoges University Hospital (5 December 2022/No. 588-2022-244). Informed consent was obtained from all participants prior to their involvement in the study.

References

Arimoto, A. (2020). An international and comparative perspective of the academic profession's development: With a focus on R-T-S nexus in the world and Japan. *Higher Education Forum, 17*, 151–175.

Barraket, J. (2005). Teaching research method using a student-centred approach? Critical reflections on practice. *Journal of University Teaching & Learning Practice, 2*(2), 17–27. https://doi.org/10.53761/1.2.2.3

Black, P., & Wiliam, D. (2009). Developing the theory of formative assessment. *Educational Assessment, Evaluation and Accountability, 21*(1), 5–31.

Black, P., & Wiliam, D. (2018). Classroom assessment and pedagogy. *Assessment in Education: Principles, Policy & Practice, 25*(6), 551–575. https://doi.org/10.1080/0969594X.2018.1441807

Boyd, W. E., O'Reilly, M., Bucher, D., Fisher, K., Morton, A., Harrison, P. L., Nuske, E., Coyle, R., & Rendall, K. (2010). Activating the teaching-research nexus in smaller universities: Case studies highlighting diversity of practice. *Journal of University Teaching & Learning Practice, 7*(2) Retrieved from http://ro.uow.edu.au/jutlp/vol7/iss2/9

Boyer Commission. (1998). *Reinventing undergraduate education: A blueprint for America's research universities*. State University of New York at Stony Brook. Retrieved from https://files.eric.ed.gov/fulltext/ED424840.pdf

Cantor, A., DeLauer, V., Martin, D., & Rogan, J. (2015). Training interdisciplinary "wicked problem" solvers: Applying lessons from HERO in community-based research experiences for undergraduates. *Journal of Geography in Higher Education, 39*(3), 407–419. https://doi.org/10.1080/03098265.2015.1048508

Côté, L., Laurin, S., & Sanche, G. (2018). Echanger de la rétroaction avec les étudiants [Exchanging feedback with students]. In I. T. Pelaccia (Ed.), *Comment (mieux) superviser les étudiants en sciences de la santé dans leurs stages et dans leurs activités de recherche? [How can health science students be (better) supervised in their placements and research activities?]* (pp. 81–109). De Boeck Supérieur.

Ekmekci, O., Hancock, A. B., & Swayze, S. (2012). Teaching statistical research methods to graduate students: Lessons learned from three different degree programs. *International Journal of Teaching and Learning in Higher Education, 24*(2), 272–279.

Firth, D. R., Derendinger, M., & Triche, J. (2024). Cheating better with ChatGPT: A framework for teaching students when to use ChatGPT and other generative AI bots. *Information Systems Education Journal, 22*(3), 47–60. https://doi.org/10.62273/BZSU7160

Furze, L., Perkins, M., Roe, J., & MacVaugh, J. (2024). The AI Assessment Scale (AIAS) in action: A pilot implementation of GenAI-supported assessment. *Australasian Journal of Educational Technology, 40*(4), 38–55.

Gilmore, J., Lewis, D. M. G., Maher, M., Feldon, D., & Timmerman, B. E. (2015). Feeding two birds with one scone? The relationship between teaching and research for graduate students across the disciplines. *International Journal of Teaching and Learning in Higher Education, 27*(1), 25–41. Retrieved from http://www.isetl.org/ijtlhe/

Gonsalves, C. (2025). Contextual assessment design in the age of generative AI. *Journal of Learning Development in Higher Education, 34*, 1–14.

Gretton, S., Raine, D., Hurkett, C., Williams, D., Harvey, C., & Symons, S. (2022). Revisiting the research-teaching nexus framework: Two case studies introducing research into program level, undergraduate teaching. *International Journal of Teaching and Learning in Higher Education, 33*(2), 259–272. Retrieved from https://files.eric.ed.gov/fulltext/EJ1345570.pdf

Griffiths, R. (2004). Knowledge production and the research-teaching nexus: The case of the built environment disciplines. *Studies in Higher Education, 29*(6), 709–726. https://doi.org/10.1080/0307507042000287212

Guetterman, T. C., Creswell, J. W., Deutsch, C., & Gallo, J. J. (2019). Process evaluation of a retreat for scholars in the first cohort: The NIH mixed methods research training program for the health sciences. *Journal of Mixed Methods Research, 13*(1), 52–68.

Healey, M. (2005). Linking research and teaching to benefit student learning. *Journal of Geography in Higher Education, 29*(2), 183–201. https://doi.org/10.1080/03098260500130387

Healey, M., & Jenkins, A. (2009). *Developing undergraduate research and inquiry. Research report to the Higher Education Academy*. Higher Education Academy. Retrieved from https://www.advance-he.ac.uk/knowledge-hub/developing-undergraduate-research-and-inquiry

Healey, M., Jordan, F., Pell, B., & Short, C. (2010). The research-teaching nexus: A case study of students' awareness, experiences and perceptions of research. *Innovations in Education and Teaching International, 47*(2), 235–246. https://doi.org/10.1080/14703291003718968

Jenkins, A., Healey, M., & Zetter, R. (2007). *Linking research and teaching in disciplines and departments*. Higher Education Academy.

Kaeedi, A., Nasr Esfahani, A., Sharifian, F., & Moosavipour, S. (2023). The quantitative and qualitative study of the effectiveness of the problem-based learning approach in teaching research methods. *Journal of University Teaching & Learning Practice, 20*(5). https://doi.org/10.53761/1.20.5.06

Leary, S., & Ness, A. (2021). Teaching research methods to undergraduate dental students. *Journal of University Teaching and Learning Practice, 18*(2), 7.

Lopatto, D. (2007). Undergraduate research experiences support science career decisions and active learning. *CPE-Life Sciences Education, 6*(4), 297–306. https://doi.org/10.1187/cbe.07-06-0039

Macheridis, N., Pihl, A. F., Paulsson, A., & Pihl, H. (2024). Students' experiences of the research-teaching nexus. *Tertiary Education and Management, 30*, 1–16. https://doi.org/10.1007/s11233-023-09129-8

Mandel, L. H. (2017). Experiencing research firsthand: The "unClassroom" experiential learning approach to teaching research methods in an LIS master's program. *Journal of Education for Library and Information Science, 58*(4), 187–201.

Merrill, M. (2006). First principles of instruction. *Educational Technology Research and Development, 50*(3), 43–59.

Nhem, D. (2023). So, is there a teaching-research nexus in Cambodia? Evidence from EFL students at one public university. *Research in Post-Compulsory Education, 28*(1), 48–69. https://doi.org/10.1080/13596748.2023.2166692

Page, E., Meyers, G., & Krahe Billings, E. (2024). Theory to practice: An assessment framework for generative AI. *Intersection: A Journal at the Intersection of Assessment and Learning, 5*(4), 114–126.

Paufler, N. A. (2023). Preparing scholarly practitioners to use improvement science: A systematic, iterative, and reflective approach to teaching applied quantitative research methods. *Impacting Education: Journal on Transforming Professional Practice, 8*(2), 10–15.

Peachey, A. A., & Baller, S. L. (2015). Ideas and approaches for teaching undergraduate research methods in the health sciences. *International Journal of Teaching and Learning in Higher Education, 27*(3), 434–442.

Roberts, P., Ertubey, C., McMurray, I., & Robertson, I. (2012). Developing a psychology undergraduate research community in a new university. *Psychology Teaching Review, 18*(2), 82–93.

Robertson, J. M., & Kingsley, B. E. (2015). Teaching research methods to encourage the transition from "reluctant scientist" to psychologist: A longitudinal study. *Psychology Teaching Review, 21*(1), 44–55.

Sambell, K. (2010). Enquiry-based learning and formative assessment environments: Student perspectives. *Practitioner Research in Higher Education, 4*(1), 52–61.

Scarfe, P., Watcham, K., Clarke, A., & Roesch, E. (2024). A real-world test of artificial intelligence infiltration of a university examinations system: A "Turing Test" case study. *PLoS One, 19*(6), e0305354. https://doi.org/10.1371/journal.pone.0305354

Seymour, E., Hunter, A., Laursen, S. L., & Deantoni, T. (2004). Establishing the benefits of research experience for undergraduates in the sciences: First findings from a three year study. *Science Education, 88*, 493–534. https://doi.org/10.1002/sce.10131

Slapcoff, M., & Harris, D. (2014). The Inquiry Network: A model for promoting the teaching-research nexus in higher education. *Canadian Journal of Higher Education, 44*(2), 68–84.

Slavin, R. E. (1978). *Using student team-learning*. Guide for teachers, Johns Hopkins University.

Slavin, R. E., & Karweit, N. (1979). *An extended cooperative learning experience in elementary school. Report No CSOS-E-290*. Johns Hopkins University.

Tadesse, E. F., & Khalid, S. (2023). Are teachers and HE are on the same page? Calling for a research–teaching nexus among Ethiopian and Pakistani academics. *Journal of Applied Research in Higher Education, 15*(1), 130–151. https://doi.org/10.1108/JARHE-09-2021-0348
Topaz, M., Stiglic, G., Pruinelli, L., Fukahori, H., Miyagawa, S., Michalowski, M., Song, J., O'Connor, S., Peltonen, L.-M., & Ronquillo, C. (2024). The ChatGPT effect: Nursing education and generative artificial intelligence. *Journal of Nursing Education, 64*, e40. https://doi.org/10.3928/01484834-20240126-01
Vafadar, M., & Moradi Amani, A. (2024). Academic education in the era of generative artificial intelligence. *Journal of Electronic and Electrical Engineering, 3*, 110. https://doi.org/10.37256/jeee.3120244010
Wagner, C., Garner, M., & Kawulich, B. (2011). The state of the art of teaching research methods in the social sciences: Towards a pedagogical culture. *Studies in Higher Education, 36*(1), 75–88. https://doi.org/10.1080/03075070903452594
Weenink, K., Aarts, N., & Jacobs, S. (2023). 'I need a grant but spend time on teaching': how academics in different positions play out the teaching–research nexus in interdependence with their contexts. *European Journal of Higher Education, 14*(3), 489–507. https://doi.org/10.1080/21568235.2023.2221839
Werse, R., & Smith, J. C. (2025). Nothing new under the sun: Generative AI and educator anxiety over academic dishonesty. *Impacting Education: Journal on Transforming Professional Practice, 10*(1), 90–95. https://doi.org/10.5195/ie.2025.484
Willett, L., Rosevear, G. C., & Kim, S. (2011). A trial of team-based versus small-group learning for second-year medical students: Does the size of the small group make a difference? *Teaching and Learning in Medicine, 23*(1), 28–30. https://doi.org/10.1080/10401334.2011.536756
Woolf, J. (2017). An analytical autoethnographical account of using inquiry-based learning in a graduate research methods course. *Canadian Journal for the Scholarship of Teaching and Learning, 8*(1), 5. Retrieved from https://files.eric.ed.gov/fulltext/EJ1134157.pdf
Yazdani, S., Shirvani, A., & Heidarpoor, P. (2021). A model for the taxonomy of research studies: A practical guide to knowledge production and knowledge management. *Archives of Pediatric Infectious Diseases, 9*(4), e112456. https://doi.org/10.5812/pedinfect.112456
Zhang, L.-F., Horta, H., Jung, J., & Postiglione, G. A. (2020). The research-teaching nexus: Not merely an enduring myth. *Higher Education Forum, 17*, 69–97.

Bérangère Laroudie holds a Ph.D. in Education and Training Sciences. She works as a Training Manager at IFSI—CHU de Limoges, France. Her areas of interest are the professionalization of nurses, competence-oriented pedagogy, and learner motivation.

Guy Tchibozo is a research associate at LISEC UR2310, the education research center of the University of Strasbourg (France). He is the Director of Analytrics and Editor of *Education Thinking*. His research interests are in education policy, vocational education and training, and quantitative analysis, with an emphasis on school-to-work transition, dynamics analysis, competence-oriented approaches in education and training, and the policies for vocational education and training in the European Union. https://gtsite.xyz/1/.

Chapter 11
Simulation in Mixed-Reality Learning Environments: Safe Spaces for Pre-Service Teachers to Practice Classroom Management

Therese M. Cumming, Hee Min Lee, and Jordana F. Hoenig

Abstract According to the literature and anecdotal data, early career teachers often feel unprepared to cope with the realities of today's classroom, especially in the area of classroom management. Although they typically participate in a series of practicum training throughout their university studies, the usefulness of these experiences varies, as it is dependent upon the quality of the supervising teacher, the make-up and culture of the classroom, and the preparation the student receives prior to these placements. We have identified AI in the form of simulations in mixed-reality learning environments as a possible solution to a lack of preparation and practice in managing challenging classroom behavior. The aims of this chapter are threefold: to briefly review the literature about simulations in mixed-reality learning environments in teacher education; to describe a pilot study at one university that examined the efficacy of these simulations to support pre-service teachers in the development of de-escalation skills; and to discuss practical implications and future directions of this type of AI technology in teacher education.

Keywords Classroom management · Simulation · Teacher training · Technology integration

There is a long and storied history of technology use to prepare pre-service teachers in the classroom. It began as early as the 1950s and 60s, when educational television programs started to be used for teacher training to deliver content and instructional techniques to a wider audience of educators (Bates, 2015). The advent of educational technology in the 1980s saw the introduction of computer-based instruction in some teacher preparation programs, followed by the integration of educational technology courses, covering topics such as instructional design and the use of

T. M. Cumming (✉) · H. M. Lee · J. F. Hoenig
University of New South Wales, Sydney, NSW, Australia
e-mail: t.cumming@unsw.edu.au

G. Tchibozo (ed.), *International Perspectives of Generative AI in Education*, Advances in Artificial Intelligence in Education 3,
https://doi.org/10.1007/978-3-031-99804-1_11

software in the classroom in the 1990s (Hirtz, 2021). The rise of the internet in the 1990s paved the way for online learning. Teacher education programs started to offer courses and professional development opportunities through online platforms. This allowed educators to access resources and collaborate with peers remotely (Hirtz, 2021).

In the beginning of the twenty-first century, interactive whiteboards became popular in classrooms, providing teachers with interactive tools to enhance their presentations (Saltan & Arslan, 2019). Multimedia resources, including educational videos and digital simulations, were increasingly used in teacher preparation programs. The rise of mobile technology in the late 2000s precipitated the development of educational applications to support teacher training that could be accessed any time anywhere (Cumming et al., 2013). In recent years, virtual reality (VR) and augmented reality (AR) have been explored for teacher training. These immersive technologies offer realistic simulations and scenarios for practicing teaching strategies and classroom management (Samuelsson et al., 2022).

Mixed-reality simulation (MRS) has been increasingly used to prepare teachers for inclusive classrooms (Southgate et al., 2018). The use of mixed reality, which combines elements of both virtual and augmented reality, offers immersive and interactive experiences that can enhance teacher training in various ways (Luke et al., 2021a). MRS can be defined as educational settings that combine elements of both the physical world and virtual or augmented reality (Luke et al., 2021a). This technology integrates real-world surroundings with computer-generated sensory input, allowing learners to interact with both physical and digital elements simultaneously. Mixed-reality environments offer a spectrum of experiences, ranging from purely physical reality to purely virtual reality, with varying degrees of augmentation in between (Mikeska et al., 2021).

Mixed-reality simulations provide learners with the ability to interact with physical objects in the real environment while also engaging with a simulation (Mikeska et al., 2021). For instance, the student teacher can use a whiteboard in their physical space while interacting with virtual students in the virtual environment. MRSs provide dynamic and responsive simulations, allowing students to practice skills in a controlled and realistic virtual environment. Another advantageous feature is MRS' adaptability and customization. The learning content and level of difficulty can be tailored to individual needs, providing personalized learning (Mikeska et al., 2021). Lastly, MRS offers a safe space for pre-service teachers (PST) to practice pedagogy, communication, and classroom management (Luke et al., 2021b).

MRS has been applied in preparing teachers for inclusive classrooms in a variety of ways (Christensen et al., 2011; Landon-Hays et al., 2020; Luke & Vaughn, 2021). The first, and the focus of this chapter, is simulated learning environments, which provide teachers with realistic virtual classrooms where they can encounter diverse student profiles, with different learning abilities, backgrounds, and needs. Teachers can then practice classroom management using inclusive strategies, adapting their teaching methods to cater to various student needs, and addressing the needs of students with disabilities.

SimLab and Mursion, two MRS that provide simulated learning environment, use AI-driven avatars that interact with students in real-time, providing a realistic and immersive teaching experience. The AI technology behind these two MRS enables these avatars to respond dynamically to the actions and questions of the users, creating a more engaging and effective learning experience. This integration of AI helps in providing instant feedback, assessing performance, and tailoring the simulations to meet specific learning objectives. Mursion and SimLab both collect and analyze data on user interactions and performance to identify areas where users may need additional support. This allows for continuous improvement of the training programs (Murdoch University, n.d.; Mursion, 2025).

MRS enable teachers to engage in interactive scenarios within the mixed-reality environment, make decisions and see the immediate consequences of their actions (Landon-Hays et al., 2020). These scenarios can be tailored to be related to classroom management, adapting lesson plans for diverse learners, and implementing individualized education plans (IEPs). MRSs can also be used to support pre-service teachers in building empathy and understanding, as they can incorporate narratives and perspectives from students with different abilities, fostering empathy and understanding among pre-service teachers (Rappa & Ledger, 2022). MRSs can provide immediate feedback to pre-service teachers, allowing them to reflect on their actions and refine their practice (Landon-Hays et al., 2020). This has the potential to encourage pre-service teachers to incorporate all-important feedback and reflection into their everyday practice.

Situated Learning Theory

The use of simulations in mixed-reality learning environments can be underpinned by situated learning theory (Lave & Wenger, 1991). This theory emphasizes the importance of learning within the context of authentic and meaningful experiences. According to this theory, learning is situated in social and physical environments, and knowledge is constructed based on the activities and interactions occurring in these real-world contexts. The first of the theory's key principles is contextual learning, or the idea that knowledge is best acquired situated in a specific context by engaging in authentic tasks. For instance, the student teaching in an actual classroom under the supervision of a teacher, compared to microteaching, where student teachers practice teaching by demonstrating a snippet of a lesson to their fellow students and university teacher. The theory challenges traditional views of cognition by asserting that thinking and learning are inseparable from the context in which they occur. Knowledge is not abstracted from the world but is deeply tied to the situations in which it is used.

Social Participation is another principle of situated learning theory. Learning is viewed as a social activity where individuals engage in communities of practice, where members of the community share a common interest, engage in joint activities, and learn from each other through collaboration and interaction (Lave &

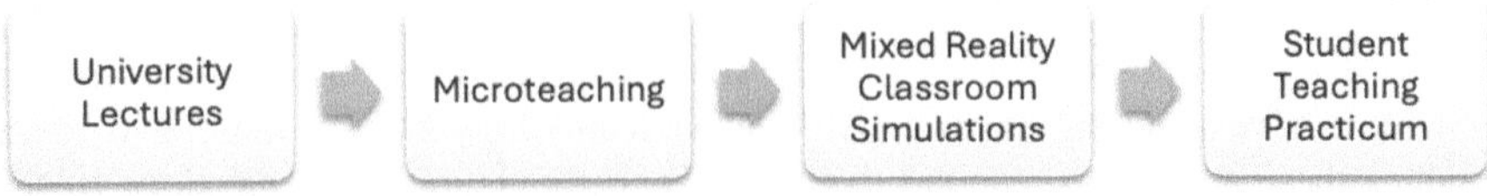

Fig. 11.1 Continuum of authentic learning activities in teacher education

Wenger, 1991). This can be illustrated by considering a class of pre-service teachers or a group of teachers in a school. Rather than seeing learning as the acquisition of fixed knowledge, situated learning theory views learning as a process of becoming a member of a community and adopting the practices, language, and values associated with that community.

The theory introduces the concept of legitimate peripheral participation, which suggests that newcomers start by participating in the periphery of a community's activities and gradually move toward more central roles as they acquire knowledge and skills (Lave & Wenger, 1991). This concept can also be illustrated by the example of student teachers, who begin their practica observing in a classroom and being supervised by the classroom teacher, and as time goes on, they are given greater responsibility and the opportunity to teach the class. This experience also contributes to mutual engagement, or shared experiences, discussions, and problem-solving within a social context.

Overall, Situated Learning Theory highlights the interconnectedness of learning and the environment in which it takes place. It argues for a more holistic and contextually embedded approach to education, promoting the idea that learners benefit most when they are actively engaged in meaningful, real-world experiences within a social community. While mixed-reality simulations are not authentic contexts, they provide students with a realistic simulated version that can be used to prepare students for their real-life practicum and practice (Ledger et al., 2022). See Fig. 11.1 for a representation of the continuum of authentic learning experiences in teacher education.

The aims of this chapter are threefold: to briefly review the literature about simulations in mixed-reality learning environments in teacher education, to describe an exploratory study at one university that examined the efficacy of these simulations to support pre-service teachers in the development of de-escalation skills, and to discuss practical implications and future directions of this type of artificial intelligence (AI) technology in teacher education.

Context

There are significant challenges for pre-service teachers, educators, and schools which compelled our research into using mixed-reality simulations in university teacher training programs. The post-pandemic teacher shortage and the limited opportunities for real-world training required an immediate and coherent response.

By gathering empirical evidence about the effects of MRS to support tertiary students' classroom management skills and self-efficacy, we identified the benefits of artificial intelligence for tertiary education courses. The prospect of alleviating the pressure on the education system and strengthening PSTs' readiness for the workforce bodes well for all stakeholders: supervising teachers, students, schools, and the PSTs themselves.

The stressors of competing school demands, ever-increasing workloads, and disruptive student behavior have impacted widespread teacher attrition (Arthur & Bradley, 2023). This is a common problem that has placed pressure on pre-service teachers to fill the gap. Both primary and secondary school teachers, however, are insufficiently prepared to manage students' mis (Delamarre et al., 2021). As PSTs, they need access to efficient, consistent, and effective opportunities for skill development, which are possible with AI technologies (Walters et al., 2021). They need experience with different scenarios, adapted to children's diverse needs, to develop confidence in managing behavioral problems in the classroom.

Ordinarily, school placements provided pre-service teachers with the necessary opportunities and experience to practice and develop content knowledge, skills, and performance. It is widely believed, however, that these practicums have limited potential. The practicum experiences are restricted by infrequency, time constraints, and limited student autonomy while teaching in a classroom that is not theirs (Walters et al., 2021). They characteristically provide limited teaching experience and guided supervision, in part due to disparate school priorities, demands of curriculum reform or an extensive curriculum, restrictive timetables, and the lack of availability of coaches and mentors. When it is impossible for pre-service teachers to enter schools, such as during the recent global pandemic, mixed-reality simulations are beneficial to them (Luke et al., 2021a). MRS can help compensate for the limitations of practicums by providing relevant teaching experiences (Luke et al., 2021b).

Furthermore, issues around equitable access and digital inclusion may prevail in schooling and, by implication, in tertiary education. In Australia, for example, an extensive Commonwealth/Federal Government research report into AI and emerging mixed realities in education, stated that there are few professional learning resources and opportunities with AI and emerging technologies for PSTs, classroom teachers, and school leaders (Southgate et al., 2018). Right now, AI is said to be in the early stages of development and application in schools, and thereby tertiary education. The recommendation is that educators develop foundational knowledge of using artificial intelligence to empower students to thrive in an AI world (Southgate et al., 2018).

Until now, microteaching has been the common model for tertiary teacher training. It involves a scaled-down teaching experience or roleplay with a micro class, a 5-to-20-min lesson, and specific predetermined objectives (Allen & Eve, 1968). To date, it has been seen as raising the level of the teachers' competencies by offering conditions for actual teaching, reduced lesson complexity, reduced task focus, a high degree of control, expanded and immediate feedback (D. Allen & Eve, 1968). Scholars are now recommending redesigning pedagogical strategies in teacher education with the integration of technologies available through AI (e.g., Luke & Vaughn, 2021). MRS would be useful course additions, to combat the limited authenticity, complexity, and realism of microteaching (Spencer et al., 2019). The research has shown, for example, that PSTs in the simulated learning environment demonstrated increased self-efficacy and use of high leverage practices related to differentiation for individual students' needs, strategic teaching, peer collaboration, and providing collegial feedback (Landon-Hays et al., 2020). The benefits extend to university educators, who can observe PSTs, give corrective and constructive feedback, and provide coaching instruction to prepare students for potentially challenging classroom realities (Luke & Vaughn, 2021).

Surprisingly, using simulations to improve pre-service teachers' pedagogical practices and teaching skills is not a new idea. Over a decade ago, one group of researchers explored the rationale for simSchool as a dynamic teacher education game for preparing early childhood teachers and teacher candidates who had prior experience working with K-12 students with disabilities (Christensen et al., 2011). As a direct outcome of working with simulated students in the Sim environment, the researchers found larger gains in PSTs' instructional self-efficacy than in traditional teacher preparation activities. In a second study conducted in 2012, researchers explored the impact of using TeachME™ Lab (TML) virtual classroom simulation on early childhood teachers' science teaching self-efficacy beliefs (Bautista & Boone, 2015). Practicing in a mixed-reality teaching environment, they found a significant increase in self-efficacy and science teaching outcome expectancy beliefs. The current study brings a new perspective to the conversation, regarding the social validity of MRS and the impact on PSTs' classroom management skills using this type of AI technology in teacher education.

Mixed-reality simulations have a wide range of applications and benefits to pre-service teacher preparation. They provide opportunities for targeted practice of instructional skills in special education, early childhood, primary, and secondary school teaching specializations, and across content strands. They can be customized for the broad range of students and educational challenges such as class disengagement and inappropriate behaviors (Ledger et al., 2022). Simulation scenarios can be modified to provide interactions with co-teachers, parents/caregivers, and IEP meetings. Overall, these experiences bridge the gap between initial teacher training and real application, whereby PSTs engage in situated learning and reflective practice, resulting in increased self-efficacy, teaching strategies, and learning outcomes (Ledger et al., 2022).

Safe Spaces

Mixed-reality simulations serve as approximations of practice that provide pre-service teachers with a safe space to hone their skills in structured virtual learning environments (Rappa & Ledger, 2022). The possibilities for customization, coaching, mentoring, collaboration, and feedback make them ideal for tertiary students' learning and skill development (Mikeska et al., 2021). Simulations provide valid models for depicting an inclusive classroom with a variety of mixed-ability students (Christensen et al., 2011). The tool mitigates any impact of inexperience of the PSTs on real students by providing pre-service teachers interaction with realistic student avatars prior to entering the classroom (Fischetti et al., 2022). Additionally, simulation technology gives teacher educators the opportunity for direct observation and assessment of pre-service teachers in a safe context without the risk of negative effects on actual students (A. Allen & Stecker, 2023).

To prepare for employment in schools, PSTs need to experience challenging student behaviors and diversity in less pressured environments. They will be expected to teach students with a variety of interests, backgrounds, needs, abilities, and learning preferences in an inclusive classroom. The simulations allow pre-service teachers to explore and reflect on various approaches to different scenarios in a safe, controlled, and realistic classroom environment (Fischetti et al., 2022). They have the advantage of being brief, available to practice multiple times, web-based so they are portable, easy to implement, and available online from anywhere in the world (A. Allen & Stecker, 2023). These practice-based spaces give PSTs time in a non-threatening and relevant environment to think critically about managing complex classroom situations (Dixon et al., 2019). They enable concurrent peer and instructor observation, feedback, and coaching (Fischetti et al., 2022) and focus the pre-service teachers on effective planning, teaching, class management, and evaluation of practice (Fischetti et al., 2022). Instructional coaching, during or after the session, is especially helpful for PSTs to examine their management skills within a safe space and make changes that heighten their self-efficacy in addressing students' behaviors and needs. When MRS is integrated into the teacher education curriculum, students can safely experiment, practice, and refine their skills (Luke & Vaughn, 2021).

Instructional Practice

In the literature, it is well-known that the use of mixed-reality simulations in tertiary learning improves pre-service teachers' metacognitive awareness and insights into the complexities of teaching (e.g., Luke et al., 2021a; Sebastian & Krishnamachari, 2023). This is reflected in a study which showed that PSTs' use of MRS in tertiary education courses increased their perceived knowledge, skills, and confidence over time as well as their actual performance (Hirsch et al., 2023). In another study, use of the simSchool platform increased PSTs' understanding of student diversity, exceptionalities, classroom management, and differentiated instruction (Johnston & Collum, 2020). Engaging in interactive scenarios provided PSTs opportunities for real-time interaction and decision-making, synchronous consultation and feedback, and the ability to witness the immediate consequences of their actions (Ledger et al., 2022).

With repeated practice, the quality of PSTs' teaching improves, as evidenced by their increased pedagogical knowledge, strategic planning, feedback to students, differentiation, and collaboration (Landon-Hays et al., 2020). Furthermore, the use of MRS decreased PSTs' performance anxiety (Fischetti et al., 2022) and increased their confidence, self-efficacy, and emotional, motivational, and cognitive classroom readiness (Fischetti et al., 2022). To illustrate this, two research studies found that 3 h of virtual simulation training followed by 3 weeks of fieldwork develops PSTs' efficacy beliefs in teaching mathematics as much as 3 weeks of training with real students, and significantly more than micro-teaching with colleagues or peers (Samuelsson et al., 2022). Not surprisingly, researchers concluded that simulation training is a valid practicum preparation (Bardach et al., 2021), a supplement (Larson et al., 2020) or even an alternative to real-life classroom contexts (Ersozlu et al., 2021).

According to the literature, simulation provides a twenty-first century approach to pre-service teachers' skill development in instruction, communication, and behavior management (Donehower Paul et al., 2019; Larson et al., 2020). The approach is timely in this age of professional scrutiny when teachers are expected to understand and personalize learning for a myriad of students, classes, and grades. PSTs report feeling ill-equipped to especially address challenging behaviors (Delamarre et al., 2021). As a result of MRS, researchers saw an increase in PSTs' understanding of diversity, students with exceptionalities, differentiated instruction, and classroom management (Johnston & Collum, 2020). Simulations facilitated the pre-service teachers' skill development and assisted with planning for diverse learners, understanding the pedagogy of personalized learning, and engaging with classroom management (Fischetti et al., 2022). Below, we illustrate these through the description of a pilot study.

Case Study

The authors of this chapter teach as part of their university's compulsory undergraduate and postgraduate courses in classroom management. They recognized two things. First, no matter how good the classroom management course, many pre-service teachers (anecdotally and in the literature) enter their first classroom practicum placement feeling unprepared to manage student behavior. Secondly, although several universities in Australia and the United States use mixed-reality simulations in their pre-service teaching programs, few focus on classroom management.

In addition, the social validity of using MRSs in teacher preparation programs has not really been studied in the literature. Social validity refers to "the social significance of intervention goals, social acceptability of intervention procedures, and social importance of intervention effects. Social validity assessments can provide researchers with information that can inform revisions and refinements to interventions" (Common & Lane, 2017; p. 73). In our opinion, if our students did not find the simulations useful, there was no point in using them, so it was important to us to conduct action research as we implemented simulations via *SimLab* to support our students in practicing classroom management, more specifically de-escalating behavior in a safe environment with plenty of opportunities for feedback and reflection. The questions that guided the study were:

1. How does practicing classroom management skills in mixed-reality learning environments affect pre-service teachers' classroom management self-efficacy?
2. Is the practice of using mixed-reality learning environments to support pre-service teachers to develop their classroom management skills socially valid?

A mixed methods study, employing both quantitative and qualitative survey questions appeared to the authors to be the most appropriate means to answer the questions.

Procedures

After receiving ethics approval from our university's ethics committee, we invited students to participate in the study. All students in the undergraduate and postgraduate classroom management courses were required to participate in the simulations, however participation in the study was voluntary. Students that decided to participate clicked on a link to access the online survey and provided their consent online. In total, 26 students agreed to participate in the study.

The Norwegian Teacher Self-Efficacy Scale or NTSES (Skaalvik & Skaalvik, 2007) was used to examine the effects of the simulation on teacher self-efficacy, pre- and post-simulation. The post-test also contained open-ended questions to measure the social validity of the simulation activities. The original NTSES scale is a scale that measures self-efficacy across 6 domains within the teaching industry: (1) Instruction, (2) Adapt Instruction to Individual Needs, (3) Motivate students, (4) Maintain discipline, (5) Cooperate with colleagues and parents, and (6) Cope with change. For our study, only the Cope with Change domain was not measured, as it did not pertain to the simulations. Each domain consisted of 4 items, totaling 20 items overall. An overall instruction, "How certain are you that you can" was given and each item was rated on a 4-point Likert scale ranging from (1) not certain at all, to (4) absolutely certain.

To measure the social validity of the simulation, a modified version of the Social Validity questions (Carroll & St. Peter, 2014) was used as an open-ended questionnaire. The original open-ended questions were modified to focus specifically on the simulation. For example, "How do you feel about allowing students to choose which behavior support plan they will experience?" was changed to "How did you feel about using the simulation to practice de-escalating student behavior?" A total of 7 questions were asked to measure social validity.

SimLab

The researchers chose *SimLab,* (Murdoch University, n.d.) a mixed-reality simulation environment, as the most appropriate platform for their students, as it was cost-effective and readily available in Australia. *SimLab* uses Zoom as its online platform. It is an online classroom with five student avatars. The avatars are approximately middle school age, so can represent upper primary or lower high school students. A professional actor controls the student avatars' actions and vocalizations, giving each avatar a distinct personality representing different cultures and abilities. This happens in real time, providing a realistic classroom environment and individualized experience for each student teacher.

Students were instructed to prepare a 10-min lesson in their chosen subject area. They were also instructed to make the experience as realistic as possible, including dressing up as a teacher, using a whiteboard to teach the lesson, and treating the avatars as if they were real students. They were provided with profiles for each avatar that detailed their individual personalities and abilities, so they would know what to expect and how to approach each one. The sessions were designed to last 30 min, with two students attending each session, so they could observe each other's lessons and provide feedback after. They were given a time slot and a link to an online session conducted via Zoom. When they entered the session, they were facing a table with five student avatars (see Fig. 11.2).

Fig. 11.2 SimLab virtual classroom with student avatars

After they completed their lesson and provided feedback to their online partner, students were instructed to complete the online survey if they were willing to participate in the study.

The simulation scenarios were designed based on Colvin's Escalation Cycle (Colvin & Sugai, 2018). The scenarios were used for the students to practice methods of de-escalation while they taught a 10-min lesson. According to Colvin and Sugai (2018), there are 7 behavior escalation stages: (1) Calm, (2) Trigger, (3) Agitation, (4) Acceleration, (5) Peak, (6) De-Escalation and (7) Recovery. Due to the limitations of the simulation platform (students could not leave their seats, touch one another, throw things, etc.), each simulation scenario only escalated to the third stage, Agitation.

Results

A total of 26 teacher education students agreed to participate in the study. Of the 26 participants, seven did not complete the NTSES survey, so they were removed from the analysis.

Analyses of NTSES Post Simulation

To examine the teacher self-efficacy post simulation, frequency and descriptive analyses were conducted on the 5 domains.

The data were collated according to the 5 domains and the mean and standard deviations of the subgroups are as follows, Instruction (M = 11.74, SD = 1.37), Maintain Discipline (M = 9.89, SD = 2.72), Adapt Instruction to Individual Needs (M = 11.00, SD = 2.16), Motivate (M = 11.37, SD = 1.89), and Cooperate (M = 12.11, SD = 1.85). (see Table 11.1). We calculated Cronbach's alphas (α) of the NTSES subscales, and they ranged from acceptable to good, where Instruction $\alpha = 0.7$, Maintain Discipline $\alpha = 0.9$, Adapt Instruction to Individual Needs $\alpha = 0.9$, Motivate $\alpha = 0.8$ and Cooperate $\alpha = 0.8$.

Table 11.1 Descriptive statistics for NTSES domains

	N	*M*(SD)
NTSES domains		
Instruction	19	11.74 (1.37)
Maintain discipline	19	9.89 (2.72)
Adapt instruction to individual needs	19	11.00 (2.16)
Motivate	19	11.37 (1.89)
Cooperate with colleagues and parents	19	12.11 (1.85)

Instruction

In the instruction domain, 78.5% of the participants expressed feeling quite certain of their ability to explain complex themes in a manner accessible to even the low-achieving students. Additionally, 68.42% expressed feeling quite certain they could provide effective guidance and instruction to students of varying abilities. A note-worthy, 73.68% of participants reported feeling quite certain of their capacity to address students' questions. Finally, 78.95% of the participants felt quite certain they could explain the subject matter so that most of the students could understand the basic principles.

Adapt Instruction to Individual Needs

In the Adapt Instruction to Individual Needs domain, 73.68% of student participants felt quite certain they could organize schoolwork to adapt instruction and assignments to individual needs. Of the participants, 52.36% felt quite certain they could provide realistic challenges for all students, even in the mixed ability classes. 57.89% of the participants felt quite certain they could adapt instruction to the needs of the low ability students while they attend to the needs of the other students in the class. Finally, 57.89% of the participants felt quite certain they could organize classroom work so that both low and high ability students work with tasks that are adapted to their abilities.

Motivate

In the Motivate domain, 62.96% of the participants felt quite certain they could get all the students in class to work hard with their school work. 63.16% of the participants felt quite certain they could wake the desire to learn even among the students in the low achieving group. A significant, 73.68% of the participants felt quite certain they could get students to do their best when working with difficult problems. Finally, 68.42% of the participants felt quite certain they could motivate their students who show low interest in schoolwork.

Maintain Discipline

In the Maintain discipline domain, 47.37% of participants felt quite certain they could maintain discipline in any school class or group of students. 36.84% of the participants felt they were quite uncertain they could control even the most aggressive students. 44.44% of the participants felt they were quite uncertain they would get the students with behavioral problems to follow classroom rules. Lastly, 47.37% of the participants felt quite certain they could get all the students to behave politely and also respect the teachers.

Cooperate with Colleagues and Parents

In the Cooperate with colleagues and parents domain, 52.63% of the participants felt quite certain they could cooperate well with most parents and 73.68% of the participants felt quite certain they could find adequate solutions to conflict with other teachers. Next, 68.42% of the participants felt certain they could collaborate constructively with parents of students with behavioral problems. Finally, 68.42% of the participants felt quite certain they could cooperate effectively and constructively with other teachers, for example, teaching in teams.

Qualitative Analysis

The qualitative survey question responses were thematically analyzed (Braun & Clarke, 2006) using inductive coding to identify emerging themes relevant to the research questions. Coding began with multiple close readings of the data, which was then coded according to issues potentially relevant to the research questions (Clarke & Braun, 2017). The coded data was then grouped and synthesized according to overarching themes that they represented, allowing for the identification of four key themes: (a) benefits, (b) applications to future practice, (c) disadvantages, and (d) ways to improve.

Benefits

Students overall found participation in the simulation beneficial, with 14 students making comments about its effectiveness. One respondent clearly appreciated getting a sense of what managing a real classroom would feel like, when they commented, "I think it opens your eyes to how overwhelming behavioral management can become and the importance of de-escalating a situation." Others appreciated the authenticity of the simulation, using terms such as, "vivid simulation," "realistic situation," and the statement, "the low-level behaviors were authentic and the range of student personalities were realistic."

Student participants appreciated the fact that the simulations provided them with a safe place to practice the behavior support strategies they were learning in class. As one student put it, "It is awesome to be able to try these out without the stress of it being a live classroom." Another acknowledged that the experience was challenging but better in a simulated environment, as they learned, "My teaching was really affected by the disruptions and the behavior could have easily escalated."

Other benefits mentioned by student respondents included being able to collaborate with their peers and provide and receive feedback from them. Comments included, "instant response to the situation," and ".... there was someone else that I was completing the simulation with and the peer feedback." Students also felt that the technology was an advantage, as it allowed for interactive experience that was different every time.

Applications to Future Practice

Overall, students expressed that they could apply their learning from the simulations to their future practice. Many felt that participating in the simulation allowed them to be better prepared for various situations later. Several participants responded that they would remember the peer feedback they received and use it to improve in real situations. One student commented, "I will better respond with wisdom, experience, and strategy when I face different types of students in a real classroom."

Disadvantages

The majority of remarks about the disadvantages of simulations were related to the technology and its limitations. One aspiring music teacher felt that the scenario was difficult for their subject, as the students did not have instruments, etc. Other comments were about the limitations of Zoom, and the fact that the student avatars could not leave their seats. A few students realized that the online platform limited the nature of the management and de-escalation strategies they could implement: "I was unable to effectively use a range of strategies that I would in the classroom which I find effective with low level behavior management (eye contact, proximity supervision etc.)," and "There were some de-escalation skills that couldn't be practiced." Two participants mentioned that the student avatars were too rude and asked questions that they considered to be too personal.

Ideas for Improvement

When asked how the experience could be improved, a total of five students felt that no improvement was necessary. Others mentioned the timing of the simulations within the term and still others thought the simulation should have been longer. Students recommended more involvement of education professionals in both the controlling of the avatars and the provision of feedback. Interestingly, some students called for the avatars to display more challenging behaviors, while others would have preferred the avatars to be more polite and compliant.

Discussion

The results of the literature review and pilot study suggest some concrete positive aspects of using MRS in pre-service teacher education. They also highlighted some barriers to using simulations. These are discussed below, as well as limitations, implications for practice, and directions for future research.

Positives

The scenarios in MRS can be custom made for course requirements, and adapted for parent-teacher communication, student-specific disabilities, and co-teaching relationships (Luke & Vaughn, 2021; Spencer et al., 2019). In Australia, this facilitates a clear and direct link between the learning experiences enabled by MRS and the Australian Professional Standards for Teachers (Australian Institute for Teaching and School Leadership, 2017), specifically: (1) Know students and how they learn, (2) Know the content and how to teach it, (3) Plan for and implement effective teaching and learning, and (4) Create and maintain supportive and safe learning environments. MRS can support initial teacher education in preparing students to meet the Standards.

PSTs see the potential for MRS to increase their confidence, provide an environment to make mistakes without feeling guilty or overwhelmed, and improve their pedagogical skills (Dixon et al., 2019). When PSTs enter their practicums and early career teaching positions with the knowledge, experience, and confidence they gain from participating in the MRS, it reduces the burden to mentor teachers (Dixon et al., 2019) and can even be used to reduce practicum placement of PSTs in their junior years (Dixon et al., 2019). The PSTs in the current study felt that MRS is a socially valid way to practice their classroom management skills in a safe space.

Limitations and Barriers

Ledger et al. (2022) summarized the limitations of MRS as: (a) time & cost, (b) translating existing models to virtual worlds, (c) technical difficulties, (d) possible exposure to inappropriate content, (e) the necessity of learning how to navigate the virtual environment, (f) feeling anxiety and incompetence learning new technology, (g) issues with effective communication in a virtual space, and (h) students' acceptance (or reluctance) to learn in a virtual interface. The majority of these barriers can be addressed proactively once the Initial Teacher Education (ITE) provider is aware that they exist.

Perhaps the largest barrier, as it is mentioned often in the literature and also experienced in the pilot study, is that MRS is time and resource intensive (Cohen et al., 2020; Ledger et al., 2022). One solution to this would be to propose government funding of MRS in the education sector. Another solution may present itself in the development of generative AI to the point where the live interactor is no longer necessary.

Implications for Practice and Future Research

Right now, we are well-served to capitalize on AI technologies to prepare PSTs to manage challenging behaviors and establish productive classrooms. Exploring the research findings (including, but not limited to, those presented in this chapter) enables discussion of future directions for the use of AI in tertiary education. While MRS is arguably an effective and socially valid way to provide PSTs with teaching practice in a safe environment, there are cautions as well as implications for practice. As voiced by Samuelsson et al. (2022), MRS should be considered as preparation, support, or extension of practical classroom experience, not a substitute. While this form of experiential learning was especially welcomed during the global pandemic, it is but only one part of the authentic learning continuum.

Teacher educators must continuously "keep up" with the development of a variety of AI technologies. When considering the potential uses, one must also consider the ethics of using such technology (Southgate et al., 2018). It is important for educators to make themselves aware of the variety of frameworks and guidelines available for educators regarding the use of AI by both teachers and students to ensure transparent processes and accountability are in place at all levels of education.

The research around the affordances and effectiveness of MRS is still in its infancy. The literature reviewed in this chapter, as well as the pilot study highlight some areas that would benefit from future research. More research is necessary to explore how MRSs transfer to the actual classroom and whether the teaching, communication, and management skills learned in those environments are maintained. Future research could also address other areas of teaching practice, as well as how the MRS benefits teaching in specific subject areas. There is currently no research results available on the benefits of the number or length of practice sessions.

It would be beneficial for ITE providers to be able to access research into the effectiveness of MRS at different stages of the teaching degree and in career development, as in professional learning for in-service teachers, particularly when there are changes in school pedagogies, practices, or enrolments. Overall, the sparse number of publications in the area identified by Ledger et al. (2022) suggests more empirical studies are needed. In addition to the suggestions above, researchers will have to take the ever-changing development of AI into account.

Conclusion

The literature review outlines the great interest of simulations in mixed-reality learning environments on teacher education. The pilot study discussed in this chapter highlights the efficacy of these simulations in supporting pre-service teachers in developing essential skills, such as classroom management and de-escalation techniques. The integration of artificial intelligence technology in teacher training programs shows promise in addressing the challenges faced by educators and schools, especially when real-world training opportunities are limited.

Furthermore, the qualitative analysis of student responses underscores the benefits of simulation-based learning, providing a safe space for practicing behavior support strategies and gaining valuable insights into real classroom scenarios. The chapter emphasizes the importance of continuous professional development for teacher educators to stay abreast of AI technologies and ethical considerations in their implementation.

Looking ahead, future research is needed to explore the transferability of skills learned through mixed-reality simulations to actual classroom settings and to investigate the effectiveness of different teaching practices enhanced by AI technology. By leveraging the potential of AI technologies, teacher education programs can better prepare pre-service teachers to manage challenging behaviors, establish productive learning environments, and adapt to evolving pedagogical practices. This chapter sets the stage for further exploration and innovation in the use of artificial intelligence in tertiary education, paving the way for enhanced teacher training and student learning outcomes.

Competing Interests The authors have no conflicts of interest to declare that are relevant to the content of this chapter.

Ethics Approval This study was performed in line with the principles of the Declaration of Helsinki. Approval was granted by the Ethics Committee of the University of New South Wales (23 March 2023/HC230003). Informed consent to participate was obtained from individual participants.

References

Allen, D. W., & Eve, A. W. (1968). Microteaching. *Theory Into Practice, 7*(5), 181–185. https://doi.org/10.1080/00405846809542153

Allen, A. A., & Stecker, P. M. (2023). Using mixed-reality simulation in teacher preparation in reading. *Intervention in School and Clinic, 59*(1), 59–65. https://doi.org/10.1177/10534512221130077

Arthur, L., & Bradley, S. (2023). Teacher retention in challenging schools: Please don't say goodbye! *Teachers and Teaching, 29*(7–8), 753–771. https://doi.org/10.1080/13540602.2023.2201423

Australian Institute for Teaching and School Leadership. (2017). *Australian professional standards for teachers*. Retrieved from https://www.aitsl.edu.au/teach/standards

Bardach, L., Klassen, R. M., Durksen, T. L., Rushby, J. V., Bostwick, K. P., & Sheridan, L. (2021). The power of feedback and reflection: Testing an online scenario-based learning intervention for student teachers. *Computers & Education, 169*, 104194. https://doi.org/10.1016/j.compedu.2021.104194

Bates, A. W. (2015). *Teaching in a digital age: Guidelines for designing teaching and learning*. BCcampus. Retrieved from https://opentextbc.ca/teachinginadigitalage/chapter/section-8-1-a-short-history-of-educational-technology/

Bautista, N. U., & Boone, W. J. (2015). Exploring the impact of TeachME™ lab virtual classroom teaching simulation on early childhood education majors' self-efficacy beliefs. *Journal of Science Teacher Education, 26*(3), 237–262. https://doi.org/10.1007/s10972-014-9418-8

Braun, V., & Clarke, V. (2006). Using thematic analysis in psychology. *Qualitative Research in Psychology, 3*(2), 77–101. https://doi.org/10.1191/1478088706qp063oa

Carroll, R. A., & St. Peter, C. (2014). Methods for assessing social validity of behavioral intervention plans for children with attention deficit hyperactivity disorder. *Acta de Investigación Psicológica, 4*(3), 1642–1656.

Christensen, R., Knezek, G., Wood, T. T., & Gibson, D. (2011). simSchool: An online dynamic simulator for enhancing teacher preparation. *International Journal of Learning Technology, 6*(2), 201. https://doi.org/10.1504/IJLT.2011.042649

Clarke, V., & Braun, V. (2017). Thematic analysis. *The Journal of Positive Psychology, 12*(3), 297–298. https://doi.org/10.1080/17439760.2016.1262613

Cohen, J., Wong, V., Krishnamachari, A., & Berlin, R. (2020). Teacher coaching in a simulated environment. *Educational Evaluation and Policy Analysis, 42*(2), 208–231. https://doi.org/10.3102/0162373720906217

Colvin, G., & Sugai, G. (2018). *Seven stages of behavioral escalation: A preventive approach*. Pacific Northwest Publishing.

Common, E. A., & Lane, K. L. (2017). Social validity assessment. In J. K. Luiselli (Ed.), *Applied behavior analysis advanced guidebook: A manual for professional practice* (pp. 73–92). Elsevier Academic Press. https://doi.org/10.1016/B978-0-12-811122-2.00004-8

Cumming, T., Draper Rodriguez, C., & Strnadová, I. (2013). Aligning iPad applications with evidence-based practices in inclusive and special education. In S. Keengwe (Ed.), *Pedagogical applications and social effects of mobile technology integration* (pp. 55–78). IGI Global, IGI Global. https://doi.org/10.4018/978-1-4666-2985-1.ch004

Delamarre, A., Shernoff, E., Buche, C., Frazier, S., Gabbard, J., & Lisetti, C. (2021). The interactive virtual training for teachers (IVT-T) to practice classroom behavior management. *International Journal of Human-Computer Studies, 152*, 102646. https://doi.org/10.1016/j.ijhcs.2021.102646

Dixon, R., Hall, C., & Shawon, F. (2019). Using virtual reality and web conferencing technologies: Exploring alternatives for microteaching in a rural region. *Northwest Journal of Teacher Education, 14*(1). https://doi.org/10.15760/nwjte.2019.14.1.4

Donehower Paul, C., Bukaty, C. A., & Dieker, L. (2019). Teacher professional learning using simulation: A Delphi study. *Teacher Development, 24*(1), 21–32. https://doi.org/10.1080/13664530.2019.1694574

Ersozlu, Z., Ledger, S., Ersozlu, A., Mayne, F., & Wildy, H. (2021). Mixed-reality learning environments in teacher education: An analysis of TeachLivE™ research. *SAGE Open, 11*(3). https://doi.org/10.1177/21582440211032155

Fischetti, J., Ledger, S., Lynch, D., & Donnelly, D. (2022). Practice before practicum: Simulation in initial teacher education. *The Teacher Educator, 57*(2), 155–174. https://doi.org/10.1080/08878730.2021.1973167

Hirsch, S. E., Griffith, C. A., Kelley, M. H., Carlson, A., & McKown, G. (2023). Increasing preservice teachers' knowledge and skills using a mixed-reality simulator: The tale of two studies. *Teacher Education and Special Education, 46*(3), 204–222. https://doi.org/10.1177/08884064231154028

Hirtz, S. (2021). The history of instructional technology in education. In *Education for a digital world: Advice, guidelines, and effective practice from around the globe*. BCcampus. Retrieved from https://open.umn.edu/opentextbooks/textbooks/356

Johnston, V., & Collum, D. (2020). Understanding diversity and the educational needs of students with exceptionalities: A case study of simSchool. *International Journal of Smart Technology and Learning, 2*(2/3), 198–216. https://doi.org/10.1504/ijsmarttl.2020.112159

Landon-Hays, M., Peterson-Ahmad, M. B., & Frazier, A. D. (2020). Learning to teach: How a simulated learning environment can connect theory to practice in general and special education educator preparation programs. *Education Sciences, 10*(7), 184. https://doi.org/10.3390/educsci10070184

Larson, K. E., Hirsch, S. E., McGraw, J. P., & Bradshaw, C. P. (2020). Preparing preservice teachers to manage behavior problems in the classroom: The feasibility and acceptability of using a mixed-reality simulator. *Journal of Special Education Technology, 35*(2), 63–75. https://doi.org/10.1177/0162643419836415

Lave, J., & Wenger, E. (1991). *Situated learning: Legitimate peripheral participation*. Cambridge University Press. https://doi.org/10.1017/CBO9780511815355

Ledger, S., Burgess, M., Rappa, N., Power, B., Wong, K. W., Teo, T., & Hilliard, B. (2022). Simulation platforms in initial teacher education: Past practice informing future potentiality. *Computers & Education, 178*, 104385. https://doi.org/10.1016/j.compedu.2021.104385

Luke, S. E., & Vaughn, S. M. (2021). Embedding virtual simulation into a course to teach parent–teacher collaboration skills. *Intervention in School and Clinic, 57*(3), 182–188. https://doi.org/10.1177/10534512211014873

Luke, S. E., Ford, D., Vaughn, M., & Fulchini-Scruggs, A. (2021a). Using mixed reality simulation and roleplay to develop preservice teachers' metacognitive awareness. *Journal of Technology and Teacher Education, 29*(3), 389–413.

Luke, S. E., Ford, D. J., Vaughn, S. M., & Fulchini-Scruggs, A. (2021b). An online field experience using mixed reality virtual simulation. *Journal of Research on Technology in Education, 55*(2), 324–343. https://doi.org/10.1080/15391523.2021.1962452

Mikeska, J. N., Howell, H., Dieker, L., & Hynes, M. (2021). Understanding the role of simulations in K-12 mathematics and science teacher education: Outcomes from a teacher education simulation conference. *Contemporary Issues in Technology and Teacher Education, 21*(3), 781–812.

Murdoch University. (n.d.). *SimLab: A mixed reality learning environment for teaching preparation and professional learning*. Retrieved from https://www.murdoch.edu.au/pages/simlab

Mursion. (2025). The upskilling platform for a future-ready workforce. Retrieved from https://www.mursion.com

Rappa, N., & Ledger, S. (2022). Pre-service teachers' reflections on their challenging experiences interacting with a parent avatar: Insights on deepening reflection on the simulation experience. *Journal of Education for Teaching, 49*(2), 311–325. https://doi.org/10.1080/02607476.2022.2061339

Saltan, F., & Arslan, K. (2019). The new generation of interactive whiteboards: How students perceive and conceptualize. *Participatory Educational Research, 6*(2), 93–102. Retrieved from https://files.eric.ed.gov/fulltext/EJ1236334.pdf

Samuelsson, M., Samuelsson, J., & Thorsten, A. (2022). Simulation training-a boost for preservice teachers' efficacy beliefs. *Computers and Education Open, 3*, 100074. https://doi.org/10.1016/j.caeo.2022.100074

Sebastian, R., & Krishnamachari, A. (2023). Unlocking the potential of introduction to teaching courses through simulations. *Teaching and Teacher Education, 133*, 104276. https://doi.org/10.1016/j.tate.2023.104276

Skaalvik, E. M., & Skaalvik, S. (2007). Dimensions of teacher self-efficacy and relations with strain factors, perceived collective teacher efficacy, and teacher burnout. *Journal of Educational Psychology, 99*(3), 611–625. https://doi.org/10.1037/0022-0663.99.3.611

Southgate, E., Blackmore, K., Pieschl, S., Grimes, S., McGuire, J., & Smithers, K. (2018). *Artificial intelligence and emerging technologies (virtual, augmented and mixed reality) in schools: A research report*. University of Newcastle, Australia.

Spencer, S., Drescher, T., Sears, J., Scruggs, A. F., & Schreffler, J. (2019). Comparing the efficacy of virtual simulation to traditional classroom role-play. *Journal of Educational Computing Research, 57*(7), 1772–1785. https://doi.org/10.1177/0735633119855613

Walters, S. M., Hirsch, S. E., McKown, G., Carlson, A., & Allen, A. A. (2021). Mixed-reality simulation with preservice teacher candidates: A conceptual replication. *Teacher Education and Special Education, 44*(4), 340–355. https://doi.org/10.1177/08884064211001453

Therese M. Cumming is a Professor of Special Education and Deputy Head of School, Learning and Teaching at UNSW Sydney. She is also the Academic Lead Education at the UNSW Disability Innovation Institute and a Scientia Education Academy Fellow. Her teaching and research focus on promoting the use of evidence-based practices to support the learning and behavior of students with disabilities and the use of technology to create inclusive, accessible, and engaging learning environments.

Web of Science Researcher ID: A-9957-2010.

University of New South Wales: https://research.unsw.edu.au/people/professor-terry-cumming

Google Scholar: https://scholar.google.com.au/citations?user=yuTleRgAAAAJ

Research Gate: https://www.researchgate.net/profile/Therese-Cumming

Hee Min Lee (Ellen) is a Lecturer in Educational Psychology and Special Education at UNSW Sydney. Her teaching and research are centred around Cognitive Load Theory and particularly focused on applying Cognitive Load effects to support students with disabilities in a learning environment. She is also passionate about teaching Educational Psychology and Special and Inclusive Education to undergraduate and postgraduate students.

Web of Science Researcher ID: HSE-8951-2023

Research Gate: https://www.researchgate.net/profile/Hee-Min-Lee

Jordana F. Hoenig is an early-career researcher in Education at the University of New South Wales. Her school leadership and research focus on implementing diverse pedagogies and evidence-based practices to support students' development in primary, secondary, and tertiary education settings.

University of New South Wales: https://www.unsw.edu.au/hdr/jordana-hoenig

Research Gate: https://www.researchgate.net/profile/Jodie-Hoenig

Chapter 12
Generative AI Cascading Effect Framework for the Global South: Exposing Pedagogical Gaps in Teacher Education

Matthew Nyaaba

Abstract Using Ghana as a case study, this chapter proposes a conceptual framework positioning Generative Artificial Intelligence (GenAI) as a catalyst for transforming entrenched teacher education systems in the Global South. For decades, teacher preparation has been dominated by content-heavy instruction, a "content refuge" that masks persistent deficits in practical training, resource provision, and sustained professional development. The integration of GenAI offers the potential to strengthen content mastery to the extent that such avoidance strategies become untenable, compelling stakeholders, including lecturers, policy makers, and educational institutions, to confront their long-neglected responsibilities in delivering high-quality teacher education. The framework identifies eight interrelated domains through which GenAI could drive systemic change toward this goal: strengthening pedagogical modeling; improving resource acquisition; enhancing performance-based assessment; reducing resistance to change; advancing digital literacy; fostering critical thinking; promoting sustained professional development; and encouraging collaborative learning. If adopted strategically in teacher education, GenAI can help to achieve what decades of reform have failed to deliver due to implementation infidelity; producing teachers with demonstrable competencies who, in turn, will prepare students for the demands of the future workforce, close skills gaps, and reduce unemployment. These latent potentials, however, require intentional and well-structured integration of GenAI into teacher education systems. Future research should empirically evaluate GenAI's impact within each domain of the framework to generate context-specific evidence that can guide sustainable, equitable, and scalable integration across the Global South.

Keywords Ghana · Global South · Pedagogical modeling · Pre-service teachers

M. Nyaaba (✉)
University of Georgia, Athens, GA, USA
e-mail: matthew.nyaaba@uga.edu

G. Tchibozo (ed.), *International Perspectives of Generative AI in Education*, Advances in Artificial Intelligence in Education 3,
https://doi.org/10.1007/978-3-031-99804-1_12

Teacher education programs across Ghana and other parts of the Global South have long been trapped in a cycle of content-heavy instruction, despite decades of reforms aimed at holistic teacher preparation. In Ghana, the transformation from certificate to diploma and finally to 4-year bachelor's degree programs was designed to integrate pedagogical modeling, performance-based assessments, and practical skills development (Graham, 2013; Mpuangnan, 2020; T-TEL, 2017). Yet these reforms have largely failed to dislodge the entrenched "content refuge," an environment where teacher educators shield themselves from implementing challenging pedagogical innovations by defaulting to familiar lecture-based instruction (Adarkwah, 2021; Akyeampong, 2017a; Annan, 2020). This persistent focus on content delivery has allowed stakeholders to avoid addressing critical gaps in practical training and innovative pedagogies, viewing them as secondary to content acquisition (Melek & Schmidt-Crawford, 2024; Nketsia et al., 2020).

The implementation challenges are multifaceted and deeply rooted. Teacher educators often lack training and experience in innovative, learner-centered pedagogies, having themselves been trained under traditional systems emphasizing rote learning affect their capacity to practical teaching approaches (Antwi-Boampong, 2018; Darling-Hammond, 2016). Futhermore, the overwhelming course loads, large class sizes, and administrative burdens further constrain teacher educators' ability to implement interactive teaching methods (Annan, 2020; Gregory & Lodge, 2015). This is coupled with institutional resistance to change, coupled with cultures that prioritize content coverage over pedagogical innovation, compounds these challenges (Jost, 2015; Khosa & Makuvire, 2021). Additionally, many programs lack the resources and technological infrastructure necessary to support active, experiential learning (Asare & Nti, 2014; Mpuangnan, 2020; Nyaaba et al., 2021).

Many countries in the Global South (such as Ghana) adopted progressive approaches, including curriculum frameworks grounded in constructivist and experiential learning theories for their teacher education programs (Bada & Olusegun, 2015; Kolb et al., 2014). In these progressive approaches, emphasis was placed on core transferable skills including digital literacy, critical thinking, collaboration, and communication (Addae-Kyeremeh & Boateng, 2024; Schendel et al., 2023). Assessment approaches were largely situated within performance-based assessments, comprising portfolios (30%) and projects (30%) alongside traditional exams (40%), are designed to foster authentic learning (NTC, 2017; T-TEL, 2017). However, implementation remains superficial. The progressive elements are often undermined by traditional teaching methods, creating a disconnect between curriculum aspirations and classroom realities (Buabeng et al., 2020; Ntumi et al., 2023). This gap has produced graduates ill-equipped for modern teaching demands, widening the divide between education and industrial needs (Omoso & Odindo, 2020; Quansah et al., 2019).

The emergence of Generative AI (GenAI) presents an unprecedented disruption to this entrenched system. Recent studies demonstrate GenAI's potential in supporting content learning, lesson planning (see Chaps. 13, 14, and 18 of the present book), and resource generation (Lee & Zhai, 2024; Markos et al., 2024; Nyaaba et al., 2024a). This paper presents a framework suggesting how GenAI's support for content knowledge acquisition can trigger cascading effects across teacher education systems. When GenAI assumes responsibility to support content delivery, the traditional sanctuary of teacher educators, it dismantles the protective barrier that has allowed poor pedagogical practices to persist (Kasneci et al., 2023; Su & Yang, 2023). This technological disruption initiates a domino effect across eight interconnected domains: supporting content knowledge, promoting pedagogical modeling, facilitating performance-based assessments, reducing resistance to change, enhancing resource acquisition, encouraging digital literacy and critical thinking, supporting teacher professional development, and aligning teaching with industrial needs (Chen et al., 2024; Liang & Wu, 2024; Zhang & Zhang, 2024). As our framework illustrates, GenAI forces stakeholders to confront long-avoided responsibilities, potentially achieving the transformative change that policy reforms alone could not deliver.

Reforms of Initial Teacher Education in Ghana

The reform of initial teacher education in Ghana has been a gradual yet significant process, marked by a shift from certificate and diploma programs to a more comprehensive 4-year bachelor's degree (Graham, 2013; Mpuangnan, 2020; T-TEL, 2017). This transformation aimed to address inadequacies in the previous teacher education systems, which were heavily content driven with limited focus on practical pedagogical training. Under the former certificate programs, the emphasis was on rapidly preparing teachers to meet the growing demand for educators in basic schools (Addae-Kyeremeh & Boateng, 2024). However, the need for higher-quality education, more skilled teachers, and alignment with international standards led to the introduction of diploma programs and ultimately the 4-year degree (Addae-Kyeremeh & Boateng, 2024; Ntumi et al., 2023). The bachelor's degree program was designed to offer a more holistic approach to teacher preparation by integrating both content and pedagogy with extended periods of teaching practice, ensuring that PSTs develop the skills necessary for effective classroom teaching in diverse settings (Jiang, 2023).

This transition was formalized through the passage of the Colleges of Education Act 2012 (Act 847), which elevated the status of Colleges of Education to tertiary institutions (Buabeng et al., 2020; T-TEL, 2017). This legislative reform enabled these institutions to offer degree-level qualifications, marking a significant step forward from the previous diploma structure. The new 4-year program combines content courses, pedagogical training, and comprehensive practicum experiences, including both on-campus peer teaching and off-campus field practice (T-TEL,

2017). The primary objective is to ensure that PSTs graduate with both a deep understanding of subject matter and the practical skills needed to engage students effectively in modern classroom environments (Mpuangnan, 2021). However, challenges such as limited resources, resistance to change, and infrastructural deficits persist, impeding the full realization of the potential benefits of the 4-year degree program (Issaka et al., 2022; Kuyini & Mangope, 2011).

Theoretical Framework of Initial Teacher Training in Ghana

The theoretical framework underlying initial teacher training in Ghana is based on constructivist and experiential learning theories (Bada & Olusegun, 2015; Kolb et al., 2014). This framework emphasizes the development of reflective practitioners who can adapt to diverse classroom situations (Kolb et al., 2014). Constructivism serves as the foundation for the curriculum, highlighting the importance of active learning, where students construct their own understanding rather than passively receiving information. This focus on learner-centered pedagogies encourages PSTs to engage critically with content, challenge assumptions, and create meaning through hands-on activities and real-world teaching experiences (Shah, 2020). Kolb et al.'s (2014) theory of experiential learning further supports this approach by providing a structured model for learning through doing. The practicum and field placements embedded within the program give PSTs the opportunity to reflect on their experiences, refine their teaching practices based on feedback, and continuously improve their skills. Additionally, the integration of pedagogical content knowledge (PCK) ensures that teachers are not only experts in their subject areas but also skilled in delivering that content effectively in the classroom (Hu et al., 2024; Pinamang, 2016).

Core and Transferable Skills in Initial Teacher Training in Ghana

The 4-year initial teacher education program in Ghana places significant emphasis on the development of core and transferable skills. These essential competencies include digital literacy, critical thinking, collaboration, communication, personal development skills, respect for diversity, and accountability (Addae-Kyeremeh & Boateng, 2024; Mpuangnan, 2020). Integrated across the curriculum, these skills are designed to equip PSTs with tools to address cross-cutting issues such as equity and inclusion. For instance, digital literacy is promoted by offering opportunities for PSTs to engage with technology, surf the internet, and present their findings using modern digital tools (Ministry of Education, 2017; Quaicoe & Pata, 2020). This focus is crucial in ensuring that future educators can leverage technology to enhance learning in increasingly digital classroom environments.

Critical thinking is nurtured through reflective practices, data collection and analysis, enabling PSTs to develop problem-solving abilities essential for navigating complex teaching challenges (Asare & Nti, 2014; Schendel et al., 2023). Collaboration is encouraged through group projects and presentations, fostering teamwork and building positive relationships between schools and communities (Schendel et al., 2023). Communication skills, considered a vital component of effective teaching, are honed through activities that require PSTs to present, examine, and challenge misconceptions, as well as articulate their teaching philosophies (Asare & Nti, 2014; Schendel et al., 2023).

The program also highlights personal development and inquiry skills, particularly through action research, where PSTs learn to gather and analyze data, then initiate interventions tailored to the needs of individual learners or small groups. Respect for diversity and individual differences is reinforced through reflective practices that encourage PSTs to design inclusive interventions. Moreover, honesty and accountability are ingrained in the program, requiring PSTs to collect accurate data on learners and present findings responsibly. Together, these core and transferable skills form the foundation for developing educators who are not only proficient in pedagogy but also capable of adapting to the demands of a diverse and dynamic teaching profession.

Pedagogical Modeling

Pedagogical modeling refers to the practice where teacher educators demonstrate effective teaching strategies and techniques to PSTs, showing how educational theories can be translated into real classroom practice (Struyven et al., 2010; Swennen et al., 2008). In developing countries such as Ghana, this modeling is crucial as it equips future teachers with the skills and understanding needed to implement progressive teaching methods (Campbell et al., 2015). However, a significant challenge arises when teacher educators themselves rely on traditional, lecture-based approaches, despite promoting modern, student-centered strategies like multimedia integration and active learning (Struyven et al., 2010). This gap leaves PSTs with strong theoretical foundations but limited hands-on experience in applying these innovative methods in the classroom. Pedagogical modeling requires teacher educators to demonstrate how learner-centered approaches can be adapted to various teaching contexts, including resource-constrained environments (Ponet et al., 2023). The goal is to help PSTs to see the practical application of progressive teaching techniques, preparing them to create dynamic, engaging classrooms, which traditional methods might have undermined.

Performance-Based Assessment

Performance-based tasks are integral to assessing students' abilities by engaging them in practical activities such as projects, presentations, or portfolios (Buabeng et al., 2020; Elam, 1972). These assessments provide a more authentic measure of students' knowledge and skills, as they allow for the demonstration of real-world application and critical thinking, beyond what standardized tests can offer (Harris, 1997). In many developing countries, such as Ghana, while performance-based assessment is acknowledged in the education system, its implementation remains limited, particularly in teacher education programs (Asare & Nti, 2014; Mpuangnan, 2020). The only widely respected form of authentic performance-based assessment in these programs is the practicum or supported teaching in schools (STS), where PSTs are assessed on their ability to teach in actual classroom environments (Abdul-Karim et al., 2023; Otoo et al., 2021; T-TEL, 2017). Other forms of performance-based assessments are often underutilized, despite their potential to enhance the practical readiness of future teachers.

In the current reform in teacher education in Ghana, the three assessment components for each course largely emphasize performance-based assessments as follows: Continuous assessment based on a subject portfolio (30%) and a subject project (30%), supplemented by Summative assessment in the form of an end-of-semester exam (40%) (NTC, 2017). Subject portfolios are used to collect and showcase student teachers' best work, demonstrating their growth and providing evidence of their developing skills in relation to Course Learning Outcomes (CLO) and National Teaching Standards (NTS). Subject projects, on the other hand, offer opportunities for student teachers to engage deeply in real-world problems, fostering independent learning, collaboration, and cross-disciplinary understanding (NTC, 2017; T-TEL, 2017). The end-of-semester examinations assess both content and professional knowledge, ensuring standardized and equitable assessment practices across institutions (NTC, 2017). These comprehensive assessments aim to reduce the reliance on rote learning and enhance the quality of education delivered by future teachers (Ntumi et al., 2023).

Challenges Facing Pedagogical Modeling in Teacher Education

The implementation of pedagogical modeling in teacher education in developing countries faces substantial barriers that impede its effectiveness. Macro systemic and political challenges hamper efforts to integrate innovative teaching practices. Institutional factors also play a crucial role. This section explores the key institutional-level challenges, focusing on stakeholders such as teacher educators, whose practices and attitudes significantly influence the effectiveness of curriculum implementation.

Lack of Training and Experience in Innovative Pedagogies

A critical issue in the effective implementation of pedagogical modeling is the lack of training and experience among teacher educators in innovative, learner-centered pedagogies (Darling-Hammond, 2016). Many educators in Ghana were themselves trained under traditional, lecture-based systems that emphasized rote learning over interactive pedagogy (Akyeampong, 2017b; Annan, 2020). While reforms in Ghana have introduced new teacher education programs, transitioning from certificate to diploma and degree qualifications, these changes have not fully addressed the gaps in experiential training due to the lack of practical teaching abilities by teacher educators (Antwi-Boampong, 2018). Most teacher educators continue to rely on outdated methods, limiting the opportunities for PSTs to observe or practice innovative, inclusive, and learner-centered teaching techniques (Adarkwah, 2021; Nketsia et al., 2020). As a result, the disconnect between theoretical concepts and practical classroom applications remains a significant challenge, despite reforms aimed at promoting pedagogical modeling.

High Course Loads and Limited Time

Another barrier to pedagogical modeling is the overwhelming course loads, large class sizes, and limited time available to teacher educators (Gregory & Lodge, 2015). In Ghana, many teacher educators often manage large class sizes and are burdened with administrative duties of marking and grading, research expectations, and community engagements (Annan, 2020; Gregory & Lodge, 2015). These demands make it difficult for educators to dedicate the necessary time and effort to implement interactive, experiential teaching methods and performance-based assessments (Asare & Nti, 2014). The pressure to cover extensive material in a limited time often leads teacher educators to default to lecture-based instruction (Buabeng et al., 2020). Consequently, PSTs graduate with a strong theoretical foundation but limited hands-on experience in applying student-centered teaching practices which eventually affect K-12 students.

Resistance to Change and Institutional Culture

Resistance to change is a significant obstacle in the adoption of pedagogical modeling (Jost, 2015). In many cases, both teacher educators and institutions are reluctant to fully embrace innovative, learner-centered approaches. In Ghana, while this could partly be attributed to infrastructure deficit, the traditional attitudes toward education remain prevalent, with a continued focus on content delivery and standardized examination results (Antwi-Boampong, 2018). Teacher educators who have not received sufficient professional development in innovative teaching methods may feel uncomfortable with or resistant to adopting these practices. Institutional cultures that prioritize efficiency, research output, and content coverage over pedagogical innovation further compound this resistance (Khosa & Makuvire, 2021).

Lack of Resources and Infrastructure

The lack of access to resources and infrastructure is another challenge that affects the implementation of pedagogical modeling in Ghana. Many teacher education programs are under-resourced, lacking the necessary tools, materials, and technological infrastructure to support active, experiential learning (Asare & Nti, 2014; Mpuangnan, 2020). Digital resources such as smart boards or learning management systems are often absent, limiting opportunities for educators to create engaging, hands-on learning experiences (Aboyinga & Nyaaba, 2020).

Recent Studies on Generative AI in Teacher Education

Recent studies on the integration of GenAI in teacher education have explored its use, benefits, and challenges, particularly from the perspective of PSTs. Markos et al. (2024) investigated the perceptions of 257 PSTs in Greece, focusing on GenAI strengths, weaknesses, opportunities, and threats. The findings revealed that while PSTs viewed GenAI as a valuable tool for self-directed learning and content support, concerns were raised about accuracy and the potential for over-reliance on GenAI tools. Nyaaba et al.'s (2024a) study in Ghana with 167 PSTs highlights the positive perceptions of GenAI among PSTs. They use it as a learning tool that improves their content knowledge, assists in lesson planning, and enhances access to teaching resources. Lee and Zhai (2024) explored how 29 PSTs integrated ChatGPT into science lesson plans, identifying its diverse applications across domains like Biology, Chemistry, and Earth Science. Although the lesson plans scored well on an AI-technological pedagogical and content knowledge (AI-TPACK) rubric, the study noted the underutilization of ChatGPT's full capabilities and improper use of AI-generated information.

In addition to student perceptions, teacher educators have shown increasing interest in integrating GenAI into their instructional practices. Another study by Nyaaba and Zhaı (2024) examined the professional development needs of teacher educators in Ghana, which revealed varying levels of familiarity with GenAI tools by teacher educators. The teacher educators acknowledged GenAI's potential in grading and generating classroom materials. Challenges such as high costs, limited training, and ethical concerns hindered widespread adoption. These studies collectively emphasize that GenAI has potential roles in transforming teacher education programs particularly in developing countries.

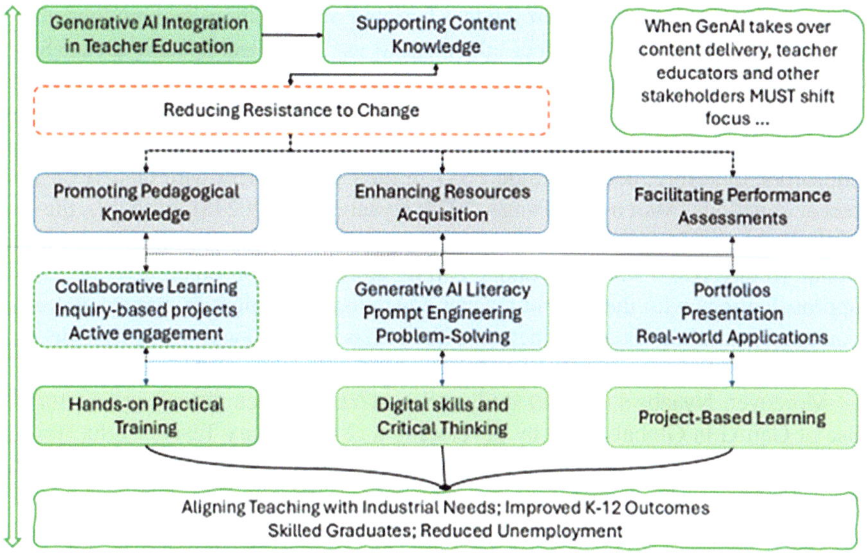

Fig. 12.1 The cascading effect of generative AI's role in transforming teacher education in the Global South

Role of Generative AI: The Cascading Effect Framework

In this study, GenAI's role is defined as both direct and indirect in the transformation of the teacher training system, which has traditionally been limited by content-heavy instruction, resistance to innovative pedagogies, and insufficient emphasis on pedagogical modeling and performance-based assessments. The term "cascading effects" refers to a chain reaction where one initial change (GenAI's support for content knowledge) triggers subsequent transformations across multiple interconnected domains, with each change reinforcing and amplifying the others. The framework presented here (See Fig. 12.1) demonstrates how GenAI's direct support for content knowledge serves as the catalyst that dismantles the "content refuge," triggering these cascading effects across eight interconnected domains.

Supporting Content Knowledge

Research has shown that GenAI is highly capable of supporting content-based learning while facilitating personalized learning experiences. GenAI has the potential to efficiently synthesize content, offering the opportunity to reduce reliance on static, restrictive materials. Pre-service teachers are increasingly turning to tools like ChatGPT to help with their content learning and teaching, making these tools valuable supplements for teacher educators to use in subject-specific areas (Su & Yang, 2023). For instance, a study by Kasneci et al. (2023) indicates that GenAI can effectively support PSTs in content knowledge acquisition and task development. However, careful oversight is required to ensure high-quality outcomes. Teacher educators, therefore, need to guide PSTs in their engagement with GenAI on content acquisitions (Marengo & Pange, 2024; Nyaaba et al., 2024a). With this, the role of the teacher educator evolves into that of a facilitator, moving away from traditional lecture-based teaching and creating more time for other activities. This approach aligns with the current teacher education curriculum in many developing countries including Ghana, where the focus has shifted away from rigid lecture notes or pamphlets towards lesson plans and digital inquiry (T-TEL, 2017).

Moreover, Nyaaba's (2025a) study emphasizes strong empirical support for the use of GenAI in Global South by developing a '21st Century Teacher Educator for Ghana GPT' for use by Ghanaians. This customized tool demonstrates that GenAI transformation can respect and incorporate local contexts through a glocalized design approach that integrates indigenous languages including *Twi*, *Dagbani*, *Mampruli*, and *Dagaare*, alongside culturally relevant pedagogical examples. This evidence suggests that breaking the content refuge through GenAI implementation need not result in cultural erasure or the imposition of Western pedagogical models.

Promoting Pedagogical Modeling

The potential of GenAI to support content knowledge also allows teacher educators to spend less time on direct content instruction and more time on pedagogical modeling. This is particularly important in countries such as Ghana, where the education system has historically focused on lecturing, often at the expense of hands-on, practical training (Addae-Kyeremeh & Boateng, 2024; Annan-Brew & Arhin, 2022). With GenAI supporting content delivery tasks, teacher educators can shift their focus toward demonstrating how to teach effectively through practical applications. Practical activities such as collaborative learning, inquiry-based projects, and other pedagogical modeling as enshrined in the teacher education curriculum could be realized (Kolb et al., 2014; Wu et al., 2024). When teacher educators have the opportunity to show PSTs how to engage students in active learning, critical thinking, and problem-solving activities; they prepare PSTs to meet the challenges of the modern classroom (NTC, 2017).

Reducing Resistance to Change

One of the significant challenges in teacher education is the persistence of dominant teaching practices, with educators often resisting pedagogical change (Jost, 2015). As GenAI supports content delivery, teacher educators will have little choice but to engage with other essential aspects of teaching, particularly those related to practical application and modeling, which have previously been neglected (Addae-Kyeremeh & Boateng, 2024). This is because the dominant teaching practices centered on content delivery will lose their value. If students can easily acquire content knowledge outside of the classroom through GenAI, the focus of in-class teaching must shift towards practical and hands-on learning, such as pedagogical modeling. This will become a critical component of teacher education, as students will seek out classes not for content repetition, but for the skills and strategies they can only gain through active modeling and engagement.

Facilitating Performance-Based Assessments

Standardized testing has long dominated teacher education (Angrist & Guryan, 2004; Nyaaba, 2025b; Rimfeld et al., 2019). With the influence of GenAI on content-based learning, teacher educators will no longer have the option to rely solely on lecture-driven teaching, pushing them toward a more practical and culturally responsive assessment (Nyaaba et al., 2024b). This shift will naturally lead to a rethinking of assessment strategies, moving away from standardized testing and toward performance-based assessments, as recommended in the curriculum. For example, teachers may focus more on project-based assessments, portfolios, and presentations which align with student-centered, practical learning approaches (NTC, 2017; T-TEL, 2017). This transformation will better prepare PSTs for the realities of modern classrooms, where practical application and performance are key to student success.

Enhancing Resources Acquisition

As teachers move away from delivering content that can easily be accessed through GenAI, they will need to enrich their teaching practices through practical and modeling approaches. As posited by Singh and Hiran (2022), GenAI offers significant benefits in higher education by providing flexible learning opportunities for students, and personalized feedback on assessments. This shift will potentially encourage teacher educators to actively seek out and incorporate diverse resources and materials that enhance learning in more dynamic ways (Nyaaba et al., 2024b). This is to say, teacher educators will be compelled to explore appropriate resources to support the interactive and experiential components of their classes, moving beyond just content delivery to creating more engaging and hands-on learning environments. Moreover, Li et al.'s (2024) study pointed out that GenAI can possibly assist teacher educators by automating and aligning Open Educational Resources (OER) for their lessons, thus reducing the manual effort of searching for teaching resources. With reference to GenAI reducing the burden of content delivery, teachers will no longer be able to avoid focusing on the practical aspects of their teaching, and the need for suitable teaching materials and resources will become more pronounced. This shift will push educators and institutions to address any gaps, ensuring that classrooms are well-equipped for modern, resource-rich teaching and learning experiences.

Encouraging Digital Literacy and Critical Thinking

Generative AI can play a crucial role in fostering digital literacy and critical thinking skills among PSTs. For instance, Zhang and Zhang's (2024) study highlight the role of GenAI in improving digital literacy and critical thinking. As GenAI becomes more integrated into teacher education programs, it will encourage PSTs to engage with digital tools and resources, enhancing their ability to navigate and use technology effectively in their learning and teaching. Moreover, Suriano et al. (2025) demonstrate that PSTs interaction with GenAI can reinforce complex critical thinking and problem-solving skills. Furthermore, teacher educators can also use GenAI to create scenarios or problems that require PSTs to analyze, evaluate, and apply their knowledge to solve real-world challenges (Liang & Wu, 2024). In contexts such as Ghana, this role of GenAI will foster the digital literacy and critical skills components enshrined in the teacher education curriculum through GenAI literacy and prompt engineering.

Aligning Teaching with Industrial Needs

The potential long-term impact of these changes on the education system should not be underestimated. As PSTs become more confident in applying their knowledge and skills through pedagogical modeling and practical teaching, they will be more motivated to teach and engage their students in meaningful ways (Omoso & Odindo, 2020). As decisions around incorporating GenAI into teacher education are made, equipping teachers with the right tools and approaches, the education system will help address key challenges like the lack of skilled personnel and unemployment. For example, Quansah et al.'s (2019) study on the gap between academia and industry in Ghana highlights that most graduates felt inadequately prepared with practical skills, as their education focused primarily on memorization and passing exams, rather than experiential learning. This study underscores the pressing need for a transformative teacher education program that will prioritize relevant, hands-on skills that meet job market demands. GenAI's role in supporting content delivery has a cascading effect of this change that will lead to improved K-12 student learning outcomes and greater alignment between teacher education and societal and industrial needs. Over time, these improvements will ensure that teacher education programs remain responsive to the evolving needs of both students and the workforce, addressing challenges such as unemployment and skills gaps.

Supporting Teacher Professional Development

Generative AI has the potential to significantly enhance teacher professional development (PD), foster continuous growth and innovation in teaching methods. In the context of Ghana, where the new curriculum has established PD sessions aimed at improving teaching practices, the effectiveness of these sessions has often been limited due to factors such as time constraints, lack of resources, and the traditional focus on content delivery. Teacher professional development needs to be strengthened in Ghana (Akyeampong, 2017a; Sambo, 2020). Siminto et al.'s (2023) study shows that GenAI can serve as a valuable tool in enhancing teacher educators' professionalism by offering quick access to educational resources, providing training recommendations, facilitating collaboration in teaching planning and aiding teacher educators in accessing real-time information and planning. GenAI can help create a more self-directed PD model, where teacher educators are not solely reliant on scheduled sessions but can engage with learning tools at their own pace (Chen et al., 2024). Moreover, the impact will extend to strengthening the core purpose of PD sessions, encouraging teacher educators and institutions to take these sessions more seriously and invest in their professional growth.

Conclusion and Recommendations

This study presented a framework showing how GenAI can trigger cascading transformations in teacher education across the Global South, particularly in Ghana, where content-heavy instruction has served as a refuge from pedagogical reform. The framework reveals how GenAI's support for content knowledge acquisition can dismantle the protective barrier that has allowed teacher educators and stakeholders to avoid implementing challenging pedagogical practices despite decades of reform attempts. By assuming responsibility for content delivery, GenAI eliminates the option to default to lecture-based methods, compelling stakeholders to confront long-neglected responsibilities across eight interconnected domains: pedagogical modeling, performance-based assessments, resource acquisition, resistance to change, digital literacy, critical thinking, professional development, and industrial alignment.

The cascading effects identified in this framework suggest that when content delivery ceases to be an escape route, teacher educators must redirect their efforts toward hands-on training, collaborative learning, and authentic assessments, precisely the practices that policy reforms have failed to implement. This shift of accountability mechanism promises to break the cycle of producing teachers with limited classroom-ready skills, ultimately improving K-12 learning outcomes and addressing the persistent gap between education and industrial needs. Successful implementation of this framework requires coordinated action across multiple levels. Teacher education institutions must prepare for this fundamental shift by developing policies and infrastructure that support hands-on learning rather than the excessive lectures. Teacher educators need intensive, practical professional development that goes beyond workshops to help them master GenAI critical literacy, pedagogical modeling, project design, and authentic assessment through experiential learning. Also, a clear guideline for GenAI integration is needed to support preservice teachers responsible for GenAI use, effective prompt writing and critical evaluation of GenAI outputs. This study lays the groundwork for future empirical research to evaluate GenAI's impact within each domain of the framework, generating contextspecific evidence to inform sustainable, equitable, and scalable integration across the Global South.

Competing Interests The author has no conflicts of interest to declare that are relevant to the content of this chapter.

References

Abdul-Karim, H., Yakubu, S., & Salifu, Z. S. (2023). The attitude of mentees of Gambaga College of Education and their mentors towards the Supported Teaching in Schools (STS) Programme. *Teacher Education and Curriculum Studies, 8*(2), 109–116.

Aboyinga, J., & Nyaaba, M. (2020). Factors that ensure motivation in virtual learning among college of education students in Ghana: The emergency remote teaching (ERT) during Covid'19 pandemic. *European Journal of Research and Reflection in Educational Sciences, 8*(9), 1–9.

Adarkwah, M. A. (2021). "I'm not against online teaching, but what about us?": ICT in Ghana post Covid-19. *Education and Information Technologies, 26*(2), 1665–1685.

Addae-Kyeremeh, E., & Boateng, F. (2024). New national teacher education curriculum in Ghana: Successes and challenges. In M. M. C. Shohel & A. Mortby (Eds.), *Practitioner research in college-based education* (pp. 233–266). IGI Global.

Akyeampong, K. (2017a). Learning to teach in Ghana: Lessons from institution-based teacher education for the African context. In I. M. Akiba & G. K. LeTendre (Eds.), *International handbook of teacher quality and policy* (pp. 478–491). Routledge.

Akyeampong, K. (2017b). Teacher educators' practice and vision of good teaching in teacher education reform context in Ghana. *Educational Researcher, 46*(4), 194–203.

Angrist, J. D., & Guryan, J. (2004). Teacher testing, teacher education, and teacher characteristics. *American Economic Review, 94*(2), 241–246.

Annan, J. K. (2020). Preparing globally competent teachers: A paradigm shift for teacher education in Ghana. *Education Research International, 2020*, 8841653. https://doi.org/10.1155/2020/8841653

Annan-Brew, R., & Arhin, D. (2022). Perceived challenges faced by student-teachers (prospective teachers) from universities and colleges in Ghana during off-campus teaching practice. *Journal of Advances in Education and Philosophy, 6*(9), 498–505.

Antwi-Boampong, A. (2018). Faculty perspectives on barriers of blended-learning adoption: A Ghana technology university college case study. In *Edulearn18 Proceedings* (pp. 9352–9361).

Asare, K. B., & Nti, S. K. (2014). Teacher education in Ghana: A contemporary synopsis and matters arising. *SAGE Open, 4*(2). https://doi.org/10.1177/2158244014529781

Bada, S. O., & Olusegun, S. (2015). Constructivism learning theory: A paradigm for teaching and learning. *Journal of Research & Method in Education, 5*(6), 66–70.

Buabeng, I., Ntow, F. D., & Otami, C. D. (2020). Teacher education in Ghana: Policies and practices. *Journal of Curriculum and Teaching, 9*(1), 86–95.

Campbell, T., Oh, P. S., Maughn, M., Kiriazis, N., & Zuwallack, R. (2015). A review of modeling pedagogies: Pedagogical functions, discursive acts, and technology in modeling instruction. *Eurasia Journal of Mathematics, Science and Technology Education, 11*(1), 159–176.

Chen, E., Lee, J. E., Lin, J., & Koedinger, K. (2024). GPTutor: Great Personalized Tutor with large language models for personalized learning content generation. In *Proceedings of the Eleventh ACM Conference on Learning@Scale, Atlanta, GA*.

Darling-Hammond, L. (2016). Research on teaching and teacher education and its influences on policy and practice. *Educational Researcher, 45*(2), 83–91.

Elam, S. (1972). Performance-based teacher education: What is the state of the art? *Quest, 18*(1), 14–19. https://doi.org/10.1080/00336297.1972.10519731

Graham, C. K. (2013). *The history of education in Ghana: From the earliest times to the declaration of independence*. Routledge.

Gregory, M. S.-J., & Lodge, J. M. (2015). Academic workload: The silent barrier to the implementation of technology-enhanced learning strategies in higher education. *Distance Education, 36*(2), 210–230.

Harris, L. B. (1997). *Using performance-based assessment to improve teacher education*. Paper presented at the Annual Meeting of the Association of Teacher Educators (77th, Washington, DC, February 15–17, 1997).

Hu, B., Zheng, L., Zhu, J., Ding, L., Wang, Y., & Gu, X. (2024). Teaching plan generation and evaluation with GPT-4: Unleashing the potential of LLM in instructional design. *IEEE Transactions on Learning Technologies, 17*, 1471–1485. https://doi.org/10.1109/TLT.2024.3384765

Issaka, C. A., Nyaaba, M., & Iddrisu, F. A. (2022). Attitudes and concerns of pre-service teachers' about inclusive education enshrined in the new four-year basic education curriculum in Ghana. *European Journal of Education and Pedagogy, 3*(1), 89–94.

Jiang, A. (2023). Developing teachers with global capabilities: A paradigm shift in teacher education in Ghana. *Journal of Theory and Practice of Contemporary Education, 3*(10), 9–15.

Jost, J. T. (2015). Resistance to change: A social psychological perspective. *Social Research: An International Quarterly, 82*(3), 607–636.

Kasneci, E., Seßler, K., Küchemann, S., Bannert, M., Dementieva, D., Fischer, F., Gasser, U., Groh, G.L., Günnemann, S., Hüllermeier, E., Krusche, S., Kutyniok, G., Michaeli, T., Nerdel, C., Pfeffer, J., Poquet, O., Sailer, M., Schmidt, A., Seidel, T., …, & Kasneci, G. (2023). ChatGPT for good? On opportunities and challenges of large language models for education. *Learning and Individual Differences, 103*, 102274. https://doi.org/10.1016/j.lindif.2023.102274

Khosa, M. T., & Makuvire, C. (2021). Barriers to the effective curriculum implementation: Secondary school teachers speak out. *IJO–International Journal of Educational Research, 4*, 41–60.

Kolb, D. A., Boyatzis, R. E., & Mainemelis, C. (2014). Experiential learning theory: Previous research and new directions. In R. J. Sternberg & L. Zhang (Eds.), *Perspectives on thinking, learning, and cognitive styles* (pp. 227–247). Routledge.

Kuyini, A. B., & Mangope, B. (2011). Student teachers' attitudes and concerns about inclusive education in Ghana and Botswana. *International Journal of Whole Schooling, 7*(1), 20–37.

Lee, G.-G., & Zhai, X. (2024). Using ChatGPT for science learning: A study on pre-service teachers' lesson planning. *IEEE Transactions on Learning Technologies, 17*, 1683–1700. https://doi.org/10.1109/TLT.2024.3401457

Li, Z., Pardos, Z. A., & Ren, C. (2024). Aligning open educational resources to new taxonomies: How AI technologies can help and in which scenarios. *Computers & Education, 216*, 105027. https://doi.org/10.1016/j.compedu.2024.105027

Liang, W., & Wu, Y. (2024). Exploring the use of ChatGPT to foster EFL learners' critical thinking skills from a post-humanist perspective. *Thinking Skills and Creativity, 54*, 101645.

Marengo, A., & Pange, P. J. (2024). Envisioning general AI in higher education: Transforming learning paradigms and pedagogies. In D. Guralnick, M. E. Auer, & A. Poce (Eds.), *Creative approaches to technology-enhanced learning for the workplace and higher education*. Springer.

Markos, A., Prentzas, J., & Sidiropoulou, M. (2024). Pre-service teachers' assessment of chatgpt's utility in higher education: Swot and content analysis. *Electronics, 13*(10), 1985. https://doi.org/10.3390/electronics13101985

Melek, Z., & Schmidt-Crawford, D. (2024). GenAI in teacher education: Teacher educators' views on AI in pre-service teacher education. In J. Cohen & G. Solano (Eds.), *Proceedings of Society for Information Technology & Teacher Education International Conference* (pp. 817–825). Association for the Advancement of Computing in Education (AACE).

Ministry of Education. (2017). *National teacher education curriculum framework: The essential elements of initial teacher education*. Accra.

Mpuangnan, K. N. (2020). Trends in the development of Ghanaian teacher education. In K. Pushpanadham (Ed.), *Teacher education in the global era* (pp. 239–255). Springer. https://doi.org/10.1007/978-981-15-4008-0_15

Mpuangnan, K. N. (2021). *Evaluation of basic teacher education curriculum in Ghana* (Doctoral Dissertation. Maharaja Sayajirao University of Baroda (India)).

Nketsia, W., Opoku, M. P., Saloviita, T., & Tracey, D. (2020). Teacher educators' and teacher trainees' perspective on teacher training for sustainable development. *Journal of Teacher Education for Sustainability, 22*(1), 49–65.

NTC. (2017). *National teacher's standards for Ghana—Guidelines*. Ministry of Education. https://ntc.gov.gh/wp-content/uploads/2021/12/NTS.pdf

Ntumi, S., Agbenyo, S., Tetteh, A., Yalley, C. E., Yeboah, A., & Nimo, D. G. (2023). Teacher preparedness and implementation of the national pre-tertiary education curriculum framework in Ghana. *Journal of Educational Research and Practice, 13*(1), 251–269.

Nyaaba, M. (2025a). Glocalizing generative AI in education for the Global South: The design case of 21st Century Teacher Educator AI for Ghana. *arXiv preprint arXiv:2504.07149*.

Nyaaba, M. (2025b). A framework for automated assessment item generation using generative AI. In *2025 AAAS Annual Meeting*. https://aaas.confex.com/aaas/2025/meetingapp.cgi/Paper/34727

Nyaaba, M., & Zhai, X. (2024). Generative AI professional development needs for teacher educators. *Journal of AI, 8*(1), 1–13.

Nyaaba, M., Aboyinga, J., & Akanzire, B. N. (2021). Pre-service parents teachers' attitude and perceived challenges about inclusive education in Ghana: The Ghanaian Inclusive Education Policy. *American Journal of Educational Research, 9*(6), 341–346. https://doi.org/10.12691/education-9-6-3

Nyaaba, M., Shi, L., Nabang, M., Zhai, X., Kyeremeh, P., Ayoberd, S. A., & Akanzire, B. N. (2024a). Generative AI as a learning buddy and teaching assistant: Pre-service teachers' uses and attitudes. *arXiv preprint arXiv:2407.11983*.

Nyaaba, M., Zhai, X., & Faison, M. Z. (2024b). Generative AI for culturally responsive science assessment: A conceptual framework. *Education Sciences, 14*(12), 1325. https://doi.org/10.3390/educsci14121325

Omoso, E., & Odindo, F. (2020). TPACK in teacher education: Using pre-service teachers' self-reported TPACK to improve pedagogic practice. *International Journal of Education and Research, 8*(5), 125–138. https://www.ijern.com/journal/2020/May-2020/12.pdf

Otoo, A. K., Kwarteng, P., Eshun, I., & Bordoh, A. (2021). Social studies teacher-trainees' competencies in supported teaching in schools in the central region of Ghana. *Journal of Social Sciences and Humanities, 7*(3), 187–195.

Pinamang, I. (2016). *Pre-service teachers' content knowledge (CK) and pedagogical content knowledge (PCK) in teaching geometric transformation* (Master's Thesis submitted to the University of Education, Winneba).

Ponet, B., Vantieghem, W., Tack, H., & Vanderlinde, R. (2023). 'Let's teach as we preach': The design of a professional development initiative to support teacher educators' responsiveness to diversity. *Education Sciences, 13*(7), 755. https://doi.org/10.3390/educsci13070755

Quaicoe, J. S., & Pata, K. (2020). Teachers' digital literacy and digital activity as digital divide components among basic schools in Ghana. *Education and Information Technologies, 25*(5), 4077–4095.

Quansah, F., Ankoma-Sey, V. R., & Asamoah, D. (2019). The gap between the academia and industry: Perspectives of university graduates in Ghana. *International Journal of Education and Research, 7*(3), 63–72.

Rimfeld, K., Malanchini, M., Hannigan, L. J., Dale, P. S., Allen, R., Hart, S. A., & Plomin, R. (2019). Teacher assessments during compulsory education are as reliable, stable and heritable as standardized test scores. *Journal of Child Psychology and Psychiatry, 60*(12), 1278–1288.

Sambo, B. I. (2020). Myths and realities about early childhood education: A case study of early childhood education in Kano municipal, Kano state, Nigeria. *Journal of Teaching and Teacher Education, 8*(1), 67–77.

Schendel, R., McCowan, T., Rolleston, C., Adu-Yeboah, C., Omingo, M., & Tabulawa, R. (2023). Pedagogies for critical thinking at universities in Kenya, Ghana and Botswana: The importance of a collective 'teaching culture. *Teaching in Higher Education, 28*(4), 717–738.

Shah, R. K. (2020). Concepts of learner-centred teaching. *Shanlax International Journal of Education, 8*(3), 45–60. https://doi.org/10.34293/education.v8i3.2926

Siminto, S., Sri Dewi, L., & Suhari, M. (2023). Teacher professionalism development strategy through ChatGPT support in the context of education management. *Journal of Contemporary Administration and Management, 1*(3), 150–155. https://doi.org/10.61100/adman.v1i3.65

Singh, S. V., & Hiran, K. K. (2022). The impact of AI on teaching and learning in higher education technology. *Journal of Higher Education Theory and Practice, 22*(13). https://doi.org/10.33423/jhetp.v22i13.5514

Struyven, K., Dochy, F., & Janssens, S. (2010). 'Teach as you preach': The effects of student-centred versus lecture-based teaching on student teachers' approaches to teaching. *European Journal of Teacher Education, 33*(1), 43–64.

Su, J., & Yang, W. (2023). Unlocking the power of ChatGPT: A framework for applying generative AI in education. *ECNU Review of Education*, 20965311231168423.

Suriano, R., Plebe, A., Acciai, A., & Fabio, R. A. (2025). Student interaction with ChatGPT can promote complex critical thinking skills. *Learning and Instruction, 95*, 102011.

Swennen, A., Lunenberg, M., & Korthagen, F. (2008). Preach what you teach! Teacher educators and congruent teaching. *Teachers and Teaching, 14*(5–6), 531–542.

T-TEL. (2017). *National teacher education curriculum framework*. https://t-tel.org/download/national-teacher-education-curriculum-framework/

Wu, D., Zhang, S. L., Ma, Z. Y., Yue, X. G., & Dong, R. K. (2024). Unlocking potential: Key factors shaping undergraduate self-directed learning in AI-enhanced educational environments. *Systems, 12*(9), 332. https://doi.org/10.3390/systems12090332

Zhang, J., & Zhang, Z. (2024). AI in teacher education: Unlocking new dimensions in teaching support, inclusive learning, and digital literacy. *Journal of Computer Assisted Learning, 40*(4), 1871–1885.

Matthew Nyaaba is a Ph.D. candidate in the Department of Educational Theory and Practice, University of Georgia, Athens, USA, where he serves as a Research Assistant on the Grow Your Own Teachers project and as an affiliate Research Assistant at the AI4STEM Education Center. Matthew's research addresses a critical challenge in STEM education: the lack of assessment grounded in students' cultural and contextual realities, which has discouraged many K-12 students from pursuing STEM-related programs. He developed a Generative AI framework for culturally responsive science assessment (CRSciA) to support prompt engineering and the development of GenAI tools. https://orcid.org/0000-0002-3341-1055. matthewnyaaba@gmail.com *or* matthew.nyaaba@uga.edu.

Part IV
Planning Lessons and Assessing Knowledge While Reducing Burnout and Increasing Productivity

Chapter 13
Generative Artificial Intelligence as a Collaborative Lesson Planning Tool for Novice Teachers: Emerging Perspectives

Beverly B. Ray and Esther Ntuli

Abstract The integration of generative artificial intelligence (GenAI) into educational practices holds immense promise but remains an underexplored area. Specifically, research exploring strategies to enhance teachers' skills in lesson planning, enabling timely interventions and targeted support for academic success, remains an under-researched area. This study employs an exploratory research approach to examine the perspectives of secondary level novice teachers' (n = 11) regarding the use of GenAI as a collaborative lesson planning tool. Specifically, written reflections are examined to gain an understanding of the challenges and opportunities associated with the use of GenAI as a collaborative lesson planning tool. An analysis of the willingness to continue its use is provided as well. This study begins the process of assessing GenAI's efficacy as a collaborative partner for novice teachers learning to write effective lesson plans.

Keywords Secondary education · Teacher preparation · Technology integration

Generative artificial intelligence (GenAI) is a computational model designed to do things that, in the past, were unique to human cognition. These tasks encompass complex tasks, such as thinking about problems, proposing solutions or recommendations, making predictions, recognizing and explaining data trends, seeing and describing the content of images, and creating new content using a process of prompt engineering.

Awareness of generative artificial intelligence rocketed to the forefront of educators' consciousness in the early months of 2023. However, a significant number of K-12 educators remain uncertain about the implications of GenAI for their professional practice. Many educators fail to realize that aspects of GenAI, in the form of

B. B. Ray (✉) · E. Ntuli
Idaho State University, Pocatello, ID, USA
e-mail: beverlyray@isu.edu

G. Tchibozo (ed.), *International Perspectives of Generative AI in Education*, Advances in Artificial Intelligence in Education 3,
https://doi.org/10.1007/978-3-031-99804-1_13

big data, cloud computing, and machine learning (ML), already impact their daily lives (Zhai et al., 2021) and professional practice. In fact, the emergence of GenAI technologies, such as ChatGPT, GPT-4, Google Gemini, and Microsoft CoPilot, has positioned GenAI as a global force influencing all sectors of society including the education sector.

The rapid diffusion and accelerated adoption of GenAI across education has resulted in a mix of excitement and concern among educators, with some viewing GenAI as a catalyst for transformative educational change (Flogie & Aberšek, 2015; Lacity & Willcocks, 2017) and others viewing it as a disruptive technology that should be banned or limited in educational settings. Some educators are alarmed, while others are excited by the possibilities, both known and unknown. Consensus as to whether this change will be beneficial or detrimental remains elusive at present. Whether GenAI will function as an accelerant for the emergence of a new twenty-first century educational revolution remains to be seen.

Given disparate perspectives on GenAI within the educational contexts, coupled with limited use or understanding of AI across K-12 schools prior to 2023, examining educators' perspectives is critical to assuring effective use and integration. Successful integration requires educators to recognize GenAI's potential within a pedagogical context and be able to harness its use in ways that promote both learning and productivity. Recognition hinges on a comprehensive understanding of GenAI and a conviction in its effectiveness as a collaborative teaching and learning tool (Su et al., 2023). Further, effective use implies that teachers can model ethical and effective GenAI usage, set clear educational objectives for learners, devise and implement assessment strategies, and prioritize the use of GenAI to cultivate students' higher-order cognitive skills.

Further, educators' understanding and use of GenAI is of global importance as is knowing what GenAI is and what it is not. Effective, fair, and ethical integration on a global scale requires knowledgeable educators capable of recognizing and correcting misunderstandings that currently exist about GenAI. This study seeks to shed light on teachers' thinking about GenAI in order to suggest ways to improve education about where we are now and where we may or may not be heading with AI. Together, educators have an opportunity to educate a global citizenry that will decide what AI will or will not be. An educated citizenry can also decide how society will or will not use AI. Yet many do not know they have this privilege or obligation. Globally, knowledgeable educators can contribute to these efforts.

Literature Review

The intersection of GenAI and education has garnered scholarly interest in recent years, with a focus on leveraging GenAI to enhance learning. This literature review explores various ways in which GenAI has been used in education. These applications extend beyond personalized learning to include streamlining assessments, optimizing assessments, and generating data driven insights that enhance learning.

GenAI as a Learning Tool

Previously, some researchers argued that the integration of GenAI in education carries significant value (Liu et al., 2017; Loeckx, 2016; Seldon & Abidoye, 2018). Across time, GenAI innovations paved the way for the development of personalized tutorial systems, revolutionizing the learning landscape. These systems, equipped with some aspects of GenAI functionalities, extend beyond learning monitoring and present developmentally congruent tasks. They also provide timely and relevant feedback, feature user-friendly interfaces to further enhance the learning experience (du Boulay, 2016; Huang et al., 2023), and contain intuitive interfaces to ensure that learners progress through the curriculum at their own pace (the Appendix summarizes some of the popular GenAI adaptive platforms/tutorial systems that adapt learning to the student's pace). Using GenAI's analytical capabilities to interpret individual learning pace, patterns, and preferences, educators gain valuable data that enhance their ability to customize instructional planning to meet the personalized needs of every learner. This process leads to the construction of novel educational content and resources (du Boulay, 2016).

Educators have also been able to construct new academic content based on GenAI interaction with learners, saving teachers' time and effort that could, instead, go into more creative academic pursuits. In terms of improving learning, there is limited research currently available. Still, recent research suggests positive possibilities for learning. For example, Holmes et al. (2023) report GenAI's efficacy for collaborative learning and as a continuous assessment tool. Grimes and Warschauer (2010) found that teachers had a positive attitude towards the use of GenAI, as it saves them time by marking students' essays and identifying areas for improvement so that students can hone their writing skills. Collaborative writing was also cited as a positive outcome (Calvo et al., 2010). However, issues have been noted as well. For example, Loeckx (2016) reported concerns about using GenAI in collaborative/participatory learning environments where students are not only learning but also co-creating content and assessments because the lines between the instructor and students' roles can fade with GenAI usage.

Educators' Perceptions of GenAI

A thorough understanding of educators' perspectives regarding the integration of GenAI as a teaching and learning tool is key to understanding its utility within the educational context (Humble & Mozelius, 2022; Lindner & Berges, 2020). Educators' perceptions, whether positive or negative, provide insight as to whether or to what extent educators are willing to incorporate GenAI technology into their instructional practices (Papadakis, 2021; Yang & Chen, 2023). Educators are instrumental in assimilating new technologies into classrooms (Saltan & Arslan, 2017). However, research documents a greater prevalence of use and positive perspectives about GenAI tools among students when compared to teachers (Shepman & Rodway, 2022; Zhang & Dafoe, 2019). This underscores the need for educators to consider GenAI's efficacy in various ways, including as a lesson plan supporting tool, and to understand GenAI's functionality, or utility, for learning. This understanding is key for the successful modeling of effective and ethical use by students (Lindner & Berges, 2020). While recent evidence suggests positive perspectives and positive outcomes (Kim et al., 2021; Zhang & Tur, 2024), other researchers report concerns regarding the implementation of GenAI in the classroom (Akgun & Greenhow, 2022). For example, research reported by Nazaretsky et al. (2021) and Shepman and Rodway (2022) suggest that educators are concerned about the potential negative impact of GenAI on their professional practice. These concerns range from ethics to the fear of being replaced by GenAI. In addition, concerns about usefulness, usability, and trustworthiness (Choi et al., 2023) have been reported, as well as concerns about the quality of pedagogical design and assessment (Loeckx, 2016). In addition, a limited knowledge base of GenAI continues to fuel teacher reluctance (Choi et al., 2023).

Many researchers are reporting positive perspectives among educators. Often, these perspectives come after experience of using GenAI (Kong et al., 2023). Others report increases in teacher productivity and advances in student learning (Copfer, 2020). GenAI can assist educators with tasks such as lesson planning and rubric creation, grading, and communication, allowing teachers to devote more time to instructional planning and other critical tasks (Homolak, 2023; also see Chaps. 14–18 of this book). For example, by using GenAI as a tool, educators can enhance their understanding and use of a variety of teaching strategies (Chiu et al., 2023), including adaptive teaching strategies. Lameras and Arnab (2021) posits that GenAI can be used to support lesson planning, predict student performance, and assess performance, and serve as a collaborative professional development tool. Because of these supports, the authors argue that GenAI will ensure rather than threaten teachers' job security.

Theoretical Framework

The research is grounded in the theoretical framework proposed by Gibson et al. (2023), which presents a model for the development of GenAI applications to bolster learning at three distinct levels: individual (micro), knowledge communities (meso), and cultural groups (macro). This research focuses on the macro level, drawing on Vygotsky's (1978) perspective of culturally and collaboratively mediated human activity. At the macro level, six roles of AI in enhancing the learning process are identified. Specifically, the research aligns with two of these roles: (a) AI to enhance goals and planning by clarifying objectives and identifying routes to achieve stated aims, and (b) use of GenAI to facilitate the formation and evolution of cross-cutting communities, enabling expert communities to integrate with other fields of knowledge through innovation and collaboration.

As educators engage in lesson planning using a collaborative tool, they are privy to GenAI-mediated suggestions for innovative interdisciplinary curriculum and assessment strategies, enabling them to achieve the learning goals they have set for their students. Moreover, GenAI suggestions allow for differentiation and contextualization of content using learning materials with a local and global connection. This not only fosters learning in cross-cutting communities but also prepares students for a future global workforce. The feedback mechanisms embedded within the macro-level of lesson planning enhance the effectiveness of novice teachers' lesson plans and introduce fresh perspectives on lesson content and delivery methods. Vygotsky's (1978) theory, which includes the concept of cognitive apprenticeship, is also a key component of this study. Its mentorship concept involves an expert and a novice working together on challenging tasks, with the expert guiding the novice in tackling the task. In this study, novice teachers worked under the direction of an expert instructor who modeled and provided guidance on effective ways of thinking about and utilizing GenAI as a planning tool.

Study Purpose

The significance of this study lies in the increasing use of GenAI technologies across education and in the need for novice teachers to develop GenAI-specific content knowledge and technical literacy. Developing and honing these skills are crucial for effective planning, execution, and assessment of lessons. The design of GenAI-assisted lesson plans, aimed at early identification of potential challenges, could enable novice K-12 educators to intervene early and offer targeted assistance to ensure the academic success of their learners. However, the use of GenAI as a collaborative tool for novice educators is an area currently under-researched. Consequently, this study seeks to bridge the knowledge gap on how novice educators perceive and understand the usefulness of GenAI as a collaborative lesson planning tool. To achieve this goal, educators' experiences, beliefs, and willingness to use GenAI are examined. Understanding novice educators' experiences and concerns assists teacher educators to assess the viability of GenAI as a collaborative tool. Specifically, the following research questions are examined:

1. What are novice teachers' perspectives regarding the challenges and opportunities of integrating the use of GenAI as a collaborative lesson planning tool?
2. To what extent are novice teachers willing to continue using GenAI as a collaborative lesson planning tool?

Method

This exploratory study used a sequential research design to examine the perspectives of novice secondary level (n = 11) teachers regarding the efficacy of GenAI as a collaborative lesson planning tool. The data reported here comes from teachers' responses to a Likert-scale survey questionnaire, administered before and after experiencing GenAI, and written reflections of their perceptions. Analyses of teachers' pre- and post-experience views allowed for the identification of the challenges and opportunities associated with integrating GenAI into collaborative lesson planning. Internal Review Board approval was obtained prior to the start of the research project.

Participants

Data were collected from novice secondary level teachers enrolled in an instructional technology course as part of the Master of Arts degree program at a university in the Intermountain Region of the continental United States. The program, housed in a college of education, is aimed primarily at teachers in rural and remote school districts.

Participants were graduates of a variety of non-STEM undergraduate programs, including History and Social Science, English, art, and humanities. All were seeking both a master's degree and initial secondary level teacher certification. At the time of the study, all participants were employed on emergency contracts in K-12 public schools, meaning they were hired temporarily with full teaching responsibility while working toward initial teacher licensure. All 11 were serving as the teacher of record for a classroom with an expectation that they would secure permanent employment upon completing the licensing program. Pseudonyms were used to protect participant privacy.

Setting

At the time of the study, participants were enrolled in a course taught fully online, incorporating synchronous and asynchronous teacher-directed instruction and peer-to-peer learning through small group assignments and discussion forum posts. Additional assignments involved independent work. The course served as an opportunity for the instructor to both model and scaffold use of AI as a collaborative lesson planning tool. The classwork was aligned with the International Society for Technology in Education (ISTE)'s Standards for Educators (Crompton, 2017), and course activities were disaggregated into learning modules reflective of ISTE standards. Aspects of the educational use of GenAI were integrated across several assignments. Early in the semester, the ethical use of GenAI and the basics of prompt writing were introduced. Participants began their study of GenAI by writing a pre-reflective discussion forum post outlining their prior knowledge of GenAI and their expectations for using this technology for collaborative lesson planning. Next, participants engaged in activities focused on understanding ethical GenAI use, culminating in video reviews of selected GenAI Chatbots. All 11 reviewed and later used ChatGPT as a collaborative tool for lesson planning. Data were collected near the end of the academic term allowing participants to learn about GenAI, engage with it, and reflect on the experience of using it as an educational tool.

Lesson Planning Process

Participants learned about and honed their lesson planning skills across the semester using GenAI as a supporting tool. Lesson planning was broken into a series of stages, and reflective checkpoints were incorporated at key junctures. The reflections expressed at the checkpoints form an important part of the data examined in this study.

Participants worked through various stages of designing and refining their lesson planning skills while using GenAI as a collaborative or supportive tool. The stages involved the identification of topic and standards, creation of an initial or draft GenAI-generated lesson plan, contextualization of that lesson within their specific learning environment, revision and integration of context within a second draft lesson, followed by iterative revisions to ensure that their final lesson plans aligned with programmatic lesson planning goals. Throughout the process, participants documented their learning reflecting in writing on their experiences. They also honed their prompt writing skills across time, learning how to formulate effective prompts to align lesson topics with learning goals and directing the GenAI bot to generate and refine the lesson plan across subsequent revisions. As a part of the process of improving the initial draft lesson plan, participants completed a learning context assignment without the aid of GenAI. This asked them to revise the GenAI lessons to focus on their learners' specific learning needs. Once completed and graded by the instructor, this classroom specific learning context was then used to further refine the initial lesson plans. Next, participants assessed each of their GenAI outputs against the programmatic lesson plan grading rubric. This rubric is aligned with national accreditation standards for initial teacher licensure and is used in several courses in the program. Self-assessing their work at this juncture empowered them to act as human experts responsible for evaluating the GenAI's output based on their knowledge of effective lesson planning. More immediately, it also allowed them to identify potential areas for improvement so that they might use GenAI as a tool to improve their final lesson planning grades. This step-by-step process was intended to provide participants with an understanding of the role of human intervention and expertise when using GenAI as an educational tool.

Instrumentation

In addition to the qualitative written reflections collected across the semester, participants responded to a short questionnaire. The goal of the questionnaire was to assess their perceptions before and after using GenAI. The two-part questionnaire was designed based on the theoretical writings of leading instructional and technology theorists (Gibson et al., 2023; Mishra & Koehler, 2006; Vygotsky, 1978). The first section included open-ended questions that asked students to reflect on challenges and opportunities. The second part was a holistic assessment of GenAI, with data collected pre and post use. The scale for the numerical questions ranged from "1 = Strongly Disagree" to "5 = Strongly Agree," with "3 = Not Sure" functioning as the scale's midpoint. The pre-and post-assessment data gathered from the survey were then analyzed to determine whether the teachers' perceptions regarding AI changed significantly after use.

Content validity was confirmed by two experts during the questionnaire development process. The first, a teacher education and instructional technology professional, taught at the middle school level for 12 years and in teacher education for 18 years. The second, an expert who teaches undergraduate and graduate-level courses in GenAI, instructional technology, and learning theory, has worked in higher education for 25 years. Both experts validated the appropriateness of the indicators on the survey for early career teachers. Further, the second expert verified the alignment with learning theory and provided helpful background knowledge on GenAI.

Data Analysis

The data derived from the questionnaire were primarily qualitative, with some numerical data derived from the small set of Likert-scale items. Additional data came from the written reflections collected across the semester. Expert readers analyzed the qualitative data using a general inductive method (Thomas, 2006). They read and reread the narrative data, identifying emergent themes and patterns. Individual results were cross validated using a process of simple agreement among the raters. The pre- and post-experience responses to the Likert scale items were first analyzed using descriptive statistics and provided information regarding participants' perceptions regarding using GenAI.

Results

Discussion of results is organized around three emergent categories: (1) challenges, (2) opportunities, and (3) willingness to continue using GenAI as a collaborative tool. Overall, agreement regarding willingness to continue using GenAI as a collaborative lesson planning tool was unanimous.

Challenges

Several challenges were identified. First, a majority of participants viewed the GenAI-generated lesson plans as broadly written or generic in scope, with little evidence of adaptations for diverse K-12 students' learning needs. Alex's comments are illustrative of this finding: "The challenge that I saw when using [Gen]AI to generate lesson plans is that the lesson plans that are made are very broad. They are very generic and don't adapt the lesson to the students in your class." Quinn agreed, elaborating on her perspectives regarding GenAI's lack of understanding of her learning context:

> One challenge of using [Gen]AI to create a lesson plan like this is [its] inability to know or understand the specific dynamics of my class and what my class has been doing leading up to the current lesson or unit. [It] is good at creating a general and broad skeleton of a lesson plan that could fit within a number of classes.

Quinn further elaborated on her concerns, stating:

> ...it would be wrong to assume that the lesson plan is good for immediate use. Despite being well-detailed and drawn out, I had to go through and double-check timing, scheduling, verbiage, and general details to ensure a plan like that would be appropriate for my students and their specific needs.

Second, some considered the need for specificity when asking questions or formulating prompts as a concern. They reported that it was challenging to prompt the GenAI in order to obtain useful lesson plans that fit their instructional needs. Another challenge identified by all involved was the need to know the difference between an effective and an ineffective lesson plan. For example, Sam wrote, "I need to have a pretty good idea of what I want or need before going to [Gen]AI for help." Further, Sam reported needing to "be very specific in what questions or prompts I used to be able to get a useful product that fits my needs." Others reported that it took some time and effort to read through, critique, and formulate a plan to revise GenAI-generated lesson plans. For example, Harper wrote, "One thing I noticed was [that] the lesson plans were fairly generic and sometimes needed a lot of extra prompts or time or thought on my part to get them where I wanted them." Harper further reflected that "[i]t also takes time to read through the lesson plan and think about if it has all of the elements I need." Others wrote about the need to ensure alignment with state standards, with Emerson reflecting that "[m]aking sure the lesson plan generated accurately matches the standards you will be teaching and assessing is challenging."

To a lesser degree, concerns about generating lesson plans for students with special needs or IEPs emerged, with one reporting that the AI-generated lesson plan would only reflect one IEP at a time. Another expressed concern as to whether the GenAI-generated lesson can provide the same level of personalization as a lesson plan created by a teacher. A small number of concerns regarding issues associated with ethics, potential usage costs, and the value of expertise were reported as well. The following quote from Shannon is broadly illustrative of these reflections:

> One concern I have is the possibility of inaccuracies in information, resources, and best teaching practices that could easily be overlooked. It is impressive how [it] can produce a lesson plan within minutes which makes it an attractive piece of technology to use. Considering that, the more comfortable you are and the greater trust you gain with [it], it may become easier to overlook errors or inaccuracies. In addition to that, the errors and inaccuracies may not be as obvious over time as the machine learns but would still have implications.

Opportunities

Opportunities, or benefits, of using GenAI as a collaborative tool for lesson planning were identified by all participants. These benefits identified include time savings, which could be redirected toward other tasks, including grading; the generation of ideas that could spark creative thought; the utilization of a familiar, standard lesson planning structure by GenAI; and opportunities for educators to revise, or hone, existing lesson plans. For instance, Jamie wrote,

> One huge benefit is that [it] is way less time consuming when writing lesson plans. Using [Gen]AI, a lesson plan can be written in detail in as little as 5 min. Saving time allows teachers to spend their time helping students or grading work, etc.

Similarly, Riley reflected that, "[w]ith enough practice and fine tuning, [GenAI] would be a huge time saver when developing a lesson plan." Hayden reflected on the benefit of using GenAI to customize and adapt lessons, writing:

> If I practice with it, and get more experienced at using GenAI, it can be a huge time saver for me. Teaching is a profession that takes so much time to do, and GenAI can help me with logistical tasks. It can put in a lot of details that would take me a long time to consider without me thinking too much about it.

Jude agreed, asserting that "[a]fter it is made… all I…have to do is adapt it to exactly what I want it to cover," A few found it useful in terms of generating new ideas for improving teachers' pre-existing lesson plans, with Shannon reflecting:

> An advantage of using GenAI to assist in lesson planning is that it provides a solid draft that can easily be tweaked or adjusted. This can be a huge time saver for teachers. Planning and writing lessons take a lot of time that teachers don't have. [Gen]AI can absorb some of the initial grunt work for lesson planning, saving time for teachers.

Nicky further elaborated: "…lessons can be incredibly interactive and if properly prompted, it can help meet standards as well objectives." Harper agreed, reflecting:

> I think I will use it to help guide me when making a lesson plan. Finding the standards that match the lesson plan is hard for me, GenAI quickly matches up standards. This will save me a lot of time.

Willingness

All 11 participants expressed a willingness to continue using GenAI as a collaborative lesson planning tool. However, the depth of willingness varied. The following quotes illustrate the range within this trend, with Channing providing one of the more nuanced positive statements of willingness:

> I will absolutely use [it] to assist me in the lesson-planning process. I believe that you can become a more creative teacher using [Gen]AI to help structure your lessons as you will not always think the exact same as the system does, and if you don't like how a lesson looks you can always click the 'regenerate' button to have it design a completely new and different lesson plan structure and activates.

Chris' response indicates a slightly more measured tone:

> I might continue to use…[GenAI] for brainstorming and possibly for creating a first rough draft to build on, but I don't think I will ever use it to generate a lesson plan and use that same lesson plan without extensive editing and customization.

Finally, Shannon's response reflects a mix of both caution and willingness: "[c]autiously yes. GenAI is a sleek tool and there are more emerging AI technologies that are being designed specifically for education and teachers."

Limitations

The sample size was relatively small, which is an important limitation to bear in mind when reviewing and discussing the results. It may be that a larger number of participants, such as primary school students or students of educational technology, would have produced different results. Further, it is important to note that the materials used in this study assessed only the written reflections shared by participants and not necessarily their full or actual thinking. Because data were created within a course setting, participants may have responded in ways that they perceived to be academically desirable. It might be that a more formalized study involving different research methods such as observation, survey research, or oral interviews might have resulted in different results. As such, the results cannot be generalized, but they remain viable in terms of identifying areas for future research.

Discussion

Reframing Challenges as Opportunities

Several themes initially seen as challenges by students can be reframed as opportunities for growth. These opportunities invite participants to engage in reflection and personal development. One such theme revolves around the intricate nature of

GenAI lesson planning, which prompts or encourages participants to delve into understanding their own students' learning styles, the complexity of curriculum content, and various instructional methods, including pacing and differentiation strategies tailored to individual student needs. Furthermore, participants enhance their expertise in lesson planning by studying beforehand, discerning the characteristics that distinguish an ineffective plan from an effective one. As articulated by Sam, "… I need to have a pretty good idea of what I want or need before going to [Gen]AI for help." Sam needed to have a clear idea before seeking assistance from GenAI. This underscores the importance of readiness in lesson planning, a quality always expected of educators.

Additionally, teachers are inherently tasked with crafting questions that not only assess students' understanding but also determine when and how to increase the complexity of instructional materials and teaching methods. Similarly, GenAI necessitates teachers to fine-tune questions or prompts to generate meaningful and contextualized lesson plans. This aligns with Sam's observation, stating that she "also need[ed] to be very specific in what questions or prompts [she] use[d] to be able to get a useful product that fits [her] needs."

Willingness

Participant quotes imply that the inclination to use GenAI as a planning tool, and possibly increase its usage, is influenced by the participants' familiarity with the technology, encompassing both technical proficiency and an understanding of how the GenAI tool operates. Additional findings indicate that the willingness to use AI is influenced by anticipated outcomes such as the ability to "*save time*" in lesson planning and GenAI's capacity to swiftly offer potential solutions to the areas that participants grapple with. This is reinforced by Avery's statement, "… [f]inding the standards that match the lesson plan is hard for me, [It] quickly matches up standards. This will save me a lot of time."

Additional insights from the reflections indicate that when participants embrace GenAI as a tool, they are willing to dedicate time and effort to contextualize, or tailor, GenAI generated lesson plans to their classroom needs, striving for optimal outcomes. A quote summarizing this dedication states:

> when I teach several classes I might continue to use [Gen]AI programs like ChatGPT for brainstorming and possibly for creating a first rough draft to build on, but I don't think I will ever use it to generate a lesson plan and use that same lesson plan without extensive editing and customization.

Similarly, some participants understood that as they are willing to continue use, they need to think carefully about GenAI's use and its impact on their future practice.

Implications for Practice

Novice teachers often grapple with the demands of formalized lesson planning, while simultaneously striving to create engaging, standards-based learning experiences for their students. In this context, GenAI emerges as a valuable tool—one that can streamline tasks such as curriculum planning, lesson development, and assessment. However, it is crucial for teacher educators to recognize that GenAI is a tool. While GenAI offers the opportunity to increase efficiency, it is not a replacement for the expertise of an experienced teacher. Instead, GenAI functions as a starting point tool that can be customized via prompting to hone lessons and meet the unique needs of individual students. Its effectiveness hinges on the user's ability to prompt it effectively.

Participants in our study found GenAI helpful for generating ideas and saving planning time, yet they expressed concerns about mastering the necessary prompting skills. To integrate GenAI successfully into education, teacher educators must provide scaffolded experiences that not only teach the technical aspects of GenAI but also explore its ethical implications. And since its effectiveness hinges on the user's ability to prompt it effectively, effective prompt engineering must be taught as well. As awareness and adoption of GenAI grow among educators, understanding and evolving perspectives on its role remain a fascinating area of exploration. Novice teachers, despite their initial struggles with formalized planning, can leverage GenAI to enhance curriculum design, lesson creation, and assessment. The key lies in harnessing GenAI's potential while maintaining the human touch that defines effective teaching.

Conclusions

Technology is constantly evolving, and new tools that help teachers create engaging and effective lesson plans are evolving as well. It is important for novice teachers to learn how to evaluate and use emerging technologies, such as GenAI. Integration of GenAI as a collaborative lesson planning tool for novice teachers can lead to more complex uses across time. The results suggest that GenAI offers opportunities to improve teaching practice while giving K-12 students the chance to receive a high-quality, inclusive education. GenAI serves as a useful collaborative tool for lesson planning as it functions as a starting point tool that can be customized to create, or hone, standard-aligned lessons that meet the needs of individual learners. As a collaborative tool, however, current versions of GenAI rely on teacher expertise to assure content accuracy, inclusion, and pedagogical effectiveness. By leveraging GenAI as a collaborative tool, teachers can also save time and generate fresh ideas for their lessons. However, while our study explores the integration of GenAI as a collaborative tool, it has broader implications for teacher education. At present, fundamental issues related to successful integration of GenAI, including structured teacher training, professional development workshops, and mentoring, remain unresolved. Further, while many of the challenges and opportunities identified in this study are universal in nature, as demonstrated by an emerging global research base (e.g., Papadakis, 2021; Yang & Chen, 2023), teachers' concerns about special needs or exceptional students, as revealed in this study, highlight GenAI's inability to understand the unique learning context of each individual learner and of each individual classroom's learning environment. It is important for educators and policy makers to be aware of GenAI's inability to respond to the local learning context, as each classroom, regardless of its local situation, functions as a unique learning environment.

Formal consideration and research on these aspects is essential if full integration is to occur. As such, this study contributes to the conversation. Teacher educators should consider the findings from this study as they navigate the intersection of GenAI and effective teaching practices.

Further, the study suggests a serious and global need for professional development for educators. Educating educators about AI is the first step in forming an informed citizenry capable of understanding where we are and where we are going with AI. This education, which includes knowledge of machine learning, LLMs and theoretical AI, should also include the understanding that we, as global citizens, have the power and obligation to decide whether natural resources are diverted to AI, as well as the power and obligation to decide how best to deploy AI ethically and equitably throughout society. In other words, a willingness to act now and in the future with regard to the development and integration of AI into global society is essential to ensure the safe, equitable and ethical integration of AI.

Competing Interests The authors have no conflicts of interest to declare that are relevant to the content of this chapter.

Ethics Approval This study was performed in line with the principles of the Declaration of Helsinki, with a formal approval of Exemption, Post 2018-Rule (US Code of Federal Regulations Title 45 Part 46.102(d)) granted by the Internal Review Board of Idaho State University on 2 Feb. 2024 (IRB FY2024 No. 140).

Appendix: Generative Artificial Intelligence Tools Used with Students

AI Tool	Description	Citations
Adaptive Learning Platforms		
DreamBox	An adaptive math program that adjusts difficulty based on a student's performance, fostering individualized learning	Foster (2023), Grams (2018)

AI Tool	Description	Citations
ABCmouse	An adaptive learning platform that tailors content to individual students, helping them develop early literacy and numeracy skills	Amin et al. (2023), Thai and Ponciano (2016) , Ponciano (2016)
Lexia	An adaptive learning platform that provides personalized content based on students' abilities. The tool adapts to students' progress, ensuring they receive content tailored to their needs	McMurray (2013), Macaruso and Walker (2008)
Educational Games and Chatbots		
Kodable	A game-based platform that introduces learners to coding concepts, promoting problem solving and critical thinking	Papadakis (2021), Lennon et al. (2022)
Osmo and ScratchJr	AI-powered educational games that engage learners in interactive and entertaining activities	Liu and Kromer (2020)
Chatbots for Reading assistance	AI-driven chatbots provide personalized reading support, helping young learners with comprehension and fluency	Liu et al. (2022)
Virtual Tours		
RoboKind's Milo	AI-driven virtual tutors like RoboKind's Milo assist educators in providing one-on-one support to learners with special needs. These AI avatars can adapt their teaching methods to cater to individual learning styles	
Speech recognition and language tools		
Google's speech-to-text functionality	AL-based speech recognition tool that supports language acquisition and literacy development. This tool helps young learners improve their pronunciation and reading skills	Su and Zhong (2022)
Duolingo	A language learning app that employs AI-driven gamification to engage learners	Papadakis and Kalogiannakis (2019)

References

Akgun, S., & Greenhow, C. (2022). Artificial intelligence in education: Addressing ethical challenges in K-12 settings. *AI and Ethics, 2*(3), 431–440.

Amin, A., Shidujaman, M., & Wang, B. (2023). Improving HCI on cognition for children with intelligent UI/UX. In International Conference on Human-Computer Interaction (pp. 355–366). Cham: Springer Nature Switzerland.

Calvo, R. A., O'Rourke, S. T., Jones, J., Yacef, K., & Reimann, P. (2010). Collaborative writing support tools on the cloud. *IEEE Transactions on Learning Technologies, 4*(1), 88–97.

Chiu, T. K., Moorhouse, B. L., Chai, C. S., & Ismailov, M. (2023). Teacher support and student motivation to learn with artificial intelligence (AI) based chatbot. *Interactive Learning Environments*, 1–17.

Choi, S., Kang, H., Kim, N., & Kim, J. (2023). How does AI improve human decision-making? Evidence from the AI-powered Go program. *Evidence from the AI-Powered Go Program*

(October 1, 2023). USC Marshall School of Business Research Paper Sponsored by iORB. https://ide.mit.edu/wp-content/uploads/2021/09/SSRN-id3893835.pdf
Copfer, A. (2020, January 7). *Teaching tools for success in the classroom*. The Learning Center by Collier Industries. https://www.nametag.com/learning-center/teachingtools
Crompton, H. (2017). *ISTE standards for educators: A guide for teachers and other professionals*. ISTE/ASCD.
Du Boulay, B. (2016). Artificial intelligence as an effective classroom assistant. *IEEE Intelligent Systems, 31*(6), 76–78.
Flogie, A., & Aberšek, B. (2015). Transdisciplinary approach of science, technology, engineering and mathematics education. *Journal of Baltic Science Education, 14*(6), 779–790.
Foster, M. E. (2023). Evaluating the impact of supplemental computer-assisted math instruction in elementary school: A conceptual replication. *Journal of Research on Educational Effectiveness*, 1–25.
Gibson, D., Kovanovic, V., Ifenthaler, D., Dexter, S., & Feng, S. (2023). Learning theories for artificial intelligence promoting learning processes. *British Journal of Educational Technology, 54*, 1125–1146.
Grams, D. (2018). *A quantitative study of the use of DreamBox learning and its effectiveness in improving math achievement of elementary students with math difficulties* (Doctoral dissertation, Northcentral University. ProQuest Dissertations Publishing). https://www.proquest.com/docview/2016788666
Grimes, D., & Warschauer, M. (2010). Utility in a fallible tool: A multi-site case study of automated writing evaluation. *The Journal of Technology, Learning and Assessment, 8*(6), 1–44. https://ejournals.bc.edu/index.php/jtla/article/view/1625
Holmes, W., Bialik, M., & Fadel, C. (2023). *Artificial intelligence in education*. Globethics Publications.
Homolak, J. (2023). Opportunities and risks of ChatGPT in medicine, science, and academic publishing: A modern Promethean dilemma. *Croatian Medical Journal, 64*(1), 1–3. https://doi.org/10.3325/cmj.2023.64.1
Huang, X., Zou, D., Cheng, G., Chen, X., & Xie, H. (2023). Trends, research issues and applications of artificial intelligence in language education. *Educational Technology & Society, 26*(1), 112–131.
Humble, N., & Mozelius, P. (2022). The threat, hype, and promise of artificial intelligence in education. *Discover Artificial Intelligence, 2*(1), 22. https://link.springer.com/journal/44163/volumes-and-issues/2-1
Kim, J., Giroux, M., & Lee, J. C. (2021). When do you trust AI? The effect of number presentation detail on consumer trust and acceptance of AI recommendations. *Psychology & Marketing, 38*(7), 1140–1155.
Kong, H., Wang, K., Qiu, X., Cheung, C., & Bu, N. (2023). 30 years of artificial intelligence (AI) research relating to the hospitality and tourism industry. *International Journal of Contemporary Hospitality Management, 35*(6), 2157–2177.
Lacity, M., & Willcocks, L. P. (2017). *Robotic process automation and risk mitigation: The definitive guide*. SB Publishing.
Lameras, P., & Arnab, S. (2021). Power to the teachers: An exploratory review on artificial intelligence in education. *Information, 13*(1), 14.
Lennon, M., Pila, S., Flynn, R., & Wartella, E. A. (2022). Young children's social and independent behavior during play with a coding app: Digital game features matter in a 1: 1 child to tablet setting. *Computers & Education, 190*, 104608. https://www.scholars.northwestern.edu/en/publications/young-childrens-social-and-independent-behavior-during-play-with-
Lindner, A., & Berges, M. (2020). Can you explain AI to me? Teachers' pre-concepts about artificial intelligence. In *2020 IEEE Frontiers in Education Conference (FIE)* (pp. 1–9). IEEE. https://doi.org/10.1109/FIE44824.2020.9274016

Liu, F., & Kromer, P. (2020). Early age education on artificial intelligence: Methods and tools. In *Proceedings of the Fourth International Scientific Conference "Intelligent Information Technologies for Industry (IITI'19)"* (pp. 696–706). Springer.
Liu, M., Rus, B., & Liu, L. (2017). Automatic Chinese factual question generation. *IEEE Transactions on Learning Technologies, 10*(2), 194–204. https://eric.ed.gov/?id=EJ1146019
Liu, C. C., Liao, M. G., Chang, C. H., & Lin, H. M. (2022). An analysis of children's interaction with an AI chatbot and its impact on their interest in reading. *Computers & Education, 189*, 104576.
Loeckx, J. (2016). Blurring boundaries in education: Context and impact of MOOCs. *The International Review of Research in Open and Distributed Learning, 17*(3), 92–121.
Macaruso, P., & Walker, A. (2008). The efficacy of computer-assisted instruction for advancing literacy skills in kindergarten children. *Reading Psychology, 29*(3), 266–287.
McMurray, S. (2013). An evaluation of the use of Lexia Reading software with children in year 3, Northern Ireland (6-to 7-year olds). *Journal of Research in Special Educational Needs, 13*(1), 15–25.
Mishra, P., & Koehler, M. J. (2006). Technological pedagogical content knowledge: A framework for teacher knowledge. *Teachers College Record, 108*(6), 1017–1054.
Nazaretsky, T., Cukurova, M., Ariely, M., & Alexandron, G. (2021). Confirmation bias and trust: Human factors that influence teachers' attitudes towards AI-based educational technology. In *AI for Blended-Learning: Empowering Teachers in Real Classrooms Co-located with 16th European Conference on Technology Enhanced Learning (ECTEL 2021). Bozen-Bolzano, Italy*. https://discovery.ucl.ac.uk/id/eprint/10141423/
Papadakis, S. (2021, June). The impact of coding apps to support young children in computational thinking and computational fluency. A literature review. *Frontiers in Education, 6*, 657–895. https://www.frontiersin.org/journals/education/articles/10.3389/feduc.2021.657895/full
Papadakis, S., & Kalogiannakis, M. (Eds.). (2019). *Mobile learning applications in early childhood education*. IGI Global.
Ponciano, L. (2016). Improving Outcomes for At-Risk Prekindergarten and Kindergarten Students with a Digital Learning Resource. https://www.academia.edu/download/53118735/Improve_Outcomes_with_a_Digital_Learning_Resource.pdf
Saltan, F., & Arslan, K. (2017). A comparison of in-service and pre-service teachers' technological pedagogical content knowledge self-confidence. *Cogent Education, 4*(1), 311501.
Seldon, A., & Abidoye, O. (2018). *The fourth education revolution*. University of Buckingham Press.
Shepman, A., & Rodway, P. (2022). The general attitudes towards Artificial Intelligence Scale (GAAIS): Confirmatory validation and associations with personality, corporate distrust, and general trust. *International Journal of Human–Computer Interaction, 39*(13), 2724–2741. https://doi.org/10.1080/10447318.2022.2085400
Su, J., & Zhong, Y. (2022). Artificial intelligence (AI) in early childhood education: Curriculum design and future directions. *Computers and Education: Artificial Intelligence, 3*, 100072. https://doi.org/10.1016/j.caeai.2022.100072
Su, J., Ng, D. T. K., & Chu, S. K. W. (2023). Artificial intelligence (AI) literacy in early childhood education: The challenges and opportunities. *Computers and Education: Artificial Intelligence, 4*, 100124. https://doaj.org/article/8a4dd4e973584a31b71a0c182173441f
Thai, K. P., & Ponciano, L. (2016). Improving outcomes for at-risk prekindergarten and kindergarten students with a digital learning resource. *Journal of Applied Research on Children: Informing Policy for Children at Risk, 7*(2), 8. https://www.academia.edu/download/53118735/Improve_Outcomes_with_a_Digital_Learning_Resource.pdf
Thomas, D. (2006). A general inductive approach for analyzing qualitative evaluation data. *American Journal of Evaluation, 27*, 237–246. https://doi.org/10.1177/1098214005283748
Vygotsky, L. S. (1978). *Mind in society: Development of higher psychological processes* (M. Cole, V. Jolm-Steiner, S. Scribner, & E. Souberman, Eds.). Harvard University Press. https://doi.org/10.2307/j.ctvjf9vz4

Yang, T. C., & Chen, J. H. (2023). Pre-service teachers' perceptions and intentions regarding the use of chatbots through statistical and lag sequential analysis. *Computers and Education: Artificial Intelligence, 4*.
Zhai, X., Chu, X., Chai, C. S., Jong, M. S. Y., Istenic, A., Spector, M., Liu, J.-B., Yuan, J., & Li, Y. (2021). A review of artificial intelligence (AI) in education from 2010 to 2020. *Complexity, 2021*(1). https://doi.org/10.1155/2021/8812542
Zhang, B., & Dafoe, A. (2019). Artificial intelligence: American attitudes and trends. *Available at SSRN 3312874*.
Zhang, P., & Tur, G. (2024). A systematic review of ChatGPT use in K-12 education. *European Journal of Education, 59*(2), e12599.

Beverly B. Ray is a faculty member in the Department of Teaching and Educational Studies at Idaho State University (ISU). She has expertise in instructional technology use and practice, with a focus on current and emerging technologies. Professor Ray is a former K-12 educator and has delivered professional development programs to schools in the United States and globally. beverlyray@isu.edu.

Esther Ntuli is a faculty member in the Department of Teaching and Educational Studies at Idaho State University (ISU). She has expertise and training in curriculum and instruction, early childhood education, and instructional technology. Her research interests are centered around technology use and practice in early childhood instruction, teacher development, assessment methodologies, and the implementation of equitable and inclusive teaching practices.

Chapter 14
Empowering Teachers Through GenAI-Created Lesson Plans

Domenica Spadoni and Gina L. Solano

Abstract Many teachers experience burnout due to the overwhelming demands of their roles, with lesson planning being a significant contributor. This qualitative study explores the potential of GenAI-created lesson plans to alleviate this burden in the case of high school teachers. GenAI tools can help educators develop comprehensive lesson plans, potentially reducing stress, and saving time. The study was carried out in New York's Lower East Side. MagicSchool.ai was chosen among other possible AI tools to carry out the study. The study's participants implemented three GenAI-created lesson plans over the course of 3 weeks. They evaluated the effectiveness of these lessons using a rubric, and provided detailed feedback. Following the implementation, participants were interviewed to assess whether the GenAI-created plans effectively met their teaching responsibilities. The findings indicate that the tool shows promise in empowering teachers and streamlining the lesson planning process. AI tools could be instrumental in helping teachers balance their professional duties, reduce burnout, and improve overall productivity. By identifying the benefits of AI in lesson planning, this research offers insights into how schools might increasingly integrate AI technology to support educators.

Keywords Action research · Lesson planning · Teacher burnout · Technology integration

Teachers are often burnt out because they must take on many responsibilities and different roles to be effective. These roles come with their sets of problems and paperwork to handle as well. A national survey in the United States indicated that many teachers are looking for new AI tools and tricks to help lighten their workload (Langreo et al., 2023). This highlights that teachers are feeling the strain of their jobs and are turning to AI for help in alleviating this stress.

D. Spadoni · G. L. Solano (✉)
State University of New York (SUNY) Oneonta, Oneonta, NY, USA
e-mail: Dspadoni@schools.nyc.gov; Gina.solano@oneonta.edu

G. Tchibozo (ed.), *International Perspectives of Generative AI in Education*, Advances in Artificial Intelligence in Education 3,
https://doi.org/10.1007/978-3-031-99804-1_14

Lesson plans are an ideal place to start making teaching easier. The school where this study was conducted requires teachers to submit their lesson plans each week, which means that teachers need to be at least a full week ahead in their planning. The lesson plans must include all the materials that will be used, and all the ways they will be tiering and differentiating their lessons. This process can feel very oppressive. In fact, through personal communication with one of the researchers, a colleague claimed that these weekly lesson plans are "the worst part of the job" (English teacher, personal communication, 2023). However, as AI is capable of creating new lesson plans or rejuvenating pre-existing ones, it could provide a productive way for teachers to implement effective lesson plans, while also saving them time and effort (Paykamian, 2023).

Problem Statement

Teaching is a profession that requires its workers to do many different jobs every day. These different jobs require creating and grading assessments to show how students have mastered the content, providing special services for each student's needs, and designing lessons that are supported by prior scaffolding and comply with state standards. Camera (2022) found that 52% of teachers claimed that they "always" or "very often" feel burnt out at work. This makes "…K-12 and higher education the two industries with the highest rate of burnout" (Camera, 2022, para. 1).

Lesson plans are a major cause of stress for educators. At the school where this study took place, they are due weekly and may be scrutinized by the administration. Just one lesson plan can be upwards of ten pages for just one day, which amounts to a lot of work. In addition to writing these lesson plans, teachers are also expected to partake in meetings, committee work, take on after school advising responsibilities, and much more as part of their professional responsibilities. This can result in overwhelming feelings of stress.

However, GenAI may be able to help alleviate some of the stress that comes along with writing effective lesson plans. A researcher stated that, "AI lesson plan generators can scan through a wealth of content related to the topic at hand providing educators with ready-made resources. This eliminates the need for hours of resource hunting and enables quick access to high-quality content" (Turner, 2023, para. 2). These AI generators give educators access to lesson plans that can be effective and adaptable to meet the differentiation needs of each student, all by typing a simple prompt.

The school where this study took place is an urban charter school in New York. Teachers at this school feel that submitting weekly lesson plans is the most stressful aspect of their job. A staff member explained that having to submit weekly lesson plans has major negative impacts on teachers' personal lives, as they often need to take the lesson planning work home, thus reducing time spent with family or friends (Special Education teacher, personal communication, 2023). Many teachers are feeling burnt out, so introducing AI lesson planning could be a great way to help alleviate much of this stress and allow them to stop dreading every Thursday (the day lesson plans must be turned in).

The goal of this qualitative study was to understand teachers' perceptions and use of AI for lesson plans. There is a need for an increased understanding of how GenAI-created lesson plans can benefit teachers so that they can avoid feelings of burnout, as well as create and discover new ways to teach content. By having this increased understanding, educators can feel more effective and confident in their lesson plans, while being less stressed.

While a range of AI-powered content generation tools are currently available, the most popular of which is ChatGPT (Kothari, 2024), MagicSchool.ai was selected for this study because it has been specifically designed to meet the needs of educators, including in particular lesson planning and the reduction of burnout, which is in line with the aim of the present study.

This action research project addressed the following questions:

- What are teachers' perceptions about using GenAI for lesson planning and material creation?
- How have teachers used MagicSchool.ai to support and fulfill teaching responsibilities?

Theoretical, Conceptual, and Technical Background

The ever-growing responsibilities of teachers can be felt in school districts worldwide (Agyapong et al., 2022). The United States is already dealing with a massive teacher shortage (Sutcher et al., 2019). Lesson plans and other responsibilities can play an important role in increasing stress and reducing teachers' effectiveness. This study followed a Participatory Action Research model.

Participatory Action Research Theory

Participatory Action Research Theory (PAR) is a research approach that emphasizes the importance of experiential knowledge in addressing challenges and imagining and applying alternative solutions (Cornish et al., 2023). In this study, the problem is the workload induced by lesson planning. The alternative solution is represented by GenAI-created lesson plans.

PAR is a research-based transformative process. It enacts change by having both researchers and participants collectively work together to make positive changes and establish a sense of community. The two main components of PAR are (a) ensuring that both researchers and participants are engaged and (b) enacting change in real-world issues to help benefit all parties involved (Chevalier & Buckles, 2019).

In this study, participants utilized AI in their planning. This helped alleviate their workloads and created a positive technology-based school community. PAR thus helped enacting social change and making sure all voices are heard through collaboration and cooperation.

Teacher Burnout

Burnout is a very harmful condition. Job-based burnout is caused when employees are not feeling stimulated or satisfied by their jobs, and feel that the job is becoming too stressful, or that they are becoming detached from it (Saloviita & Pakarinen, 2021). When teachers feel too stressed or detached from their jobs due to experiencing burnout, researchers have noted that their physical and mental health is at risk. This leads to their students experiencing negative academic and behavioral outcomes (Wentzel, 2010) and beginning to perform lower academically (Saloviita & Pakarinen, 2021).

Unfortunately, teacher burnout is only becoming more common (also see the chapter by Ross in this book). One study found that 52% of K-12 teachers in the U.S. report feeling burnout (Craft, 2023). That burnout is not only hurting the teachers, but it is leaving a massive gap in the teaching field, with employers unable to fill positions. Studies have shown that teacher burnout has a connection to the number of teachers quitting the profession (O'Brennan et al., 2017). Research has also proven that "the percentage of teachers choosing early retirement or a career change has gone up by 55% in the last 30 years" (Craft, 2023, para.6). These vacant positions are only increasing, and a growing number of students are left without educators.

AI Teacher Productivity Assistants

AI can offer teachers multiple ways to streamline their work and enhance their productivity, thus functioning as productivity assistants. AI assistants can help teachers assessment and grading, personalize learning, and create lesson plans, all of which are lengthy, but incredibly vital parts of the job. AI is now capable of creating rubrics and using them to grade assignments, and even provide automated feedback and comments on students' papers. One study deduced that "Artificial intelligence is now as good as a human at evaluating a standard five-paragraph essay and giving feedback on its logic and persuasion" (Baffour, 2023, para. 2), with both the AI programs and human graders producing similar scores and comments but with the AI doing so much quicker. However, most AI grading sites will include the comment to "use professional discretion," meaning that teachers can use the grades as a starting point but must review them before releasing them to students. As far as feedback is concerned, most AI grading software can provide meaningful feedback, but most teachers find it too complicated and difficult for their students to understand exactly what to correct (Nolan & Vang, 2023, para.6). Teachers should therefore consult the comments, then modify them to make them easier to use for their students. Still, the ability to upload assignments to AI for initial grading can free up a lot of time for educators. This free time can then be used for other essential aspects of their work. By removing this massive pressure on educators, burnout can be significantly reduced.

Another major struggle of teaching that AI can assist educators with is providing personalized learning experiences. Personalized learning experiences consist of educators creating learning experiences that are personalized to the needs of individual students. This means that the objectives, aims, and activities are geared to fit that specific student's skills and growth goals (Shemshack et al., 2021). By using AI, educators can simply ask assistants to generate lessons, assessments, or goal plans that will meet a student's specific interests and needs, thus allowing them to tailor individualized lessons and learning experiences. This can yield incredible benefits for students, and reduce the teacher's workload (Lokare & Jadhav, 2023). By streamlining this process, teachers can provide effective personalized learning experiences, while still avoiding the feelings of burnout that come along with creating such time-consuming materials.

AI assistants can benefit teachers in almost all the work that they do. Another major benefit of using AI is to facilitate communication with parents, allowing communication through the learning management system, sending progress reports and even deadline reminders to parents (Stone, 2024). This form of AI support can greatly alleviate the workload of educators, while also keeping parents and teachers informed about students' progress. This AI usage is on the rise, with research finding that four out of ten educators have begun using AI inside their classrooms with the goal of reducing their workload (Adame, 2023). AI lesson plans can come with the ability to automate grading and feedback for the lesson, let the lesson be personalized to each student's needs, collect the data from the lesson, and then communicate the data to key stakeholders to ensure a child's success.

MagicSchool.ai Teaching Assistant

MagicSchool.ai's promoters claim that their tool can save teachers up to 10 h a week doing the behind-the-scenes paperwork and lesson creation that is leading many teachers to feel burnt out and uninspired (www.magicschool.ai/). The program consists of 54 options for AI creation. Popular choices include a lesson plan generator, unit plan generator, rubric generator, text rewriter tools, multiple-choice quizzes, test generators, essay prompt creators, and vocabulary list generators. The website offers everything a teacher would need to create during the school year. The site itself is "…designed to save teachers time and help prevent teacher burnout by assisting them as they differentiate, write assessments, write IEPs, communicate, and more…" (Ofgang, 2023, para. 6). To use it, educators simply pick what they need to help create, give basic information (i.e., grade level, standards, length, and content area), and the site will create one for them. It is free and backed by The Family Educational Rights and Privacy Acts and Children's Online Privacy Protection Rule, as well as state privacy laws. This platform was chosen for this study because of its user-friendly interface and wide range of options. Although there are other GenAI tools designed for education, such as CuriPod (presentation tool), ClassPoint (presentation tool), Khan Academy (personalized learning), and Quillbot (writing assistant), none of them contain a lesson plan generating tool like MagicSchool.ai. While other popular GenAI tools like ChatGPT and Perplexity.ai can create lesson plans, MagicSchool.ai was selected because it was designed specifically for educators to create lessons aligned to state and national standards, and contains over 60 other tools to help reduce teacher workload.

Method

For this qualitative study, high school teachers were invited to create lesson plans through MagicSchool.ai and evaluate them. The research design may depart from an established set of methodologies or assumptions, allowing for knowledge to be socially constructed (Kahlke, 2014, para. 14). This means that it allows for human interactions to shape its findings. This study utilized qualitative data, such as observations and discussion, which allowed the teacher participants to share multiple perspectives and interpretations.

The participants for this study were selected through a purposeful sample. A purposeful sample allows the researcher to select participants who can best understand the research problem (Creswell, 2012). Teachers from the faculty at an urban New York high school who were experiencing burnout from creating weekly lesson plans were invited to participate via email. Eleven teachers gave consent to be participants. However, as the study progressed, three of them dropped out, resulting in this study having eight participants. These remaining participants were teachers of a wide array of subjects and were of varying years in their teaching careers.

The recruitment email explained the details of the study, the timeline, and what would be asked of the participants. The teachers who expressed interest were invited to a professional development (PD) session where they could learn more about MagicSchool.ai. The researchers then led a 45-min professional development meeting, where they explained the study in greater detail, the timeline, the requirements, and gave an overview and tutorial on how to use the platform. Once done, teachers who wished to participate signed a consent form and received their three hard copy rubrics (see rubric form in Appendix 1). The rubrics asked participants to rank each GenAI-created lesson plan on a scale from highly effective to ineffective on varying criteria.

The eight participants then created and taught three lesson plans created using MagicSchool.ai. After each lesson, they completed a rubric ranking the lesson's effectiveness. Once the 3 weeks were over, interviews with the participants were scheduled. These interviews were audio-recorded and consisted of the participants being asked ten questions (see Appendix 2). The ten questions ranged from general opinions on the use of AI for lesson planning to more specific questions on how AI-created lesson plans work in the classroom.

In line with the Participatory Action Research theory, the rubric was developed by considering what makes an effective lesson plan, and by addressing what needs to be changed to benefit the teachers creating them. For example, is the GenAI-created lesson plan relevant and engaging? Did it reduce workload? Was it easy to implement? The aim was to ensure specific, multi-level feedback that would help maintain the effectiveness of the research. (Creswell, 2012). The rubric contained a ranked order scale from highly effective to ineffective. It also contained a space for participants to leave comments sharing their reasoning. This allowed teachers to reflect and rank how well each lesson plan went and share why. As the rubrics were returned, they were paper clipped to the participant's consent form and stored in a locked filing cabinet.

Interviews are the ideal protocol when collecting participants' personal accounts, responses, and attitudes toward a situation (Paradis et al., 2016). The interview questions allowed participants to elaborate and clarify their responses (Creswell, 2012). By doing this, more information was gained, and it ensured that all data was clear and concise. The interviews took place a week after the completion of the lesson plan implementation. The interviews helped ensure that all data was understood and explained. These interviews were held in person. Both the researcher and participant had a set of questions in front of them. This was the first time the participant had seen the questions. The interview's audio was recorded, and no identifying information was included.

Data Analysis

The data was analyzed in accordance with the standard qualitative data analysis process. Firstly, the data was prepared for analysis by transcribing the interview audio files (Creswell, 2012). Audio mp4 files were uploaded onto Microsoft Word and transcribed using the transcribe tool. The researchers went through it and verified that the transcriptions were accurate. The data was then coded (Creswell, 2012). To do this, the answers given by the participants were marked "P" (positive), "N" (neutral) or "NE" (negative). For example, Participant D's sentence "I am glad it [Magicschool.ai] exists" would be coded as P. The sentence "…ChatGPT gives me a little better layout than the MagicSchool. I felt like with MagicSchool I had to…keep rephrasing things to get it [to work]" would be coded as NE. Then, a more in-depth analysis was conducted by documenting key themes, quotes, and concepts from each interview. Further analysis was conducted in comments that participants left on the rubrics. Then, the rankings of the rubric were analyzed by creating four separate tables, for lesson plan 1, lesson plan 2, lesson plan 3, and the three lesson plans combined. The researchers then documented how many times in each trial the lesson's criterion was ranked highly effective, effective, and ineffective. This allowed them to deduce the effectiveness through the percentages and identify trends in how the rankings changed as participants produced each lesson. This study used inductive coding, meaning that themes emerged as the researchers sifted through the data. This inductive coding process allowed the researchers to identify the main themes of the study.

Results

The data analyzed was 24 rubrics and eight transcribed interviews. As can be seen from Table 14.1, across all rubric criteria (120 responses in all), the AI lesson plans were rated as "Highly Effective" 70 times, "Effective" 46 times, and "Ineffective" 4 times. The AI lesson plans had the most frequent rating of being highly effective in the "Student Engagement" section (16), followed by a tie between the "Reduced Workload" and "Ease of Implementation" criteria (both 15). The AI lesson plans were ranked as "Highly Effective" 12 times each in their "Relevance" and "Meet[ing] of Teacher and Student Needs." The criterion with the lowest number of "Ineffective" ratings is "Ease of Implementation" (0). The other criteria all received 1 "Ineffective" score each. Overall, the AI lesson plans received positive ratings, with "Highly Effective" being the most frequent assessment for all criteria (70/120), and were ranked as a highly effective resource in 58.33% of cases. They were ranked ineffective in 3.33% of cases.

Through interview analysis, there were three common themes discovered. These themes were identified because they were the most repeated in all interviews. The themes discovered include the effectiveness of AI lesson plans, their positive impact on teaching practice, and increased student engagement.

Efficiency of AI Lesson Plans

One of the key findings of this study is the ability of the AI assistant to streamline course planning. Before this study began, all participants expressed that the creation of lesson plans was daunting and stressful. MagicSchool.ai was introduced to test if it would alleviate some of this stress. Participant E declared to be "...glad [MagicSchool.ai] exists. It helps me a lot because it takes me a long time to do lesson plans and being able to use any kind of AI, at least as a place to start, makes it much smoother." Participant F shared that MagicSchool.ai "...streamlines the process while increasing the quality, and that is priceless." Based on the rubric data, AI lesson plans had the second highest amount of "Highly Effective" ratings when it came to their ability to reduce a teacher's workload.

Other participants shared that by having lesson plans created efficiently and timely, they were able to shift their focus. The drawn-out creation of lesson plans

Table 14.1 Rubric results

Rubric criteria	# of times AI lesson plans ranked "Highly Effective"	# of times AI lesson plans ranked "Effective	# of times AI lesson plans ranked "Ineffective"
Lesson plan 1			
Reduced workload	4	3	1
Relevance	3	4	1
Student engagement	5	3	0
Ease of implementation	4	4	0
Meets teacher & student needs	3	4	1
Lesson plan 2			
Reduced workload	5	3	0
Relevance	6	2	0
Student engagement	6	1	1
Ease of implementation	6	2	0
Meets teacher & student needs	6	2	0
Lesson plan 3			
Reduced workload	6	2	0
Relevance	3	5	0
Student engagement	5	3	0
Ease of implementation	5	3	0
Whole study results			
Reduced workload	15	8	1
Relevance	12	11	1
Student engagement	16	7	1
Ease of implementation	15	9	0
Meets teacher & student needs	12	11	1

can prevent teachers from concentrating on other aspects of their practice. Participant A, an Economics & Government teacher and a Special Education provider, claimed:

> A lot of time I just feel like I have to get other stuff done for like my 'first job,' which is the economics class and then they [individualized education plan (IEP) students] come second. So now I can give more attention to what I couldn't give attention to.

Another participant, a tenth grade Special Education provider felt similarly. "I went from spending, let's say, for ELA (English Language Arts), maybe 2–3 periods a day creating SDI [specially designed instruction] for the week, and with the AI, it generated it for me in seconds". They further elaborated that with this extra time, they can focus on the more important paperwork like observation notes, Individual

Education Plans (IEPs) for student accommodations, and running records, rather than needing to prioritize the lesson planning work.

Positive Impact on Teaching Practice

Several participants came to see MagicSchool.ai as a personal assistant. Participant E, who teaches a Careers and Finances class, explicitly stated "…at the end of the day [MagicSchool.ai] gives me an assistant in a way that I didn't have one before." Participants expressed that this virtual assistant facilitated many processes for them, such as giving creative ideas, more content, and even clearly defining their requirements as educators. Participant B stated that "… [the site] was definitely beneficial because it laid out the gradual release", thus referring to the teaching strategy recently adopted in the school where the research was conducted, where the teacher provides a lot of support at the beginning of the lesson and gradually helps students become independent in their learning. MagicSchool.ai was able to provide a clearer representation of gradual release and how to use it in the classroom. Participant D, who teaches a ninth-grade History course, explained that "…there are teachers like myself that are not very creative and [using MagicSchool] at least gives you an idea." Participant F, who has been teaching for over 20 years stated to have been "…working the same amount of hours, but…producing so much more for the kids and… able to meet the goals of the initiative" after implementing MagicSchool.ai for teaching.

Many participants expressed that having a virtual assistant like MagicSchool.ai can reduce levels of burnout. Participant A stated:

> It greatly reduced my workload… The first time I [used MagicSchool.ai] and I rolled out the lesson plan with the materials I felt like I was missing something. I was like, I know I missed a step. It was just weird because I feel like all that [time] I usually spend was just gone and I feel like I had more time. I had more time in my day, and I just didn't have to like worry about creating this entire lesson plan.

In a clarifying question, the respondents explained that they felt as if they were missing a step in the lesson plan creation process because they could not believe all the work was done for them and ready to be implemented so quickly. Participant C had a similar response, claiming that the AI lesson plans allowed them to focus on completing other aspects of their job, so MagicSchool.ai "definitely saved" them from potential burnout. Participant E claimed that the major benefit of MagicSchool.ai is that "it allows us to reclaim our time." Similarly, Participant A explains that:

> there is an issue with teachers and like having burnouts more and more lately because of the demands… Teachers take on more of the demands now…So I just think that this [MagicSchool.ai] will help teachers want to stay in teaching.

Increased Student Engagement

Participants also found that MagicSchool.ai's lesson plans assisted them in differentiating their lesson plans, thus resulting in more engaged students. Differentiation entails educators or providers tailoring instruction to meet individual student's needs. Participant C stated that "...IEP kids... said that the lessons that I did with [MagicSchool.ai] were easier for them to understand." Similarly, Participant F said he was able to offer "...different activities in a learning packet [the daily worksheets stapled together]. That means[...] in each learning packet, they can choose two different pathways. That's so much content that I wouldn't be able to deliver to them [without MagicSchool.ai]." Differentiation gives students a choice based on their individual needs. Having an increased ability to differentiate lesson plans can increase accessibility.

AI lesson plans had the most frequent rating of being "Highly Effective" in the "Student Engagement" section. Participant G claimed that the lessons "...were very interactive for the kids, especially the discussion questions that the app generated. It helped with participation. Some of the activities actually got children who are usually quiet to be more talkative and responsive." Others, like Participants C and A, had students making the lessons into friendly competitions. Participants B, G, and H found students making strong connections to key concepts while still having fun.

Discussion

The data gathered from these instruments was sufficient to answer the study's research questions. The study's first question asked about teachers' perceptions of using AI for lesson planning and material creation. By having teachers rank their lesson plans, the researchers gathered a definitive score of how teachers felt the AI lesson plans went. The interviews consisted of asking teachers more specifically about their feelings towards AI lesson plans, if they plan to use the site again, and if they would recommend it to other staff members. This allowed the researchers to get a clear understanding of teachers' perceptions of using AI in lesson planning. The second question asked how teachers have used MagicSchool.ai to support and fulfill their teaching responsibilities. This was answered in the rubric as participants shared the AI lesson plans alongside the rubric. The rubric also allowed participants to make comments on the lesson. This is where many of them explained what the lesson did well or was missing and how this had affected the time they had spent planning. In the interviews, participants were directly asked how AI lesson planning met their responsibilities and impacted their workload. The two methods of data collection yielded enough data to meet saturation and answer the study's research questions.

Teachers' Perceptions About Using AI for Lesson Planning and Material Creation

The participants' perceptions were highly positive. They felt that their lessons were streamlined, making the process of creating them more efficient. By having lesson planning take less time, they shifted the focus of their teaching practice. Participants could now focus on aspects of their practice that are often neglected. They were able to prioritize paperwork, grading, and special education reports, among other things. They interpreted MagicSchool.ai as being highly effective in reducing their workload and engaging students. Participants found themselves avoiding feelings of burnout, while still engaging their students. Participant H claimed that they "...will use [MagicSchool] every day, every week, all the time, and this is not because I'm big into AI, but because it's really helped me." This, combined with the fact that lesson plans were ineffective in reducing a teacher's workload only once during the entire study period, shows just how beneficial they are, and how many teachers enjoyed using them. This directly ties into the findings of Paykamian (2023) about how educators at several institutions are effectively using AI tools for lesson planning. Teachers felt that MagicSchool.ai was a positive force in lesson planning and material creation.

How Teachers Have Used MagicSchool.ai to Support and Fulfill Teaching Responsibilities

MagicSchool.ai helped participants to fulfill their responsibilities as educators. Participant E explained not to have, in the past, turned in the weekly lesson plans because having felt it was too time-consuming and an unnecessary practice. This resulted in conflict with the school's administration. However, because MagicSchool.ai made the lesson plans quickly and effectively, Participant E could now meet this requirement.

Another way the site supported teachers was by helping them to create lessons. Participant E explained that some classes have a pre-made curriculum or a textbook that teachers can teach out of, however, "...I don't have that benefit, so I have to make everything up. This [MagicSchool.ai] is really great for that because it kind of streamlines the process." Participant G felt similar. MagicSchool.ai was able to create content for a new class that does not have any pre-existing curricula, thus saving the teacher time and effort, while still capturing the students' attention. In addition, it was also able to take preexisting material from classes and let teachers learn how to teach it in new ways. For example, Participant H, who has been teaching for 52 years said that MagicSchool.ai "...opens up my intelligence... I didn't know that I could do it [teaching] this way."

Teachers also increased their levels of differentiation and support for special education students through this site. Participants C, D, and F, all stated that they were able to modify assignments to better meet students' needs. This is in line with the view of Shemshack et al. (2021) that technological tools play a major role in personalizing learning. This relates to the PAR framework because the issue of lengthy lesson plans was solved through MagicSchool.ai. Teachers felt that their needs were met, often even exceeded.

Further Research Is Needed

Using AI to plan lessons is not an easy solution for teachers. Rather, it is a matter of using their resources wisely and undergoing their own technological training to improve their practice. This study shows the benefits of using MagicSchool.ai for lesson planning, although additional research is needed to determine if AI-created lessons are more effective and better designed than teacher-created lessons. While new AI tools are making lesson planning easier for educators, the lessons are not perfect and still require editing (Powell & Courchesne, 2024; van den Berg & du Plessis, 2023). Although an AI tool can produce a lesson plan in a few seconds, researchers have noted that lessons may contain inaccurate components, missing information, and falsified, or hallucinated resources (Fui-Hoon Nah et al., 2023), or even plagiarized content (Kasneci et al., 2023). MagicSchool.ai recognizes these limitations and provides a disclaimer that asks educators to check for bias and accuracy. AI may do 80% of the lesson planning, but teachers are still expected to put in 20% of the work to place the final touches on a lesson (MagicSchool.ai, n.d.).

Even though AI lesson plans may prove useful, there are still drawbacks to their use, which makes it vital to critically evaluate what it produces and to understand that an AI is not meant to replace the expertise of a teacher (Cooper, 2023). Teachers play a crucial role in assessing, refining, and customizing lesson plans and materials to ensure effective teaching. Although ChatGPT can offer specific and pertinent information, it lacks the ability to provide the emotional support and personal interaction essential for teaching (Zhai, 2023).

Additional research is also needed to thoroughly evaluate the effectiveness of the MagicSchool.ai lesson plans. Future studies could analyze student outcomes from classes where AI-created lesson plans were used and then compare the data with results from classes that followed traditional lesson plans. Qualitative data is needed from more schools and teachers who are using MagicSchool.ai lessons to determine how the lessons are engaging students and their perceived effectiveness. Conducting a comparative analysis of AI-generated lessons with those created by teachers that examined how the lessons aligned with standards, promoted creativity, integrated differentiation, and provided options for different learning styles would provide data that could help evaluate their effectiveness. By objectively evaluating the AI-created lessons, researchers could better understand their strengths and weaknesses, which would ensure a thorough evaluation.

Transferability and Generalizability

Conducted in New York's Lower East Side, this qualitative study involved teachers implementing three GenAI-created lesson plans over 3 weeks, evaluating their effectiveness, and providing detailed feedback. The context of this study, an urban charter school with a high demand for detailed weekly lesson plans, contrasts with other educational settings where lesson planning requirements and technological access may vary. For instance, schools with less stringent lesson planning protocols or limited access to AI tools might not experience the same level of benefit. However, the positive impacts observed in this study suggest that with appropriate adaptation, such as ensuring access to technology and providing training, the benefits of AI in lesson planning could be transferable to other educational contexts. This adaptability is crucial for maximizing the potential of AI tools in diverse educational environments and addressing the unique challenges faced by different schools.

Conclusion

The aim of this study was to understand teachers' perceptions and use of AI for lesson planning and burnout mitigation. The study aimed to answer two research questions, "What are teachers' perceptions of using AI for lesson planning and materials creation?" and "How have teachers used MagicSchool.ai to support and fulfill their teaching responsibilities?". Study participants created lesson plans using MagicSchool.ai and then taught them. A rubric was then used to evaluate the effectiveness of each plan. Participants then took part in evaluation interviews. The results of the study were positive. AI lesson plans were found to be highly effective in creating lesson plans that engaged students, increased teacher time and reduced teacher burnout. These positive results invite further research to explore the benefits and drawbacks of AI-generated lessons.

Currently, AI "is poised to have lasting effects on how teachers plan their daily lessons" (Powell & Courchesne, 2024, p. 12). However, tools such as MagicSchool.ai are not intended to replace the knowledge, expertise and personality of a teacher trained in effective teaching strategies and who knows how best to help students succeed.

Teachers looking to save time and find quick lesson ideas should consider that an AI-generated lesson still requires a professional to refine it. Unmotivated teachers may place an over-reliance on AI which would dramatically diminish the personalization and expertise of a professionally trained teacher (van den Berg & du Plessis, 2023). Using AI to design a lesson plan is a helpful starting place, but teachers are still needed to fill in the gaps and provide the contextual knowledge that an AI tool cannot provide. Integrating AI into teaching practices may well prove imperative to cultivating excellence in education. Nevertheless, the use of AI to support teachers must be approached strategically, maintaining the teacher at the center of creating effective learning experiences.

Competing Interests The authors have no conflicts of interest to declare that are relevant to the content of this chapter.

Appendices

Appendix 1: Empowering Teachers through GenAI-Created Lesson Plans Rubric

Content Area:

Grade Level:

Lesson Topic:

Lesson Number:

Directions: Use this rubric after you implement an AI lesson plan inside your classroom. Answer honestly and use the comment box if you have a specific experience you want to share or elaborate on why you ranked the criteria the way you did.

Criteria	Highly Effective	Effective	Ineffective	Comments
Reduced workload	The teacher experienced a significant reduction in workload due to the GenAI-created lesson plan	The teacher experienced some reduction in workload with the GenAI-created lesson plan	The teacher did not observe any reduction in workload The teacher felt the GenAI-created lesson plan added to their workload	
Relevance	The GenAI-created lesson plan was highly relevant to the subject matter and aligned with the curriculum	The GenAI-created lesson plan was mostly relevant to the subject matter and aligned with the curriculum	The GenAI-created lesson plan was not relevant to the subject matter and did not align with the curriculum	
Student engagement	The GenAI-created lesson plan consistently engaged students and fostered active participation	The GenAI-created lesson plan somewhat engaged students and encouraged participation	The GenAI-created lesson plan failed to engage students and lacked opportunities for participation	
Ease of implementation	The teacher found the GenAI-created lesson plan extremely easy to implement, requiring minimal preparation	The teacher found the GenAI-created lesson plan relatively easy to implement, with some preparation required	The teacher found the GenAI-created lesson plan difficult to implement, requiring extensive preparation	
Teacher and student needs	The GenAI-created lesson plan fully met both the teacher and student needs, addressing their specific requirements	The GenAI-created lesson plan partially met the teacher and student needs, addressing some of their specific requirements	The GenAI-created lesson plan did not meet the teacher and student needs, failing to address their specific requirements	

Appendix 2: Empowering Teachers Through GenAI-Created Lesson Plans Interview Questions

Instructions: Thank you for taking part in my research study. Before we begin, make sure you have signed the consent form. As a reminder, the interview will be recorded so that I may transcribe it afterward for analysis. You are encouraged to answer each question; however, you are not required to answer any questions you do not want to. Your participation is voluntary, and we can end at any time. Do you have any questions?

1. Please describe your experience using AI tools to create lesson plans.
2. What is your opinion about using AI assistants to help teachers use their time more effectively?
3. Now that you have taught three GenAI-created lessons, how do you feel they turned out?
4. How did teaching the AI generated lesson plans turn out? Were they any better, worse, or about the same compared to your own lessons?
5. What are your current perceptions about using AI in lesson plans?
6. Would you recommend more staff utilize this tool? Why or why not?
7. Did AI lesson plans affect your workload as an educator? How?
8. Did you enjoy using GenAI-created lesson plans? Why or why not?
9. Did you find GenAI-created lesson plans to be beneficial? Why or why not?
10. Did GenAI-created lesson plans benefit your teaching practice? Why or why not?

References

Adame, D. (2023, September 21). AI is taking off in classrooms. Here's how one Boston teacher is using it. *GBH*. https://www.wgbh.org/news/education-news/2023-09-21/how-one-teacher-uses-artificial-intelligence-in-his-boston-classroom

Agyapong, B., Obuobi-Donkor, G., Burback, L., & Wei, Y. (2022). Stress, burnout, anxiety and depression among teachers: A scoping review. *International Journal of Environmental Research and Public Health, 19*(17). https://doi.org/10.3390/ijerph191710706

Baffour, P. (2023, September 17). AI can grade a student essay as well as a human, but it cannot replace a teacher. *The 74*. https://www.the74million.org/article/ai-can-grade-a-student-essay-as-well-as-a-human-but-it-cannot-replace-a-teacher/

Camera, L. (2022, June 13). Educators report highest level of burnout among all other industries. *U.S. News*. https://www.usnews.com/news/education-news/articles/2022-06-13/educators-report-highest-level-of-burnout-among-all-other-industries

Chevalier, J. M., & Buckles, D. (2019). Pragmatic, psychosocial and critical PAR. In I. J. M. Chevalier & D. J. Buckles (Eds.), *Participatory action research: Theory and methods for engaged inquiry* (2nd ed., pp. 37–60). Routledge.

Cooper, G. (2023). Examining science education in ChatGPT: An exploratory study of generative artificial intelligence. *Journal of Science Education and Technology, 32*, 444–452. https://doi.org/10.1007/s10956-023-10039-y

Cornish, F., Breton, N., Moreno-Tabarez, U., Delgado, J., Rua, M., Aikins, A. D., & Hodgetts, D. (2023). Participatory action research. *Nature Reviews Methods Primers, 3*, 34. https://doi.org/10.1038/s43586-023-00214-1

Craft, S. (2023, February 2). Teacher burnout statistics. ThinkImpact.com. https://www.thinkimpact.com/teacher-burnout-statistics/#:~:text=The%20percentage%20of%20teachers%20choosing,they%20should%20have%20been%20paid

Creswell, J. W. (2012). *Educational research: Planning, conducting, and evaluating quantitative and qualitative research* (4th ed.). Pearson.

Fui-Hoon Nah, F., Zheng, R., Cai, J., Siau, K., & Chen, L. (2023). Generative AI and ChatGPT: Applications, challenges, and AI-human collaboration. *Journal of Information Technology Case and Application Research, 25*(3), 277–304. https://doi.org/10.1080/15228053.2023.2233814

Kahlke, R. M. (2014). Generic qualitative approaches: Pitfalls and benefits of methodological mixology. *International Journal of Qualitative Methods, 13*(1), 37–52. https://doi.org/10.1177/160940691401300119

Kasneci, E., Seßler, K., Küchemann, S., Bannert, M., Dementieva, D., Fischer, F., Gasser, U., Groh, G.L., Günnemann, S., Hüllermeier, E., Krusche, S., Kutyniok, G., Michaeli, T., Nerdel, C., Pfeffer, J., Poquet, O., Sailer, M., Schmidt, A., Seidel, T., …, & Kasneci, G. (2023). ChatGPT for good? On opportunities and challenges of large language models for education. *Learning and Individual Differences, 103*, 102274. https://doi.org/10.1016/j.lindif.2023.102274

Kothari, S. (2024, September 12). Top generative AI tools: Boost your creativity. *Simplilearn.* https://www.simplilearn.com/tutorials/artificial-intelligence-tutorial/top-generative-ai-tools

Langreo, L., McFarlane, L., & Meisner, C. (2023, August 28). Can AI improve instruction? 3 teachers share how they use it. *Education Week.* https://www.edweek.org/technology/can-ai-improve-instruction-3-teachers-share-how-they-use-it/2023/08

Lokare, V. T., & Jadhav, P. M. (2023). An AI-based learning style prediction model for personalized and effective learning. *Thinking Skills and Creativity, 51*, 101421. https://doi.org/10.1016/j.tsc.2023.101421

MagicSchool.ai. (n.d.). Frequently asked questions. *MagicSchool.* https://www.magicschool.ai/faq

Nolan, H. G., & Vang, M. C. (2023, June 14). Can AI help teachers with grading? *EdSurge.* https://www.edsurge.com/news/2023-06-14-can-ai-help-teachers-with-grading

O'Brennan, L., Pas, E., & Bradshaw, C. (2017). Multilevel examination of burnout among high school staff: Importance of staff and school factors. *School Psychology Review, 46*(2), 165–176. https://doi.org/10.17105/SPR-2015-0019.V46-2

Ofgang, E. (2023, October 19). 12 AI tools beyond CHATGPT that can save teachers time. *TechLearning Magazine.* https://www.techlearning.com/news/10-ai-tools-beyond-chatgpt-that-can-save-teachers-time

Paradis, E., O'Brien, B., Nimmon, L., Bandiera, G., & Martimianakis, M. A. (2016). Design: Selection of data collection methods. *Journal of Graduate Medical Education, 8*(2), 263–264. https://doi.org/10.4300/JGME-D-16-00098.1

Paykamian, B. (2023, September 6). Professors find AI most useful for lesson plans, discussions. *Government Technology.* https://www.govtech.com/education/higher-ed/professors-find-ai-most-useful-for-lesson-plans-discussions.

Powell, W., & Courchesne, S. (2024). Opportunities and risks involved in using ChatGPT to create first grade science lesson plans. *PLoS One, 19*(6), e0305337. https://doi.org/10.1371/journal.pone.0305337

Saloviita, T., & Pakarinen, E. (2021, October 27). Teacher burnout explained: Teacher-, student- and organization-level variables. *Teaching and Teacher Education, 97*, 103221. https://doi.org/10.1016/j.tate.2020.103221

Shemshack, A., Kinshuk, & Spector, J. M. (2021). A comprehensive analysis of personalized learning components. *Journal of Computers in Education, 8*, 485–503. https://doi.org/10.1007/s40692-021-00188-7

Stone, A. (2024, August 20). 3 technologies to facilitate parent-teacher communication: Create clear channels for communication without adding work for K-12 educators. *EdTech*

fFocus on K-12. https://edtechmagazine.com/k12/article/2024/08/3-technologies-facilitate-parent-teacher-communication
Sutcher, L., Darling-Hammond, L., & Carver-Thomas, D. (2019). Understanding teacher shortages: An analysis of teacher supply and demand in the United States. *Education Policy Analysis Archives, 27*(35) https://eric.ed.gov/?id=EJ1213618
Turner, R. (2023, September 11). How can teachers save time using AI lesson plan generators? *Twin Science.* https://www.twinscience.com/en/teacher-tips/how-can-teachers-save-time-using-ai-lesson-plan-generators/#:~:text=AI%20lesson%20plan%20generators%20can%20assist%20teachers%20in%20starting%20with,to%20creating%20plans%20from%20scratch
van den Berg, G., & du Plessis, E. (2023). ChatGPT and generative AI: Possibilities for its contribution to lesson planning, critical thinking and openness in teacher education. *Education Sciences, 13*(10), 998. https://doi.org/10.3390/educsci13100998
Wentzel, K. R. (2010). Students' relationships with teachers. In J. L. Meece & J. S. Eccles (Eds.), *Handbook of research on schools, schooling, and human development* (pp. 75–91). Routledge.
Zhai, X. (2023). ChatGPT for next generation science learning. *XRDS: Crossroads, The ACM Magazine for Students, 29*(3), 42–46. https://doi.org/10.1145/3589649

Domenica Spadoni (SUNY Oneonta University) is an English teacher in New York. She has experience teaching ninth, tenth, and twelfth-grade general education English, New York State Regents preparation classes, and composition courses. Ms. Spadoni has earned her bachelor's in Secondary Education: English. She was awarded the Secondary Education Department Achievement Award in that program. She has received her master's as a K-12 Educational Technology Specialist and was awarded the Educational Technology Graduate Program Academic Achievement Award. Ms. Spadoni's research focuses on artificial intelligence in the world of education. Dspadoni@schools.nyc.gov.

Gina L. Solano is a university professor of Educational Technology at SUNY Oneonta. Her research focuses on the professional development of educators in the field of technology, AR/VR/XR, generative AI, innovative technologies, and using technology to support mindfulness education. She teaches courses on research, digital media, educational technology, STEM, multimedia, online learning, and instructional design. She has presented on a variety of technology topics at national and international conferences on virtual reality, digital badges, digital storytelling, digital design, gamification, augmented reality, and geospatial technologies, among others. She has directed several service-learning programs, community outreach, and international student trips. Gina.solano@oneonta.edu. https://orcid.org/0009-0001-3970-5193.

Chapter 15
An Exploratory Study on the Use of GenAI in Higher Education as Support for Teachers' Feedback of Written Assignments

Stefanie A. Hillen

Abstract Artificial intelligence (AI) applications are increasingly used in various fields. Reviews by Okonkwo and Ade-Ibijola (Computers and Education: Artificial Intelligence, 2, 100033, 2021), Pérez et al. (Computer Applications in Engineering Education, 28(6), 1549–1565, 2020), and Cunningham-Nelson et al. (The 30th Annual Conference for the Australasian Association for Engineering Education (AAEE 2019): Educators Becoming Agents of Change: Innovate, Integrate, Motivate. Engineers Australia, 2019), demonstrate the variety and potential quality of chatbots and AI applications in education. This chapter examines whether and how generative AI (GenAI) can help educators provide feedback on student assignments as part of their learning. While helping students learn GenAI is often discussed, the main focus here is on supporting educators. This exploratory study's objective is to demonstrate the potential benefits of various GenAI approaches as digital tools for teachers, considering specific educational intents such as the production of written feedback reports, the analysis of assessment criteria, and the development of rubrics. The results show that GenAI can support instructors' feedback or assessment work if prompting and assessment alignment are appropriately considered.

Keywords Cognitive tool · Feedback · Prompt engineering · Teacher support

Generative Artificial Intelligence applications (GenAI) or Chat(ro-)bots are developed to facilitate communication and interaction between humans and machines (Yenduri et al., 2023). Efforts and initiatives are underway to improve their architecture for educational purposes (Sjöström et al., 2018). Generative AI has significant

S. A. Hillen (✉)
Department of Education, University of Agder, Kristiansand, Norway
e-mail: stefanie.a.hillen@uia.no

G. Tchibozo (ed.), *International Perspectives of Generative AI in Education*, Advances in Artificial Intelligence in Education 3,
https://doi.org/10.1007/978-3-031-99804-1_15

strengths and weaknesses. It poses challenges, including the risks of misinformation, ethical violations, and lack of originality. One major concern is the risk of facilitating plagiarism when students easily develop text through GenAI in learning contexts (Rudolph et al., 2023).

Reviews by Okonkwo and Ade-Ibijola (2021), Pérez et al. (2020), Lizarraga et al. (2023), and Cunningham-Nelson et al. (2019) demonstrate the wide range and the quality of chatbots/GenAI applications in education. Still, while applications for students are being implemented and researched, applications specifically for assessment by teachers are not as widely focused on, with only 6% of GenAI supporting assessment activities (Okonkwo & Ade-Ibijola, 2021, pp. 5–6). This chapter argues that GenAI can offer a cognitive partnership—in the sense of Salomon (1988)—to support teachers' work if GenAI is thoughtfully implemented (Hillen, 2023). The research question is: What kind of support can the use of GenAI in higher education provide for teachers in their assessment and feedback role?

The writing tools used here, for instance, Gemini, are Generative Artificial Intelligence-based applications that can be used in education, for educational purposes, and in educational settings. This exploratory study intends to use existing GenAI applications to support educational objectives, tasks, and processes, rather than to create, analyze or use autonomous educational bots (Edubots, 2022). At the beginning of 2023, when the writing of this chapter began (Hillen, 2023), most universities had not yet created their own applications or established legal and safe access to GenAI. This chapter has been influenced by the testing and development of different GenAI tools (see Table 15.1) that were available at that time. Some of these have undergone further development (e.g., ChatGPT), while others have simply changed their names (Bard has become Gemini, Bing has become Copilot), or both.

Legal and Ethical Considerations

Some countries or institutions have banned students from using AI writing tools. For instance, Russia, China, North Korea, Cuba, Iran, and Syria have prohibited their use (Martindale, 2023). Several school districts in the US have also banned the use of AI writing tools, expressing concerns about plagiarism and false information. Steps have been taken by universities in India and France to ban the use of ChatGPT. Educational institutions that support the use of such writing robots as ChatGPT have implemented specific rules and conditions to prevent plagiarism and protect data use. A common description one can find in higher education institutions is: "Writing robots, such as ChatGPT, may be used as a legal aid for exams where all support materials are allowed. Submitting text, calculations or any other content that has been copied directly from a writing robot without citing the source is considered to be presenting someone else's work as your own, and therefore cheating." (University of Agder, 2023, author's own translation). Interestingly no guidelines or regulations were provided for instructors or lecturers at that time. These regulations

Table 15.1 Research approaches, tools, learning groups, specifications, and notes

Approach	AI Tools/ LLMs	Participants	Specification	Annotations
(1a) Midterm assignment approach Spring 2023	Bard; Bing; GPT 3,5; GPT 4	Bachelor students ED 007, n = 13	Questionnaire-based comparison of respective usefulness of (i) teacher written, (ii) GenAI-supported written, and (iii) oral (through zoom) feedback	Different feedback opportunities were appreciated but none of them was specifically preferred by the students
(1b) Midterm assignment approach Spring 2023	Bard; Bing; GPT 3,5; GPT 4	Bachelor students ED 007, n = 13	Teachers' assessment criteria are used as prompt	Bard generated wrong results and even it was asked to correct these mistakes
(2) Assignment with simulated grading and explanation writing Fall 2023	Bing; GPT 3,5; GPT 4	Two teachers. Bachelor students ED 009, n = 28	(a) Structured prompt using assignments' wording. (b) Comparison of teacher and GenAI simulated grading	The comparison showed that the simulated GenAI-grading did not generate useful results
(3) Midterm assignment feedback Fall 2023	Bing/Copilot; GPT 3,5; GPT 4	Master students ED 008, n = 22	Structured prompt, Use of LMS to provide feedback	The feedback is experienced as too unspecific by the native speaking students
(4) Midterm assignment Rubrics Feedback Spring 2024	Gemini; Copilot GPT 3,5; GPT 4	Bachelor students ED 007, n = 28	Structured prompt by rubrics	Students asked for extended written feedback besides the shorter annotations already given in the LMS

have since been redefined, and are now more nuanced (University of Agder, 2024), taking into account the variety of examination contexts. Courses for teachers on the technical, ethical and legal aspects of GenAI have also been introduced.

When considering ethical aspects, it is important to keep in mind that a Generative Pre-trained Transformer (GPT), such as the one described by Yenduri et al. (2023), is trained by its developers and may therefore be influenced by their biases and choice of sources (Ekin, 2023). This could potentially perpetuate traditional role models, ethnic biases, and unhealthy power dynamics. Ekin (2023) states that one needs to be aware of potential biases that the tool may contain based on the data and sources they have been trained on. Teachers need to critically evaluate AI-generated content and ensure that it does not reinforce stereotypes or contain biased information.

To maintain the integrity of the assessment process, educators should also keep themselves informed of developments in the use of GenAI in education and continually improve their practices to ensure that their use of GenAI enhances, rather than compromises, the potential quality of student assessment.

Theoretical Baseline and Empirical Research in the Educational Landscape

As mentioned above, GenAI applications specifically designed for teacher assessment are not widespread. A keyword-based literature search in ORIA (a Norwegian electronic library tool) shows the following research and publication distribution ratio: a literature search on 'Edubots' resulted in 93 hits, while only 19 were related to 'edubots and teachers', and only 11 hits were found for the search topics 'edubots, teachers, and assessment'. If one dives deeper into these research papers, assessment is considered as a direct feedback tool without a teacher as mediator. Additionally, the papers discuss how assessment needs to be reconsidered in light of students using GenAI to prepare or write exam papers (Lacey & Smith, 2023) or how students can use for their own quiz-like applications (Sreelakshmi et al., 2019). Lacey and Smith (2023), for example, highlight that the assessment of students' performance is likely to change: "Students may be required to produce drafts and document searches and prompt strategies" (p.125); or that they will have to reflect on a given analysis and critique the source material, so students will be given other roles and tasks in academia with GenAI.

The study by Sreelakshmi et al. (2019) reports on a student-friendly chatbot that helps children learn fact-based topics by allowing them to ask questions and create quick practice quizzes. It takes an uploaded document as input. The bot combines two views: one simply checks how many key words from the question appear in each sentence (word matching), while the other looks at the overall meaning. By balancing these two views, the chatbot keeps its answers and quizzes tightly connected to what the child has just learned and thus reports on their performance.

A paper by Cunningham-Nelson et al. (2019) presents two short -response GenAI tools for classroom implementation: an FAQ chatbot that responds to common student inquiries, thereby acquiring course expertise while reducing teacher workload, and a short-response quiz bot that administers short quizzes, identifies misconceptions in students' written responses, and guides them to relevant resources through subsequent dialogue.

The specific perspective of how GenAI can be used to support teachers in improving qualitative and individual feedback is little or only partially addressed. When it is discussed, it is usually in the context of improving administrative efficiency.

The roots of GenAI for teachers can be traced back to tutorial systems (TS) in the 1960s (Opwis, 2001), which later evolved into intelligent systems supported by AI, known as ITS. At that time, computerized assessment was also a significant component, but it was primarily considered from a quantitative perspective. A more recent approach is the development of computer-aided testing systems (CAT), that provide automated feedback based on Bloom's cognitive taxonomy (Barker, 2011). Barker's efforts have resulted in four prototypes for objective testing. The automated feedback system uses a simple marking scheme and can be used in any subject. The subject tutor must create it as a text file according to a template. Marks for each option and feedback statements are stored in a database. The teacher marks each question, creating an individual feedback file applied automatically to each learner.

Even more advanced is the AI-driven Automatic Essay Scoring system, AES, (Susanti et al., 2023; Celik et al., 2022). Both papers conducted reviews on AES, while Celik's group conducted a review of the teachers' actual use of GenAI. The earlier study identified three areas of use for teachers: planning, implementation, and assessment. According to their review, GenAI helps teachers in exam automation and essay scoring and in decision-making on student performance. "It was found that an automated essay scoring system can not only significantly improve the effectiveness of essay scoring but also make the scoring more objective" (Celik et al., 2022, p. 7).

Another interesting approach is the development of a formative self-assessment tool for students, providing them with a safe environment for individual and self-directed learning (Durall & Kapros, 2020). Here, students can be in control without the pressure of being judged. From an inclusion point of view, GenAI have been considered as a potentially inclusive environment, accessible to people with special needs.

Approaches utilizing GenAI for automated assessment are also being developed. These chatbots ask students questions, but require short written answers (Ndukwe et al., 2019). Automated assessment of short text using GenAI is intended to scale this process, making it interactive and engaging for students. However, it does not serve as an assistive tool for educators in their daily work of providing feedback and assessment.

Therefore, the focus of this paper is on how to support teachers and instructors in delivering better qualitative assessments that incorporate the learning potential of written feedback for students. This is not meant to administer or to replace the teachers' educational autonomy and duty to carry out their own assessment and feedback tasks. One intention is to reduce the routine parts of providing feedback, while allowing more space and time for better, more adapted, more detailed, and more personalized written feedback. As assessment can sometimes lead to cognitive dissonance or disagreement (Goldring et al., 2015), it is important to provide text-based feedback with careful consideration. Constructive feedback can also be motivating (Hattie & Timperley, 2007) and can influence further learning.

To summarize the research intention: From the perspective of university lecturers and examiners, the project aims to provide better feedback or assessment of students' written assignments with the support of GenAI as a cognitive tool.

The Prompt, a Crucial Component in the Use of Chatbots to Support Written Feedback and Assessment Routines

An important prerequisite for working usefully with GenAI is the proper and considered use of prompts. This has influenced the approaches used and presented in this paper. A prompt is a way of addressing a GenAI application by creating and formulating a specific task or a question. The use of prompts needs to be carefully considered, because "we reap what we sow". Several types of prompts are available to address different purposes and styles of answers. It is important to adhere to the principles outlined in publications developed by experienced language modelers for GenAI (Atlas, 2023). The literature describes a variety of handling principles, but typically there are three to six basic ones: These include choosing words carefully, defining the conversation's purpose and focus, being concise and specific, and providing context. It is important to maintain a formal tone, use precise language, and adhere to established standards and units. Other recommendations include the following three main components:

– role (the perspective which should be taken and the level of expertise),
– task (the task, the objective the GenAI should conduct),
– form (presentation format for the result of the task).

Ekin (2023, p. 4) presents five factors that influence prompt engineering.

(a) User intent: Clarifying the user's goal and desired output helps to design a prompt that aligns with the user's expectations.
(b) Consider the purpose of the interaction, whether it is for information retrieval, content generation, or problem-solving.
(c) Model understanding: To craft effective prompts, it is important to understand chatbot's strengths and limitations. It is important to note that a chatbot may not always provide accurate or comprehensive information. Familiarize yourself with the model.
(d) Domain specificity: To enhance output accuracy, one needs to use specific concepts, technical terms, and contexts in specialized areas to guide the GenAI tool to better responses.
(e) Clarity and specificity: To ensure accurate responses, it is important to provide clear and specific messages, to give direct instructions, and to avoid vagueness or ambiguity. Specifying constraints is important, which means that it is helpful to define any specific requirement, such as response length or format, to guide bot's outputs more precisely.

As one can see, the recommendations and advice offered have some overlap in their purpose. Regardless of the specific approach taken, creating a prompt requires thoughtful reflection. Documentation and training programs are available for prompt engineering (Ekin, 2023).

Improvement, Organization, Transparency and Prompting

The study emphasizes that GenAI in education can serve not only as a tool to improve students' learning opportunities, but also as a means of enabling teachers to improve individualized feedback on distinct types of student work. In addition, intending to *improve* the quality of written feedback can help the teacher to better *organize* feedback using clearly articulated categories, becoming aware of the importance of differentiating the quality of performance, e.g., by using rubrics as a part of a prompt. Particularly, in times of accountability, prompt engineering can also be helpful in promoting clarity and transparency while ensuring alignment of assessment to the curriculum. The need to create a clear, concise prompt leads the teacher to reflect on the curriculum and the specificity and clarity of the guidelines given or developed for student learning. The prompt can then also be derived from the course- or learning outcome description. This *transparency* can be supported by the use of rubrics developed collaboratively with students to enhance their understanding of expectations. In addition, teachers can use written feedback for essays or assignments that are similar for all students. This is a common *organizing* practice for university lecturers, as assignments often ask about the same problem, project, or phenomenon.

Methods, Research Instruments and Sources

This exploratory study is based on the application of different approaches, which are outlined in Table 15.1. These approaches can be understood as an incremental development. In the case of prompt engineering, a guiding principle was to make the prompt more structured and to identify differences in language use. The experiences made, as well as participation in courses about GenAI, informed this research. Therefore, this research can be understood as exploratory qualitative classroom-based research. As a data corpus, student assignments and reports from four courses of a University in Norway (ED 007-009 from spring semester 2023 to 2024) were used. The last column of Table 15.1 is further explained in the results section.

The first approach, Feedback on midterm assignments/English, (1b), utilized data from an international university course taught in English at the Bachelor level. The students' midterm assignments varied in terms of the topic chosen by the students. These assignments served as a platform for written, GenAI-supported individual feedback. Due to the erroneous results generated by Bard, it was replaced by Bing/Copilot. Prior to this, a pre-study was conducted on students' feedback preferences (1a). The findings indicated that students were largely undecided as to which method was most appropriate for obtaining feedback, provided they were offered several options and combinations of options.

The second approach (2) refers to another international undergraduate course taught in English. All students were given the same assignment. GenAI-supported marking reports and explanations were provided to students to explain the quality and grading of their assignments after receiving their results. Every student has the right to request a written 'explanation' of the assignment results. Teachers often have to provide these explanations to students who request them, which can be time-consuming.

The third approach (3), feedback on midterm assignments/Norwegian, which involves providing individual written feedback on midterm assignments in the students' mother tongue, was used for a Master level course in Education.

The fourth approach (4), which involved providing feedback based on a rubric prompt for midterm assignments in English, was used 1 year later in the same international university course at the Bachelor level as in approach (1b). This time the feedback included rubrics, citations, and page numbers of the essay assignment.

Analysis, Findings and Discussion

To begin this exploratory research, we first need to find out about how students want to receive their feedback, and to ensure that the intention to offer appropriate feedback and explanations meets their needs and wishes, and is accepted by the students themselves. Studies on feedback (Agricola et al., 2020, p. 7) show that effective feedback needs to respect the timing, format and overall, the preferences of the students.

The Preference study (1a) looked at three types of feedback: oral feedback via zoom, short written feedback, and explicit written feedback supported by GenAI. In this study, the students were asked to outline their individual perceptions of the usefulness of feedback (Appendix 1). The students were deliberately not informed that the explicit written feedback was mainly generated with the support of GenAI.

The teacher made individual adjustments and corrections, as GenAI is not error-free and is not pedagogically trained. The combined written feedback, both short and extended, was delivered to the student in one go. Students were then asked to rate the usefulness of the written feedback and compare it with the usefulness of the Zoom feedback. The results showed no clear tendency, except that students preferred each type of combined feedback, presumably to have a variety of feedback from which to learn.

Midterm Assignment Feedback: The Use of Iterative Prompt

After clarifying students' preferences and perceived usefulness of oral and written feedback, the midterm assignments feedback was investigated (Approach 1b in Table 15.1). It was of particular interest to analyze how the prompt was fed by the criteria (Box 15.1). This prompt was used to provide extended written feedback on the midterm assignment in the same international bachelor course, Spring 2023, where the preferences were analyzed. The criteria and guidelines provided to the students were applied for assignment, in line with the principles of pedagogical honesty and instructional alignment, as defined by Polikoff and Porter (2014), and the principles of prompt formulation (see above).

Box 15.1 Prompt Specification Using Assignment Guidelines, and the GenAI-Generated Answer

Examiners Prompt: Please assess the following data collection report which should include the following parts:

1. A clear Index with page numbers
2. Information about the school
3. Description of the phenomenon to be observed (including research question)
4. Observation methods and timeline for the observation
5. Description of the observation tool
6. Description of the findings (data collected)
7. Information about further work to be done
8. Coherence between the criteria mentioned above
9. The paper respects the 3000-word limit
10. Appropriate references are added and correct
11. Appendix is added

GenAI answer:

Data Collection Report Assessment

The following criteria were used to assess the data collection report:

1. **Clear Index with Page Numbers**
   - *The report lacks a well-structured index. Including an index with clear page numbers is essential for navigation and readability.*
2. **Information about the School**
   - *The report provides insufficient details regarding the school where the data collection took place. More context about the school, such as its size, location, and student demographics, would improve the comprehensiveness of the report.*
3. **Description of the Phenomenon to be observed (Including Research Question)**
   - *A description of the phenomenon being observed is not adequately outlined. The research question should be clearly stated to guide the observation and analysis.*

(continued)

Box 15.1 (continued)

4. **Observation methods and timeline for the observation**
   - *The report does not offer enough information on the observation methods used or the timeline of the observation. Specifying the method (e.g., participant observation, structured observation) and the timeline (e.g., dates and duration of the observation) is necessary for transparency and reproducibility.*
5. **Description of the observation tool**
   - *The observation tool is not described in the report. This is a crucial omission, as the effectiveness and relevance of the data collection largely depend on the tools used (e.g., checklists, questionnaires).*
6. **Description of the findings (data collected)**
   - *While the report does include some findings, they are not adequately detailed. A more structured presentation of the data collected, including both quantitative and qualitative results, would enhance clarity and allow for better interpretation.*
7. **Information about further work to be done**
   - *There is little to no information on future steps. Recommendations for further research or next steps in the data collection process should be included to indicate a clear trajectory for the study.*
8. **Coherence between the criteria mentioned above**
   - *The coherence between the various sections of the report is lacking. The report should logically flow from one section to the next, ensuring that each criterion is adequately addressed.*
9. **Word limit adherence (3000 words)**
   - *The report does not clearly indicate whether it respects the maximum word count of 3000 words. It is essential to remain within this limit to ensure conciseness and focus.*
10. **Appropriate and correct references**
    - *The report does not include the necessary references. Proper citations of relevant literature are required to support the methodology and findings.*
11. **Appendix**
    - *The report includes an appendix, but its contents are not sufficiently detailed. The appendix should offer additional material that supports the main text, such as raw data, observation tools, or supplementary documentation.*

(continued)

Box 15.1 (continued)

Overall AI Assessment:

Based on the initial review, several criteria are missing or inadequately addressed. To provide a complete assessment, access to the full report would be necessary. As noted, critical sections such as the observation tool description and references are either absent or incomplete.

Box 15.2 Prompt Example—Combined Report

TASK: Please grade critically the essay. The essay should ... (original assignment description here) .... Mention if the amount of words max. 3000 is respected, the index, the research question, the theory and the topic, the conclusion, if literature is integrated. ROLE: The simulated is on bachelor's level with grades A to F (excellent to fail). Respect the grades definition. FORM: Do it explicitly and add a summarized part in which you do use the six criteria specified in the rubric and number it. Use specific examples ...

The criteria—derived from the assignment's writing guidelines—used in the prompts were applied iteratively until all important aspects were included to see how the extended written feedback evolved and became 'complete'.

In the early stages of using GenAI for feedback, one of the results was that teachers could use the GenAI-generated feedback as a guide to write the shorter, more personalized feedback in their own words. From the teachers' point of view, this was an effective form of support.

Investigation on Grading and Explanation: The Use of a Combined Prompt

In the Grading and Explanation approach, i.e. Approach (2) in Table 15.1, the prompt writing was modified. The course was taught by two teachers and twenty-two students participated. The prompt (Box 15.2) was designed to assist the teachers in the assessment process, which included assigning grades and eventually explaining them. The prompt consisted of two parts. It asked to generate an explicit written report followed by a structured brief summary.

The prompt was developed based on the original task and criteria given and adjusted to the format needed to be supportive for the teacher's final assessment report. It provided the explanation if the student asked for it. Finally, the teacher's written explanation report was based on the extended report and the summary. The

Box 15.3 AI-Generated Structured Short Report with Grades

STUDENTS CODE XXXX

The essay "Outdoor Education" compares outdoor education in Norway and Spain. Here's a critical assessment:

1. **Word Count**: Exceeds 3000-word limit, impacting conciseness and focus. Grade: C
2. **Index**: Clearly structured, facilitating easy navigation. Grade: A
3. **Research Question**: "What are the benefits of outdoor education? Should Spain take more advantage of nature and learning outside like Norway?"—Relevant and well-articulated. Grade: A
4. **Theory and Topic**: Incorporates theories from sources like Beate and Iversen (2023) but could benefit from deeper analysis. Grade: B
5. **Conclusion**: "Spain might gain by utilizing nature more and adopting a Norwegian-style school system"—Effective synthesis but lacks critical examination. Grade: B+
6. **Literature Integration**: Good use of sources like Noriega (2018) for comparative analysis but limited in scope and diversity. Grade: B

Overall, while the essay is well-structured and addresses the research question, the wordiness, limited theoretical depth, and scope of literature review affect its overall effectiveness. Grade: B/B+

prompt was tried out in Bard (Gemini) and Copilot. Bard produced wrong results which were caused by wrong interpretation of the criteria included in the prompt. Additionally, a comparison of grades was conducted using the GenAI results and the grades assigned by the two examiners in person.

There are two examiners because the university's grading regulations prescribe that grading should always be conducted by two examiners, both an internal and an external one. As previously stated, the prompt asked not only for a qualitative written feedback (Part 1), but also for a short report with simulated grades (Part 2), in this case from A to F (excellent to fail). Box 15.3 below shows an example of the prompt's output.

Grading Comparison

To evaluate the extent to which chatbot grading can support teacher grading, will be shown in the following comparison (see Table 15.2). While the grades themselves are not difficult to understand and to operationalize because they are described in the national university's grading system (see Appendix 2), it is important to question how GenAI weighs these grades. Hence, this requires careful consideration.

To be able to conduct this small statistical comparison, the scores were scaled as numbers from 1–6. The comparison showed different statistical ranges.

Table 15.2 Comparison between the teacher-assigned grades and those generated by GenAI

Student Exam ID	Teacher grading 'letter format'	Teacher grading 'numerical format'	GenAI grading 'letter format'	GenAI grading 'numerical format'	Statistical measure	Teacher grading	GenAI grading
01	C	3	C	3	n = 22		
02	E	5	B	2	Range	5	3
03	B	2	B	2	Variance	1.2866941	0.38134431
04	A	1	B	2			
05	A	1	B	2			
06	C	3	B	2			
07	A	1	C	3			
08	A	1	B	2			
09	E	5	B	2			
10	D	4	B	2			
11	...	...	...	...			
⋮	...	...	...	...			
22	...	...	...	...			

Compared to the two-teacher grading with a range of grades of "5", the smaller range of just "3" generated by GenAI is too narrow to allow a fine differentiation between students' respective performances, and to distinguish, for example, between cases of insufficient knowledge and those of poor argumentation. This small statistical investigation, using 'range' and 'variance', demonstrates the unsatisfactory discriminatory power of the GenAI-attributed grades, even though the university's grading definitions (Appendix 2) were included in the prompt. It is important to note that GenAI only organizes, administers, and has access to information, but the system itself is not an *expert*. Still, the GenAI results can assist teachers during the grading process by providing specific explanations. The GenAI tool can quickly identify criteria of interest (e.g. research questions or literature used) in students' work (Box 15.1). This key information easily provides an overview of the assessment criteria chosen for in-depth analysis. Teachers assigning grades or writing explanatory reports can orient themselves based on the GenAI report to dive deeper into the many pages of an essay before writing a personal feedback report.

Midterm Assignment Feedback/Native Language: Structured Prompt

The third approach (3) was not satisfactory for the students because they felt that they did not receive valuable feedback. One preliminary explanation is that the GenAI tool did not generate semantically appropriate native language. Even after the teacher rewrote the feedback generated by GenAI, the feedback did not meet the students' expectations. In the overall evaluation of this course, the students have clearly expressed their dissatisfaction with the written midterm assignment feedback they received. As previously discussed, prompt design is a critical factor. Therefore, it is also necessary to review the prompts and the assignment's wording as well. The prompt wording in this course was taken directly from the assignment (a text-based task in the mother tongue), and was accompanied by the other two key components needed for precision: the "role" and the "form" of the prompted report.

On the one hand, it is worth asking whether the assignment's wording was rather too open, and therefore not specific or clear enough and eventually had to be reformulated by the teachers. Interestingly, the assignment results themselves were satisfying, as confirmed by the second examiner in person. On the other hand, it is important to keep in mind that the ability to construct academic knowledge in an 'open-ended assignment' can be expected of Master students. Therefore, the assignment itself seems to have been appropriate for the students' capabilities but not for GenAI's prompt output to generate appropriate feedback.

Midterm Assignment Feedback/English: The Use of the Rubric-Based Prompt

Assessing and providing feedback is a time-consuming challenge. It is important to identify and address the specific aspects, such as quotations or reflective, literature-based discussions, that indicate whether the assignment criteria and guidelines have been met. To address this issue, this prompt approach includes quotations and page numbers as well as rubrics that complement the GenAI output. Citations and page numbers make it easy for the teacher to trace and identify where and on what GenAI has evaluated the student's work. This prompt approach builds on the experience and challenges of approaches 1a, 1b, 2 and 3 already presented. In this approach, the structured prompt also incorporated a rubric. Rubrics are commonly used pedagogical tools to categorize, indicate, or assess learner performance or knowledge. In this study the rubric served additional pedagogical purposes. The rubric was shared with the students so that they could understand the expectations, and the feedback given. The literature reports instances where rubrics were developed in collaboration with students (however, this was not the case in the research presented here), enhancing their awareness and acceptance of being assessed using a rubric (Cockett & Jackson, 2018). In general, a rubric comprises three components (Cockett & Jackson, 2018): assessment criteria, statements indicating the quality, and eventually a scoring manual. The rubric used here was generated electronically with the help of GenAI, but the content and criteria components had to be thoroughly developed in advance by the instructor for later use by the GenAI tool. The prompt comprised two parts. The first part was the description of the student's task or goal, as well as the length and format of the prompt's output, i.e. the same structure as the prompt presented in Box 15.2. The second part was the rubric itself (Table 15.3). Finally, the study examined the perceived usefulness of the rubrics (see Appendix 3). It is difficult to draw a general conclusion as only three out of the 27 expected responses were received, likely due to the approaching end of the semester. Anyhow, these three responses indicated that written feedback is preferred to the rubric, while a combination is preferred overall.

In the output of this prompt, specific sections can now be easily located using page numbers and references taken from the student report. The rubric accompanied the written feedback. The purpose of this rubric is to make it easier for students to understand the written comments.

One significant finding is that lecturers can now quickly gain an overview and insight into their students' work. They can then analyze the crucial aspects of the students' work in depth. This allows them to provide concise, written-rubric combined feedback supported by the GenAI, "in partnership" (Salomon et al., 1991).

Summary and Conclusion

This exploratory analysis aimed to investigate the usefulness of different approaches related to supporting teachers' daily work of written feedback and assessment. Teachers' assessment and feedback work meets an important requirement but is time-consuming. Examiners need to identify and address specific aspects, such as reflective, literature-based discussions or citations by the students that indicate whether the assignment criteria and guidelines have been met. This analysis highlights the potential benefits, challenges, and pitfalls of using GenAI-based feedback in four different teaching conditions and approaches. The approaches were developed and applied to generate case-based research findings.

As potential benefit, GenAI can provide support by quickly identifying different types of criteria which do function as core indicators of quality in the students' work. One of the challenges and responsibilities is to better engineer prompts that can include citations and page numbers, and to create rubrics that complement GenAI's structured report output. These anchors, for instance, page numbers, allow the lecturer to easily track and identify on what and where GenAI has assessed the student's work. Hence, the teachers' work assigning grades or writing explanatory reports can use the GenAI reports as a guide to dive deeper into the many pages of an essay to finally write personalized feedback reports. An example of a pitfall, tried out in one of these approaches (Approach 3), would be to use "open assignments" that would probably respond well to students' intellectual abilities, but wouldn't work (yet) for GenAI applications.

As well does prompt writing serve as a form of quality assurance. Prompt writing causes the teacher to reflect on the clarity and transparency of the learning task that students are responding to, while ensuring that the assessment is aligned with the

Table 15.3 Part II of the prompt: rubric with categories of student performance

Criteria	Excellent (A)	Very Good (B)	Good (C)	Satisfactory (D)	Needs Improvement (E)	Fail (F)
Word count	Within 4000 words, concise and comprehensive	Within 4000 words, mostly concise	Slightly exceeds 4000 words but all content relevant	Approaches 4000 words but includes some irrelevant details	Exceeds 4000 words with redundancy	Significantly exceeds or falls short of 4000 words, with many irrelevant sections
Index	Index is well-organized, accurate, and easy to navigate	Index is organized with minor inaccuracies	Index is clear with some organizational flaws and writing errors	Index is present but lacks the specification of the content	Index is poorly organized and somewhat inaccurate	No index provided or completely unusable
Introduction	Engaging and clearly stating the report's purpose and relevance	Clearly states the report's purpose with good relevance	Adequately introduces the purpose and relevance	Introduction lacks some clarity or detail	Introduction is vague and incomplete	No introduction or fails to introduce the report
Observation question	Perfectly articulated and highly relevant to the field	Clearly articulated and relevant to the field	Clearly stated but could be more closely tied to the field	Stated but lacks some relevance to the field	Vaguely stated, lacking specific relevance	No clear observation question or completely irrelevant
Method	Methodology is exemplary, perfectly suited, and well-explained	Methodology is well-suited and clearly explained	Methodology is appropriate with good explanation	Methodology described but lacks detail or clarity	Methodology is poorly suited or inadequately described	No methodology described or completely inappropriate
Presentation of findings	Findings are excellently presented and analytically insightful	Findings are very well presented with good analysis	Findings are well presented with adequate analysis	Findings presented but analysis is basic	Findings are poorly presented and superficially analyzed	Findings are not presented or irrelevant
Use of figures and tables	Excellent use, enhancing clarity and integration	Very good use, generally enhances text	Good use, adds value and mostly integrated	Adequate use, but integration could be better	Limited or ineffective use, adds little value	No effective use or completely misaligned with content

Criteria	Excellent (A)	Very Good (B)	Good (C)	Satisfactory (D)	Needs Improvement (E)	Fail (F)
Summary and conclusion	Insightful and comprehensive, fully addressing the observation question	Thorough. Addresses very well the observation question	Adequately addresses the observation question	Provides a basic summary and conclusion	Incomplete or unclear, partially addresses the question	Fails to summarize or conclude appropriately
Use of literature	Excellent range and integration of relevant literature	Very good use of appropriate literature	Good use of literature to support claims	Satisfactory use, but not fully exploited	Minimal or inappropriate use of literature	No relevant literature used or misuse of sources
Language use	Impeccable academic language and tone	Very good language use with minor errors	Good language use with some errors	Satisfactory language with occasional errors	Language use needs improvement. Frequent errors	Poor language use, severe impact on readability

curriculum. The need to create a clear, concise prompt leads the teacher to reflect on the curriculum and the specificity and clarity of the guidelines given or developed for student learning.

Repeating the research question, 'What kind of support can the use of GenAI in higher education provide for teacher written feedback and assessment?', the following conclusion can be drawn. As mentioned above, GenAI can assist teachers in obtaining an overview of students' submissions and questions. This is crucial because teachers are frequently involved in administrative tasks, which can impede their ability to concentrate on essential assessment tasks and processes required for providing adequate feedback. The support is *twofold*. On the one hand it provides a writing grid, which of course mirrors the quality of the prompt designed. The grid helps to evaluate students' assignments, together with the 'informative anchors' provided, for writing feedback in more depth and with more focus. On the other hand, prompt writing can be constructive, creative, and evaluative as it leads to reflection on one's own work in education, such as the construction of assignment items and questions that need as well to take the curriculum alignment into account. The responsibility of professional teachers, and their commitment to their profession, should not be called into question using GenAI. Instead, GenAI can be considered as a cognitive tool that can help to strengthen and stress their commitment.

Limitations, Reflections and Outlook

A limitation of the study is that several types of GenAI were intentionally tested and used to support teachers' assessment tasks and feedback at the beginning, with little prior academic and empirical knowledge from research studies. In addition, the GenAI applications make use of different language models (LLMs) and are pretrained differently (Patil & Gudivada, 2024), which may have led to different outcomes. Another limitation is that few questionnaires were returned, so they represent only a small proportion of all students' views. Another limitation was the analysis of the less well-defined assignments for students although an 'open-ended assignment' could be expected to be performed by Master's level students. Thus, the assignment may have been appropriate for the students' capabilities but not for GenAI's—for the time being. However, as GenAI knowledge bases develop, their pretraining and adaptability to users' needs will increase. Users themselves will also become more proficient in engineering prompts for better results.

Acknowledgement Special thanks to the project Consense (https://consense.uia.no/) which inspired me to conduct this research.

Competing Interests The author has no conflicts of interest to declare that are relevant to the content of this chapter.

Appendices

Appendix 1: Questionnaire on Students' Feedback Preferences

What kind of feedback helped you, and to what extent?		Please mark one of the six options for each question!
The oral advising via zoom	Helped me	Not at all □ □ □ □ □ □ to a great extent
The explicit written feedback	Helped me	Not at all □ □ □ □ □ □ to a great extent
The short written feedback	Helped me	Not at all □ □ □ □ □ □ to a great extent
A combination of oral advising and short-written feedback	Helped me	Not at all □ □ □ □ □ □ to a great extent
A combination of all three feedback types	Helped me	Not at all □ □ □ □ □ □ to a great extent

Appendix 2: Definition of Grades

A/Excellent—An excellent performance, clearly outstanding. The candidate demonstrates excellent judgement and a very high degree and independent thinking
B/Very good—A very good performance. The candidate demonstrates sound judgement and a high degree of independent thinking
C/Good—A good performance in most areas. The candidate demonstrates a reasonable degree of judgement and independent thinking in most important areas
D/Satisfactory—A satisfactory performance, but with significant shortcomings. The candidate demonstrates a limited degree of judgement and independent thinking
E/Sufficient—A performance that meets the minimum criteria, but no more. The candidate demonstrates a very limited degree of judgement and independent thinking
F/Fail—A performance that does not meet the minimum academic criteria. The candidate demonstrates an absence of both judgement and independent thinking

Appendix 3: Students' Perceived Usefulness of Feedback Types

Items	Less useful—1 2 3 4 5 6—more useful
The feedback through the rubrics is useful	(please fill in a number between 1 and 6): 4
The feedback through the written comments is useful	(please fill in a number between 1 and 6): 6
Feedback through the written comments along with the rubrics marked by the teacher is useful	(please fill in a number between 1 and 6): 6
The feedback only through the rubric marked by the teacher is useful	(please fill in a number between 1 and 6): 4

References

Agricola, B. T., Prins, F. J., & Sluijsmans, D. M. A. (2020). Impact of feedback request forms and verbal feedback on higher education students' feedback perception, self-efficacy, and motivation. *Assessment in Education: Principles, Policy & Practice, 27*(1), 6–25. https://doi.org/10.1080/0969594X.2019.1688764

Atlas, S. (2023). *Chatbot prompting: A guide for students, educators, and an AI-augmented workforce*. Amazon KDP Self-Publication, ASIN B0BV1XT5D6. ISBN-13: 9798376508602.

Barker, T. (2011). An automated individual feedback and marking system: An empirical study. *Electronic Journal of E-Learning, 9*(1), 1–14. https://files.eric.ed.gov/fulltext/EJ930249

Celik, I., Dindar, M., Muukkonen, H., & Järvelä, S. (2022). The promises and challenges of artificial intelligence for teachers: A systematic review of research. *TechTrends, 66*, 616–630. https://doi.org/10.1007/s11528-022-00715-y

Cockett, A., & Jackson, C. (2018). The use of assessment rubrics to enhance feedback in higher education: An integrative literature review. *Nurse Education Today, 69*, 8–13. https://doi.org/10.1016/j.nedt.2018.06.022

Cunningham-Nelson, S., Boles, W., Trouton, L., & Margerison, E. (2019). A review of chatbots in education: Practical steps forward. In *The 30th Annual Conference for the Australasian Association for Engineering Education (AAEE 2019): Educators Becoming Agents of Change: Innovate, Integrate, Motivate. Engineers Australia.*

Durall, E., & Kapros, E. (2020). Co-design for a competency self-assessment chatbot and survey in science education. In *Learning and Collaboration Technologies. Human and Technology Ecosystems: 7th International Conference, LCT 2020, Held as Part of the 22nd HCI International Conference, HCII 2020, Proceedings Part II* (pp. 13–24).

Edubots. (2022, January 31). *Best practices of pedagogical chatbots in higher education*. Faculty of Organization and Informatics, in collaboration with the consortium partners in the project. Erasmus+. https://uploads-ssl.webflow.com/5eb417ec5e1a81e0e30258a0/6241a9addc2a994a9b1018ec_WP5_D6_Whitepaper_Best_Practices_of_Chatbots_in_higher_education.pdf

Ekin, S. (2023). Prompt engineering for ChatGPT: A quick guide to techniques, tips, and best practices. https://doi.org/10.36227/techrxiv.22683919.v1

Goldring, E. B., Mavrogordato, M., & Haynes, K. T. (2015). Multisource principal evaluation data: Principals' orientations and reactions to teacher feedback regarding their leadership effectiveness. *Educational Administration Quarterly, 51*(4), 572–599. https://doi.org/10.1177/0013161X14556152

Hattie, J., & Timperley, H. (2007). The power of feedback. *Review of Educational Research, 77*(1), 81–112. https://doi.org/10.3102/003465430298487

Hillen, S. A. (2023). *An exploratory study on the use of chatbots in higher education as support for teachers' assessment of written midterm assignments*. Paper presentation. ECER 2023. Glasgow, Scottland.

Lacey, M., & Smith, D. (2023). Teaching and assessment of the future today: Higher education and AI. *Microbiology Australia, 44*, 124–126.

Lizarraga, C., Aguayo, R., Quiñonez, Y., Reyes, V., & Mejia, J. (2023). A new proposal for virtual academic advisories using chatbots. In J. Mejia, M. Muñoz, Á. Rocha, & V. Hernández-Nava (Eds.), *New perspectives in software engineering. CIMPS 2022* (Lecture Notes in Networks and Systems) (Vol. 576, pp. 233–242). Springer. https://doi.org/10.1007/978-3-031-20322-0_16

Martindale, J. (2023, 12 April). *These are the countries where ChatGPT is currently banned.* https://www.digitaltrends.com/computing/these-countries-chatgpt-banned

Ndukwe, I. G., Daniel, B. K., & Amadi, C. E. (2019). A machine learning grading system using chatbots. In S. Isotani, E. Millán, A. Ogan, P. Hastings, B. McLaren, & R. Luckin (Eds.), *Artificial intelligence in education* (pp. 365–368). Springer. https://doi.org/10.1007/978-3-030-23207-8_67

Noriega, J. (2018). La estrategia del mínimo operante como apoyo a las acciones de promoción de salud en la escuela primaria. In X Congreso Internacional de Investigación y Práctica Profesional en Psicología XXV Jornadas de Investigación XIV Encuentro de Investigadores en Psicología del MERCOSUR. Facultad de Psicología-Universidad de Buenos Aires. https://www.aacademica.org/000-122/105.pdf

Okonkwo, C. W., & Ade-Ibijola, A. (2021). Chatbots applications in education: A systematic review. *Computers and Education: Artificial Intelligence, 2*, 100033. https://doi.org/10.1016/j.caeai.2021.100033

Opwis, K. (2001). Instructional technology: Cognitive science perspectives. In N. J. Smelser & P. B. Baltes (Eds.), *International encyclopedia of the social & behavioral sciences* (pp. 7573–7577). Pergamon. https://doi.org/10.1016/B0-08-043076-7/01476-5

Patil, R., & Gudivada, V. (2024). A review of current trends, techniques, and challenges in large language models (LLMs). *Applied Sciences, 14*(5), 2074. https://doi.org/10.3390/app14052074

Pérez, Q. J., Daradoumis, T., & Marquès Puig, J. M. (2020). Rediscovering the use of chatbots in education: A systematic literature review. *Computer Applications in Engineering Education, 28*(6), 1549–1565. https://doi.org/10.1002/cae.22326

Polikoff, M. S., & Porter, A. C. (2014). Instructional alignment as a measure of teaching quality. *Educational Evaluation and Policy Analysis, 36*(4), 399–416. https://doi.org/10.3102/0162373714531851

Rudolph, J., Tan, S., & Tan, S. (2023). ChatGPT: Bullshit spewer or the end of traditional assessments in higher education? *Journal of Applied Learning and Teaching, 6*(1), 342–363. https://doi.org/10.37074/jalt.2023.6.1.9

Salomon, G. (1988). AI in reverse: Computer tools that turn cognitive. *Journal of Educational Computing Research, 4*(2), 123–139. https://doi.org/10.2190/4LU7-VW23-EGB1-AW5G

Salomon, G., Perkins, D. N., & Globerson, T. (1991). Partners in cognition: Extending human intelligence with intelligent technologies. *Educational Researcher, 20*(3), 2–9. https://doi.org/10.3102/0013189X020003002

Sjöström, J., Aghaee, N., Dahlin, M., & Ågerfalk, P. J. (2018). Designing chatbots for higher education practice. In *Proceedings of the 2018 AIS SIGED International Conference on Information Systems Education and Research* (p. 4) https://aisel.aisnet.org/siged2018/4

Sreelakshmi, A. S., Abhinaya, S. B., Nair, A., & Jaya Nirmala, S. (2019). A question answering and quiz generation chatbot for education. In *2019 Grace Hopper Celebration India (GHCI)* (pp. 1–6). https://doi.org/10.1109/GHCI47972.2019.9071832

Susanti, M. N., Ramadhan, A., & Warnars, H. L. (2023). Automatic essay exam scoring system: A systematic literature review. *Procedia Computer Science, 216*, 531–538.

University of Agder. (2023, January). *Use of AI in examinations*. https://www.uia.no/student/eksamen/linkeblokksamling/under-eksamen/plagiat-og-fusk-paa-Eksamen

University of Agder. (2024, May 30). *Artificial intelligence in assignment writing*. https://www.uia.no/english/studies/for-students/examinations/ai-in-assignment-writing.html

Yenduri, G., Ramalingam, M., Chemmalar, S. G., Supriya, Y., Srivastava, G., Maddikunta, P. K., DeeptiRaj, G., Jhaveri, R. H., Prabhadevi, B., Wang, W., Vasilakos, A. V., & Gadekallu, T. R. (2023). Generative pre-trained transformer: A comprehensive review on enabling technologies, potential applications, emerging challenges, and future directions. *ArXiv abs/2305.10435*.

Stefanie A. Hillen holds a Ph.D. in business education and is a full professor at the Department of Education, University of Agder, Norway. She has been a visiting professor at Florida State University and the University of Nebraska at Omaha. Her research interests include technology-enhanced learning, general and ICT didactics, and didactics in vocational education. Professor Hillen leads the research group on school development, evaluation and digital assessment. She teaches courses in career and professional theory and international and general education. She also advises doctoral students in vocational education. ORCID: https://orcid.org/0000-0002-3245-2592, URL: https://www.uia.no/kk/profil/stefanah. Email: stefanie.a.hillen@uia.no.

Chapter 16
Identifying GenAI Effectiveness: Grading Elementary Writing

Tyler Harnish and Gina L. Solano

Abstract This chapter looks at the viewpoints of educators on the use of Generative Artificial Intelligence (GenAI) in grading writing pieces of 3rd–5th grade students. The purpose is to explore the efficacy and accuracy of using GenAI to grade written assignments of students to determine if it is an effective tool. A qualitative descriptive study was conducted in an elementary school in a school district in the Southern Tier of New York State. The participants were tasked with using two different GenAI tools to grade the same versions of student papers based on a New York State-given rubric. Participants answered various questions in the form of a questionnaire and an interview to assess the effectiveness of the technology. The results showed that the majority expressed optimism about the experience, and a common agreement emerged that AI's grading capabilities are satisfactory. Nonetheless, the occasional errors and absence of personality were deemed too significant to definitively assert that GenAI could entirely supplant the role of a teacher in grading written pieces. This study could help provide evidence to promote or discourage the use of GenAI technology in schools as a grading aid.

Keywords Action research · Assessment · Grading · Rubrics

Generative Artificial Intelligence (GenAI) has been invading the education world in recent years. The media have given this technology a negative connotation, portraying it as a way for students to cheat on their homework (Alasadi & Baiz, 2023). However, GenAI can also be an opportunity for teachers in their assessment and grading functions. Several small U.S. school district technology teams are exploring the possibility of GenAI assisting with teacher workloads. Using technology to

T. Harnish · G. L. Solano (✉)
State University of New York (SUNY) Oneonta, Oneonta, NY, USA
e-mail: Tharnish@cppasd.com; Gina.solano@oneonta.edu

G. Tchibozo (ed.), *International Perspectives of Generative AI in Education*, Advances in Artificial Intelligence in Education 3,
https://doi.org/10.1007/978-3-031-99804-1_16

grade written work is one way GenAI could be used. This study will evaluate the effectiveness of GenAI used by teachers for grading elementary students' written work.

Background to the Problem

In 2023, the average teacher in the United States spent more time at work grading assignments for their classes than their contractual hours dictated by their contracts (Steiner et al., 2023). A typical teacher might be allowed to leave work according to their contract at 3:15 p.m. each day. However, on average, these teachers leave the classroom at 4:30 p.m. (4th grade teacher, personal communication, September 2023). This includes time spent during preparation periods, as well as before class. This contributes to teachers feeling overworked and burnt out (Steiner et al., 2023) and fuels the national teacher shortage.

Assessment and grading are one of the factors behind teachers' work overload. One of the main pieces of grading in 5th grade elementary school is assessing student writing. This process takes longer than others because each individual student's work takes time to process, reflect on, and offer suggestions to improve their writing. This represents a potential opportunity to use GenAI for grading. However, while GenAI is a possible solution, it is not without controversy.

A study by Kumar (2023) illustrated the dilemma of using GenAI to grade. Arguments against using GenAI in this role involve the cost of commercial GenAI tools, privacy rights, legality of sharing students' work, and the ethics of using an agent other than the professor to grade (Kumar, 2023). Kumar's research was conducted at a higher education university. The case described a professor who was beyond busy and wanted to utilize GenAI to help grade students' work and make grading more efficient. The professor utilized Dall-E and ChatGPT. The study concluded that educators will have to place themselves on the continuum between two poles: ignoring GenAI tools and educating about GenAI tools. The professor reasoned that not using GenAI at this time would be a safe bet.

This case study brought to light the complexity of using this relatively new technology. Even though this study focused on higher education versus elementary, the findings are germane.

Another pertinent study about GenAI focused on the advantages and disadvantages of different GenAI methods when it comes to assessing and grading collaboration (Tomić et al., 2023). This other study delved into GenAI grading of essays and collaborative projects.

The school where the present research was conducted is a suburban elementary school in the southern tier of western New York. The school services students with individual devices such as Chromebooks. In the school, each teacher is given a laptop that they can wirelessly connect to their smartboards. The school district has an active teacher-led technology team. This functional team meets monthly to discuss issues and concerns facing the district's schools. GenAI has been a topic of focus at one of the meetings (Technology Director, personal communication, May, 2023).

During the meeting, there were multiple discussions on how to use GenAI as well as setting district guidelines on how students can and cannot utilize GenAI in the classrooms. Teachers being able to utilize GenAI in the classrooms on a district level was also discussed, and generated a lot of interest. This was tabled as GenAI is too new for the district to adopt it as a standard grading practice, with the need for more evidence highlighted. This action research project is directly relevant to the district in its ongoing inquiry for teacher utilization of GenAI for grading purposes. This study will be identifying two different GenAI tools that will be used to see which one the teacher participants deem more effective, if any.

As McKinsey (2024) put it: "Generative artificial intelligence (GenAI) describes algorithms (such as ChatGPT) that can be used to create new content, including audio, code, images, text, simulations, and videos" (para. 1). Lawton (2023) tells us that generative AI was actually introduced as early as the 1960s. It was not until 2014, with the introduction of a specific type of learning algorithm, that GenAI really took off, being able to create authentic and convincing images, videos and sounds of real people. GenAI continually learns what the user wants it to do, and becomes smarter as the user interacts with the tool. GenAI should be capable of grading a writing assignment that is given with a rubric. The two GenAI tools evaluated in this study are MagicSchool.ai and ChatGPT.

As described by Reimers (2023), MagicSchool.ai is a GenAI-powered educational platform that was specifically designed with teachers in mind. The platform allows the users to create different sets of documents (such as lesson plans, rubrics, and assessments) and ask questions to receive answers that would be more beneficial to an educator than to other professions. Hook (2023) tells us that MagicShool.ai promises to help educators save time by automating the task of lesson planning, among other tools, including a powerful grading functionality.

ChatGPT, as described by Hetler (2023), is a GenAI chatbot that uses natural language processing to create a humanlike conversation. This GenAI tool is capable of numerous tasks from answering questions you have, to creating new pieces of work like a quiz or a lesson plan. Ortiz (2023) wrote that ChatGPT is also capable of composing essays, describing art in detail, and having philosophical conversations. How you use the tool is up to your imagination.

This qualitative study investigates the effectiveness of GenAI grading from the point of view of teachers at a suburban elementary school in Western New York. GenAI presents a way that can help reduce teacher burnout, and eventually reduce the national teacher shortage (Post, 2024). Reducing burnout could in turn make teachers more effective in their instruction. Teachers could refocus on improving the quality of teaching and providing better support for their students. According to Kumar (2023), professors at higher education also are willing to utilize the technology; however, they are unsure how the public would react and if it is time for the technology to be integrated into colleges, let alone the public education system.

Further research and results are needed before a decision can be made on whether or not to utilize this new technology. Lawton (2023) emphasizes the need for more research to be able to make a more ethical decision on GenAI involvement in education. More action research studies could provide much needed data on whether

GenAI could be an effective tool for giving feedback and grading (U.S. Department of Education, 2023).

The purpose of this study is to understand teachers' perspectives on the use of GenAI when grading writing assignments to determine if it is an effective tool for teacher usage. The question that will guide this study is: How effective are different GenAI tools in grading elementary writing?

Literature Review

Research on GenAI for assessment and grading highlights benefits and drawbacks. GenAI is being used in education to provide intelligent tutoring systems, learning analytics, and online tutoring. Alam (2021) mentioned that GenAI could use analytics to track student progress and provide personalized recommendations to the students for improvement.

Alam (2021) also discussed the idea that GenAI can power chatbots that are able to answer student questions about a course or assignment in real time, unlike educators who can take hours to respond, while students need these clarifications to be able to continue working on their assignments. Rutner and Scott (2022), who conducted a study about the application of GenAI in online grading of student discussion boards also noted that GenAI can provide students with immediate feedback. This latter study was prompted by the increased use of online learning during the COVID-19 pandemic, which highlighted the need for efficient grading methods for asynchronous discussions. GenAI reduced the workload on instructors while providing timely feedback to students (Rutner & Scott, 2022). Results from this study indicated a mixed response from students, with some appreciating the quick feedback while others were concerned about the accuracy and fairness of an AI assessing their work. Based on these findings, Rutner and Scott (2022) suggested that GenAI should be used to complement rather than replace human grading.

Another set of benefits that could come from GenAI technologies include more objective feedback to the learners. One of the age-old drawbacks to teachers' grading of writing is its subjectivity. Teachers might give better grades to writing that is more appealing to them. GenAI tools might help mitigate this. In the study by Rutner and Scott (2022), the participating teachers found that GenAI contributed to the consistency of marks between students. Kumar (2020) and Tomić et al. (2023) highlighted GenAI's ability to grade without bias and that it can provide consistent feedback thus resulting in higher-quality work. However, a drawback highlighted by Stoica (2022) is that the results generated by GenAI tools may reproduce the biases contained in the data with which these tools were trained.

Pack et al. (2025) investigated the effectiveness of GPT-4 in providing corrective feedback in a writing course. The researchers compared the feedback provided by the instructors with that from GPT-4. They discovered that the instructors' feedback was more reliable than that of the GenAI tool. Still, they suggested that despite the limitations, with ongoing improvements and better prompt engineering, GenAI tools could eventually assist educators in managing the time-consuming task of providing accurate written feedback.

Another limitation of GenAI is that humans inherently have more of a creative side that GenAI may not be capable of detecting currently. This could cause an error when the algorithm for the grade does not have the pre-trained data necessary to make that correct judgment. GenAI is such a new technology that no solution currently exists to guarantee a flawless assessment (Stoica, 2022).

Alam (2021) also discussed the challenges and ethical considerations of using AI in education, which may cause a loss of human interaction. The author warned of the need for cautious implementation to ensure equity and accessibility when using GenAI.

Babitha et al. (2022) delved into the topic of accessibility. They made clear the many challenges of accessibility and disabilities that are inherent in education. GenAI tools have proved useful for improving the writing skills not only of general education students, but also of special education students (Babitha et al., 2022). GenAI is also suited to overcome some of the accessibility and disability challenges through online delivery.

Barrett and Pack (2023) investigated the perceptions of both students and educators regarding the integration of generative AI tools in academic writing. Based on a survey of 68 educators and 158 university students, the study revealed little disagreement between the two groups on the acceptable use of GenAI in various stages of the writing process, such as brainstorming, outlining, writing, revising, feedback, and evaluating. While some participants recognized the potential benefits of GenAI, others expressed concerns about academic integrity and the readiness of educational institutions to manage these technologies. The findings underscored the need for explicit guidelines and professional development for teachers to effectively incorporate GenAI in educational settings. The study concluded that clear policies and ongoing dialogue are essential to ensure the responsible and effective use of GenAI tools in education.

Some other concerns of using GenAI tools involve its cost as well as privacy and other ethical issues (Kumar, 2023).

Finally, GenAI can provide the support needed to students as they write their assignments. Online AI tools, such as Grammarly and QuillBot, work simultaneously with the writer to provide grammar and punctuation corrections, as well as suggestions for improving the sentence structure or phrasing. These tools, along with other AI writing assistants have shown positive improvements in students' writing quality, content, and organization (Marzuki et al., 2023). However, a study conducted by Ironsi and Solomon Ironsi (2025) experimented using ChatGPT in a writing course to determine if it could help to improve their writing skills. The authors determined that while the GenAI tool was helpful in providing ideas for writing assignments, it did not improve their overall writing skills.

Method

A qualitative action research approach was chosen for this study because it enabled the researchers to explore the problem in depth and gain insight into the social world (Creswell, 2015). The authors of this chapter adhere to the view that qualitative (action) researchers must accept "the risks and challenges of the interpretive mode" because in doing so they can "demonstrate to others (and reassure ourselves) that, in spite of their undistinguished origins, our works and the implications to be drawn from them are socially significant" (Mills, 2018, p. 203).

Qualitative data was collected through interviews and evaluations and then was analyzed in a complex manner, allowing the ability to continually refine the questioning and data collection process to better understand the educators' perceptions, opinions, and experiences.

Participants

Five teachers were participants in the study. Two fourth-grade teachers, a third-grade teacher, a fifth-grade teacher, and a special education teacher. These individuals were chosen based on a purposeful sampling because they had to meet specific criteria to be included. The approach followed that of Creswell (2015), who stated: "In qualitative research, we identify our participants and sites on purposeful sampling, based on places and people that can best help us understand our central phenomenon" (p. 205). Thus, the participants in the study were ones that are required in the school to grade their student's writing pieces on the rubric scale that the GenAI utilized as well. These individuals were best suited to answer the study questions.

Procedures

After the participants were recruited, the next step was to have them fill out a pre-check evaluation to determine their experience in the use of GenAI. This helped to determine if they needed to be taught how to utilize the GenAI tools. Then, they were provided with three different pieces of student work, the first one well-constructed, the second semi-well-constructed, and the third poorly written. They were asked to utilize ChatGPT to grade the different pieces.

Following the grading, the participants read the feedback and scores that the GenAI generated. They took the time to fill out an evaluation questionnaire. This helped to characterize their reactions to the usability and results of the technological tool and determine its efficacy. Then, the participants repeated the same process with MagicSchool.ai. Finally, the participants who so wished were invited to take part in an interview to help determine their overall thoughts about how effective the GenAI tools were at grading the writing samples.

Instruments

A study by Braun et al. (2020), stated that "questionnaire studies were more appealing to potential participants than face-to-face interviews or laboratory studies." Utilizing a questionnaire format is likely to attract more teachers to share their feedback and participate in the study. A questionnaire was therefore developed and used (see Appendix 1).

Nevertheless, this study also used interviews (see Appendix 2), as "They permit participants to describe detailed personal information" (Creswell, 2015 p. 218). The study thus obtained more detailed information. While most participants filled out the questionnaire, their responses were thin. In contrast, fewer people agreed to an interview, which was more time-consuming, but yielded more data.

Data Analysis

The data collected was analyzed through reduction into different codes and themes. These themes were set to match the research question. Data reliability was examined (Mills, 2018).

Results

Analysis of the data revealed three themes corresponding to the research question and framework, i.e.: quality of the grading, ease of use, and alignment to the teachers' standards.

Theme 1: Quality of AI-Based Grading and Teacher-Based Grading

There was a difference between ChatGPT and MagicSchool.ai in the alignment of their gradings to that of teachers. Some participants (P1, P4) thought that MagicSchool.ai aligned more with a teacher's grading than ChatGPT. Teacher (P2) stated, "MagicSchool.ai certainly looked more like a response from a teacher. It was written in paragraph form vs. bullet points." Three participants (P1, P2, P3) disagreed with a score that was given to a student by ChatGPT. ChatGPT gave a student a score of 1 while the participants stated that they would have given that student a 0.

Theme 2: Ease of Use

Throughout the process, the participants found the technology tools easy to utilize. "There were no challenges when it came to using the GenAI," (P3). "All that is needed to complete the process is the ability to copy-paste into the GenAI" (P2). Another participant, (P4), went a step further to say that "MagicSchool.ai was much more intuitive." Some said that "the perceived ease of use was much greater than they had originally anticipated" (P5). It can be said that the overall experience of using the two different GenAI tools was simplistic and extremely user-friendly.

Theme 3: Alignment to Teacher Standards

The final theme highlighted by the study was alignment with the standards of the educators based on their rubrics and personal teaching pedagogy. One of the main aims of using GenAI was to take over feedback to the students on behalf of the educators. P2 believed that the feedback provided by the GenAI gave zero depth and was not detailed enough to provide the students with sufficient information to know how to improve their writing. The GenAI could be beneficial in correcting grammar components, but the feedback is not specific enough (P2, P5). One of the main weaknesses of the technology was that, in the absence of the entire book or story, it was impossible to know whether the details of the text were sufficiently precise (P1, P4, P3). Another participant found that GenAI would be a great addition to teachers' own grading of the grammar in written responses but not replacing the grading process from educators (P4).

Discussion

In response to the research question ("How effective are different GenAI tools in grading elementary writing?), the study participants pointed to different avenues. One of the main conclusions that was drawn was the ease of use that GenAI technology offers. Some participants (P2, P3) stated that the tools were user-friendly. Others (P1, P4) noted that the process was easier than previously thought. According to Reimers (2023), MagicSchool.ai's response generator features a convenient "quick copy" button for effortless pasting. The goal of the tool is to be an easy-to-use tool for teachers and that seems to be accomplished.

However, another important conclusion was that the GenAI tools' output failed to align with the educators' standards. One of the main complaints from the participants was the lack of depth behind the feedback. This echoes Stoica's (2022) observation that GenAI's grading is not guaranteed against flawed assessments. While there was a consensus that GenAI models had shortcomings in terms of feedback and assessing the quality of the graded assignments, the educators were aware that this is a new technology. Stoica (2022) had mentioned that additional prerequisites that could enhance GenAI's proficiency as a grading tool include ensuring that it provides personalized feedback. A few participants (P2, P3) shared similar thoughts that a graded writing piece should be based on a student's specific needs and the GenAI did not accurately reflect this enough.

Transferability and Generalizability

Conducted in a suburban elementary school in the Southern Tier of New York State, this qualitative study examines the efficacy and accuracy of GenAI in grading student work based on a New York State rubric. Contrasting this context with similar educational settings, such as higher education or under-resourced schools, highlights differences in technological access and the specific needs of students and educators. For instance, while higher education institutions may have more resources to implement and refine AI tools, under-resourced schools might struggle with access to the necessary technology and training. These contextual differences suggest that while the positive impacts observed in this study could be transferable, they would require adaptation to local conditions. Ensuring equitable access to technology and providing adequate professional development for educators are essential steps for effectively integrating AI tools in diverse educational environments. This adaptability is crucial for maximizing the benefits of AI in education and addressing the unique challenges faced by different educational contexts.

Conclusion

This study investigated the initial opinions of 3–5th grade teachers who utilized GenAI to grade student writing pieces. The results and mentioned opinions could be used by other elementary teachers and GenAI developers to help them formulate their own perceptions of GenAI's effectiveness (compared to that of teachers) in terms of grading student writing, giving feedback, and scoring.

AI technology in the educational world is very controversial. Arguments against using GenAI to grade student papers involve cost, privacy, legality, and ethics (Kumar, 2023). There are many arguments that can be made as to why GenAI should be left out of the classroom. The teachers who participated in this study were eager to see how the technology would fare against their own perceptions of how the writing pieces should be graded. While most were very optimistic about the experience, there was a consensus that GenAI is not very good at grading. The few mistakes and lack of personality were too definitive to truly say that GenAI could duplicate a teacher's job at grading writing pieces. GenAI is a relatively new technology and will undoubtedly go through several iterations that will overcome these shortcomings. There is little doubt that one day GenAI will be able to offer quality assistance to educators in this area, but that day is not here yet.

Competing Interests The authors have no conflicts of interest to declare that are relevant to the content of this chapter.

Appendices

Appendix 1: Evaluation Questionnaire

- What are your initial impressions of GenAI?
- In your opinion, how effective was the GenAI tool in accurately grading the writing pieces?
- How closely did the GenAI tool's grading align with how you would typically assess and grade these writing pieces manually?
- How user-friendly and intuitive did you find the GenAI tool for grading writing pieces? Did you encounter any challenges in using it?
- How would you rate the quality and depth of feedback provided by the GenAI tool in guiding students on how to improve their writing?
- Can you envision incorporating this GenAI grading tool into your regular teaching practices for assessing students' writing? Why or why not?
- How do you anticipate your students reacting to receiving feedback from a GenAI tool compared to feedback from you as their teacher?

Appendix 2: Interview Questions

- Initial impressions: What were your initial thoughts or impressions when using the GenAI grading tools for the first time to evaluate students' writing pieces?
- Comparison of GenAI tools: How would you compare the feedback provided by the two AI tools in terms of accuracy, relevance, and alignment with the rubric criteria?
- Effectiveness in grading: In your opinion, how effective were the GenAI tools in accurately grading the writing pieces based on the given rubric?
- Alignment with teacher assessment: How closely did the GenAI tools' grading align with how you would typically assess and grade these writing pieces manually?
- Ease of use and efficiency: How user-friendly and intuitive did you find the GenAI tools for grading writing pieces? Did you encounter any challenges in using them?

- Feedback quality: How would you rate the quality and depth of feedback provided by the GenAI tools in guiding students on how to improve their writing?
- Potential integration into teaching: Can you envision incorporating either of these GenAI grading tools into your regular teaching practice for assessing students' writing? Why or why not?
- Student engagement and acceptance: How do you anticipate your students reacting to receiving feedback from a GenAI tool compared to feedback from you as their teacher?

References

Alam, A. (2021, December). Should robots replace teachers? Mobilisation of AI and learning analytics in education. In *2021 International Conference on Advances in Computing, Communication, and Control* (pp. 3.1–12). https://ieeexplore.ieee.org/document/9697300

Alasadi, E., & Baiz, C. (2023). Generative AI in education and research: Opportunities, concerns, and solutions. *Journal of Chemical Education, 100*(8), 2965–2971. https://pubs.acs.org/doi/abs/10.1021/acs.jchemed.3c00323

Babitha, M. M., Sushma, C., & Gudivada, V. K. (2022). Trends of Artificial Intelligence for online exams in education. *International Journal of Early Childhood Special Education, 14*(1) https://www.researchgate.net/publication/360513613_Trends_of_Artificial_Intelligence_for_Online_Exams_in_Education

Barrett, A., & Pack, A. (2023). Not quite eye to AI: Student and teacher perspectives on the use of generative artificial intelligence in the writing process. *International Journal of Educational Technology in Higher Education, 20*(1), 59. https://doi.org/10.1186/s41239-023-00427-0

Braun, V., Clarke, V., Boulton, E., Davey, L., & McEvoy, C. (2020). The online survey as a qualitative research tool. *International Journal of Social Research Methodology, 24*(6), 641–654. https://doi.org/10.1080/13645579.2020.1805550

Creswell, J. (2015). *Educational research: Planning, conducting, and evaluating quantitative and qualitative research* (4th ed.). Pearson.

Hetler, A. (2023). *What is ChatGPT.* Tech Target. https://www.techtarget.com/whatis/definition/ChatGPT

Hook, S. (2023). *What is Magic School AI*? PC Guide. https://www.pcguide.com/ai/magic-school-ai/

Ironsi, C. S., & Solomon Ironsi, S. (2025). Experimental evidence for the efficacy of generative AI in improving students' writing skills. *Quality Assurance in Education, 33*(2), 237–252. https://doi.org/10.1108/QAE-04-2024-0065

Kumar, A. (2020). *AI's new role in education: Automated grading*. eLearning Industry. https://elearningindustry.com/artificial-intelligence-new-role-in-education-automated-paper-grading

Kumar, R. (2023). Faculty members' use of artificial intelligence to grade student papers: A case of implications. *International Journal for Educational Integrity, 19*, 9. https://edintegrity.biomedcentral.com/articles/10.1007/s40979-023-00130-7

Lawton, J. (2023). *What is generative AI? Everything you need to know*. TechTarget. https://www.techtarget.com/searchenterpriseai/definition/generative-AI

Marzuki, Widiati, U., Rusdin, D., Darwin, & Indrawati, I. (2023). The impact of AI writing tools on the content and organization of students' writing: EFL teachers' perspective. *Cogent Education, 10*(2). https://doi.org/10.1080/2331186X.2023.2236469

McKinsey. (2024). *What is generative AI?* McKinsey & Company. https://www.mckinsey.com/featured-insights/mckinsey-explainers/what-is-generative-ai

Mills, G. (2018). *Action research: A guide for the teacher researcher* (6th ed.). Pearson.

Ortiz, S. (2023). *What is ChatGPT and why does it matter? Here's what you need to know*. ZDnet. https://www.zdnet.com/article/what-is-chatgpt-and-why-does-it-matter-heres-everything-you-need-to-know/

Pack, A., Hartshorn, K. J., Escalante, J., & Gillette, N. (2025). How well can GenAI (GPT-4) provide written corrective feedback on English-language learners' writing? *International Journal of English for Academic Purposes: Research and Practice, 5*(1), 7–26. https://doi.org/10.1186/s41239-023-00427-0

Post, R. (2024, February 1). *How can AI help solve the teacher shortage*? American Association of School Personnel Administrators. https://www.aaspa.org/news/how-can-ai-help-solve-teacher-shortages#:~:text=Technology%20and%20AI%20are%20often,that%20can%20reduce%20their%20workload

Reimers, P. (2023). *MagicSchool offers 40+ time-saving AI tools for teachers*. Technotes. https://blog.tcea.org/magicschool/

Rutner, S., & Scott, R. (2022). Use of artificial Intelligence to grade student discussion boards: An exploratory study. *Information Systems Education Journal, 20*(4), 4–18. https://files.eric.ed.gov/fulltext/EJ1358299.pdf

Steiner, E. D., Woo, A., & Doan, S. (2023). *All work and no pay—Teachers' perceptions of their pay and hours worked: Findings from the 2023 State of the American Teacher Survey*. RAND Corporation. https://www.rand.org/pubs/research_reports/RRA1108-9.html

Stoica, E. (2022). *A student's take on challenges of AI-driven grading in higher education*. University of Twente. https://essay.utwente.nl/91784/1/Stoica_BA_EEMCS.pdf

Tomić, B., Kijevčanin, A., Ševarac, Z., & Jovanović, J. (2023). An AI-based approach for grading students' collaboration. *IEEE Transactions on Learning Technologies, 16*(3), 292–305. https://doi.org/10.1109/TLT.2022.3225432

U.S. Department of Education. (2023). *Artificial intelligence and future of teaching and learning: Insights and recommendations*. https://www.ed.gov/sites/ed/files/documents/ai-report/ai-report.pdf?utm_content=&utm_medium=email&utm_name=&utm_source=govdelivery&utm_term=

Tyler Harnish is a General Elementary Education Teacher in the Southern Tier of New York State, teaching 5th Grade education. Mr. Harnish is on the teacher technology team for his school district, also serving on the District Technology committee, which contributes to create policies for the district to follow. Mr. Harnish earned his B.A. in Elementary Education, achieving a dual certification in General and Special Education. He has earned a master's degree as an Educational Technology Specialist from SUNY Oneonta. Mr. Harnish's research in his master's program has delved into the world of technology acceptance in Artificial Intelligence in the school system. Tharnish@cppasd.com.

Gina L. Solano is a university professor of Educational Technology at SUNY Oneonta. Her research focuses on the professional development of educators in the field of technology, AR/VR/XR, innovative technologies, and using technology to support mindfulness education. She teaches courses on research, digital media, educational technology, STEM, multimedia, online learning, and instructional design. She has presented on a variety of technology topics at national and international conferences on virtual reality, digital badges, digital storytelling, digital design, gamification, augmented reality, and geospatial technologies, among others. She has directed several service-learning programs, community outreach, and international student trips. Gina.solano@oneonta.edu. https://orcid.org/0009-0001-3970-5193.

Chapter 17
Utilizing AI to Mitigate Teacher Burnout

Austin C. Ross

Abstract This chapter explores the potential of Artificial Intelligence (AI) to alleviate teacher burnout and improve educational practices. By automating routine tasks, delivering personalized learning experiences, and supporting professional development, AI tools such as MagicSchool.ai, Eduaide.ai, ChatGPT, and Khanmigo can significantly reduce educators' workload and stress. The chapter reviews a range of AI and GenAI tools as well as a few studies, and indicates how these tools can help reduce educators' workload, stress, and burnout. The chapter outlines some suggestions for practice, administration, and policy, that may help to effectively integrate AI into education while preserving the essential human element.

Keywords Administrative burden · AI tools · Repetitive tasks · Routine tasks

The topic of utilizing AI to mitigate teacher burnout has gained significant relevance in today's educational landscape. As an educator who began teaching high school in the fall of 2014 and continued until the fall of 2022, I witnessed firsthand the growing empathy gap toward educators, which was exacerbated during the height of the pandemic. Teachers, who were once seen as pillars of the community, quickly became scapegoats for systemic issues. This shift in perception added to the already substantial pressures teachers face, including heavy workloads, lack of administrative support, emotional exhaustion, and inadequate resources. Additionally, the expectation for teachers to take work home sacrifices family time and personal well-being, further contributing to burnout. These factors collectively make it increasingly difficult for educators to remain in their profession. The integration of AI into education presents a promising solution to alleviate these burdens and support teachers in maintaining their well-being and effectiveness.

A. C. Ross (✉)
University of Arizona, Tucson, AZ, USA
e-mail: across5@arizona.edu

G. Tchibozo (ed.), *International Perspectives of Generative AI in Education*, Advances in Artificial Intelligence in Education 3,
https://doi.org/10.1007/978-3-031-99804-1_17

The primary objective of this chapter is to review a range of actionable tools that leverage recent advancements in AI, including GPT-o3, GPT-4o, and GPT-4.5. The chapter offers insights into the practical applications of AI, and the impact of these tools on reducing stress and workload. It not only addresses current challenges but also looks toward future trends and possible directions to support sustainable teaching practices. Reducing the total number of hours worked each week can have a tremendous impact on teachers' mental health and wellness, allowing them more time to re-engage with the core business that initially inspired their careers in education.

Understanding Teacher Burnout

Teacher burnout is a multifaceted issue that affects both the mind and body. It manifests as emotional exhaustion, depersonalization, and a diminished sense of personal achievement. Educators grappling with burnout often feel drained, overwhelmed, and unable to manage the demands of their profession, leading to significant mental and physical health concerns. According to a National Education Association (NEA) survey in the United States (Jotkoff, 2022), 90% of teachers report feeling burnt out, with 67% identifying it as a very serious issue. The relentless stress and demands placed on teachers exacerbate this toll, severely impacting their well-being and job satisfaction (Doan et al., 2023).

The roots of teacher burnout are varied, with workload being a critical factor. Secondary school teachers face an avalanche of administrative tasks, large class sizes, and the pressure to meet high academic standards, all of which compound their workload. The Economic Policy Institute (EPI), a Washington DC (USA) based independent non-profit think tank, highlights that increasing responsibilities and insufficient support have led to high turnover and attrition rates, further burdening the remaining staff (García & Weiss, 2019). The NEA survey reveals that 74% of teachers have had to cover for colleagues due to staff shortages, adding to their already substantial workload (Jotkoff, 2022).

A significant contributor to teacher burnout is the lack of support from administration and the broader educational system. Many teachers feel undervalued and unsupported, which heightens their stress and emotional fatigue. Scholaroo (2024) shows that worsening student-teacher ratios in numerous states make it harder for teachers to manage their duties effectively, fostering feelings of isolation and lack of support. Additionally, the declining societal respect for the teaching profession is a critical issue. Once regarded as a noble vocation, teaching has seen a reduction in societal esteem, evident in the stagnant compensation and escalating expectations placed on educators without corresponding support or recognition (García & Weiss, 2019). Artificial intelligence could help combat teacher burnout. Emerging research suggests that thoughtfully integrated educational AI may help alleviate these pressures, reducing stress and burnout while supporting professional autonomy and development (Duan & Zhao, 2024).

Artificial Intelligence in Education

AI tools have increasingly become pivotal in the education sector, revolutionizing the way teachers and students interact with content. Recent advancements in AI technology have led to the development of sophisticated tools that can assist educators in various aspects of their work, from administrative tasks to personalizing learning experiences. Major tech companies have integrated AI features into their education-related software, enabling tasks like automated grading, lesson planning, and resource management to be handled more efficiently. These developments can not only save time but also enhance the quality of education by allowing teachers to focus more on student engagement and instruction.

Importantly, many popular tools already widely used in classrooms—such as Nearpod and Pear Deck—have begun embedding AI capabilities into their platforms. Nearpod, for instance, is an interactive instructional tool that allows teachers to create multimedia-rich lessons with embedded polls, quizzes, videos, and real-time student responses. It is often used to increase student engagement and provide adequate formative assessment during live or asynchronous instruction. After integrating AI into their educational technology platform, Nearpod now supports features like auto-generated questions, adaptive content suggestions, and improved analytics to support instructional decision-making.

Administrative Tasks

AI tools are streamlining administrative tasks, significantly reducing the burden on educators. Tools like MagicSchool.ai and Eduaide.ai are popular choices among teachers for automating grading, scheduling, and resource management (Karageorgakis, 2024). By handling these repetitive tasks, such tools allow educators to reclaim valuable time that can be redirected toward more interactive and meaningful classroom experiences.

Personalized Learning

Personalized learning is one of the most impactful applications of AI in education. AI tutors such as those provided by Khan Academy and GPT-based systems can tailor educational content to meet the individual needs of students. These platforms analyze learning patterns and adapt content to ensure it is appropriately challenging and engaging for each student. This personalized approach helps in addressing the diverse needs of learners, making education more inclusive and effective (Aguilar, 2024; Karageorgakis, 2024). In Arizona, Khan Academy's AI tutor Khanmigo (also see the Mitigating Teacher Burnout section below) has recently been adopted statewide to replace a COVID-era response tutoring program initiated by Superintendent Tom Horne. The original initiative funded human tutors to help students recover from pandemic-related learning loss. However, the shift to an AI-powered platform has drawn mixed responses: while some celebrate the scalability and cost-efficiency of AI tutoring, others, including educators who relied on the program for supplemental income, have expressed concern over the sudden loss of human-centered support (KTAR News, 2024). Although no conclusive data is yet available on Khanmigo's effectiveness in closing achievement gaps for Arizona students, the shift illustrates a broader tension in education: the push for innovation on one side and the unintended consequences of workforce displacement on the other (also see Chap. 21 of the present book).

Professional Development

AI-powered platforms such as MagicSchool.ai and Eduaide.ai are reshaping professional development by offering on-demand support aligned with educators' specific roles and needs. These tools provide personalized learning modules, instructional strategy suggestions, and real-time planning assistance that help teachers bridge knowledge gaps and improve classroom practice. Rather than relying on one-size-fits-all workshops, educators can use these platforms to access targeted resources and continuously refine their skills. By using AI to tailor professional development, teachers can engage in continuous learning that is relevant to their specific needs and career goals (Johnson, 2024).

Creativity and Immersive Learning

Tools like Canva AI and MidJourney are being used in art courses to help students create innovative projects, and foster creativity and critical thinking. Additionally, AI-driven virtual simulations and augmented reality experiences are making complex subjects like history and science more accessible and engaging. These immersive learning environments not only enhance understanding but also prepare students for a future where technology plays a central role in education (Aguilar, 2024; Spector, 2024).

The integration of DALL-E into ChatGPT has further expanded the possibilities for creative expression in the classroom. Educators and students can now generate high-quality, customized images directly within ChatGPT, facilitating the creation of visual aids, infographics, storytelling elements, and artistic projects that align with curricular goals. This advancement supports a more personalized and engaging learning experience, bridging the gap between imagination and tangible outputs.

By integrating these AI tools, educators can create more efficient, personalized, and engaging learning experiences. These advancements in AI technology are helping to transform the educational landscape, making it more responsive to the needs of both teachers and students.

Mitigating Teacher Burnout

MagicSchool.ai

MagicSchool.ai is a cutting-edge tool designed to streamline and enhance various administrative and instructional tasks for educators (see Chaps. 14 and 16 in this book). One of its primary benefits is its ability to automate grading, scheduling, and resource management, which significantly reduces the time teachers spend on these routine tasks. By handling these responsibilities, MagicSchool.ai allows educators to focus more on interactive teaching and personalized student engagement, thus enhancing the overall learning experience. The tool's advanced algorithms can also provide detailed analytics and insights on student performance, helping teachers to identify areas where students need more support and to tailor their instructional strategies accordingly.

In addition to data and grading features, MagicSchool.ai offers over 50 tools designed to assist with Individualized Education Program (IEP) writing, rubric creation, parent communication, behavior intervention plans, and more. Its lesson planning functions generate standards-aligned content that can be customized to specific classroom goals. This comprehensive toolkit supports not only general educators, but also special educators, instructional coaches, and administrators. The integration of AI in managing these responsibilities can lead to a significant reduction in teacher burnout by alleviating workload and streamlining decision-making. This allows teachers to maintain a better work-life balance and dedicate more energy to creative and impactful teaching practices (Spector, 2024).

Curipod

Curipod is an AI-driven platform designed to enhance classroom interactivity and student engagement. It offers a range of tools for creating interactive presentations, quizzes, and discussions that are designed to be seamlessly integrated into any curricula. Curipod's AI capabilities enable teachers to generate content quickly, based on specific topics or learning objectives, aiming to maintain student interest and participation. The platform also provides real-time analytics on student engagement and performance, allowing educators to adjust their instructional strategies dynamically.

Recent enhancements to Curipod include the integration of real-time, rubric-aligned AI feedback, which offers students immediate, personalized insights into their work, fostering a more responsive learning environment.

By automating the creation of engaging content and providing tools for interactive learning, Curipod reduces the time teachers spend on preparing materials and grading. This is likely not only to save time but also to enhance the overall teaching and learning experience. Furthermore, the decrease in preparation and grading workload can significantly alleviate teacher burnout, as educators can allocate more time to meaningful student interactions and less to administrative tasks.

Eduaide

Eduaide is an AI-powered educational assistant that supports teachers across lesson planning, resource creation, and assessment design. The platform enables educators to generate instructional materials aligned with curriculum standards, including scaffolded objectives, differentiated texts, quizzes, and writing prompts. Teachers can also use Eduaide's built-in tools for behavior intervention ideas, vocabulary support, and question stems for higher-order thinking.

Its "Idea Generator" feature helps teachers brainstorm new approaches to classroom activities or adapt existing materials to meet the needs of English Language Learners and students with IEPs. By reducing the time spent developing materials from scratch, Eduaide empowers educators to focus more on student engagement and feedback. This reduction in preparation time and planning fatigue plays a key role in supporting teacher retention and mitigating burnout.

ChatGPT

ChatGPT has emerged as a versatile AI assistant for educators, capable of supporting a wide range of teaching tasks. Teachers use it to generate lesson ideas, draft emails, build rubrics, create exit tickets, modify texts for various Lexile levels, and design activities tailored to student interests and needs. Its conversational interface makes it an effective tool for brainstorming and rapidly refining instructional plans in real time. With the rollout of its memory feature, ChatGPT can now retain details across sessions—enabling teachers to develop ongoing instructional goals, revisit prior requests, and build long-term project plans without starting from scratch.

Because ChatGPT can respond to prompts iteratively, it enables teachers to customize outputs with greater specificity, allowing for differentiated materials and scaffolded supports. Whether used to streamline documentation or generate multiple versions of classroom activities, ChatGPT reduces decision fatigue and administrative overload. By reclaiming hours of prep time each week, educators are better able to maintain creativity, responsiveness, and balance in their practice.

Khanmigo

Khanmigo (see the Personalized Learning section above) provides real-time support for students as they work through practice problems, offering hints, Socratic questioning, and encouragement that promotes self-regulation and metacognition.

For educators, Khanmigo assists with lesson planning, formative assessment, and simulating academic conversations—for example, role-playing as a literary character or historical figure. Khanmigo represents a new model for scalable, individualized academic support. As a digital co-teacher, it has the potential to ease instructional burdens and help mitigate burnout by supporting differentiation and reducing the need for repeated reteaching.

Research on AI's Impact on Teacher Burnout

According to a survey conducted by Canva (Daff, 2024), 60% of teachers agree that AI can improve work efficiency, and 58% report that AI helps alleviate burnout. The survey highlighted that AI's roles in managing administrative tasks and personalizing learning experiences are significant contributors to these improvements. By automating routine tasks, AI allows teachers to allocate more time to instructional activities and student engagement, thereby reducing stress and workload.

Hashem et al. (2024) also explored the role of AI, specifically ChatGPT, in reducing teacher workload and preventing burnout. These authors highlighted that ChatGPT can produce lesson plans that follow the 5Es instructional model, where the emphasis is on engagement, exploration, explanation, elaboration and evaluation, making the lessons more interactive and student-centered. This approach helps in engaging students better and making learning more effective. The study also highlights the variety of areas in which AI helps teachers better meet standards while easing their workload, for example by adapting learning to the needs of diverse students or providing translation services for classrooms with multilingual students.

In a recent experimental study, Duan and Zhao (2024) found that teachers who received training in the use of educational AI tools experienced significantly lower levels of digital burnout compared to those in the control group. Posttest scores revealed substantial reductions across multiple dimensions of burnout among the experimental group. Their findings suggest that AI integration not only enhances teacher autonomy but also supports ongoing professional development in digital learning environments. The authors emphasize the importance of structured, context-sensitive training in maximizing the positive effects of AI on teacher well-being (Duan & Zhao, 2024).

Similarly, Dickey and Bejarano (2024) presented the GAIDE framework, which outlines how generative AI can assist educators in content development while minimizing cognitive overload. The GAIDE framework—which stands for Generative

AI for Instructional Development and Education—offers a structured approach for integrating generative AI into curriculum planning, consisting of five stages: Goal setting, AI tool selection, Iteration, Design refinement, and Evaluation (Dickey & Bejarano, 2024). According to these authors, "educators reported a significant reduction in the time and effort required to develop course materials, without compromising on the breadth or depth of the content" (2024, p. 1). They further note that "preliminary feedback suggests a high degree of satisfaction with the framework and an indication that the workshop objectives were largely met" (Dickey & Bejarano, 2024, p. 8). This supports the growing body of evidence that thoughtfully implemented AI tools can alleviate burnout and promote more sustainable teaching practices.

Grewe (2024) explored the potential of AI to alleviate faculty burnout and enhance teaching creativity. This author discussed the automation of routine tasks, the improvement of student engagement, and the generation of creative teaching materials as key benefits of AI. Grewe emphasized the need for thoughtful integration of AI tools to ensure they support rather than replace the human elements of teaching, promoting a healthier work-life balance for educators.

Transferability and Generalizability

This chapter is grounded in the U.S. context, particularly within a secondary teacher preparation program that seeks to mitigate early career burnout through intentional use of AI tools and reflective planning strategies. Pre-service teachers are introduced to generative AI as a support for lesson planning, differentiation, and time management—key components often cited as sources of stress during the first years in the profession. While such tools are increasingly accessible in well-connected educational systems, these strategies may differ in relevance or feasibility across international settings. In countries where teacher preparation is more centralized, tightly scripted, or where digital infrastructure is uneven, the flexibility and autonomy required to meaningfully integrate AI may be limited. Still, the broader challenge of teacher burnout is globally shared, and approaches aimed at increasing efficiency, reducing isolation, and encouraging professional agency may offer valuable entry points for adaptation across diverse educational contexts.

Conclusion and Future Directions

This chapter has examined how artificial intelligence can play a pivotal role in reducing teacher burnout and enhancing educational practices. We began by exploring the complex issue of teacher burnout, particularly its psychological and physical impacts. Factors such as extensive workloads, insufficient support, and emotional exhaustion commonly contribute to this issue. In response, AI tools are emerging as transformative solutions, reducing administrative burdens, facilitating personalized learning, and supporting continuous professional development. By automating routine tasks, these tools enable educators to dedicate more time to student engagement and direct classroom interaction—critical elements in mitigating burnout.

As demonstrated by recent statewide efforts, such as the implementation of Khanmigo in Arizona, AI is not only theoretical—it is being woven into real educational policy and practice. Likewise, tools like ChatGPT, now equipped with memory features, offer the potential for educators to sustain long-term planning conversations across the school year, reducing redundancy and decision fatigue.

To fully harness AI's benefits in this matter, a few suggestions are worth considering. Investments in technological infrastructure are necessary to ensure that all schools have access to AI resources. Continuous professional development programs would equip teachers with the skills to use AI effectively. Educational practices, administration and policies should aim to balance workloads by utilizing AI's automation capabilities to minimize repetitive tasks, thus reducing burnout risks. Ethical considerations—such as data privacy—should be prioritized to maintain trust and preserve the human aspect of teaching. Lastly, a collaborative approach involving educators, administrators, and policymakers would ensure that AI implementation actually improves the teaching and learning experience.

Finally, while the benefits of AI are clear, future studies must continue to evaluate its long-term effects on teacher satisfaction, retention, and student outcomes. A strong research-practice feedback loop will ensure these tools evolve in ways that are pedagogically sound, human-centered, and equitably accessible.

Adopting these principles could foster a healthier, more sustainable educational environment for teachers and students alike.

Competing Interests The author has no conflicts of interest to declare that are relevant to the content of this chapter.

References

Aguilar, X. (2024, January 3). *The six use cases of AI in classrooms that will change education in 2024*. UOC. https://www.uoc.edu/en/news/2024/003-six-use-cases-AI-classrooms-education-2024

Daff, C. (2024, May 7). *How teachers are using AI to battle burnout*. https://www.canva.com/newsroom/news/teacher-survey.

Dickey, M. D., & Bejarano, W. (2024). GAIDE: A framework for using generative AI to assist in course content development. In *2024 IEEE Frontiers in Education Conference (FIE)* (pp. 1–9). IEEE. https://doi.org/10.1109/FIE61694.2024.10893132

Doan, S., Steiner, E. D., Pandey, R., & Woo, A. (2023, June 21). *Teacher well-being and intentions to leave: Findings from the 2023 state of the American teacher survey*. RAND Corporation. https://www.rand.org/pubs/research_reports/RRA1108-8.html

Duan, Z., & Zhao, H. (2024). The effects of educational artificial intelligence–powered applications on teachers' perceived autonomy, professional development for online teaching, and digital burnout. *The International Review of Research in Open and Distributed Learning, 25*(1), 57–77. https://doi.org/10.19173/irrodl.v25i1.7410

García, E., & Weiss, E. (2019, March 26). *The teacher shortage is real, large and growing, and worse than we thought: The first report in "The perfect storm in the teacher labor market" series*. Economic Policy Institute. https://www.epi.org/publication/the-teacher-shortage-is-real-large-and-growing-and-worse-than-we-thought-the-first-report-in-the-perfect-storm-in-the-teacher-labor-market-series

Grewe, J. (2024). Examining ways of using ai to better support teaching faculty, mitigate burnout, and increase teaching creativity. In B. Buyserie & T. N. Thurston (Eds.), *Teaching and generative AI: Pedagogical possibilities and productive tensions*. Utah State University. https://uen.pressbooks.pub/teachingandgenerativeai/chapter/examining-ways-of-using-ai-to-better-support-teaching-faculty-mitigate-burnout-and-increase-teaching-creativity/

Hashem, R., Ali, N., El Zein, F., Fidalgo, P., & Abu Khurma, O. (2024, January 1). AI to the rescue: Exploring the potential of ChatGPT as a teacher ally for workload relief and burnout prevention. *Research and Practice in Technology Enhanced Learning, 19*, 1–26. https://doi.org/10.58459/rptel.2024.19023

Johnson, P. (2024, March 6). *Reimagine education 2024: Prepare for the future with new AI and security offers*. Microsoft Education Blog. https://educationblog.microsoft.com/en-us/2024/03/reimagine-education-2024-prepare-for-the-future-with-new-ai-and-security-offers

Jotkoff, E. (2022, February 1). *NEA survey: Massive staff shortages in schools leading to educator burnout; Alarming number of educators indicating they plan to leave profession*. NEA. https://www.nea.org/about-nea/media-center/press-releases/nea-survey-massive-staff-shortages-schools-leading-educator-burnout-alarming-number-educators#:~:text=Conducted%20by%20GBAO%20Strategies%2C%20the,they%20love%20earlier%20than%20planned

Karageorgakis, T. (2024, May 23). *Best 100 AI apps for teachers and the classroom*. Educraft. https://educraft.tech/best-100-ai-apps-for-teachers

KTAR News. (2024, March 5). *Free tutoring program ends early for Arizona students, replaced by Khan Academy AI*. https://ktar.com/arizona-news/free-tutoring-program-arizona-ends-early/5642509/

Scholaroo. (2024). *The U.S. teacher shortage 2024: A state-by-state breakdown*. https://scholaroo.com/report/teacher-shortage-by-state/

Spector, C. (2024, February 14). *How technology is reinventing K-12 education*. Stanford Report. https://news.stanford.edu/stories/2024/02/technology-in-education

Austin C. Ross is a seasoned educator with 9 years of high school teaching experience, now contributing to the academic community at the University of Arizona. He graduated from Arizona State University with a Bachelor of Arts in Secondary Education, and a Master's in English. Additionally, Austin holds a Master's of Education in Curriculum & Instruction from The American College of Education. His work focuses on enhancing pedagogical skills and fostering inclusive, equitable learning environments. His current research, "Empowering Secondary Classroom Teachers: Leveraging AI for Enhanced Pedagogical Outcomes," was presented at The National Autonomous University of Mexico in November 2023. https://orcid.org/0009-0008-2058-5348. across5@arizona.edu.

Chapter 18
Teacher Perspectives on Using Generative Artificial Intelligence to Improve Productivity in Lesson Planning, Rubric Creation, and Assessments

Shelby Grosso and Gina L. Solano

Abstract Generative Artificial Intelligence (GenAI) is increasingly permeating the field of education, offering innovative solutions to enhance instructional efficiency. GenAI tools have begun to play a pivotal role in automating routine responsibilities, such as generating emails, rubrics, answer keys, lesson plans, and unit outlines. This chapter critically examines the efficacy of different AI tools in producing educational resources, such as lesson plans, rubrics, and assessments, across various grade levels and subject areas. Three GenAI platforms—ChatGPT, MagicSchool.ai, and Perplexity.ai—were selected for analysis and evaluated by a small sample of educators (n = 5). This qualitative research employed a combination of interviews and rubric-based assessments of GenAI-created resources. Participants were tasked with reviewing and rating lesson plans, rubrics, and assessments produced by each GenAI tool, and were then interviewed for more in-depth insights into the comparative effectiveness of the platforms. The results revealed divergent preferences among participants, with each platform having its own strengths and limitations. Overall, however, the majority of participants recognized the potential of AI tools in enhancing teacher productivity.

Keywords AI effectiveness · Assessment · Rubrics · Teacher productivity

Generative Artificial Intelligence (GenAI) is the new tool that can do everything at the push of a button, but can it also easily create lesson plans, design rubrics, and create formative and summative assessments to save teachers time and help them be more productive? Many new AI platforms are designed for use in education. GenAI has a lot of qualities that can potentially benefit teachers, saving their time on lesson planning and other time-consuming tasks (Bradley, 2024). Based on their

S. Grosso · G. L. Solano (✉)
State University of New York (SUNY) Oneonta, Oneonta, NY, USA
e-mail: sgrosso@bronxexcellence.org; Gina.solano@oneonta.edu

G. Tchibozo (ed.), *International Perspectives of Generative AI in Education*, Advances in Artificial Intelligence in Education 3,
https://doi.org/10.1007/978-3-031-99804-1_18

investigation in Canada, Singapore, the United Kingdom, and the United States, Bryant et al. (2020) estimated that teachers spend approximately 50 h per week working and spend less than half of that with their students. These authors noted: "Across the four countries we studied, teachers spend an average of 11 hours a week in preparation activities. We estimate that effective use of technology could cut the time to just six hours" (p. 4). GenAI can help teachers not only to plan and prepare, but also to grade and evaluate (Akgun & Greenhow, 2021; Bailey, 2023; Celik et al., 2022; Mijwil et al., 2022). Educators also spent time checking writing and electronic work for plagiarism. AI can now be used to scan work to check for plagiarism (Slimi, 2023). Using GenAI has the potential not only to help "teachers to manage their time effectively during the course" (Mondal et al., 2023, p. 4), but also to save time for educators before, during, and after the school day.

Review of Literature

GenAI technologies are being integrated into education across the globe with the intention of improving teaching and learning experiences. Initiatives, such as the GenAI Education Frontier, focus on providing educators with tools and training to effectively use GenAI in their classrooms (Meli et al., 2024). They tout that GenAI can support personalized learning, automate administrative tasks and offer innovative ways to engage students. As with any new technology, educators need professional development to understand and use GenAI tools responsibly and ethically. GenAI tools have the potential to help teachers utilize their time more productively. The time saved by teachers using artificial intelligence can be used to meet with students, provide time to research new tools to use in the classroom, or provide time to prepare for lessons (Meli et al., 2024).

Industry experts predict that in 2025, 80% of software designers will be using GenAI tools in the development of their software, and that 50% of the world's 500 largest companies will use GenAI software for ideation, scenario planning, and decision optimization (Jump et al., 2025). They predict that in 2026, 60% of conversational AI tools will have "proactive intelligence capabilities" (para. 12), and that virtual assistants (VAs) will be involved in 50% of online sales. While in 2023 the use of GenAI in workers' tasks was 0%, by 2027 it will account for 30% of their work (Jump et al., 2025). In education, the use of virtual assistants, or tutors, is already making it possible to offer personalized teaching and suggest revisions for assignments, create lesson plans, assessments and course materials (Jump et al., 2025). According to Carnegie Learning (2025), school administrators were using GenAI more than teachers in 2024. However, GenAI use by teachers was on the rise, with ChatGPT, MagicSchool.ai and Canva being—in that order—the three most widely used tools. These trends were all 10% to 30% higher than in 2023. The use of GenAI tools is predicted to become more efficient and integrated in the near future (Carnegie Learning, 2025; Hanover Research, 2025; Jump et al., 2025).

Raj (2024) explored the transformative potential of GenAI in education and research. The study highlighted how GenAI, which can create diverse data types such as text, images, and 3D models by learning from existing patterns, is revolutionizing various industries. The study discussed the advancements in GenAI technologies like GPT and their applications in solving complex problems, creating art, and assisting scientific research. GenAI tools can also analyze data, create charts and tables, recommend research articles, and provide writing assistance. Raj (2024) emphasized the need for educational institutions to adapt these technologies to enhance learning and research outcomes, but to also be mindful about using GenAI ethically.

Nguyen and Truong (2025) conducted a systematic literature review to explore the trends and emerging themes in the effects of GenAI in education from 2021 to 2024. Their findings reported that GenAI was being used primarily for personalized learning and automated assessments. They discussed a surge in GenAI research in 2023 and 2024 that showed a rapid adoption of GenAI into educational frameworks. GenAI is being used to automate assessment, provide real-time feedback, and improve the productivity in educators (Nguyen & Truong, 2025). The researchers noted another rising trend in the use of GenAI to create educational content, lesson plans, study materials, quizzes, and assignments. Another area that GenAI has infiltrated is in gamification tools where it is assisting the creation of formative learning games and assessments.

The aim of this study is to determine whether GenAI can be implemented as a time-saving productivity tool for educators when it comes specifically to planning courses, creating rubrics, and assessments, and whether one of the main GenAI platforms currently available outperforms the others in producing lesson plans, rubrics, and assessments.

GenAI Education Tools Used in This Study

Three different technology tools were evaluated in this study. ChatGPT, Magic School.ai, and Perplexity.ai are the GenAI tools that the participants used for creating, evaluating and critiquing lesson plans and materials (assignments and rubrics). GenAI "is any type of AI that uses deep learning models to generate or create new content" (Bowen & Watson, 2024, p. 22).

ChatGPT is an AI conversational bot (chatbot) that uses natural language processing to generate human-like responses to questions and prompts (Bowen & Watson, 2024). ChatGPT can answer questions, help formulate emails, and provide written work based on the prompt that was put into it.

MagicSchool.ai is another online artificial intelligence tool that is free to use with an account. This tool was created with educators in mind. It allows for lesson planning, text leveling, rubric making, and has features such as creating professional emails, writing thank you notes, and creating social stories. MagicSchool.ai also creates many things teachers need such as math word problems, unit plan generators, and individualized education plan generators. It can produce a variety of differentiated materials, standards-aligned assessments, and save time in lesson planning (Sobehrad & Francis, 2024). With over 60 different applications provided to teachers to save time on a multitude of tasks, this GenAI tool could help to mitigate teacher burnout.

Perplexity.ai has a "discover" tab where users can ask questions and get answers on trending topics. Before GenAI, information was retrieved from browser queries, which provided users with links to resources that they then had to read in order to find the answers to their questions. Perplexity.ai provides direct answers to the questions asked.

Research Questions

Research is needed to evaluate the different GenAI tools to better understand which ones can produce quality lesson plans and complete other teachers' time-consuming tasks with results that are effective and usable (Zhang & Aslan, 2021). Saving teachers time is essential, as educators are burnt out by the time they spend on repetitive, routine tasks. This qualitative descriptive study aims to provide insights on whether educators can actually save time by using GenAI tools. It addresses the following questions:

- Can GenAI tools be used as productivity tools to create lesson plans, rubrics, and assessments for educators?
- Of the three GenAI tools tested, which one created the best lesson plans, rubrics, and assessments, and on what grounds is the judgement based?

Theoretical Background

When planning a lesson or activity, there are a lot of components that need to be involved, including a technology integration component. The Technology Pedagogical Content Knowledge (TPACK) is a framework that helps with effectively and purposefully integrating technology into the classroom (Koehler & Mishra, 2009; McGraw Hill, 2019). With TPACK, teachers can guarantee that the technology they are integrating into their classroom is going to benefit the students. The TPACK framework comprises three domains: Content Knowledge, Pedagogical Knowledge, and Technological Knowledge (Mishra & Koehler, 2006). TPACK can be used for choosing which technology to integrate into a lesson, as well as using it effectively. All three domains are interdependent and work together to effectively integrate technology. The goal of TPACK is to integrate technology and have it thought of as teaching and learning knowledge. Thinking about technology, teaching and learning separately can limit student learning. When the three domains are considered as a whole, students learn effectively (Koehler & Mishra, 2009; McGraw Hill, 2019). This study was guided by the TPACK framework.

Method

This qualitative descriptive study asked the participants to create and evaluate several common teacher tasks. Qualitative design provides the opportunity to focus on the views of the participants (Creswell & Guetterman, 2019), asking in-depth questions and enabling participants to discuss and support their thoughts, critiques, and evaluations.

Participants

A convenience sample of five teachers who agreed to take part in the study was set up. They were teachers in a suburban elementary school in New York. The approach followed Creswell and Guetterman (2019) according to which "In some educational situations, you will select individuals for your research based on who volunteers to participate or who is available" (p. 139). These participants were teachers from all different grades, from elementary through higher education. Their personal information was kept confidential by assigning each one a number in place of their name. No personal information was used that could identify them.

Procedures

The first step of the research was for the participants to use the three artificial intelligence tools to create lesson plans, rubrics, and assessments in their content areas and grade levels. One of the researchers provided an introductory training to the participants to familiarize them with the GenAI tools they would use during this study. Next, the participants used a rubric they were provided with to evaluate and critique the GenAI-created lesson plans, rubrics, and assessments. This took between 1 and 3 weeks to complete, depending on each participant. The participants focused on one of the GenAI tools at a time, to give ample time to evaluate each component. Finally, the participants, either on their own or with a researcher, completed a set of interview questions, where they shared their opinions, and suggestions about the GenAI-created lesson plans, rubrics, and assessments.

Instruments

The participants were provided with a set of directions and materials for evaluating each item. To evaluate the lesson plan, they used a lesson plan rubric (see Appendix 1). The lesson plan rubric had key components that are crucial for a lesson plan to contain. It also included a section in which participants had to explain and justify their grading results.

The next instrument was the rubric evaluation form (see Appendix 2). The rubric evaluation form is what the participants used to critique the rubrics made by the AI tools. There was space provided for their justifications on whether the rubric aligned with the activity and the lesson that was taught. The rubric documents were helpful to further the understanding of the data and make connections between the participants' evaluations.

To evaluate the assessments, participants were able to use an assessment rubric (Appendix 3). The rubric provided space where the participants could evaluate and comment on the assessments created by the GenAI tools. The goal was to identify whether there is one GenAI-created assessment that stood out above the rest of them. Another goal was to determine if any of the assessments created by GenAI tools could be used to evaluate students' knowledge of what they would have been taught.

Rubric analysis was used to allow participants to be descriptive and write their thoughts. Participants were able to formulate their critical comments, supporting and explaining their reasoning. The use of rubrics allowed the participants to do that and the researcher to follow along (Mills, 2018). From the evaluations, it was possible to find commonalities and answer the research questions.

Once the rubric-based evaluation had been completed, interviews (face-to-face and one-to-one) were conducted on participants' experiences and opinions regarding the use of GenAI tools (Appendix 4). For the participants who answered the questions on their own, one of the researchers reviewed their answers and reached out to ask follow-up questions and to ascertain if there was anything they wanted to add. This was to fully understand their perspectives on the tools and what they produced. "In qualitative research, you ask open-ended questions so that the participants can best voice their experiences unconstrained by any perspectives of the researcher or past research findings" (Creswell & Guetterman, 2019, p. 218). The instruments were validated through member-checking by confirming with the participants that their data was represented accurately.

Data Analysis

The data was organized by categorizing all 50 documents into three sections, i.e. one section per GenAI tool. For each tool, the data was first read, then organized by ideas (each of which was given a code) and then by theme. According to Maguire and Delahunt (2017, p. 3356), "A theme is characterized by its significance". A theme brings together several coded ideas. Once the codes and major themes were identified, the data results were narrowed down to three themes (Clarke et al., 2020). The themes were then aligned to answer the research questions.

Results

The data showed reoccurring themes and ideas about the artificial intelligence tools that were used. Three main themes emerged, i.e., usability, incompleteness, and weaknesses. These themes provide an overview of the strengths and weaknesses of each tool, as well as its effectiveness in the production of teaching materials.

Artificial Intelligence Usability

Several questions on the evaluation forms and in the interviews asked the participants about the usability of each tool. There were many similarities between participants. ChatGPT was mentioned repeatedly as the easiest tool of the three to use, while MagicSchool.ai was repeatedly mentioned as a difficult tool to use. A first-grade teacher stated:

> ChatGPT also has everything in one place, so once you have your lesson plan created, all you had to do was to mention that you wanted a rubric made about the lesson and an assessment made about the lesson to create those things. (Participant 5)

Participant 1, a 12th grade English teacher, stated, "[The] easiest was ChatGPT because it is just a textbox that you type what you want." The textbox was a recurring reason why ChatGPT was the easiest to use. Participant 2, a seventh-grade Math Teacher, explained "I personally thought the ChatGPT tool was easiest to use because I could stay in the section, I was originally working in." Participant 3, a kindergarten teacher, agreed that ChatGPT was the easiest, but also added in that Perplexity.ai was also easy to use. "I felt that Perplexity and ChatGPT were equally easy to use since all that needed to be done was type in the prompt and the site did the rest." All participants discussed how ChatGPT was the easiest tool to use, due to all content being located in one textbox.

Another commonality among participants on the usability of the artificial intelligence tools was that MagicSchool.ai was a difficult tool to use. MagicSchool.ai has a lot of options and generators for its users. Participant 4, a fifth-grade special education teacher, thought, "Although geared towards those in education, I found MagicSchool.ai to be too overwhelming and challenging to navigate with no prior experience." Participant 5, a first-grade teacher, went into detail about their experience using MagicSchool.ai and why it was the most difficult tool to use:

> All the information was kept separate, and the GenAI tool was unable to just take the lesson plan and make a rubric or assessment. When it came to each generator, you had to type in the specific information or components you wanted, which made Magic School.ai slightly more difficult to use. (Participant 5)

Participant 3 also acknowledged that the changing between tabs made the usage of MagicSchool.ai more difficult. "MagicSchool.ai was the most difficult because you had to go onto different sections of the website to get the lesson plan, rubric, and assessment." All participants agreed that MagicSchool.ai was a more difficult tool to use and navigate.

Using Artificial Intelligence as a Starter

The idea here is that the materials produced by GenAI still need to be edited and refined, and cannot be used as they stand. A commonality was that while the tools are okay, they all needed to be tweaked and adjusted to better fit the classroom and students. One participant explained:

> Even though I may not necessarily use the lesson plans, rubrics, or assessments these tools created alone, I might use pieces of them to act as my baseline. I could… add more detail to them or tweak them to make them useful for me and my students. (Participant 5)

Using artificial intelligence as a starting tool can help teachers save time in the planning process. Participant 2 mentioned how while creating assessments and rubrics can be time-consuming, using artificial intelligence can provide a start. "Making assessments and rubrics can be very time-consuming and even if I am given one of these from a GenAI tool and need to make changes to it, at least I am not starting from scratch."

Using GenAI as a brainstorming tool was brought up a few times by participants. Participant 3 explained:

> AI helped with the brainstorming aspect of lesson planning. I typically spend a lot of time brainstorming how to approach teaching a topic, so GenAI helped me to be more productive in that regard. However, there were bits to each lesson, ChatGPT and MagicSchool.ai specifically, that needed more touching up before teaching compared to Perplexity. (Participant 3)

Participant 4 wrote, "Overall, the GenAI tools helped my productivity by brainstorming and outlining key aspects that I hoped to accomplish within the lesson. It provided a starting point to see what information and projects would be possible within a given standard." Having an additional tool to help brainstorm or create ideas based on a topic they need to be covered can help teachers save time. Brainstorming and creating is a long and thought-out process. Having the assistance of artificial intelligence, even if the results need to be adjusted, can help.

Weaknesses and Critiques of Artificial Intelligence

While conducting the study, the participants had to use their professional expertise to critique the GenAI-created lesson plans, rubrics, and assessments. The participants identified specific components of the lesson plans that they felt were lacking. Each participant made note of important elements they believed to be missing from each material. Participant 1 found that both ChatGPT and Perplexity.ai, had objectives that lacked measurability whereas the objectives created by MagicSchool.ai were measurable. Participant 2 highlighted that objectives lack measurability and achievability for all three tools. Participant 2 also felt that the technology component of a lesson plan was absent or irrelevant in ChatGPT and Perplexity.ai, and that in MagicSchool.ai it was limited or not purposeful. Participant 3 and Participant 5 mentioned how they found differentiation to be missing from the lesson plans. Participant 5 also found scaffolding to be missing, stating:

> The one MagicSchool.ai created mentioned scaffolding for one activity of the lesson, but I would like to see the lessons talking about how to scaffold and differentiate all the activities of the lesson in order to make sure all students can participate and get the most out of the lesson. (Participant 5)

In addition, Participant 5 also felt that there was no detailed procedure: "Overall, I believe all of the lessons were missing a thorough procedure. The lesson plans should have procedures that are well-explained and explicitly show both the teacher and students' roles during the lesson." Many components go into making a strong lesson plan, and the participants found that the artificial intelligence tools were all lacking some of them.

The participants were also tasked with looking for weaknesses in the rubrics. Participant 1 found that Perplexity.ai created the rubric that was the weakest. In the rubric evaluation, Participant 1 wrote, "Weak. Look how short the descriptions are!" Participant 4 explained to have not felt that the rubric created by MagicSchool.ai was useable: "I would say that the Magic School.ai rubric stood out to me as incomplete as it only offered a general outline that served as suggestions rather than rubric statements." Participant 4 also claimed, "I believe this rubric to be poor quality as it does not provide specifics for what students must have accomplished per each section of the rubric." Finally, Participant 5 expressed both positives and negatives regarding all the rubrics, explaining in particular: "I feel like the 'Participation in Whole Group Discussion' part of the rubric is a bit redundant and not needed since the student was already graded on their engagement in all discussions prior."

Finally, the participants had to look for weaknesses within the assessments. The artificial intelligence tools created assessments that were based on the lesson plans. Several participants found multiple weaknesses with the assessments, including wrong or not covered questions. Participant 1 claimed, "ChatGPT, MagicSchool.ai, and Perplexity.ai either gave me a question that was incorrect or included questions that we did not cover in Chap. 1." Participant 5 claimed, "Magic School.ai created a lesson that only had content, but some of the questions that were asked were not about the content the lesson taught. It was about other topics that the lesson did not cover." Participant 2 gave a detailed response on the inaccuracies of the assessment ChatGPT created:

> Out of the five questions, three of them I would use on 7th-grade assessment; however, the other two I may not use for 7th grade. This is because, in questions three and five, the problems ask students to solve for the value of the variable where there are variables on each side of the equation.... Thus, I would probably adjust those two questions slightly that way there are only variables on one side of the equation. (Participant 2)

In addition to having questions that were wrong or not covered in the lesson, participants noted several other issues. Participant 3 explained when asked if any of the assessments were useable, "No, because something would have to be fixed with all of them. Perplexity's language is fine, but the formatting would need to be fixed. ChatGPT and MagicSchool.ai's formatting was fine, but the language needed to be fixed." However, not all participants found the assessments unusable and lacking. Participant 4 claimed that they are useable, although only as a quick formative assessment, not summative assessments:

> I do feel that the assessments created by all the GenAI tools are usable but only if they served as smaller formative assessments such as an exit ticket. They would be great for check-ins to monitor understanding but lack depth with its questions and variety. (Participant 4)

Participant 2 was the only participant to find an assessment fully useable. Participant 2 wrote, "Personally, I would use the Perplexity assessment because it asks a variety of questions about adding and subtracting linear expressions and it is not just problem after problem."

Discussion

The goal of this study was to see whether artificial intelligence tools can be used as a productivity tool to help teachers regain some of their time as well as determine whether there is one tool that is better than the rest. The data shows that while artificial intelligence does have the capability to create lesson plans, rubrics, and assessments, they are far from having reached the necessary maturity (at least at the time of this study). Teachers still need to make tweaks and changes based on their classroom and their professional judgement. There are components of each tool that are great and some that are lacking. The data suggests that these tools may be helpful for teachers who are unsure of what activity to do on a specific topic or have an idea but are not sure how to expand on it. These tools can be used as a productivity tool for teachers (Mijwil et al., 2022), but more as a starter tool or brainstorming tool than actually using the products made as is. This supports previous studies (Bailey, 2023; Celik et al., 2022). Many of the participants agreed that while not everything that was made by the artificial intelligence tools was either great or horrible, most products needed to be tweaked or adjusted based on the grade level, classroom needs or, sometimes, because of inaccurate information. "At times, they churn out information that might sound convincing but is irrelevant, illogical, or entirely false— an anomaly known as 'hallucination'" (Bailey, 2023, pg. 31).

As for which artificial intelligence tool is best, there was no clear-cut answer. Participants all had different opinions on what stood out to them as being the best. There was a clear winner however for useability, as all participants explained that ChatGPT was the easiest tool to use. One participant also added Perplexity.ai in addition to ChatGPT for their similar makeup. As for creating lesson plans, rubrics, and assessments, the results were mixed on which tool created the best. Several participants thought Perplexity.ai required the least amount of tweaking while others thought that Perplexity.ai was not well done. One participant wrote that MagicSchool.ai was the best while others thought it did not create quality lesson plans, rubrics, and assessments. Further research studies are needed to clarify this point and determine which artificial intelligence tool of the three studied is the best (Zhang & Aslan, 2021). Yet all the participants acknowledged that all tools had beneficial features.

The TPACK framework is written as a guideline for teachers to follow to purposefully integrate technology into the classroom. The usability of the tools is important to consider in the integration process. If an artificial intelligence tool is difficult to use, the teacher may choose to not use it or use it where it is ineffective and does not provide a purpose. Using artificial intelligence as a starting point is a great way to integrate it into the classroom. When teachers are struggling with expanding an idea or are not sure what they want to do, they can ask artificial intelligence tools for help. This can allow them to get additional ideas that they can then adjust, and change based on their classroom and the needs of everyone in the classroom.

Transferability and Generalizability

This study, conducted in a suburban elementary school in New York, highlights the potential of GenAI tools to enhance teacher productivity by automating routine tasks. This context contrasts with broader educational settings where AI integration varies significantly, such as in higher education or under-resourced schools, where access to technology and professional development may differ. These differences suggest that while the positive impacts observed in this study could be transferable, they would require adaptation to local contexts, including addressing technological access and providing adequate training for educators to effectively utilize AI tools. This adaptability is crucial for ensuring that the benefits of AI in education are equitably distributed and effectively implemented across diverse educational environments.

Conclusion

The purpose of this study was to determine whether artificial intelligence could be used as a productivity tool to assist with planning, rubrics, and assessments, and save teachers' time. The study also looked to answer whether one artificial intelligence is better at creating lesson plans, rubrics, and assessments. The participants were able to critique lesson plans, rubrics, and assessments created by ChatGPT, MagicSchool.ai, and Perplexity.ai. An overall thought among the participants was that ChatGPT was the easiest while MagicSchool.ai proved to be difficult to navigate. The participants also found several weaknesses with the materials created by the three GenAI tools. Based on all the information, none of the tools stood out as the best. Therefore, further research is called for. Finally, it was mentioned several times how artificial intelligence tools could be used as a starting point or for brainstorming. GenAI tools are not ready to be the sole creators of lesson plans, rubrics, and assessments but they provide great ideas and a baseline. Artificial intelligence can be used as a productivity tool to help teachers manage their time better and devote more time to improving the quality of teaching.

Competing Interests The authors have no conflicts of interest to declare that are relevant to the content of this chapter.

Appendices

Appendix 1: Lesson Plan Rubric

Teachers' views on using artificial intelligence to improve teacher productivity.

Participant Number:

Content Area:

AI Tool:

Lesson Topic:

Grade Level:

Directions: Use the same lesson topic, grade level, and criteria for each AI tool you test. This way, it will provide consistency and allow you to better evaluate the differences in each lesson. Once the lesson plan is generated, copy and paste it onto a new document to submit with this rubric. Please use this rubric to record your explanations and critiques on the lesson plans and materials. Add as much detail as you can to support your rating for each section. If completing it on paper and you need more room, there is space on the back of the rubric.

Criteria	Outstanding	Satisfactory	Revise	Needs improvement	Explain and justify your rating	Describe your criticism or compliments
Standards	Aligns with NYS Standards	N/A	N/A	Does Not Align NYS Standards		
Objectives	Objectives are clearly stated, measurable, achievable, and aligned with NYS Standards	Objectives are stated, measurable, achievable, and mostly aligned with NYS Standards	Objectives are stated, but may lack measurability, achievability, or alignment with NYS Standards	Objectives are unclear, not measurable, not achievable, or not aligned with NYS Standards		
Technology Integration	Technology is purposefully and appropriately integrated into the lesson, enhancing student learning	Technology is integrated into the lesson but may not always enhance student learning	Technology integration is limited or not purposeful and may not enhance student learning	Technology integration is absent or irrelevant to the lesson		
Hands-On Activity	The hands-on activity is engaging, aligns with the objectives, and enhances student understanding	The hands-on activity is engaging and aligns with the objectives but may not fully enhance student understanding	The hands-on activity is somewhat engaging and aligns with the objectives but does not enhance student understanding	The hands-on activity is not engaging, does not align with the objectives, or does not enhance student understanding		
Procedures	The procedure is well explained, thorough, and each step is clearly explained	The procedure is mostly well explained and thorough, with some steps lacking clarity	The procedure lacks clarity or thoroughness, making it difficult for others to understand and follow	The procedure is poorly explained, lacks thoroughness, and is unclear		

Appendix 2: Rubric Evaluation Form

Teachers' views on using artificial intelligence to improve teacher productivity.

Participant Number:

Content Area:

AI Tool:

Project Title:

Grade Level:

Project Description:

Directions: Use the same project, grade level, and criteria for each AI tool you test. Use each AI tool to create a rubric for your project. Copy and paste the rubric onto a document to attach to this evaluation. Please reflect upon your experience and answer each question with as much detail as you can.

1. Please describe the quality of the criteria descriptions it provided.
2. How easy or difficult was it to create the rubric for your project?
3. Is the rubric something you would actually use in your teaching? Why or why not?
4. How did using this AI tool save you time?
5. What recommendations or suggestions do you have about this AI tool in creating rubrics?

Appendix 3: Assessment Evaluation Form

Teachers' views on using artificial intelligence to improve teacher productivity.

Participant Number:

Content Area:

AI Tool:

Assessment Topic:

Grade Level:

Directions: Use the same assessment topic, grade level, and prompt for each AI tool you test. Use each AI tool to create a 5-question multiple-choice assessment on a topic of your choosing. Copy and paste the multiple-choice assessment onto a document to attach to this evaluation. Please reflect upon your experience and answer each question with as much detail as you can.

1. Please describe the quality of the questions the AI tool generated.
2. How easy or difficult was it to create the assessment for your project?
3. Is the assessment something you would actually use in your teaching? Why or why not?
4. How did using this AI tool save you time?
5. What recommendations or suggestions do you have about this AI tool for creating assessments?

Appendix 4: Interview Questions

Teachers' views on using artificial intelligence to improve teacher productivity.

Participant Number:
Content Area:
AI Tool:
Project Title:
Grade Level:

1. How was your experience using the three different Artificial Intelligence tools? Be specific.
2. Which AI tool in your opinion was the easiest to use? Which was the most difficult? Please Explain:
3. Was there a lesson plan that stood out as better than the rest?
4. What made that lesson stand out among the rest? Please be specific relating directly to the rubric.
5. What was missing from the lessons? Please be specific relating directly to the rubric.
6. Would you use any of the lessons presented in front of you to teach your students in their current state? Why or why not?
7. Do you feel that any of the assessments created by the AI tools are usable as is? Please be specific.
8. Was there any rubric that stood out as not usable or incomplete?
9. If you had to choose a lesson plan that was the best based on the rubric and your professional opinion, which would it be and why?
10. What is your overall opinion about how AI tools helped you to be more productive?

References

Akgun, S., & Greenhow, C. (2021). Artificial intelligence in education: Addressing ethical challenges in K-12 settings. *AI and Ethics, 2*, 431–440. https://doi.org/10.1007/s43681-021-00096-7

Bailey, J. (2023, September 13). *AI in education*. Education Next. https://www.educationnext.org/wp-content/uploads/2023/09/ednext_XXIII_4_bailey.pdf

Bowen, J. A., & Watson, C. E. (2024). *Teaching with AI: A practical guide to a new era of human learning*. Johns Hopkins University Press.

Bradley, T. (2024, September 18). *AI's role in saving teachers time and revolutionizing education*. Forbes. https://www.forbes.com/sites/tonybradley/2024/09/18/ais-role-in-saving-teachers-time-and-revolutionizing-education/

Bryant, J., Heitz, C., Sanghvi, S., & Wagle, D. (2020, January). *How artificial intelligence will impact K-12 teachers*. Mckinsey & Company. https://www.mckinsey.com/~/media/McKinsey/Industries/Public%20and%20Social%20Sector/Our%20Insights/How%20artificial%20intelligence%20will%20impact%20K%2012%20teachers/How-artificial-intelligence-will-impact-K-12-teachers.pdf

Carnegie Learning. (2025). *The state of AI in education 2025: Key findings from a national survey*. https://discover.carnegielearning.com/hubfs/PDFs/Whitepaper%20and%20Guide%20PDFs/2025-AI-in-Ed-Report.pdf?hsLang=en#page=2.09

Celik, I., Dindar, M., Muukkonen, H., & Järvelä, S. (2022). The promises and challenges of artificial intelligence for teachers: A systematic review of research. *TechTrends, 66*, 616–630. https://doi.org/10.1007/s11528-022-00715-y

Clarke, J. S., Porath, S., Thiele, J., & Jobe, M. (2020). *Analyzing data from your classroom*. Action Research. https://kstatelibraries.pressbooks.pub/gradactionresearch/chapter/chap6/

Creswell, J., & Guetterman, T. (2019). Specify the population and sample. In J. W. Creswell & T. C. Guetterman (Eds.), *Educational research: Planning, conducting, and evaluating quantitative and qualitative research* (pp. 139–139). Pearson Education.

Hanover Research. (2025). *2025 trends in higher education*. https://www.hanoverresearch.com/reports-and-briefs/higher-education/2025-trends-in-higher-education/

Jump, A., Bradley, A., Goodness, E., & Miclaus, R. (2025). *Emerging tech: Primary impact of generative AI on business use cases*. Gartner. https://www.gartner.com/en/doc/779868-emerging-tech-top-use-cases-for-generative-ai

Koehler, M., & Mishra, P. (2009). What is technological pedagogical content knowledge (TPACK)? *Contemporary Issues in Technology and Teacher Education, 9*(1), 60–70. https://www.learntechlib.org/p/29544/

Maguire, M., & Delahunt, B. (2017). Doing a thematic analysis: A practical, step-by-step guide for learning and teaching scholars. *All Ireland Journal of Teaching and Learning in Higher Education, 8*(3), 3351–33514. https://ojs.aishe.org/index.php/aishe-j/article/view/335/553

McGraw Hill. (2019, April 16). *What is TPACK theory and how can it be used in the classroom*? McGraw Hill. https://www.mheducation.ca/blog/what-is-tpack-theory-and-how-can-it-be-used-in-the-classroom

Meli, K., Taouki, J., & Pantazatos, D. (2024). Empowering educators with generative AI: The GenAI education frontier initiative. In *EDULEARN24. 16th International Conference on Education and New Learning Technologies, Spain*. IATED. https://doi.org/10.21125/edulearn.2024.1077

Mijwil, M. M., Aggarwal, K., Mutar, D. S., Mansour, N., & Singh, R. S. S. (2022). The position of artificial intelligence in the future of education: An overview. *Asian Journal of Applied Sciences, 10*(2). https://doi.org/10.24203/ajas.v10i2.6956

Mills, G. E. (2018). *Action research: A guide for the teacher researcher*. Pearson.

Mishra, P., & Koehler, M. J. (2006). Technological pedagogical content knowledge: A new framework for teacher knowledge. *Teachers College Record, 108*(6), 1017–1054. https://psycnet.apa.org/doi/10.1111/j.1467-9620.2006.00684.x

Mondal, H., Marndi, G., Behera, J. K., & Mondal, S. (2023). ChatGPT for teachers: Practical examples for utilizing artificial intelligence for educational purposes. *Indian Journal of Vascular and Endovascular Surgery, 10*(3), 200–205. https://doi.org/10.4103/ijves.ijves_37_23

Nguyen, T. N., & Truong, H. T. (2025). Trends and emerging themes in the effects of generative artificial intelligence in education: A systematic review. *Eurasia Journal of Mathematics, Science and Technology Education, 21*(4), em2613. https://doi.org/10.29333/ejmste/16124

Raj, A. S. (2024). *GenAI and the future of education and research*. SSRN. https://papers.ssrn.com/sol3/papers.cfm?abstract_id=4686338

Slimi, Z. (2023). The impact of artificial intelligence on higher education: An empirical study. *European Journal of Educational Sciences, 10*(1), 17–33. https://doi.org/10.19044/ejes.v10no1a17

Sobehrad, S., & Francis, R. (2024). Indistinguishable from magic: AI for educators. In J. Cohen & G. Solano (Eds.), *Proceedings of Society for Information Technology & Teacher Education International Conference* (pp. 2278–2283). Association for the Advancement of Computing in Education (AACE). https://www.learntechlib.org/primary/p/224294/

Zhang, K., & Aslan, A. B. (2021). AI technologies for education: Recent research & future directions. *Computers and Education: Artificial Intelligence, 2*, 1–11, 100025. https://doi.org/10.1016/j.caeai.2021.100025.

Shelby Grosso (SUNY Oneonta University) earned a master's degree as a K-12 Educational Technology Specialist at SUNY Oneonta. She also completed a bachelor's degree at SUNY Oneonta in a dual program for Early Childhood and Childhood Education, with a concentration in Mathematics and a minor in Educational Psychology. In college, she was the Vice President of Omicron Delta Kappa, the school's Leadership Honors Society, and the Community Service Chair of the Association for Childhood Educators International. She was also the Oneonta Connection Team Supervisor for the Admissions Office. Ms. Grosso's research focuses on how artificial intelligence can impact teacher productivity. sgrosso@bronxexcellence.org.

Gina L. Solano is a university professor of Educational Technology at SUNY Oneonta. Her research focuses on the professional development of educators in the field of technology, AR/VR/XR, innovative technologies, and using technology to support mindfulness education. She teaches courses on research, digital media, educational technology, STEM, multimedia, online learning, and instructional design. She has presented on a variety of technology topics at national and international conferences on virtual reality, digital badges, digital storytelling, digital design, gamification, augmented reality, and geospatial technologies, among others. She has directed several service-learning programs, community outreach, and international student trips. Gina.solano@oneonta.edu. https://orcid.org/0009-0001-3970-5193.

Part V
Students, AI, and GenAI: Identity Formation and Perceptions

Chapter 19
The Impact of Generative AI on Student Identity Formation

Ezechiel Thibaud

Abstract One of the many purposes of education is to facilitate students' identity formation through various social and pedagogical processes. As Artificial intelligence (AI), and especially generative AI (GenAI), are being increasingly introduced into classrooms, this chapter looks at the potential impact they may have on these processes. We first analyze the links between education and identity, then identify three dimensions of identity formation: relational, dialectical, and agential. After a quick look at the various ways GenAI can be used in education, the chapter addresses concerns regarding the possible impact of GenAI on these three dimensions. We conclude that caution is required in order to maintain mastery of certain skills necessary not only to think critically and autonomously, but also to get a robust sense of who we are.

Keywords Autonomy · Identity formation · Education

This chapter starts with the premise that one of education's roles is to facilitate student's identity formation. Education enables individuals to go through the processes that are necessary to discover the world, but also their own identity. This includes the values they hold, the traits of character they possess, as well as the relationships they form with others and with their social context(s). Artificial intelligence (AI), and generative AI (GenAI), have massively invested the education field, and students and teachers are increasingly incentivized to make use of it in various ways (OECD, 2023). AI is defined by Luckin et al. (2016, p. 14) as "computer systems that have been designed to interact with the world through capabilities (…) and intelligent behaviours (…) that we would think of as essentially human". Although AI and GenAI are often interconnected in their application, traditional AI is mainly focused on performing specific tasks, analyze data and make predictions, while

E. Thibaud (✉)
Education University of Hong Kong, Hong Kong SAR, China
e-mail: ethibaud@eduhk.hk

G. Tchibozo (ed.), *International Perspectives of Generative AI in Education*, Advances in Artificial Intelligence in Education 3,
https://doi.org/10.1007/978-3-031-99804-1_19

GenAI creates data based on already available information (Marr, 2023). It is precisely because of its creative human-like capacities that GenAI is subject to debate, especially since the introduction of Large Language Models (LLMs), which created an almost "seismic shift" in the education field (Cooper, 2023, p. 451).

However, while many have looked at the benefits as well as the ethical risks of AI in education, few have studied its potential impact on identity. We start by suggesting three main ways that education impacts identity formation, identified as relational, dialectical, and agential (Cinoğlu & Arıkan, 2012). This chapter analyses the importance of these processes for identity development and investigates the impact that GenAI may have on them if generalized in the field. We conclude that despite some benefits, the use of GenAI in education raises concerns for identity formation that should not be overlooked. At a time where AI in education seems either uncritically welcomed, or fearfully rejected, we hope to provide a moderate but realistic view of its potential consequences.

The Role of Education in Identity Formation

Identity is a complex concept, to say the least: it is vague, broad, ambiguous, and multidimensional (Flum & Kaplan, 2012). Brubaker and Cooper (2000) point out the difficulty of identifying the nature of a concept that is fluid, constructed, and multiple at the same time. When discussing personal identity, two main questions arise: the question of what makes an individual the same over time, and the question of what makes an individual different from other individuals (Flanagan & Oksenberg Rorty, 1990). Identity is also linked to moral agency: it is not only a series of traits individuals specifically possess, but also the capacity to make ethical decisions, form opinions and act accordingly. Personal identity is also to be distinguished from the various identities a person can embody, and that may conflict at times—national, sexual, racial, religious, professional, and many more (MacDonald Mishler, 1978).

Despite its complexity, identity remains a central concept of humanities and social sciences. Understanding how people form their identity(ies) is key to understanding the personal, socio-economic and political dynamics that shape an individual's self-construal and self-perception. Understanding one's own identity is essential to position oneself in the world and know the framework from which to make authentic choices. But identity doesn't have to be conceived as a set of constant traits; instead, it is a series of "traits that typically make a systematic difference to the course of a person's life, to the habit-forming and action-guiding social categories in which she is placed (…)" (Oksenberg Rorty & Wong, 1990, p. 19). Because of identity's deeply subjective dimension, we will refrain in this chapter from proposing a definition that would fit all human experiences. Instead, we will only describe some of the procedural and instrumental aspects of identity: the way identity comes about, is understood, and what aspects are necessary for the further flourishment of individuals and their society. We will do so by focusing on the role that education plays in the process: our goal is not to provide a fixed picture of identity that education should promote, but to highlight the essential tools that education can and should provide for people to identify, understand, and act based on their respective identity.

Education too is a broad and multidimensional term. There are multiple ways to educate or be educated, and all may have an impact on how we construe our identity. Much of it is formed at home, through familial and cultural traditions, hobbies, friendships, etc. We will, however, restrict our definition to the formal meaning of education, done through school or other educational institutions.

Schools' role is not restricted to acquiring academic or professional skills, it is also to help students gain a robust sense of who they are, through the provision of emotional, relational and cognitive tools. This view is not new; it follows holistic education traditions (Miller et al., 2018), but also functionalism. Holistic education focuses on whole-person development; understanding and supporting students through the complex process of their identity formation is a central part of educational practitioners' duties (Torres et al., 2009). Moral education also highlights the interconnection between educational practices and character development (Lapsley & Narvaez, 2006). As King (2009) suggests, the cognitive and moral development of the student are fundamentally intertwined and almost inseparable. Schools facilitate the development of the whole person by providing students with opportunities to connect academic content to their own lived experience and reflect on what they study (Flum & Kaplan, 2012).

The functionalist approach too points out the interrelatedness of education and identity formation. Functionalists like Durkheim (1893) believe that one function of schools is to maintain a form of social order based on value consensus, socialization and role identification in the context of the division of labor (Cookson et al., 2014; Durkheim, 1893). Identity formation, in this context, is linked to the social, economic and political environment in which students grow. Awareness of their socio-political identity, therefore, comes with and is supported by education: it is contextualized to fit the norms and expectations of a given community. Sociological theories suggest that identity is (at least partly) socially constructed, fundamentally intertwined with education, and that strong links exist between students' approach to learning and their socio-cultural background (Altugan, 2015; Bliuc et al., 2011).

Schools, broadly conceived, play a limited but significant role in the way students understand who they are, where they stand, and what social role they wish (or are requested) to play (Flum & Kaplan, 2012). This process is neither fixed nor substantive; schools don't teach students specifics about who they should be, but provide the epistemic tools for students to self-discover and make choices. We suggest that education impacts and shapes identity formation through what we identify to be a three-dimensional process: relational, dialectical and agential.

Education and the Relational Dimension of Identity Formation

Research stresses the significance of relationships for self-construal (Chen et al., 2011; Cross et al., 2000; Morgan & Korobov, 2012). Identity formation takes place through a process that allows students to understand the various bonds and relationships that constitute their environment broadly conceived (family, social, political, natural, etc.). To understand who we are is to understand the interrelatedness of our social reality. Schools, because of their socializing function, play an important role in highlighting these links. Flum and Kaplan (2012, p. 240) write that "identity formation is a product of the interrelations between the individual and the context". This idea echoes previous psychological research showing that human development happens through an integrative process of transactions between oneself and one's environment (Dewey & Bentley, 1949). Erikson (1959, 1968) is among the first to provide a comprehensive psychological account of the interconnection between psychological, personal and social aspects of identity formation. The personal dimension refers to the specific behaviors and characters that distinguish a person from another, while the social dimension is understood through the recognition of one's role within a given community (Côté & Levine, 2002). This view of the individual in context is particularly relevant in educational settings, as schools focus not only on socialization but also on the discovery of students' environment (historical, cultural, political, geographical, among others). Knowledge of one's particular socio-cultural context facilitates the recognition of one's role in the community and provides the opportunity to exercise appropriate social behaviors. As Flum and Kaplan (2012, p. 241) note, "school as a social community provides a relational web, a system of relations that create meaning".

The relational aspect of education has also been highlighted by ethicists of care, who claim that caring relations should be at the center of our ethical considerations (Noddings, 1995). Education is made of a series of encounters through which students learn to navigate the world in a caring and respectful way. The relational dimension of identity formation posits that we discover and are able to make claims about who we are based on the discovery of the various relationships that shape our interpersonal, social and moral reality.

Education and the Dialectical Dimension of Identity Formation

Identity formation also takes place through the process of learning, engaging in dialogue, and organizing thoughts. An essential aspect of our identity is the ability to make descriptive and normative claims, form personal opinions and reflect on the opinions of others. It is not a passive process, but something that emerges through negotiation (O'Boyle, 2014), as emphasized by Relational Dialectics Theory, which postulates that meaning-making "emerges from the interplay of competing discourses" (Baxter & Braithwaite, 2008, abstract). Inspired by the Socratic method of truth-seeking through dialogue, Hegelian dialectics stipulate that the process of argumentation constitutes a back-and-forth between opposite sides, often illustrated through the thesis, antithesis, synthesis model (Maybee, 2020; Woods, 2013). Dialectical learning supposes an exploration of conflicting opinions, and has been described as essential for cognitive and creative stimulation of learners (Ravenscroft et al., 2006). Exposing conflicting views allows students to compare, synthesize, prioritize, adopt or reject ideas. Through this process, students develop their own opinions, which ultimately plays a role in the discovery of where they stand on significant matters. The benefits of dialectical learning go beyond mere exposure to different views: it encourages the formation of structured, analytical and innovative thinking. It helps challenging preconceptions and old paradigms, analyzing contradictions and considering new logical possibilities (Chaves, 2007). Dialectical identity formation is the process through which students develop personal opinions through exposure to different views, which allows them to locate themselves intellectually and morally.

Education and the Agential Dimension of Identity Formation

This last dimension concerns the cultivation of autonomy and agency, considered by some to be the ultimate goal of education (Bakhurst, 2011; Dearden, 1972). For Biesta (2015, 2019) one of education's role is to engage students in a process of subjectification: to create a desire to be in the world as "subjects of initiative and responsibility rather than as objects of the actions of others" (Biesta, 2015, p. 77). Identity formation can here be understood as the capacity to understand one's own motivations and desires, in order to make authentic decisions and develop individual and collective agency. Rödl (2016, p. 84) argues that through education, children acquire a social and historical identity that equips them with personal powers: "thought, reasoning, intellect and will". Côté and Levine (2002, p. 148) stress the importance of education as "active adaptation", as opposed to "passive compliance". They argue that although the latter is more widely spread, the former is crucial for identity and value affirmation. Active adaptation is described as "agentic dispositions and behaviours that lead individuals to avoid and resist the paths of least resistance and effort offered by late modern consumer culture, and instead to actively explore their potential, build personal strengths, and sustain some sense of direction and meaning" (Côté & Levine, 2002, p. 148). Identity can be characterized by a series of projects and commitments that a person is capable of making (or refuses to make), and the ability of that person to live the life he or she finds meaningful (Flanagan & Oksenberg Rorty, 1990).

Some crucial aspects of decision-making and autonomous action are self-esteem, confidence, and trust in others (Govier, 1993). Boosting students' self-esteem does not only boost academic performance but also creates the necessary conditions for confident decision-making in the future. Who we are politically, but also who we are in the eye of others, shapes our identity as a learner (MacDonald Mishler, 1978):

trust in one's capacities, but also knowledge that our experience is shared by others becomes a way to overcome socio-political barriers. Charles Taylor (1991) argues that group identification and value commitment provide agents with a framework within which they can determine what is worthy of pursuit. The role of schools is here to provide the procedural necessary tools to identify what matters to us, reject what harms us, and take part in individual or collective actions for the realization of a meaningful life. Identity formation comes as a result of these capacities: as we confidently act in the world, we make statements about who we are.

It is important to mention that the three dimensions of identity formation we propose are not separate but interconnected: they influence each other in complex ways, resulting in the formation of a unique person. The role of education, although significant, is also limited: systemic, religious or economic forces, for example, also shape and sometimes dictate the way identity is construed (Desjardins, 2015). However, education can be considered as a way to counterbalance these forces, by equipping students with the intellectual and emotional tools to understand and sometimes resist social determinisms. To put it simply, we are who we are because we have acquired the various tools that are necessary to form an idea of who we are. The question is now to determine whether the use of GenAI in education can interfere with the acquisition of these tools.

AI Use in Education

GenAI in education remains a polarizing topic. While various education actors consider it to be a "real and present danger" (Morrison, 2023, para. 1), UNESCO (2023, para. 1) describes it as a tool that "has the potential to address some of the biggest challenges of education today". Some wonder whether GenAI will replace teachers (Chan & Tsi, 2024; also see the chapter by Singh and co-authors in this book), while others see it as an instrument for a more flexible, engaging, and inclusive form of education (Luckin et al., 2016). When first introduced, LLMs tools like ChatGPT have sparked discussions and even panic, especially regarding academic dishonesty, privacy, or the possibility that LLMs produce biased content or hallucinate (Javaid et al., 2023). On the other hand, it is sometimes praised as having the potential to revolutionize the way education is conceived (Harry & Sayudin, 2023). Our aim here is not to speculate on hypothetical apocalyptic scenarios, nor to fall for AI-solutionism. Instead, it is to discuss the potential and foreseeable impact that using GenAI in education could have on identiy formation.

There are countless ways to have a well-intended use of GenAI in education. It can be used to reduce teachers' workload (e.g. administrative duties) and provide support for students in the completion of time-consuming tasks, giving everyone more time to work together (Fullan et al., 2023). Some of the benefits mentioned include working as a personal tutor, detecting student's moods, giving emotional support, engaging students in Socratic dialogues, providing scaffolding assistance, boosting individual students' motivation by using their native language, and/or understanding cultural norms (Luckin et al., 2016; Pang et al., 2024). GenAI can be used to provide the personalized feedback and support that teachers may struggle to give due to a lack of time or overpopulated classes. Teachers might introduce AI chatbots in the classroom to assist students quickly, provide unlimited resources to answer their questions, or give individual follow-ups (Javaid et al., 2023). The hope is that this would create a more interactive, inclusive and flexible learning environment, centered around students' specific needs.

GenAI tools like ChatGPT can generate content for all kinds of pedagogical purposes, potentially rendering certain writing tasks irrelevant. It can also be used to summarize long texts, entire chapters or books, and handle large data (Javaid et al., 2023). Teachers might make use of GenAI to adapt programs and assessments based on AI-collected data on their students' progress (Baidoo-Anu & Owusu Ansah, 2023). GenAI can assist teachers in engaging in differentiated instruction, by creating challenging material for advanced students, and scaffolding support for those who need it, creating a more equitable learning environment (Cooper, 2023). AI is also easily brought home: LLMs can assist students with their homework, when parents lack time or resources.

However, it is important to remember that, despite their efficiency, LLMs only produce data based on what is already available, and are therefore limited. In addition, GenAI can hallucinate, present inaccurate facts, biased content, or simply fail to answer complex questions that have no black or white answers. Despite the various flaws that have been documented, GenAI is nonetheless considered by many to be part of the future of education. An increasing number of education professionals advocate for AI-literacy programs in elementary schools, in order to prepare students for an informed use of GenAI (Chai et al., 2021; Kim et al., 2021). This doesn't mean, however, that the use of GenAI should be uncritical and unconditional: an informed and prudent analysis of its potential effects remains crucial.

Impact of GenAI on Identity Formation

At the time of writing this chapter, the long-term effects of GenAI on students' development remain unexplored. As GenAI tools are being rapidly developed and incorporated into school curricula, we lack the distance to evaluate their long-term consequences (Holmes et al., 2023). This section draws hypotheses and explores the potential impact of GenAI on students' identity formation processes, based on the three dimensions developed above. These propositions remain speculative, but we believe that they raise important moral, social and political questions that need to be addressed.

Impact on Relational Identity Formation

GenAI and relational identity formation raise questions related to the type of exchanges that happen in the classroom. Biesta (2004) argues that education is to be understood as a process of communication between students and teachers. From this perspective, it becomes essential to determine what kind of communication should take place in schools. This seems even more crucial as GenAI is presented as a potential educational interlocutor, a personal tutor able to provide quick and personalized feedback (Mollick & Mollick, 2023). According to Biesta (2010, 2019) the phenomenon of "learnification" has redefined all educational elements in terms of learning, which has led to questioning and marginalizing the role of teachers. Guilherme (2019) follows these lines and argues that education is increasingly conceived as the acquisition of skills, rather than the process through which students form their character. According to these authors, learnification, heavily supported by the rapid and often uncritical technologization of classrooms, has neglected the importance of human interactions in the learning process. Additionally, it has been argued that the increasing digitalization of classrooms creates a detached learning environment (Laura & Chapman, 2009). From their research on the effects of what they call "compuphilia" on students' mental health and general development, Laura and Chapman (2009, abstract) straightforwardly conclude that "the more virtual the classroom becomes, the more disconnected students become". Because of its focus on learning-outcomes as the sole imperative of schools, learnification undermines the importance of human communication for student development. AI-generated feedback may present certain benefits but may also produce a more isolated learning experience; while students might learn skills and facts, they may fail to develop essential character traits that can only be discovered through human interactions. This divide is further highlighted by the distinction between instruction and education: instruction is seen as passive absorption of data for practical purposes, while education involves active engagement in one's own development (Toye, 1971). While GenAI might be good for the former, questions remain unanswered regarding its impact on the latter.

Communication with others is a key aspect of self-discovery, as it provides agents with the opportunity to position themselves and commit to cohesive worldviews (Erikson, 1968). Hohenstein et al. (2023) have studied the possible impact of GenAI on communication and language, as well as on emotional literacy. Their findings suggest that while GenAI may have a positive effect on everyday conversations, it may also alter the emotional perception of language. They conclude that interpersonal relationships are likely to be impacted by the generalization of GenAI: for example, they worry that the homogeneity of GenAI discourse used in emails or texts might make us lose sense of our personal communication style.

Emotion recognition and regulation is another crucial aspect of both education and self-construal. It is associated with children's academic success and the development of important skills (Graziano et al., 2007). On the other hand, emotional literacy—the ability to read, express and appropriately respond to emotions

(ECLKC, 2024)—is necessary to improve social behaviors and engage in questions of meaning and values (Park, 1999). While GenAI is increasingly used as an emotion-tracking tool, some argue that it fails to accurately recognize or convey certain emotions—e.g. empathy (Hoang et al., 2023; Perry, 2023).

More importantly, it might be necessary to look at whether using GenAI for emotional literacy and communication is truly desirable.

Levinas famously stressed the importance of the recognition of the Other through the concept of Face (Levinas, 1985). Face, for Levinas, represents the externality of the Other, but also what connects them to ourselves and our own moral duty. Face-to-face encounters provide a unique emotional experience that reminds us of our mutual responsibility, the need for human proximity, and the moral obligation to be at the Other's service (Edgoose & Edgoose, 2017). What Levinas teaches us through the concept of Face, is that alterity, emotions, and human communication are intertwined in the unique face-to-face experience, through which we learn who we are. Can GenAI—whether through discourses or images—ever play the role of that Other in helping us understand our unique moral duty as human beings? As we currently lack a long-term perspective to confidently answer this question, the possibility that GenAI might alter or take away the opportunity for face-to-face encounters needs to be considered. For example, GenAI is increasingly used as a mental health device. Students use it as a personal therapist (Chan, 2025; Opel et al., 2023) and despite certain advantages like accessibility and affordability, reports have highlighted the inability of GenAI to go beyond a narrow therapeutic approach or deliver any deep connection (Chan, 2025). Overall, the reported lack of genuine human engagement and empathy seems to highlight the mismatch between GenAI's appearance as a communicative agent and the reality. In the classroom, we should take seriously the risk raised by Elmessiry et al. (2023) that AI may dehumanize the learning experience and reduce it to a mere transaction.

Additionally, the question is not merely whether we can form an authentic relationship with GenAI as Guilherme (2019) notes, we also need to consider what kind of relationship should be established in education. Hoang et al. (2023, p. 3) write that "along with asking if AI can engage emotionally, the question of "what" makes meaningful emotional interactions should be addressed first". Biesta (2019, p. 551) wonders whether our subject-ness "emerges from the outside-in, as a response to what speaks to us, to what addresses us, calls us and, through this, calls us *forth*, calls us into existence and into the world". Given the importance of interpersonal relationships, emotional literacy and social interactions for identity formation and moral commitments, we have reasons to worry that the generalization of GenAI in education might interfere with the unveiling of our specific traits and our responsibility toward our fellow humans. Accurate emotion recognition might one day be made possible through GenAI, but it might also take away the unique opportunity that personal interactions represent for human and student development. In other words, the uniqueness and importance of the student-teacher relationship should not be overlooked. If teachers are irreplaceable, so is the human attention they pay to their students.

Impact on Dialectical Identity Formation

Dialectical identity formation implies negotiation and the confrontation of competing discourses (Baxter & Braithwaite, 2008; O'Boyle, 2014). Schools can create the conditions for such exploration to happen, and provide learners with opportunities to identify what matters to them, share their worldviews, and locate themselves on matters of significance. Can the introduction of GenAI alter this cognitive process, ultimately making learners lose touch with who they are, by stripping them off the opportunity to engage in such dialogue?

The dialectical experience requires critical thinking and rational skills that need to be trained. While some argue that GenAI can provide an opportunity for students to improve critical thinking (Darwin et al., 2024), this position lacks a long-term view, and is not without limits (Deng & Yu, 2023; Li et al., 2022). Concerns have been raised about the possibility that GenAI may create an echo chamber—an environment in which individuals only encounter views that coincide with their own—or provide content that lacks a nuanced understanding (Darwin et al., 2024). Hegemonic discourses may threaten the dialectical process if failing to provide conflicting or alternative views. It has been shown that the convenience of GenAI chatbots may discourage students from searching for alternative solutions, reinforcing the risk of hegemony (Parsakia, 2023). GenAI may also present biased reasonings that students, without proper training, may fail to recognize (Kusters et al., 2020). Algorithms and AI are not neutral tools but often reflect the views emerging from the data they are trained with (Stinson, 2022). Because of this, GenAI often produces a biased and sometimes discriminatory discourse, raising concerns about the perpetuation of harmful stereotypes that reinforce pre-existing dynamics of power and domination (Stinson, 2022; Xavier, 2025). Risks for the dialectical process emerge if biased information is presented as neutral or non-controversial, while students lack the *a priori* skills to identify them as biased (or for example, when they study on their own).

It has been argued that heavy use of GenAI can create overreliance and dependency, raising questions about students' capacity to obtain the same results with and without it (Iskender, 2023). This could ultimately impair critical thinking if GenAI is used not to refine but to generate ideas or argument structures (Widiati et al., 2023). A study conducted with students from Albania found a strong negative correlation between reliance on AI for school assignments and the development of problem-solving skills (Çela et al., 2024). In higher education, it has also been reported that despite LLMs' ability to provide quick and accessible learning content, overreliance on GenAI can reduce students' abillity to critically examine this content and impair their reflective skills (Melisa et al., 2025).

Overreliance on GenAI may also erode creative skills—another essential tool for the formation of our distinct identity (Dollinger & Dollinger, 2017). As linguist Naomi S. Baron points out, by relying on AI tools for creative purposes such as writing, we run the risk of decreasing our artistic voice and unique style in a process of automation that eventually "can stop us from thinking" (Baron & The Conversation, 2023).

Additionally, learning is a long-term and slow process that should not only be measured through direct outcomes without understanding the source of our mistakes. It has been shown that while GenAI can help students improve grammar on a given assignment, it is unclear whether grammar rules are assimilated or how long-lasting results will be (Widiati et al., 2023). Beyond grammar, this raises the question of the extent to which the use of GenAI, by replacing human effort and accelerating the process of creation, may actually limit the depth of students' learning.

These risks should inform us about the importance to equip students with rational and creative skills beforehand, but also raise question about whether GenAI should be used in this preparation process. There is a worry that overreliance on GenAI can erode the cognitive skills necessary for dialectical learning or affect the condition under which it takes place, by providing a hegemonic discourse, impairing creative thinking or over-assisting students in their argumentation practice, ultimately making us unsure of or disinterested in what we truly think.

Impact on Agential Identity Formation

A large part of our self-construction has to do with the way we mobilize our moral commitments to make authentic, individual or collective decisions (Korsgaard, 2009). This implies that certain skills be trained, and certain dispositions cultivated, such as autonomous decision-making, self-confidence, or collective trust.

Although GenAI can support teachers and students through decision-making, it can also lead to dependency and the erosion of certain rational skills. Ahmad et al. (2023) studied the impact of AI on student decision-making skills and laziness. They argue that AI use in education tends to minimize students' participation, which might overtime lead to a loss of traditional skills (critical thinking, innovation, creativity, etc.), but also ultimately erode responsibility. They conclude that "AI is minimizing our autonomous roles, replacing our choices with its choices, and making us lazy in various walks of life" (Ahmad et al., 2023, p. 4). Darvishi et al. (2024) argue that students tend to rely on AI tools rather than actively learn from them. They show that once AI tools are removed, students are often unable to produce results of a similar quality. These findings raise important questions about the risk that AI may disempower students rather than assist them in learning. Not only does GenAI seem to aggravate existing problems in education, but it also seems to pose a unique challenge that may have larger implications: the rational abilities mentioned are not only crucial for academic and professional success, but they also play a significant role in the formation of who we are as individuals and members of communities.

Additional concerns have emerged regarding students' self-esteem and confidence, which are crucial aspects of agency (Bandura, 1990). Back in the 1950s,

Gunther Anders already expressed the fear that technological advancements may result in a decrease in human confidence, which he called "Promethean shame" (Anders, 1956). This concept refers to the humiliation felt when humans realized that the efficiency of the machines that they created had surpassed their own. Although Anders wrote long before the emergence of AI, his words seem to remarkably echo our current concerns. The narrative of human incompetence is commonplace, and often serves as a justification for the implementation of various technological solutions. We see this, for example, in the growing popularity of behavioral nudges, in education and elsewhere (Thaler & Sunstein, 2009; Weijers et al., 2021). Nudges are a form of choice-architecture tool that seek to direct people's behavior towards a desired outcome without coercion (Thaler & Sunstein, 2009). In an argument referred to as "libertarian-paternalism", Thaler and Sunstein justify the use of nudges by the assumption that humans, because naturally prone to biases, lack the rational abilities to make good decisions for themselves and others. Nudges, AI, and other technological tools, come as a way to compensate for assumed human incompetence. But the risk of a self-fulfilling prophecy should not be overlooked: by over-relying on GenAI and technology as a way to compensate for our shortcomings, do we risk impairing our capacity to train the skills that could allow us to overcome them?

The relation between confidence and AI-trust can be understood as a mutual-reinforcement phenomenon. GenAI may affect confidence in decision-making by eroding the skills mentioned above. At the same time, low self-esteem may reinforce the belief that GenAI's decisions are superior, increasing the likelihood that it will be blindly trusted (Chong et al., 2022). Parsakia (2023, p. 73) writes that "excessive dependence on chatbots for decision-making or problem-solving might undermine an individual's confidence in their own judgment and abilities". He adds that emotionally vulnerable individuals are at higher risk: chatbots that fail to convey adequate empathy may impact their self-esteem by producing inconsiderate or harmful content. Prunkl (2024) also argues that GenAI may affect self-esteem by generating or recommending content that perpetuates negative stereotypes. We also know that using GenAI for tasks previously done by humans may affect their confidence: for example, workers who feel threatened by AI may feel robbed of their professional and personal worth (Morgan, 2023). As our tasks get increasingly handled by GenAI, we might feel not only professionally obsolete but also personally irrelevant (Puntoni & Yalcin, 2023). Finally, constant narratives about the need for GenAI to compensate for assumed human irrationality can worsen the problem by deterring people from trusting their own decision-making skills.

The link between self-confidence and blind trust in AI have been explored by Chong et al. (2022) who find correlations between AI acceptance and human self-confidence. Their research highlights that people's self-confidence directly impacts their trust in AI: the more confident a person is in their decision-making skills, the less likely they are to trust AI decisions (and *vice-versa*). Consequently, people's self-perception determines both their use of AI and their tendency to trust AI-made decisions over their own. It therefore seems that if self-confidence is not adequately boosted, there is a risk that people might blindly accept AI decisions, irrespective of their quality.

Finally, GenAI may also impact personal autonomy. Prunkl (2024) argues that AI can affect both authenticity and agency. According to her, AI systems can impair authenticity by manipulating agents into making decisions using their rational or emotional vulnerabilities (for example, by personalizing social media feeds, GenAI can influence agents to post or engage with a certain type of content). To her, the impact on agency comes from the fact that GenAI often takes on an agential role and sometimes produce results that are undesirable to humans (for example, automated loan approval or university admissions). In doing so, GenAI is seen as a force that limits people's opportunities and power of action (Prunkl, 2022). This feeling of disempowerment might be exacerbated if GenAI replaces humans for decision-making roles, or discourages people from exercising their rational skills, ultimately producing a form of moral atrophy (Schwarz, 2019). Overuse of AI for decision-making seems at odds with the very goal of education, which is in part to empower students in their self-discovery journey through the development of autonomous thinking and rational skills. The loss of confidence that may result from this overuse may impact students' self-trust but also their trust in collective solutions and actions, rendering the task of becoming informed agents irrelevant in itself. Schools should therefore consider these risks and whether they outweigh the potential benefits of using GenAI in the classroom. Teachers should consider prioritizing boosting students' self-esteem and improving their agential skills before introducing GenAI into their practice.

Conclusion

This chapter has explored the dimensions of identity formation on which education seems to have the strongest impact, and the effects of GenAI on these processes. It concludes that a cautious and conditional use of GenAI is required for identity development not to be affected: GenAI's potential negative impact on interpersonal relations, communication, argumentation or agency seems too great to ignore. To be able to structure one's thoughts is to be able to locate oneself on matters of significance. Failure to identify such position puts us at risk of moral apathy, where we no longer care what speech is given, nor do care who or what gives it, as long as a speech is being produced. AI-dependency for writing, creating and structuring arguments could lead to a form of moral disengagement, and ultimately a loss of self. This form of disempowerment could further discourage autonomous decision-making or collective deliberation and action. It is therefore crucial that education professionals take these risks seriously, and place more emphasis on developing human intelligence alongside AI literacy (Spector & Ma, 2019). Additionally, we should prioritize addressing the root cause of education long-lasting issues—understaffed schools, overpopulated classrooms, underfunded programs, etc.—before turning to GenAI with the naive hope that it will magically fix them.

Competing Interests The author has no conflicts of interest to declare that are relevant to the content of this chapter.

References

Ahmad, S. F., Han, H., Alam, M. M., Rehmat, M. K., Irshad, M., Arraño-Muñoz, M., & Ariza-Montes, A. (2023). Impact of artificial intelligence on human loss in decision making, laziness and safety in education. *Humanities and Social Sciences Communication, 10*, 311. https://doi.org/10.1057/s41599-023-01787-8

Altugan, A. S. (2015). The relationship between cultural identity and learning. *Procedia - Social and Behavioral Sciences, 186*, 1159–1162.

Anders, G. (1956). *The obsolescence of man (Vol. II): On the destruction of life in the epoch of the third industrial revolution*. Translated by Pérez, J. M. (2011). Libcom. https://files.libcom.org/files/ObsolescenceofManVol%20IIGunther%20Anders.pdf.

Baidoo-Anu, D., & Owusu Ansah, L. (2023). Education in the era of generative artificial intelligence (AI): Understanding the potential benefits of ChatGPT in promoting teaching and learning. *Journal of AI, 7*(1), 52–62.

Bakhurst, D. (2011). *The formation of reason*. Wiley-Blackwell.

Bandura, A. (1990). Perceived self-efficacy in the exercise of personal agency. *Journal of Applied Sport Psychology, 2*(2), 128–163.

Baron, S. N., & The Conversation. (2023, January 20). *Even kids are worried ChatGPT will make them lazy plagiarists, says a linguist who studies tech's effects on reading, writing and thinking*. Fortune. https://fortune.com/2023/01/19/what-is-chatgpt-ai-effect-cheating-plagiarism-laziness-education-kids-students/

Baxter, L. A., & Braithwaite, D. O. (2008). Relational dialectics theory. In L. A. Baxter & D. O. Braithewaite (Eds.), *Engaging theories in interpersonal communication: Multiple perspectives* (pp. 349–361). Sage Publications, Inc.

Biesta, G. (2004). "Mind the gap!" Communication and the educational relation. *Counterpoints, 259*, 11–22.

Biesta, G. (2010). *Good education in an age of measurement: Ethics, politics, democracy*. Routledge.

Biesta, G. (2015). What is education for? On good education, teacher judgement, and educational professionalism. *European Journal of Education, 50*(1), 75–87.

Biesta, G. (2019). Should teaching be re(dis)covered? Introduction to a symposium. *Studies in Philosophy and Education, 38*, 549–553.

Bliuc, A. M., Ellis, R. A., Goodyear, P., & Hendres, D. M. (2011). The role of social identification as university student in learning: Relationships between students' social identity, approaches to learning, and academic achievement. *Educational Psychology, 31*(5), 559–574.

Brubaker, R., & Cooper, F. (2000). Beyond "identity". *Theory & Society, 29*, 1–47.

Çela, E., Fonkam, M. M., & Potluri, R. M. (2024). Risks of AI-assisted learning on student critical thinking: A case study of Albania. *International Journal of Risk and Contingency Management (IJRCM), 12*(1), 1–19.

Chai, C. S., Lin, P.-Y., Jong, M. S.-Y., Dai, Y., Chiu, T. K. F., & Qin, J. (2021). Perceptions of and behavioral intentions towards learning artificial intelligence in primary school students. *Educational Technology & Society, 24*(3), 89–101.

Chan, C. K. Y. (2025). AI as the therapist: Student insights on the challenges of using generative AI for school mental health frameworks. *Behavioral Sciences, 15*(3), 287.

Chan, C. K. Y., & Tsi, H. Y. L. (2024). Will generative AI replace teachers in higher education? A study of teacher and student perceptions. *Studies in Educational Evaluation., 83*, 101395. https://doi.org/10.1016/j.stueduc.2024.101395

Chaves, C. A. (2007). Adult learners and the dialectical process: A validating constructivist approach to learning transfer and application. *Online Journal for Workforce Education and Development, 3*(1), 2.
Chen, S., Boucher, H., & Kraus, M. W. (2011). The relational self. In S. Schwartz, K. Luyckx, & V. Vignoles (Eds.), *Handbook of identity theory and research*. Springer.
Chong, L., Zhang, G., Goucher-Lambert, K., Kotovsky, K., & Cagan, J. (2022). Human confidence in artificial intelligence and in themselves: The evolution and impact of confidence on adoption of AI advice. *Computers in Human Behavior, 127*, 107018.
Cinoğlu, H., & Arıkan, Y. (2012). Self, identity and identity formation: From the perspectives of three major theories. *Journal of Human Sciences, 9*(2), 1114–1131.
Cookson, P., Levinson, D., & Sadovnik, A. (2014). *Education and sociology: An encyclopedia*. Routledge.
Cooper, G. (2023). Examining science education in ChatGPT: An exploratory study of generative artificial intelligence. *Journal of Science Education and Technology, 32*, 444–452.
Côté, J. E., & Levine, C. G. (2002). *Identity formation, agency, and culture: A social psychological synthesis*. Lawrence Erlbaum.
Cross, S. E., Bacon, P. L., & Morris, M. L. (2000). The relational-interdependent self-construal and relationships. *Journal of Personality and Social Psychology, 78*(4), 791–808.
Darvishi, A., Khosravi, H., Sadiq, S., Gašević, D., & Siemens, G. (2024). Impact of AI assistance on student agency. *Computers & Education, 210*, 1–18.
Darwin, Rusdin, D., Mukminatien, N., Suryati, N., Laksmi, E. D., & Marzuki. (2024). Critical thinking in the AI era: An exploration of EFL students' perceptions, benefits, and limitations. *Cogent Education, 11*(1).
Dearden, R. F. (1972). Autonomy and education. In R. F. Dearden, P. H. Hirst, & R. S. Peters (Eds.), *Education and the development of reason*. Routledge.
Deng, X., & Yu, Z. (2023). A meta-analysis and systematic review of the effect of chatbot technology use in sustainable education. *Sustainability, 15*, 2940.
Desjardins, R. (2015). The precarious role of education in identity and value formation processes. *European Journal of Education, 50*(2), 134–146.
Dewey, J., & Bentley, A. F. (1949). *Knowing and the known*. The Beacon Press.
Dollinger, S. J., & Dollinger, S. C. (2017). Creativity and identity. In I. M. Karwowski & J. C. Kaufman (Eds.), *The creative self: Effect of beliefs, self-efficacy, mindset, and identity*. Academic.
Durkheim, E. (1893). *The division of labor in society*. The Free Press, Simon and Schuster (1997).
ECLKC. (2024). *Fostering emotional literacy in young children: Labeling emotions*. Early Childhood Learning & Knowledge Center. U.S. Department of Health & Human Service. https://eclkc.ohs.acf.hhs.gov/mental-health/article/fostering-emotional-literacy-young-children-labeling-emotions
Edgoose, J. Y. C., & Edgoose, J. M. (2017). Finding hope in the face-to-face. *Annals of Family Medicine, 15*(3), 272–274.
Elmessiry, A., Elmessiry, M., & Elmessiry, K. (2023). Unethical use of artificial intelligence in education. In *EDULEARN23 Proceedings* (pp. 6703–6707).
Erikson, E. H. (1959). Identity and the life cycle [Monograph]. *Psychological Issues, 1*, 1–191.
Erikson, E. H. (1968). *Identity: Youth and crisis*. Norton.
Flanagan, O., & Oksenberg Rorty, A. (1990). *Identity, character and morality: Essays in moral psychology*. MIT Press.
Flum, H., & Kaplan, A. (2012). Identity formation in educational settings: A contextualized view of theory and research in practice. *Contemporary Educational Psychology, 37*(3), 240–245.
Fullan, M., Azorín, C., Harris, A., & Jones, M. (2023). Artificial intelligence and school leadership: Challenges, opportunities and implications. *School Leadership & Management, 44*(4), 339–346. https://doi.org/10.1080/13632434.2023.2246856
Govier, T. (1993). Self-trust, autonomy, and self-esteem. *Hypatia, 8*(1), 99–120.
Graziano, P. A., Reavis, R. D., Keane, S. P., & Calkins, S. D. (2007). The role of emotion regulation and children's early academic success. *Journal of School Psychology, 45*(1), 3–19.

Guilherme, A. (2019). AI and education: The importance of teacher and student relations. *AI & SOCIETY, 34*, 47–54.

Harry, A., & Sayudin, S. (2023). Role of AI in education. *Injurity: Interdiciplinary Journal and Humanity, 2*(3), 260–268.

Hoang, C., Meg Lee, H.-H., & Lup, D. (2023). Friend and foe: Cognitive, emotional and moral consequences of working with AI. *ESCP Impact Paper, No.2023-09-EN*. ESCP Business School.

Hohenstein, J., Kizilcec, R. F., DiFranzo, D., Aghajari, Z., Mieczkowski, H., Levy, K., Naaman, M., Hancock, J., & Jung, M. F. (2023). Artificial intelligence in communication impacts language and social relationships. *Scientific Reports, 13*, 5487.

Holmes, W., Bialik, M., & Fadel, C. (2023). Artificial intelligence in education. In C. Stückelberger & P. Duggal (Eds.), *Data ethics: Building trust—How digital technologies can serve humanity* (pp. 621–653). Globethics Publications.

Iskender, A. (2023). Holy or unholy? Interview with open AI's ChatGPT. *European Journal of Tourism Research, 34*, 3414.

Javaid, M., Haleem, A., Singh, R. P., Khan, S., & Khan, I. H. (2023). Unlocking the opportunities through ChatGPT tool towards ameliorating the education system. *BenchCouncil Transactions on Benchmarks, Standards and Evaluations, 3*(2), 100115.

Kim, S., Jang, Y., Kim, W., Choi, S., Jung, H., Kim, S., & Kim, H. (2021). Why and what to teach: AI curriculum for elementary school. *Proceedings of the AAAI Conference on Artificial Intelligence, 35*(17), 15569–15576. https://doi.org/10.1609/aaai.v35i17.17833

King, P. M. (2009). Principles of development and developmental change underlying theories of cognitive and moral development. *Journal of College Student Development, 50*(6), 597–620.

Korsgaard, C. M. (2009). Agency and identity. In C. M. Korsgaard (Ed.), *Self-constitution: Agency, identity, and integrity* (Online ed.). Oxford Academic.

Kusters, R., Misevic, D., Berry, H., Cully, A., Le Cunff, Y., Dandoy, L., Díaz-Rodríguez, N., Ficher, M., Grizou, J., Othmani, A., Palpanas, T., Komorowski, M., Loiseau, P., Moulin Frier, C., Nanini, S., Quercia, D., Sebag, M., Soulié Fogelman, F., Taleb, S., …, Wehbi, F. (2020). Interdisciplinary research in artificial intelligence: Challenges and opportunities. *Frontiers in Big Data, 3*, 577974.

Lapsley, D. K., & Narvaez, D. (2006). Character education. In K. A. Renninger, I. E. Sigel, W. Damon, & R. M. Lerner (Eds.), *Handbook of child psychology: Child psychology in practice* (6th ed., pp. 248–296). Wiley.

Laura, R. S., & Chapman, A. (2009). The technologisation of education: Philosophical reflections on being too plugged in. *International Journal of Children's Spirituality, 14*(3), 289–298.

Levinas, E. (1985). *Ethics and infinity*. Translated by Cohen, R. A. Duquesne University Press.

Li, L., Subbareddy, R., & Raghavendra, C. G. (2022). AI intelligence chatbot to improve students learning in the higher education platform. *Journal of Interconnection Networks, 22*. https://doi.org/10.1142/S0219265921430325

Luckin, R., Holmes, W., Griffiths, M., & Forcier, L. B. (2016). *Intelligence unleashed. An argument for AI in education*. Pearson.

MacDonald Mishler, M. (1978). Education and identity. *Oxford Review of Education, 4*(2), 197–203.

Marr, B. (2023, July 24). *The difference between generative AI and traditional AI. An easy explanation for anyone*. Forbes. https://www.forbes.com/sites/bernardmarr/2023/07/24/the-difference-between-generative-ai-and-traditional-ai-an-easy-explanation-for-anyone/?sh=641bd4f8508a

Maybee, J. E. (2020). Hegel's dialectics. In E. N. Zalta & U. Nodelman (Eds.). *The Stanford encyclopedia of philosophy* (Winter 2020 Edition). Stanford University.

Melisa, R., Ashadi, A., Triastuti, A., Hidayati, S., Salido, A., Ero, P. E. L., Marlini, C., Zefrin, Z., & Fuad, Z. A. (2025). Critical thinking in the age of AI: A systematic review of AI's effects on higher education. *Educational Process: International Journal, 14*, e2025031.

Miller, J. P., Nigh, K., Binder, M. J., Noval, B., & Crowell, S. (2018). *Holistic education: A brief history*. Routledge.

Mollick, E., & Mollick, L. (2023, September 25). *Student use cases for AI, Part 2: AI as personal tutor*. Harvard Business Publishing: Education. https://hbsp.harvard.edu/inspiring-minds/ai-as-personal-tutor

Morgan, K. (2023, July 18). *AI can threaten your personal identity—But it doesn't have to*. BBC. https://www.bbc.com/worklife/article/20230712-ai-can-threaten-your-personal-identity-but-it-doesnt-have-to

Morgan, E. M., & Korobov, N. (2012). Interpersonal identity formation in conversations with close friends about dating relationships. *Journal of Adolescence, 35*(6), 1471–1483.

Morrison, N. (2023, May 20). *School leaders warn AI is a 'real and present' danger to education*. Forbes. https://www.forbes.com/sites/nickmorrison/2023/05/20/school-leaders-warn-ai-is-a-real-and-present-danger-to-education/?sh=7f5391db7cea

Noddings, N. (1995). *Philosophy of education*. Westview Press.

O'Boyle, N. (2014). Front row friendships: Relational dialectics and identity negotiations by mature students at university. *Communication Education, 63*(3), 169–191.

OECD. (2023). *Is education losing the race with technology?: AI's progress in maths and reading*. OECD Publishing.

Oksenberg Rorty, A., & Wong, D. (1990). Aspects of identity and agency. In I. O. Flanagan & A. Oksenberg Rorty (Eds.), *Identity, character and morality: Essays in moral psychology*. MIT Press.

Opel, D. J., Kious, B. M., & Cohen, I. G. (2023). AI as a mental health therapist for adolescents. *JAMA Pediatrics, 177*(12), 1253–1254.

Pang, S., Nol, E., & Heng, K. (2024). *Generative AI as a personal tutor for English language learning: A review of benefits and concerns*. SSRN. https://ssrn.com/abstract=4865398

Park, J. (1999). Emotional literacy: Education for meaning. *International Journal of Children's Spirituality, 4*(1), 19–28.

Parsakia, K. (2023). The effect of chatbots and AI on the self-efficacy, self-esteem, problem-solving and critical thinking of students. *Health Nexus, 1*(1), 71–76.

Perry, A. (2023). AI will never convey the essence of human empathy. *Nature Human Behaviour, 7*, 1808–1809.

Prunkl, C. (2022). Is there a trade-off between human autonomy and the 'autonomy' of AI systems? In V. C. Müller (Ed.), *Philosophy and theory of artificial intelligence*. Springer.

Prunkl, C. (2024). Human autonomy at risk? An analysis of the challenges from AI. *Minds & Machines, 34*(2), 6.

Puntoni, S., & Yalcin, G. (2023). How AI affects our sense of self: And why it matters for business. *Harvard Business Review*. https://hbr.org/2023/09/how-ai-affects-our-sense-of-self

Ravenscroft, A., Wegerif, R., & Hartley, R. (2006). *Reclaiming thinking: Dialectic, dialogic and learning in the digital age*. Available on ResearchGate.

Rödl, S. (2016). Education and autonomy. *Journal of Philosophy of Education, 50*(1), 84–97.

Schwarz, E. (2019). Günther Anders in Silicon Valley: Artificial intelligence and moral atrophy. *Thesis Eleven, 153*(1), 94–112.

Spector, J. M., & Ma, S. (2019). Inquiry and critical thinking skills for the next generation: From artificial intelligence back to human intelligence. *Smart Learning Environments, 6*, 8.

Stinson, C. (2022). Algorithms are not neutral. *AI and Ethics, 2*, 763–770.

Taylor, C. (1991). *The ethics of authenticity*. Harvard University Press.

Thaler, R. H., & Sunstein, C. R. (2009). *Nudge: Improving decisions about health, wealth, and happiness*. Penguin Publishing Books.

Torres, V., Jones, S. R., & Renn, K. A. (2009). Identity development theories in student affairs: Origins, current status, and new approaches. *Journal of College Student Development, 50*(6), 577–596.

Toye, M. (1971). To educate ....or to instruct? *Industrial and Commercial Training, 3*(12), 588–589.

UNESCO. (2023). *Artificial intelligence in education*. https://www.unesco.org/en/digital-education/artificial-intelligence

Weijers, R. J., de Koning, B. B., & Paas, F. (2021). Nudging in education: From theory towards guidelines for successful implementation. *European Journal of Psychology of Education, 36*, 883–902.
Widiati, U., Rusdin, D., Indrawati, I., Marzuki, & Govender, N. (2023). The impact of AI writing tools on the content and organization of students' writing: EFL teachers' perspective. *Cogent Education, 10.*
Woods, J. G. (2013). Model of dialectical learning. In E. G. Carayannis (Ed.), *Encyclopedia of creativity, invention, innovation and entrepreneurship*. Springer.
Xavier, B. (2025). Biases within AI: Challenging the illusion of neutrality. *AI & Society, 40*, 1545–1546.

Ezechiel Thibaud is a lecturer at the Education University of Hong Kong, where she teaches for the Department of Education Policy and Leadership. After working as a teacher in various countries, she has obtained a Ph.D. in philosophy from Lingnan University in Hong Kong. She is primarily interested in ethics, philosophy of education, and philosophy of technology. ethibaud@eduhk.hk.

Chapter 20
Future Teachers' Perspectives on AI in Education: Insights from Bethlehem University Students

Alejandro González Cerna

Abstract This chapter examines future teachers' perspectives on the integration of Artificial Intelligence (AI) in Palestinian education amidst ongoing socio-political challenges. Focus group discussions with students and graduates from Bethlehem University's Faculty of Education revealed diverse levels of familiarity with AI, acknowledging its potential to enhance teaching and streamline administrative tasks. However, concerns about ethics, plagiarism, and over-reliance on technology were also raised. The chapter underscores the need for AI training right from the start of the initial education of future teachers, ethical guidelines, and community awareness. Despite the challenges, participants foresee AI complementing traditional teaching methods, and calling for policy and curriculum adjustments to support a balanced, holistic approach to education.

Keywords AI benefits · AI-related concerns · AI-related needs · Palestine · Prospects for Education

As the world has become increasingly aware, Palestine has undergone for the last 75 years a tremendously challenging situation that has further intensified in recent times. Education has been severely affected by the destruction of all Gaza's universities (Deconstructed, 2024) and assaults on professors and students at West Bank universities (Action Against Hunger, 2024). Restrictions to movement and the danger of violent settler attacks have forced universities in the West Bank to work on emergency online or hybrid modalities while public schools are teaching online and only 3 days a week due to the aforementioned difficulties and related financial problems. It is in this context that we embarked on the writing of the present chapter.

This chapter is grounded in the unique context of Bethlehem University, a Catholic higher education institution in the occupied West Bank, where

A. González Cerna (✉)
Bethlehem University, Bethlehem, Palestine
e-mail: acerna@bethlehem.edu

G. Tchibozo (ed.), *International Perspectives of Generative AI in Education*, Advances in Artificial Intelligence in Education 3,
https://doi.org/10.1007/978-3-031-99804-1_20

socio-political instability, infrastructural challenges, and constrained digital access shape both learning possibilities and educational objectives. Unlike institutions in more politically stable or economically advanced countries, Bethlehem University functions within a system affected by military-occupation-related restrictions and continuous humanitarian crises, which drastically influence students' daily lives, and access to educational institutions and to technology. The study's findings may resonate with broader themes in low-resource or conflict-affected educational settings, while their direct applicability to other more stable or privileged contexts may be limited. Nevertheless, the perspectives shared here offer insights for comparative research, particularly in exploring how educators conceptualize and engage with AI in complex socio-political conditions.

Many things could be considered when trying to write about the intersection of Artificial Intelligence (AI) and Education in Palestine. As a developing region, and one under military occupation, access to technology is not generalized (Mitchell, 2024); many areas in Palestine have little or no access to the internet (or even electricity), although the propagation of mobile phones has partially compensated for the shortcomings in this matter. Still, mobile connection is limited to 3G speed and some areas suffer frequent blackouts.

While it is undeniable that AI has great potential to enhance educational processes, it is also true that education in Palestine remains eminently traditional (Hussein et al., 2022) and old in its delivery methods and general conceptions. Besides, although many AI platforms have developed Arabic language modalities, most of these are based on the Literary or Modern Standard versions of the language, which is not the language people use for everyday communication in Palestine and might represent a communication barrier for some.

Government agencies, educational institutions and NGOs have long supported education in Palestine and continue to do so. Nevertheless, the undeniable and urgent humanitarian crisis in Gaza has justifiably redirected many funds and efforts towards the more immediate necessities while abandoning important—but not life-or-death—enterprises to an uncertain future.

However, the conflict context itself brings the focus back to AI and its great potential, dramatically illustrated by its military instrumentalization (McKernan & Davies, 2024).

It is in this context that the author established a dialogue with current students and recent graduates of the Faculty of Education at Bethlehem University, to explore their knowledge, opinions and perspectives on the role of AI in education in Palestine both today and in the future.

The dialogue took place in the format of a focus group with the participation of 15 individuals either current students or recent graduates of the Bachelor of Education or Higher Diploma in Education programs. The student body at Bethlehem University is highly representative of Palestinian society as it includes students from cities, villages, and refugee camps; students living in the occupied West-Bank and in the annexed occupied East Jerusalem; students of Christian and Muslim faiths; and students coming from all socioeconomic echelons of Palestinian society.

The focus group was animated by a lecturer at Bethlehem University, who promoted and moderated the participants' interventions.

The dialogues of the focus group were afterwards transcribed, analyzed and matched through a progressive process of selection and categorization in accordance with the Grounded Theory approach, which addresses a phenomenon without preconceived expectations or hypotheses but with an open mind to hear and receive from the participants and build from their shared perceptions and experiences a congruous body of knowledge.

A short list of questions was used to prompt the dialogue in the focus group while participants were allowed to express themselves freely either directly addressing the questions posed or tangentially in any direction of their choice or interest.

Research Questions

This study sought to explore the following research questions:

- What are the perceptions of future teachers in Palestine regarding the role and potential of AI in education?
- How do education students in Palestine currently use AI in their educational practices?
- What concerns or challenges do these students foresee regarding the integration of AI into Palestinian educational systems?
- How do students envision the future role of AI in their professional practices as educators?
- What are the ethical implications of AI use in education as perceived by these future educators?

Method

This study followed a qualitative approach. A total of 15 participants, all either current students or recent graduates from the Faculty of Education, were invited to share their insights. The focus group was moderated by a lecturer, who facilitated an open and dynamic conversation guided by a short list of questions designed to prompt discussion while allowing participants to express themselves freely.

The discussions were recorded, transcribed, and analyzed using Grounded Theory, a methodology that allows themes to emerge directly from the data without imposing preconceived ideas or hypotheses. Through open coding, key concepts were identified, such as AI's role in creating teaching materials and the ethical challenges it poses. Axial coding was then employed to examine the relationships between these concepts, grouping responses into categories such as "AI as facilitator of teaching efficiency" and "Challenges related to abuse or misuse of AI".

Finally, through selective coding, "The Complex Role of AI in Palestinian Education" was established as the core category all others would tie into.

Findings

When questioned about whether they had had personal direct experience in the use of Artificial Intelligence tools, the totality of the participants responded affirmatively. They were then questioned about how they would define AI.

Participant 1 said "AI stands for artificial intelligence, it means man-made, not natural, designed by a human being. Intelligence is a capacity of the brain. So, AI means a robot that has intelligence but not that of a human being".

Participant 2 shared: "It is a system that can perform tasks and resolve problems meant for humans and even go beyond that, there are so many things that are made by AIs that we didn't expect would be done like that".

Participant 3 stated: "It's an imitation of humans and the way we think in a programmed way".

The participants agreed in describing AIs as technological creations that seek to mimic human mental processes and bring solutions to diverse practical or theoretical problems.

Participant 2 shared the experience of having used an AI tool for help in writing a resume, with great success: "It came out much better than if I had done it myself alone".

When discussing the role of AI specifically in the current Palestinian educational setting, Participant 4 expressed that, in her opinion, her students in grades 3 and 4 of elementary school don't know much about AIs. Participant 5 believes that university students in Palestine are very familiar with AI technology and use it a lot, while students at lower academic levels tend not to be as familiar or informed about it. However, Participant 14 mitigated this point by stating, "Some schools try to teach students to make AIs useful, teach them how to get main ideas from AIs". Participant 3 shared:

> Last year I used to teach at a private school in Al-Ram [a village in the suburb of Jerusalem] and once I gave them an assignment and I was surprised by the answers, and I discovered that they used ChatGPT and other AIs. It was something new to me, it didn't occur to me that they would use the AI software to generate the assignment, but they did! It didn't at all represent their level of proficiency or their work, simply because it was not their work! (In response to a follow up question, he specified he was talking about 9th and 10th graders).

The same participant added that in this first experience with students using AIs for their schoolwork, he was unable to identify with a sufficient degree of certainty which students had used AIs or not, and to what extent. He indicated that he had consequently awarded low marks where the presence of AIs seemed obvious, while he had let other students off with a simple warning, given the lack of evidence. The participant also acknowledged that he didn't expect students to have no idea of what plagiarism is in the academic context, which prompted useful and necessary conversations on the subject with the students.

Participants agreed, to the surprise of the moderator, that they believe a large number of students in Palestine might be completely ignorant about how to use AI technology in any way that is meaningful to them or practical in their lives, including their school lives. This applies to younger students and lower levels. This situation gradually evolves as students move on to middle school, Tawjihi (the General Secondary Education Certificate Examination), and University, where participants consider students to be using AI very widely and for many types of school-related assignments and work, mainly those requiring extensive text development or expression in foreign or highly technical languages.

As far as teachers are concerned, participants unanimously stated that they felt that teachers in Palestine know little or nothing about the use of AI in their lives or work; they added that this assessment becomes truer as the age of the teacher increases.

Participants also discussed the different purposes for which they use AI tools, agreeing that the most prevalent are as follows:

1. Creating materials for students, i.e. quizzes, exams, and worksheets.
2. Creating exercise or evaluation items.
3. Creating original texts such as sample sentences.
4. Saving time in planning or preparation for teaching.

Participant 9 spoke of AI as a double-edged sword. It can provide good ideas but can also be used to avoid making efforts. Students can overuse it and avoid writing anything original themselves, or even thinking of an answer or solution to a problem themselves.

Participants 8 and 11 both specifically mentioned that they use AI tools when they want to find creative ideas, options or solutions that they wouldn't have found otherwise, making AI a tool that facilitates the design and application of more creative educational approaches.

Specifically speaking of the relationship between AI and Learning outcomes, participants expressed that AIs are powerful tools for providing ideas on ways to get students engaged in the learning process and truly facilitate the achievement of learning outcomes. AI tools were reported to be helpful in creating well-geared lesson plans with a variety of methods and approaches suited to different student profiles.

When questioned about the future development of AI in education in Palestine, participants agreed that it will progressively make its way into the classroom and help teachers save time they currently spend in repetitive or administrative tasks; Participant 8 in particular talked about AIs helping future teachers to design better learning strategies and optimize them in accordance to the needs of their students.

In contrast, participants recognized that AIs will also become a challenge as they make it easy for students to avoid doing work or undergoing mental processes that are important for their education and their lives in the future. Participant 13 indicated that AI detectors will develop, improve and be useful in this regard, but the effectiveness and reliability of these tools was questioned by a few participants who doubt that their detection capability will ever be sufficient to supplant that of generators in creating human-looking content.

There was an agreement amongst the participants in considering that despite the growth and development of AIs, teachers will still have a role in education that will not be taken over by technology. Participant 11 talked about the importance of the teachers' management of voice tonalities and the authority of their presence in the class as important elements that facilitate and support learning. "I think the information given by an AI is easier to forget than that given by a teacher" they expressed.

In this regard, Participant 5 stated that parents and the community at large in Palestine do not tend to prefer technology-based teaching approaches to traditional face-to-face ones. The experience of emergency online teaching during the Covid pandemic and then during the Israeli government's campaign against Gaza has reinforced the impression that online teaching is quite limited and that face-to-face teaching is to be preferred. Participants agreed that in the current Palestinian mindset, the best possible education definitely is the one that is given by a teacher in front of a classroom, while the effectiveness of other methods tends to be called into question. Participant 10 pointed out that this appreciation of traditional teaching and dismissal of other approaches is widely spread. Participant 3 agreed stating that "even if you offer new methods, people won't believe they will work". Participant 1 reflected on the difficulty of changing a mindset, much greater than that of changing a teaching method.

Participants also shared the view that parents in Palestine know little about AIs and tend to be suspicious of them as effective methods. The least technology-inclined among them might associate the idea of AI with general fears about technology. Participant 2 candidly shared "My dad hears about AI and thinks about robots taking over the world". Other parents might have more specific concerns, such as the one shared by Participant 1: "AI can mislead students, give them wrong or incomplete information." A different sort of concern emerged too, voiced by Participant 8: "Students might become lazy, they will no longer be able to think, to use their skills, to analyze, to imagine". In the same line, Participant 4 spoke about the concern of some parents about their children developing a dependence on technology. Participants agreed that these concerns of parents converge with those of teachers: misleading or false information, students becoming lazy or unable to acquire important skills, both practical and intellectual, and eventually developing a dependence on technology that will be very difficult to overcome, if at all possible.

In contrast, participants also reported another group of parents for whom grades are the only important and valid measure and outcome of education, and who might encourage their children to use and even abuse AI beyond any ethical consideration, as long as it gets them good grades on their report cards.

The risk of becoming lazy out of abusing the use of AIs is not exclusive to students. Participants in the focus group discussed how some AI tools offer tempting possibilities to teachers, such as automatic grading and even feedback provision. Participants manifested their little confidence in the ability of AIs to properly evaluate students in Palestine. Participant 2 mentioned that the personal knowledge the teacher has of the student enriches and informs the feedback given in evaluation and cannot be replaced by an artificial intelligence process. Participant 7 feared that the lack of understanding of the AI of the context of the students would also negatively affect its effectiveness in grading. As a concrete example of the aforementioned, Participant 11 shared "Students of English as a Foreign Language here often use Arabic words or expressions that the AI would never be able to understand and that might throw it off". In agreement, Participant 3 added: "I think for some questions, a human being is necessary for grading another human being". Participant 6 said "I wouldn't trust an AI to grade because students are beginners and sometimes very weak and you have to consider that to properly grade them. It is not like grading native speakers who learn to write".

To address these concerns and the challenges posed by the presence of AIs in the world of education, teachers are to develop skills such as prompt design and writing; design of criteria to establish the suitability of certain tools and their productions for education and for specific students; an interest, motivation and taste for technology that enables them to keep up to date with the developments; and an expert eye to detect signs of non-human intervention in products that are meant to be student-originals. This will all require training on the use of AI tools. Participant 7 shared: "Most classrooms in Palestine have projectors now, so teachers and principals need to learn about AIs and share with their colleagues and offer periodical training courses".

Given the limitations often and currently experienced in Palestine, though, the participants agreed that an intrinsic motivation on the part of the teacher is very important and even necessary to help them keep updated and learn on their own what won't be offered by their schools or the Ministry. Participant 10 expressed: "Teachers should always be motivated and keep updated. I don't think it's a matter of choice". And in the same tone, Participant 3 said: "I like exploring educational innovations, both for my personal benefit and to be aware of the latest tools students use, to be able to work with them and to bust them if they are cheating".

The power and scope of AI will certainly require ethical parameters to be considered in its use and presence in education. Participants agree with that, though not all of them believe Palestinian schools are ready to undertake such a mission. Participant 13 says "Schools are not ready to establish ethical parameters for the use of AIs in education. Many teachers are not aware of its capabilities and don't use it at all so they can't guide students to use it properly". In agreement, Participant 1 doubted that school colleagues, teachers or principals, had ever talked about AI and its role in education. Participant 4 agreed, stating that the only time this has happened is when a colleague, who is pursuing studies at a university, shared with them some of what he had learned at a conference. The contents of that sharing were completely new to everyone in the school for, as Participant 4 expresses "No one knew anything about it". Participant 3 adds that when asked about AI detection tools, the technician at his school knew of none, nor was he familiar with the concept of plagiarism. In view of all the above, there was general agreement that the Ministry of Education and individual schools should consider the need for training in the use of AI in education, for both students and teachers, so that teachers are both users and guides in the use of these tools by students.

As far as ethical guidelines are concerned, some participants made the distinction that university teachers are better informed and equipped to develop and implement them, while elementary school teachers may need them less, as their role rarely involves research or highly creative production.

Finally, other topics were briefly discussed during the conversation. Participants felt that AI has the potential to help make education more accessible to students with special educational needs, providing them with the support they need based on their disability or condition and helping them overcome their limitations and even learn new ways to connect with their teacher and other students.

Because of its facilitation of plagiarism and falsification, some participants manifested that AI can negatively affect the teacher-student relationship as it breaks bonds of trust. Given that AI can take over educational functions, Participant 12 believes "maybe there will no longer be a need for relationships with teachers". In contrast, Participant 9 thinks that as AI takes over some of the administrative and formal tasks of education and provides teachers with ideas and materials to improve their teaching, it will also free them to be more focused on the human aspect of education and develop more meaningful relationships with their students.

Participants were asked about the impact of AI in Education for marginalized communities, and they agreed that these communities probably know very little about this technology at the moment and don't feel it is useful or connected to their needs. Participant 6 expressed that while social media has become a kind of social "need" that has reached marginalized communities, AIs remain more of an academic tool and not as generalized. In this sense, the risk would be that, precisely due to lack of information or because it is considered of little use, the currently marginalized communities could become even more so, because they would not be able to benefit from the possibilities and facilities offered by AI.

As a conclusion participants were asked about their vision of the future of teaching with Ais. They indicated that they anticipate increased difficulties with students who lack basic skills and are accustomed to doing everything with the help of technology without developing in themselves the thinking processes or effort required. Participant 4 expects education to move from an information-centric model to a more analytical model, in which students will be expected to perform analyses that are less dependent on software. Two of the participants shared that they foresee a future where the role of AIs and technology in general is increased but other methods and tools for teaching are still in use, valued, and necessary to achieve the goals of a holistic education. According to the participants, the role of technology will keep being important in any case, and educational change will remain necessary, not only in methods and approaches that depend on the teacher but also at the level of policy and curriculum.

Discussion

The findings of the study reinforce the nature of AI in education as both a tool for innovation and a potential source of ethical conundrums, particularly in a complex socio-political environment like Palestine. Similar findings have been reported in studies by Hussein et al. (2022), which highlight the challenges of technology integration in underdeveloped educational systems.

The participants seem to hold an optimistic view of AI's role in enhancing efficiency and providing creative solutions in education. These perspectives align with research on AI's growing influence in global educational settings (Huang et al., 2021). Concerns about student dependency on AI and its potential for misuse in academic work are consistent with global discussions around academic integrity and the responsible use of technology (Selwyn, 2022).

Participants' concerns about Palestinian teachers' unpreparedness for AI use echo wider challenges in low-resource settings, where educators often lack the technological skills or infrastructure necessary to integrate AI effectively (Bali, 2023). This reflects the urgent need for professional development and policy adjustments to accommodate the realities of AI's growing role in education.

Implications and Recommendations

The long-term implications of AI in Palestinian education are diverse and multifaceted, involving both opportunities for development and ethical dilemmas. While AI can bring significant benefits in terms of efficiency, personalized learning, promotion of creativity and access to education, it also presents risks related to academic integrity, equity of access and the preservation of essential skills and teacher-student relationships. Successfully integrating AI into education will require a careful balance of all these dimensions, as well as significant policy development and teacher training tailored to both the technology itself and the values and goals of Palestinian society and its individuals.

The study also highlights the need for clear policies regarding the use of AI, the encouragement of critical thinking and creative pedagogical approaches, and the creation of supportive learning environments where students learn about and ethically utilize technology, and gain relevant knowledge, skills and values.

Although the study was limited by its small, localized sample and qualitative scope, the richness of participant narratives provides groundwork for future research. Further studies involving longitudinal methods or broader demographic samples could enhance our understanding of how teacher identity and ethical engagement with AI evolve across diverse Palestinian educational settings.

Limitations

This study was limited to 15 Palestinian English Education Students or recent graduates. All of them are currently engaged in school teaching whether full-time, part-time or on practicum.

The study is also limited by its contextual specificity, the limited access of Palestinians to technology and connectivity.

Acknowledgement Our sincere appreciation to the participating students and graduates from Bethlehem University, and to Ms. Paola Handal for her animation of the focus groups that made this study possible.

Competing Interests The author has no conflicts of interest to declare that are relevant to the content of this chapter.

References

Action Against Hunger. (2024, January 31). *Children suffer as education under attack in the West Bank and Gaza.* Retrieved from Action Against Hunger: https://www.actionagainsthunger.org/story/children-suffer-as-education-under-attack-in-the-west-bank-and-gaza/

Bali, M. (2023). *What I mean when I say critical AI literacy.* (2023, April). Retrieved September 30, 2024, from Reflecting Allowed website: https://blog.mahabali.me/educational-technology-2/what-i-mean-when-i-say-critical-ai-literacy/

Deconstructed. (2024, February 9). *No universities left standing in Gaza.* Retrieved from The Intercept: https://theintercept.com/2024/02/09/deconstructed-gaza-university-education/

Huang, S, Yang, J, Fong, S, & Zhao, Q. (2021). Artificial intelligence in the diagnosis of COVID-19: Challenges and perspectives. *International Journal of Biological Sciences, 17*(6):1581–1587. https://doi.org/10.7150/ijbs.58855. https://www.ijbs.com/v17p1581.htm

Hussein, A., Wong, S., & Bright, A. (2022, September 15). *The Palestinian K-12 education system: History, structure, challenges and opportunities.* Retrieved from Research Gate: https://www.researchgate.net/publication/363691267_The_Palestinian_K-12_Education_System_History_Structure_Challenges_and_Opportunities

McKernan, B., & Davies, H. (2024, April 3). "*The Machine did it coldly*"*: Israel used AI to identify 37,000 Hamas targets.* Retrieved from The Guardian: https://www.theguardian.com/world/2024/apr/03/israel-gaza-ai-database-hamas-airstrikes

Mitchell, R. (2024, January 9). *Palestine-Israel conflict impacts internet access three months on.* Retrieved from Internet Society Pulse: https://pulse.internetsociety.org/blog/palestine-israel-conflict-impacts-internet-access-three-months-on

Selwyn, N. (2022). The future of AI and education: Some cautionary notes. *European Journal of Education, 57*(4), 620–631. https://doi.org/10.1111/ejed.12532

Alejandro González Cerna studied Education and Religious sciences, including a Postgraduate in Lasallian Studies, Master's Degrees in Education and Lasallian Leadership, and a Ph.D. in Education from La Salle Northwest University. Dr. González Cerna taught in basic and middle schools, served as school headmaster in Mexico, and Delegate to the Council for Lasallian Educational Mission in Latin America. Since 2018 he is Professor and Dean of Education at Bethlehem University in Palestine. He is currently a facilitator of the Leadership Program for the International Association of Lasallian Universities. ORCID: 0000-0002-2031-2533. Website: www.bethlehem.edu. email: acerna@bethlehem.edu.

Part VI
Taking a Critical Step Back

Chapter 21
Critical Generative AI Literacy in Education: Inter/National Perspectives from Teacher-Research

Michael Singh, Lìpíng Niú, and Xiǎo-Lí Lǐ

Abstract The question that prompted this study was how teacher-researchers make meaning of 'critical GenAI literacy' through their professional education. To construct 'critical GenAI literacy' as the object of teacher-research, a *problem-posing method* was used to review the literature, establishing background knowledge of critical literacy and GenAI systems. The *objective* was to analyze teacher-researchers' practices of 'critical GenAI literacy' while studying for a master's degree in education. Focusing on the interconnectedness of teacher-researchers and GenAI systems, the *method* of relational socio-analysis was used to explore the multi-layered drivers for giving meaning to 'critical GenAI literacy.' The *results* indicate that teacher-researchers make meaning of 'critical GenAI literacy' by acquiring the know-how to use GenAI systems in their studies, sharing knowledge of the uses of GenAI systems in 汉语 (Hànyǔ, Hàn language), analyzing the contributions of GenAI systems to precarious employment, and evaluating the governing power of GenAI systems. A key *outcome* of this study is to show that teacher-researchers can work collaboratively to extend and deepen the meaning of 'critical GenAI literacy' by processing data and producing knowledge about the blurry and complex penetration of education and teachers' work by GenAI systems.

Keywords Automating education · Bourdieu · Critical GenAI literacy · Teacher-research

---

M. Singh (✉)
Western Sydney University, Sydney, NSW, Australia
e-mail: m.j.singh@westernsydney.edu.au

L. Niú
TESOL, Beijing, China

X.-L. Lǐ
Crown Institute of Higher Education, Sydney, NSW, Australia

G. Tchibozo (ed.), *International Perspectives of Generative AI in Education*, Advances in Artificial Intelligence in Education 3,
https://doi.org/10.1007/978-3-031-99804-1_21

This enquiry into 'critical GenAI literacy' contributes to the continuous systemic testing of the multilayered threats that generative artificial intelligence (GenAI) poses to education, educators, and those being educated. Because GenAI in automating education poses the challenge of "digital unfreedom" and threatens critical thinking and democratic education, it is necessary to craft prompts that challenge these surveillance technologies (Zuboff, 2022). Critical GenAI literacy provides teacher-researchers with a proactive tool for addressing concerns about GenAI surveillance technologies in education, including location tracking, facial identification technologies, automated speech recognition, and social media mining (Gilliard & Selwyn, 2023). This study deepens the criticality brought to the risks of GenAI in automating education identified throughout the present book (see Väkevä & Partti; Spadoni & Solano; and Thibaud).

Generative AI is embedded in early years learning because 'digital technologies and media can enable children to access global connections and resources and encourage new ways of thinking' (AGDE, 2022, p. 23). In contrast to the disadvantages of dependence on GenAI assistance, the meaningful human relationships created by teacher-led learning and learning through peer collaboration promote students' overall cognitive and social-emotional development (Darling et al., 2024). However, children's problematic, if not addictive, uses of GenAI technologies result in sleep problems (e.g., poor sleep quality, shorter sleep duration), increased internalizing and externalizing problems (e.g., depressive symptoms, problem behaviors, lower emotional intelligence); being overweight/obesity, low executive functioning, poor academic performance with lower academic achievements (ECA, 2018; Coyne et al., 2021; Liu et al., 2021; Muppalla et al., 2023; Rega et al., 2023). The rapid integration of GenAI into early childhood education raises substantial challenges (Berson et al., 2025), including those concerning:

1. governments fragmented and inconsistent framing of regulations (lack of participatory governance provisions to tailor global enforcement of GenAI to children's vulnerabilities).
2. negative impacts on children's development (fostering overreliance, manipulation, or loss of autonomy to GenAI undermines relational human learning),
3. data privacy (inadequate protections against data breaches, profiling, and misuse make significant gaps in safeguarding children),
4. algorithmic bias (fairness is being eroded by non-representative datasets, perpetuating systemic inequities, disproportionately affecting marginalized communities).

Because the problematic inter/national connections possible through GenAI in education are complex, teacher-researchers struggle with the complexities of critical GenAI literacy. Through empirical investigation and theoretical explanations of 'critical GenAI literacy,' this study contributes to the systematic, relational understanding of GenAI in automating education (Hu, 2024). A preliminary definition of critical GenAI literacy refers to the practice of questioning, critiquing, and transforming the cultural, ethical, political, and socioeconomic risks of GenAI in automating education (Veldhuis et al., 2024). Breaking with taken-for-granted ways of critical thinking, this study focuses on the dynamics in the relational structures between GenAI in automating education and inter/national GenAI systems, by analysing teacher-researchers' efforts to make meaning of 'critical GenAI literacy'.

To understand how GenAI works in education, consider the following. Artificial intelligence performs computational algorithmic tasks that include decision-making, experiential learning, pattern recognition, and understanding human languages (Banh & Strobel, 2023). Through human mediation, including user prompts, GenAI machine-driven systems produce seemingly novel and (apparently) realistic content across texts, images, video, programming code, sounds, and three-dimensional renderings for various fields of education. Educators are mindful of the many challenges that GenAI businesses pose, including expanding beyond their current practices to automate education by the disaggregation and eventual disruption of the public's education (Zarifis & Efthymiou, 2022). These challenges include their (1) having no inherent morality, (2) multiple, toxic, automation biases built into the training and inferences of GenAI systems (3) the lack of accountability, legitimacy and transparency in the training of GenAI, (4) copyright, licenses, and intellectual property issues, (5) errors, inaccuracies, contradictory and fictional content or so-called hallucinations, (6) misuse and abuse through deepfakes, misinformation, disinformation and fraud, (7) excessive energy consumption, and (8) threats to society, including over-trust in GenAI systems, job losses and undermining public trust (Mejia, 2023). These challenges are overridden by efforts to make significant advances in expanding and automating GenAI markets in educationally tailored content, operations, and services (Banh & Strobel, 2023). Educators may use 'critical GenAI literacy' to mitigate some of these risks.

This study seeks an explanation of critical GenAI literacy through addressing four interrelated concerns. First, a problem-posing literature review was used for the initial construction of 'critical GenAI literacy' as a research object. Second, the logic of this study's relational research practice is explained. Third, the results of this analysis are presented in terms of the relationships among the teacher-researchers, their positioning within GenAI in automating the education system, and the field of inter/national power relations governing GenAI enterprises.

Breaking with Pre-constructed Views of Critical GenAI Literacy

Pollock's (1957) inter/national research in Germany and the United States grappled with the tensions between fully automated, socio-economically structured production systems and the replacement of human labor. Pollock (1957, p. 247) cites Norbert Wiener, a cybernetics pioneer, whose prescient insights suggest possibilities for rethinking 'critical GenAI literacy':

> possibilities for good and for evil. We can only hand it over into the world that exists about us, and this is the world of Belsen and Hiroshima. [The] contribution we are making [is] to the concentration of power … in the hands of the most unscrupulous (Wiener cited in Pollock, 1957, p. 247).

Centering power relations, critical GenAI literacy questions the claims made about critical thinking *in* GenAI systems within and beyond education. Critical GenAI literacy problematizes taken-for-granted assumptions in the literature about using GenAI systems *for* critical thinking. Establishing the warrant for thinking critically *about* GenAI systems provides a useful reframing of the object of this research. Thinking critically about the conduct of education research *by* GenAI is socially significant, given the arguments about this issue.

Critical Thinking in *GenAI*

Karapantelakis et al. (2024) argue that critical thinking *in* GenAI systems can explain to human managers the decisions necessary for fulfilling work requirements by leveraging various data sources. However, GenAI sometimes demonstrates its artificiality by fabricating citations. Although GenAI 'does provide seemingly real sources that are supposedly listed by actual journals, upon closer inspection … many of these sources do not actually exist' (Pack & Maloney, 2023, p. 1574). The fake intelligence of GenAI systems means they generate incorrect, formulaic, and vague texts (Malinka et al., 2023). Underperforming students who use ChatGPT to complete assessment tasks struggle to persuade teachers that they produced the results themselves. Where corporate university managers allow such assessment to pass the requirements for degrees, they further the interests of those who bring the education of the public into question. To address complex problems, it is necessary to analyze and evaluate information using trustworthy knowledge for reasoning, making well-informed decisions, and debating the merits of these processes, all of which have a pivotal role in critical thinking. The assumption that critical thinking is incorporated *in* GenAI systems is questionable.

A risk posed by assuming critical thinking *in* GenAI systems is that students mistakenly believe they are encountering human intelligence rather than a form of fake intelligence (Selwyn, 2022a, 2024). The current weaknesses of critical thinking *in* GenAI systems provide grounds for breaking with the pre-constructed meaning of critical GenAI literacy.

Using GenAI for *Critical Thinking*

To a limited degree, GenAI systems may be used *for* critical thinking. However, using GenAI systems for critical thinking can endanger rather than enable such thinking. Students need to think critically about the 'solutions' provided by the

GenAI system, recognize failures in its processes, and generate an appropriate solution using suitable procedures (Barana et al., 2023). Critical thinking is the 'intellectually disciplined process of actively and skillfully conceptualizing, applying, analyzing, synthesizing, and evaluating information gathered from, or generated by, observation, experience, reflection, reasoning, or communication, as a guide to belief and action' (Barana et al., 2023, p. 378). Because critical thinking disrupts prior beliefs, Thiga (2024) explains that it requires clarity of purpose, contextual grounding, the evaluation and formulation of well-reasoned arguments based on questioning the (in)credibility of information sources, especially the anthropomorphism attributed to the mimicking of human capabilities, the hallucinations in their claims, and toxicity. GenAI reproduces political and religious biases involving class, gender, and race (Motoki et al., 2023). Uncritical thinking, including uncritical thinking about critical thinking, is characterized by the passive acceptance of information, selecting information that confirms or reinforces one's bias, and accepting sources simply because they claim to be authoritative (Thiga, 2024). Because of the complexities of critical thinking, which requires nuanced understanding, questioning norms, analyzing context, and evaluating evidence, using GenAI *for* critical thinking has limitations for cultivating robust critical thinking, for instance, among master's candidates studying education (Darwin et al., 2024).

The use of GenAI *for* critical thinking demonstrates that it is prone to producing echo chambers. Thus, human intelligence continues to be pivotal in problem-solving and problem-posing (Hu, 2024). It is necessary to break with unquestioning uses of GenAI *for* critical thinking to construct 'critical GenAI literacy' as a research object.

Thinking Critically About *GenAI Systems*

Through thinking critically about automated production systems, Pollock (1957) grappled with the socioeconomic consequences for workers being replaced by machines that operate, direct, and control processes and the outputs produced. The consequences of GenAI systems are as far-reaching as those of the Industrial Revolution, with machines guiding other machines and controlling human beings (Mejia, 2023). Thinking critically *about* GenAI systems is important because technologically driven unemployment, a long-standing feature of automation in agricultural and manufacturing industries, is now having an impact on knowledge workers (e.g., teachers), the structuring of their work, and their earnings (Dandalt, 2021). Like Pollock (1957, p. 60), those teacher-researchers who think critically *about* GenAI systems by questioning techno-solutionism are in the awkward position of warning students and colleagues of dangers that are not immediately obvious (Kouritzin et al., 2023). Through thinking critically *about* GenAI systems, about the grinding, gradual, and attritional harms of these systems, individuals may slowly recognize their inability to understand these systems and their inability to ensure their accountability (Teo, 2024).

Thinking critically *about* GenAI systems means recognizing that no one can address the ever-emerging challenges posed by the threats to people's right to privacy, freedom of expression, and freedom of thought (Aksoy & Kursun, 2024). To break with the routine, orthodox meaning given to 'critical GenAI literacy,' it is necessary to think critically *about* GenAI systems across multiple, interrelated levels of dangers to human freedoms, harms to democracy, and risks to education.

Thinking Critically About Research by *GenAI*

Thinking critically about research *by* GenAI brings into focus the multiple risks and challenges GenAI systems pose for transforming research across all disciplines (Grossmann et al., 2023). Major challenges include differentiating between research authored by humans and GenAI systems, especially given the limitations in detecting citations to fake references and manipulating research findings (Teng, 2023). Relying on GenAI systems that extract information from existing sources limit their application for making a substantial and original contribution to knowledge, posing problems of authorship (Ashraf & Ashfaq, 2024). It is necessary to inform research participants that the data they provide will be shared with the research funder, including third parties such as AI companies, and to inform them of the risks involved. Ensuring that participants understand the risks involved in data sharing is an integral part of the process of obtaining their informed consent (Bearman et al., 2023). Higher education managers, reviewers, examiners, and editors do not have the knowledge or technical expertise to detect the differences between research generated by humans and fake AI, raising concerns about the rise of substandard and fraudulent research (Watanabe, 2023). University management and policies cannot ensure transparency and accountability, busy as they are pressing teacher-researchers into ever-more record-keeping and public documentation regarding their uses of GenAI systems throughout all research processes and decision-making (Dillon & Schaffer-Goddard, 2023). Technologies cannot detect inappropriate and unethical use of GenAI systems in research, research writing, thesis examinations, and peer reviews. Managers' tendency to moral complacency towards GenAI systems threatens human researchers' capabilities and undermines their control of AI-driven processes and outcomes (Kaas, 2024).

Educational institutions that view GenAI systems as making teacher-researchers' intelligence redundant, and oppose the academic freedom to think critically, deny their institutional obligation to liberate human intelligence to address the multilayered challenges of inter/national GenAI systems.

Teacher-researchers need to reconstruct the concept of 'critical GenAI literacy' as a research object.

Methodologically, the first stage of this study focused on the preliminary construction of 'critical GenAI literacy' as the research object. Establishing the assumptions informing critical thinking and GenAI in automating education was necessary to guard against being taken in by words presented as value-neutral, orthodoxy, or common-sensical (Bourdieu & Wacquant, 1989). Innocent expressions about critical thinking in GenAI carry questionable assumptions that confuse its past representation with what is needed now. The taken-for-granted orthodoxy of using GenAI *for* critical thinking is co-terminus with a range of interests invested in seeing GenAI in automating education in certain ways. Thinking critically *about* GenAI systems raises questions about the educational value, power, and integrity of the word 'critical' as representing both an *instrument* and an *object* of analysis. Evidence of the contested and contestable nature of 'critical thinking' is recognised through thinking critically about research *by* GenAI. This provides a working framework for 'critical GenAI literacy' that recognizes GenAI systems in education as dynamic assemblages of inter/national power relations among data, ideas about education, operational management, and money-making, oriented to reassembling education and disassembling teachers' work.

The Logic of Relational Research Practice

We now extend the logic of relational research practice that this study employed to identify teacher-researchers' moves to enact, navigate, and define 'critical GenAI literacy' through collaborative self-study as part of their university work. The problem-posing method employed above to create a working framework of 'critical GenAI literacy' as the object of this research gave shape to the rationale for using evidence and conducting a multi-level, relational data analysis.

Rationale for Using Evidence

Evidence for this study was generated through collaborative *teacher-research* to enact, navigate, and define 'critical GenAI literacy' as part of our *inter/national experiences* of using GenAI systems in a self-study professional education program (Singh & Nguyễn, 2018). Three criteria informed the rationale for collecting and using this evidence. First, the program focused on teachers making a position for themselves as researchers by negotiating the tensions between their professional dispositions for research-informed practices and the structures governing the division of labor between teachers and researchers in the changing field of education. For instance, deep learning for early childhood educators goes beyond reading research to include participation in collaborative research projects that contribute to evidence-based teaching/learning practices (AGDE, 2022). Teacher-researchers engage in practitioner inquiry to contribute to knowledge necessary to inform the intentional design of children's deep learning to include 'safe and healthy digital technology use and social relationships [which] is integral to wellbeing and self-confidence' (AGDE, 2022, p. 44). Early childhood educators develop research-based knowledge of 'appropriate digital technology use and safety with children and families' (AGDE, 2022, p. 63).

Second, instead of opposing national and international perspectives of GenAI in automating education and insights from research in diverse educational contexts, this study employs a relational research method to ground the concept of 'inter/national' in context (Bourdieu & Wacquant, 1999). This relational research method made it possible to situate teachers engaging with GenAI in automating education (or not) as part of a collective struggle with the uncertainties of change borne of the multilayered fields in which they are incorporated. Research reveals how generative GenAI systems perpetuate digital neocolonial capitalism (for example, through the hierarchical dominance of a select version of American English), with its concentration of a few corporations in a few countries to amplify existing disparities in and through inter/national education (Nyaaba et al., 2024). To escape the cunning of imperialist reason, research into 'inter/national' perspectives on GenAI in automating education must be rooted in forms of knowledge that articulate critical GenAI literacy in the languages of divergent intellectual cultures.

Third, the data for this study were collected from a subset of bilingual teacher-researchers selected because of their potential influence on inter/national perspectives on GenAI in automating education, proficient in 汉语 (Hànyǔ, Hàn language) and 英语 (Yīngyǔ, English language). Reaching past the preoccupation with 英语 (Yīngyǔ), the teacher-researchers in this study engage Australia as a multilingual nation; among some 300 languages spoken in this country, 汉语 (Hànyǔ) is the second largest. The logic of this study's relational research practice meant generating prompts for bringing together languages and knowledge from divergent intellectual cultures (Dobinson et al., 2024). By crossing inter/national linguistic borders, this study contributes to research that generates educational knowledge by enhancing language maintenance, transcending the drive to marginalize teacher-researchers' primary languages and reproduce monolingual nation-states through their education systems (Singh & Lǐ, 2024).

This study's evidence was collected in the context of the tension-ridden relations between China and the US that are undermining the meaningful inter/national governance of GenAI systems, posing challenges to any coalition that centers on inter/national democratic governance (Hine, 2024). GenAI systems streamline access to information, but fall short of fully replacing human intelligence, proving inadequate in delivering in-depth and comprehensive evaluations regarding the complexities of inter/national trade (Aggarwal & Karwasra, 2025). The struggles between China and the US for the inter/national monopoly of new GenAI technologies, including those with super-powerful military applications, are eroding the sovereignty of many nations (Emery-Xu et al., 2024).

Multi-level Relational Data Analysis

Following the logic of Bourdieu and Wacquant's (1989) relational research practice, this study's analysis was framed to explicate multiple layers impacting teacher-researchers' efforts to enact, navigate, and define 'critical GenAI literacy.' This relational analysis disrupts inter/national boundaries between teachers' research into critical GenAI literacy, GenAI in automating education, and the fields of GenAI production and governance. The layers of inter/national interconnections included the disposition of teacher-researchers for 'critical GenAI literacy' given the position they occupied within the field of intern/national education, the structure of the field of intern/national education itself, and the GenAI systems' inter/national field of power.

First, the relational analysis focuses on the sociohistorical genesis of the intellectual agency of inter/national students positioning themselves as intellectual agents within the field of GenAI-mediated education. The focus is on their dispositions and trajectory as teacher-researchers generating practices of 'critical GenAI literacy' by internalising, over time, divergent conditions of possibilities. Second, the relational analysis maps the structure of relations between the positions occupied by these teacher-researchers as intellectual agents competing for the legitimate forms of authority within the inter/national teacher education field. This analysis foregrounds the relations between the characteristics of these teacher-researchers for 'critical GenAI literacy' and the structural topography configuring GenAI in automating education. Third, this relational analysis situates these teachers-researchers and the field of education vis-à-vis the inter/national field of power that dominates GenAI systemic relations. At this level, their positioning is analysed through the mediating governing power relations created by the inter/national GenAI field.

Teacher-Researchers' Critical GenAI Literacy Practices

The *results* below provide a sociolinguistic taxonomy of four themes adhering to the teacher-researchers' practices of 'critical GenAI literacy.' This analysis indicates the meaning they made of critical GenAI literacy through studying the logic of their practices. After analyzing their acquisition of the know-how to use GenAI in automating their education, we analyze their ways of sharing this knowledge using 汉语 (Hànyǔ). Analysis then turned to the contributions of GenAI systems to changes in the teacher-researchers' work, leading to an analysis of the governing power of GenAI systems in education. This multi-level relational data analysis captures the interactions between the bilingual teacher-researchers' practices of critical GenAI literacy as embedded within the field of GenAI in automating education and situated within the larger national/international field of GenAI. This analysis suggests teacher-researchers benefit from honing their critical GenAI literacy by extending their knowledge and deepening their intelligence, rather than simply developing skills for using GenAI in automating education.

Acquiring Know-How to Use GenAI in Automating Education

Table 21.1 indicates that the teacher-researchers acquired the know-how for using GenAI through prior professional education, thus, the sociohistorical products of GenAI in automating education. This history gave them the disposition, competencies, or capabilities to position themselves at the entry-level of a GenAI-saturated education field. Further, using GenAI to automate their education proved effective in streamlining their work of generating assignments and securing academic credit. These GenAI systems provided convenient, fast, and seemingly accurate answers to the assessment challenges. Apparent productivity improved, as these GenAI systems saved them the time and effort required for deep learning.

Table 21.1 Acquiring know-how through using GenAI systems for professional learning

中国留学生专业是常用的工具Common GenAI systems used by inter/national teachers majoring in education	使用的具体目的和用途 Purposes and applications of GenAI systems used	好处的体现 Benefits of using GenAI systems
Grammar correction software	Check for grammatical and spelling mistakes Correct punctuation errors Improve sentence structure	Improve the quality and readability of writing. Enhance credibility. Minimize plagiarism
Paraphrase software	Quickly reword text by replacing certain words with synonyms and paraphrases Restructure or rephrase sentences	Save time and intellectual effort to rewrite content manually Maintain the original meaning of the sentences using a different expression form Create 'unique' sentences, reducing the likelihood of plagiarism Gradually expand vocabulary by using different words and phrases to express the same meaning
Reference generator software	Generate references automatically	Reduce the tedium and errors of writing citations manually
Translation software	Translates certain written sentences in 英语 (Yīngyǔ) and words into汉语 (Hànyǔ). Translates intended汉语 (Hànyǔ) content into 英语 (Yīngyǔ)	Improves understanding of the content of the literature Improves the efficiency of writing

However, teachers' reliance on GenAI systems for obtaining answers limited their learning to spelling words and making correct use of grammar and did little to advance their inclination to think critically about the myriad issues at stake. Without GenAI in automating their education, teachers could not perform as well on the assignments or advance their capabilities for securing employment in teaching.

GenAI augmented learning is meant to be combined with the creative intelligence of these teacher-researchers. However, teacher-researchers' reliance on GenAI in automating their education hinders their professional development, especially the exercise of critical AI literacy, a key employability skill. By prioritizing the speed of productivity over in-depth learning, the teacher-researchers' work lacks originality and attention to the ethics of applying GenAI systems in their work. Further, the lack of systematic, critical thinking about the answers provided by GenAI systems leads them to a shallow understanding of the topic. However, teacher education graduates need higher-order skills to use digital technology to secure employment (Mahfoodh & Hashim, 2021). The recruitment of digital talent is part of many organizations' strategies to realize digital transformation (Gilch & Sieweke, 2021). Professional learning courses are designed to generate synergies between their teachers' education and prospective employment (Kouritzin et al., 2023). However, by reconstituting education and work, GenAI systems disrupt the relationship between education and jobs, provoking efforts to reconstruct the missing links.

Sharing Knowledge of GenAI Systems in 汉语 (Hànyŭ)

Table 21.2 illustrates the teacher-researchers' disposition for using their multilingual capital in their studies, including the use of GenAI systems in 汉语 (Hànyŭ). GenAI systems such as CNKI and CQVIP (academic search engines in Hànyŭ) empower students to exercise control over the languages used in their professional education, potentially extending the freedom with which they use their languages for generating and communicating knowledge. Efforts by teacher-researchers to mediate or otherwise mitigate the hierarchical power relations between their primary language (e.g., 汉语, Hànyŭ) and the inter/nationally dominant language (英语, Yīngyŭ) mirror the broken relationship between education and work born out of the globalization of GenAI systems. Teaching 英语 (Yīngyŭ) as a local Australian language finds its educational appeal in the questionable belief that speaking one language, specifically 英语 (Yīngyŭ), creates more harmonious inter/national relations (between the US and Canada, for instance) (Singh & Huang, 2013).

The assumption that 英语 (Yīngyŭ) per se builds bonds among people by bridging the gaps between speakers of different languages is questionable. The struggles to establish an educational relationship between teacher-researchers' primary and secondary languages are paralleled by the disruption to the relationship between their professional education and conditions of employment as teachers, including a salary commensurate with the investment they make in continuing professional

Table 21.2 Using 汉语 (Hànyǔ) and GenAI in automating teacher education

背景 Contexts	引发使用双语的情况 Situations triggering the use of bilingualism	双语解释的体现和好处Manifest benefits of bilingualism
Students studying 英语 (Yīngyǔ) at universities in China speak汉语 (Hànyǔ)		
Lecturers conduct classes primarily in 英语 (Yīngyǔ) All class participants can speak汉语 (Hànyǔ)	Teachers find concepts presented in 英语 (Yīngyǔ) difficult to understand	Lecturers switch to汉语 (Hànyǔ) to provide explanations of concepts to ensure comprehension
	Lecturers speak 英语 (Yīngyǔ) too quickly for teachers to keep up with, and have problems in note-making	Teachers use a combination of 英语 (Yīngyǔ) and汉语 (Hànyǔ) to make notes For example, a combination of 英语 (Yīngyǔ) and 汉语 (Hànyǔ) is used to remember the definition of 'syntax': 是研究的语言学分支 (structure of sentences and phrases in a language)
	Teachers find it difficult to remember 英语 (Yīngyǔ) pronunciation, e.g., [r]; [æ]; [e]	To remember the pronunciation of 英语 (Yīngyǔ) phonetics, a combination of Pīnyīn and Hànyǔ is used For example, students use 拼音 (Pīnyīn) notation to learn the phonetic symbols. e.g., [r]-rou; [æ]- 大口ai; [e]-小口ai
Inter/national student-teachers at Australian universities speak汉语 (Hànyǔ)		
During lectures and tutorials, the lecturer conducts the entire session in 英语 (Yīngyǔ)	Teachers have difficulties understanding certain content	Teachers discuss handouts and express opinions in汉语 (Hànyǔ) in face-to-face groups when attending tutorials (tutors did not discourage this practice) Teachers' discussions enhance understanding and facilitate effective communication
Teachers encounter problems when completing assignments after class	Teachers cannot relate course content to assignments, nor analyze them	Lecturers encourage teachers to form a 微信 (Wēixìn, WeChat) group for each course Teachers communicate in汉语 (Hànyǔ) their relational analyses of course content and assignments
Some Lecturers speak 英语 (Yīngyǔ) and汉语 (Hànyǔ)	Teachers encounter difficulties in understanding concepts, how to analyze assignment requirements, and the course connections with career trajectory	Teachers ask Lecturers for guidance in汉语 (Hànyǔ), who then explain in their primary language
Translation	Writing difficulties caused by barriers created by 英语 (Yīngyǔ)-only policy practices	Some teachers plan and draft assignments in汉语 (Hànyǔ) and then translate them into 英语 (Yīngyǔ) for submission via Turnitin

(continued)

Table 21.2 (continued)

背景 Contexts	引发使用双语的情况 Situations triggering the use of bilingualism	双语解释的体现和好处Manifest benefits of bilingualism
Translation and analysis	Doing assignments in 英语 (Yīngyǔ) only adds to the time required	Translate articles into汉语 (Hànyǔ) before reading them carefully Analyze content by comparing the translation with the original articles
Reading research in汉语 (Hànyǔ) (e.g., CNKI, CQVIP)	Used to understand topics when doing assignments	Some teachers choose to read literature in汉语 (Hànyǔ) before delving into 英语 (Yīngyǔ) literature when working on assignments

learning. The hierarchical power relations among languages adhere to the commodification of communications through GenAI in automating education. However, multilingualism enhances the possibilities for optimizing humanity's collective capabilities by ensuring the production and dissemination of research-based knowledge.

GenAI systems are trained on data from and absorb knowledge embedded in a limited selection of humanity's 7000 languages. Along with the academic erosion of the valorization of students' primary language, the challenges of AI-driven unemployment are corroding the intellectual and socio-economic valorizations of teachers' advanced education (French & Armitage, 2020). In 英语 (Yīngyǔ)-only monolingual teacher education, the use of GenAI systems in the 汉语 (Hànyǔ) is not made explicit or recognized. However, these GenAI systems provide teacher-researchers spaces for them to use the funds of knowledge from their repertoire of languages to engage in professional learning, thereby contributing to the struggles over the hierarchical power relations among languages (AGDE, 2022; Dobinson et al., 2024). Thoughtful uses of GenAI in automating teacher education entail sharing, via translation, the interesting knowledge produced by teacher-researchers working in 汉语 (Hànyǔ) and providing contextual knowledge about their research. At stake here is the monitoring and control by corporatized universities, autocratic GenAI systems, and oligarchic governments of teacher-researchers' use of their multilingual capital in education. The growing surveillance of lecturers, teachers, and students' online activities using classroom management software, social media surveillance, and education apps is driven by the commercialization and commodification of GenAI in automating education.

Normalizing such GenAI surveillance (not learning technologies) is problematic because it undermines democratic education and digital rights, while invading privacy to appropriate personal property through data harvesting. This relational socio-analysis moved from this empirical account of the accelerating extension and amplification of GenAI systems across the languages of education to the production and reproduction of inter/national power relations.

GenAI Systems Contribute to Teacher-Researchers' Precarious Employment

Table 21.3 indicates that some of the work, once performed by teacher-researchers (e.g., paraphrasing), is being replaced by GenAI systems. The inscription of GenAI in automating education is changing teachers' work, for instance, by using automated facial recognition technology to register, monitor, and manage students' attendance (Rensfeldt & Rahm, 2023). As a result of GenAI in education, teachers' work now encompasses surveilling students' platform activities, including assessments, follow-ups, and grading as well as 'the behavior of themselves and others based on the data provided by the systems' prognostics and dashboards' (Rensfeldt & Rahm, 2023, p. 35). The use of GenAI in education automates teachers' work, rearranges how teaching is performed, and how learning is experienced. Network-based platforms draw from the inter/national online labor workforce to employ teachers as temporary, on-demand, or project workers in areas such as language education. The intelligence of education system employees, such as teachers and researchers, is being mimicked by using GenAI systems, creating openings for management to make human workers redundant. Claims for using GenAI in automating education stress the inadequacies of the teacher workforce being compensated by automating parts of teachers' work (Selwyn, 2022b). However, replacing teachers' work by using GenAI in the automation of education disregards the requirement for humanly situated knowledge (Selwyn et al., 2021).

Using GenAI in automating education contributes to marked employment problems for students, the rising generations of workers, and teachers, including redundancies (Selwyn, 2022a, 2024). Replacing skilled human workers by adopting GenAI systems adds to technologically driven unemployment (Jung et al., 2024). The extent and duration of GenAI-driven unemployment among teachers depend

Table 21.3 GenAI systems replace aspects of teacher-researchers' work

Specific types of automated machinery	Work done
Grammar correcting tools	Analyzes and (supposedly) corrects written assignments by identifying and correcting spelling, grammar, and syntax errors (using a narrow version of American 英语 (Yīngyǔ), and punctuation mistakes, and (worryingly) provides stylistic and vocabulary suggestions
Paraphrasing tools	Rephrase the sentences and paragraphs from the original article while (supposedly) preserving their original meaning and (possibly) maintaining academic integrity
Reference generating tools	Automatically formatting and organizing the (un)necessary information for citation and listing references
Translation tools	Translate text from one language to another automatically (from a limited range of human languages), using machine learning algorithms and natural language processing to 'understand' context, tone, and nuances, resulting in human-like (but not human) accurate translations

upon the capabilities of the GenAI systems and the governing circumstances controlling their administration (Al Ghazali et al., 2024). As GenAI in education becomes seemingly more sophisticated, technologically driven changes in the structuring of teachers' work and as job substitution increases, teachers' collective bargaining power diminishes and exacerbates income inequality (Dandalt, 2021). For those educators and teachers rendered unemployed, there is a long delay between being made redundant and creating new forms of human jobs that provide commensurate employment (Pollock, 1957).

GenAI systems are involved in the incremental, continuous, and slow colonization of more and more of teacher-researchers' work. The micro-interactions in teacher-researchers' professional learning, such as acquiring the know-how to use the GenAI system for education, in both 英语 (Yīngyǔ) and 汉语 (Hànyǔ), are embedded in structured relations meant to replace aspects of teacher-researchers' work. The use of GenAI in automating education is part of a larger process that has different purposes.

The Governing Power Relations of GenAI in Automating Education

Table 21.4 widens the lens to situate teacher-researchers' practices of critical GenAI literacy within a multilayered, hierarchical field of the power relations governing GenAI in automating education. Working in conjunction with the state, global GenAI corporations are privatizing the education of the public, digital citizens, leaving little defense of democratic education. The interests of GenAI systems are in capturing and exploiting education for capitalist accumulation and sociopolitical control (Eastman & Hansen, 2021). GenAI systems are privatizing public education using adaptive learning technology to transform the conception of knowledge,

Table 21.4 The governing power of GenAI in automating education

Software types	GenAI systems	Owner
Grammar correction	Grammarly	Developed by Grammarly Incorporated, which is headquartered in San Francisco (USA)
Paraphrase	Quillbot	Acquired by Silicon Valley's Course Hero on August 21, 2021
	Chatgpt	OpenAI, an AI research laboratory founded in 2015 by Sam Altman and others, including Elon Musk and Peter Thiel
Reference generator	MyBib	Owner unknown
Translation	Google Scholar	Google is a subsidiary of Alphabet Inc., a US multinational technology corporation
	Deepl	DeepL SE, headquartered in Germany
	Youdao (有道)	NetEase (網易) is based in China

learning, and teachers' work; biometric pedagogies to locate the cultural politics of learning in the body; and digital surveillance technologies to enhance impact (Saltman, 2020). Teacher-researchers can expand on the few-shot prompting to explore the road to digital unfreedom via GenAI in automating education, through shaping authoritarian controls to influence people to think alike while reinforcing their ignorance and weakening their critical thinking.

Using GenAI in automating education poses significant challenges and socioeconomic risks inter/nationally for diverse societies and individuals. GenAI systems are a site of inter/national struggles and contestation, being part of the post-neoliberal de-structuring of the public's education to ensure the sociopolitical reproduction of the imperatives of capital accumulation (Dandalt, 2021). GenAI systems focus on consumer demand to generate revenue through the attention economy. Surveillance capitalism involves collecting and commodifying personal data using these GenAI systems to supply online goods and services (Zuboff, 2022). Money is made from low-quality, sensational clickbait, using algorithms to produce filter bubbles that amplify misinformation and encourage students or teachers to embrace mundane, polluted information (Suiter & Culloty, 2021). Given the profit motive, there is warrant for caution in talking up GenAI in automating education (Selwyn, 2022b). As it has more in 'common with a totalitarian way of life than with a democratic way of life,' Pollock (1957, p. 217) anticipated that automation would contribute to the day-to-day running of societies controlled by authoritarian principles. GenAI systems already concentrate power among those who favor authoritarian rather than democratic forms of government, prompting teacher-researchers to question the evil they do, rather than the good (Schroeder, 2020).

Critical GenAI literacy raises new concerns about teacher-researchers' responsibility as socially moral beings and our educational work of actively and deliberately protecting a human society that values criticality. Teacher-researchers bring critical GenAI literacy to work on constituting the meanings, values, and practices for the defence of education, democratic education, and democracy in the face of the technological turn to the privatization of the public's education through for-profit GenAI systems. Thinking critically, there is more to GenAI in automating education than moral and social issues.

Teacher-Researcher's Reflexive Socio-Analysis

Teacher-researcher reflexivity is integral to the logic of Bourdieu and Wacquant's (1992, pp. 104–107) relational research practice. Reflexivity addresses potential dangers of misrecognition in the research process. Here. the focus of our reflexivity is identifying possibilities for furthering the break with pre-given constructions of critical GenAI literacy by rethinking GenAI in automating education in new ways.

As teacher-researchers, our inter/national educational trajectories and bilingual cognitive structures orient our thinking and practices of 'critical GenAI literacy.' Questioning taken-for-granted presuppositions about 英语 (Yīngyǔ)-only education created spaces for the possible reconstitution of our sociolinguistic practices as teacher-researchers. More can be done to make critical GenAI literacy worthwhile by using the funds of knowledge that come with their multilingual capabilities to problematize the tensions posed by 英语 (Yīngyǔ)-only monolingualism advanced by GenAI in automating education (AGDE, 2022). There is more to critical GenAI literacy than questioning the output of GenAI systems and establishing those claims that are meaningless, nonsensical, or useless misinformation or disinformation. Critical GenAI literacy questions the amplification, legitimation, and reproduction of biases by GenAI systems because of inequities in their impact and their constraints on imagining alternative futures. To be valuable, teacher-researchers can extend critical GenAI literacy to explore disruptions to their work by GenAI systems, especially their fragmentation and degradation of their funds of knowledge in multiple languages. Critical GenAI literacy leverages human insights and ingenuity to explore questions confronting socially significant educational issues, such as the over-trust invested in GenAI systems at the expense of demands for public accountability.

The uses of GenAI in automating the education field provide grounds for reflexivity regarding the imperative to think beyond the prevailing *orthodoxy*, which is the only one acknowledged and legitimised in this field. Initially, we did not understand our place as teacher-researchers working with GenAI in automating education or our placement in the continuing historical collaborative struggles with management systems across education. Moving from individual to collective teacher-research provides a means for knowing what we are doing to free ourselves (and others) from the naivete associated with our lack of consciousness of the spaces of possibilities for thinking otherwise. Working together, teacher-researchers can generate knowledge across languages, contributing to the pursuit of intellectual freedom from the constraints and challenges of GenAI systems in automating education. Mindful that definitions of 'critical GenAI literacy' are contestable, collective reflections on the limits of the intellectual box in which our taken-for-granted thinking about it is imprisoned provide grounds for extending its contestability. Reflexivity has a key function in education and education research, namely, understanding the freedom inherent in the constraints of GenAI systems.

The inter/national GenAI system that exists in a dynamic power relationship with us as teacher-researchers provides a focus for reflexivity rather than merely as an object of contemplation. Here, critical GenAI literacy may be defined as teacher-researchers' capability to collaborate in critically evaluating the inter/national governance mechanisms of GenAI systems for automating the education systems of nation-states. America's nationalist modes of GenAI production are now pitched in multilayered struggles with the so-called international (i.e., Chinese) production (Hine, 2024). Contemporary struggles over the category 'inter/national' are driven by interests wedded to the nation-state, with most GenAI, even the most 'international' ones, being American (for the moment) (Aggarwal & Karwasra, 2025). The previous generation of strategies for the inter/nationalisation of GenAI by the cosmopolitan elites no longer correspond with the American nation-state's socioeconomic hierarchies. Current strategies aim to revalue the nation-state's capital, in a continuing struggle to reproduce the evolving techno-oligarchic structure internationally (Emery-Xu et al., 2024). Knowingly, or not, teachers are embedded in the struggles over the inter/national governance of GenAI systems. These struggles connect with long historical struggles between nation-states and their modes of (capital) production.

Conclusion

This reflexivity about the potential dangers of misrecognizing critical GenAI literacy brings us back to the prompts we posed in the introduction about GenAI in automating education. By working collectively, teacher-researchers contribute to the struggles to free humans from illusions about critical GenAI literacy (including the illusion that we do not have any illusions) and make it difficult to passively and unconsciously contribute to systemic domination through GenAI in automating education. Constructing 'critical GenAI literacy' as an object of research means breaking with taken-for-granted antecedents and procedures that are exhausted or restrict the production of new practices. Emerging critical GenAI literacy craft prompts that challenge the (in)adequacies of education research (including research into critical GenAI literacy) that create divisions by failing to situate classrooms within education systems and inside the inter/national systems of power relations governing GenAI. Seeing 'critical GenAI literacy' in a new way makes it possible to think about and act on these differently. Doing so makes it possible to teach and study the dynamics of the inter/national structures of GenAI systems governing the automation of education, and the redefinition of educational structures.

Competing Interests The authors declare that they received no research grants or other support from funding agencies for this publication, are not presently nor do they anticipate employment by any organization that may gain or lose financially through this publication; have no interests by which they may gain or lose financially through this publication, and have no other professional or personal interests that could impart bias on this publication.

Ethics Approval Western Sydney University, Human Research Ethics Committee approval number (H) 1096996: Research-Oriented School Engaged Teacher Education: A Longitudinal Case Study.

References

AGDE [Australian Government Department of Education]. (2022). *Belonging, being and becoming: The Early Years Learning Framework for Australia (V2.0)*. Australian Government Department of Education for the Ministerial Council.

Aggarwal, V., & Karwasra, N. (2025). Artificial intelligence v/s human intelligence: A relationship between digitalization and international trade. *Future Business Journal, 11*(1), 1–16.

Aksoy, D., & Kursun, E. (2024). Behind the scenes: A critical perspective on GenAI and open educational practices. *Open Praxis, 16*(3), 457–470.
Al Ghazali, S., Zaki, N., Ali, L., & Harous, S. (2024). Exploring the potential of ChatGPT as a substitute teacher: A case study. *International Journal of Information and Education Technology, 14*(2), 271–278.
Ashraf, H., & Ashfaq, H. (2024). The role of ChatGPT in medical research: Progress and limitations. *Annals of Biomedical Engineering, 52*(3), 458–461.
Banh, L., & Strobel, G. (2023). Generative artificial intelligence. *Electronic Markets, 33*(1), 1–17.
Barana, A., Marchisio, M., & Roman, F. (2023). Fostering problem solving and critical thinking in mathematics through generative artificial intelligence. In *International Association for Development of the Information Society. 20th International Conference on Cognition and Exploratory Learning in the Digital Age*.
Bearman, M., Ryan, J., & Ajjawi, R. (2023). Discourses of artificial intelligence in higher education: A critical literature review. *Higher Education, 86*(2), 369–385.
Berson, I., Berson, M., & Luo, W. (2025). Innovating responsibly: Ethical considerations for AI in early childhood education. *AI, Brain and Child, 1*(1), 2.
Bourdieu, P., & Wacquant, L. (1989). Towards a reflexive sociology: A workshop with Pierre Bourdieu. *Sociological Theory, 7*(1), 26–63.
Bourdieu, P., & Wacquant, L. (1992). *An invitation to reflexive sociology*. University of Chicago Press.
Bourdieu, P., & Wacquant, L. (1999). On the cunning of imperialist reason. *Theory, Culture & Society, 16*(1), 41–58.
Coyne, S., Shawcroft, J., Gale, M., Gentile, D., Etherington, J., Holmgren, H., & Stockdale, L. (2021). Tantrums, toddlers and technology: Temperament, media emotion regulation, and problematic media use in early childhood. *Computers in Human Behavior, 120*, 106762.
Dandalt, E. (2021). Automation, job security, and teacher employment in the United States. *Labor Law Journal, 72*(1), 41–49.
Darling, M., Owusu, S., Botchwey, M., & Asenso, D. (2024). The dark side of artificial intelligence: The negative effects on learning. *Journal of Artificial Intelligence, Machine Learning and Neural Network., 4*(6), 47–62. https://doi.org/10.55529/jaimlnn.46.47.62
Darwin, R., Mukminatien, N., Suryati, N., Laksmi, E., & Marzuki. (2024). Critical thinking in the AI era: An exploration of EFL students' perceptions, benefits, and limitations. *Cogent Education, 11*(1), 2290342.
Dillon, S., & Schaffer-Goddard, J. (2023). What AI researchers read: The role of literature in artificial intelligence research. *Interdisciplinary Science Reviews, 48*(1), 15–42.
Dobinson, T., Dryden, S., Dovchin, S., Gong, Q., & Mercieca, P. (2024). Translanguaging and "English only" at universities. *TESOL Quarterly, 58*(1), 307–333.
Eastman, N., & Hansen, E. (2021). Classroom exchanges: Big data and the commodification of educational communication. *Education and Culture, 37*(1), 76–93.
ECA [Early Childhood Australia]. (2018). *Statement on young children and digital technologies*. ECA. https://doi.org/10.23965/ECA.001
Emery-Xu, N., Jordan, R., & Trager, R. (2024). International governance of advancing artificial intelligence. *AI & Society, 40*, 3019–3044. https://doi.org/10.1007/s00146-024-02050-7
French, M., & Armitage, J. (2020). Eroding the monolingual monolith. *Australian Journal of Applied Linguistics, 3*(1), 91–114.
Gilch, P., & Sieweke, J. (2021). Recruiting digital talent: The strategic role of recruitment in organisations' digital transformation. *German Journal of Human Resource Management., 35*(1), 53–82.
Gilliard, C., & Selwyn, N. (2023). Automated surveillance in education. *Postdigital Science and Education, 5*(1), 195–205.
Grossmann, I., Feinberg, M., Parker, D., Christakis, N., Tetlock, P., & Cunningham, W. A. (2023). AI and the transformation of social science research. *Science, 380*(6650), 1108–1109.

Hine, E. (2024). Governing Silicon Valley and Shenzhen: Assessing a new era of artificial intelligence governance in the United States and China. *Digital Society, 3*(3), 50.
Hu, Y. (2024). Generative AI, communication, and stereotypes: Learning critical AI literacy through experience, analysis, and reflection. *Communication Teacher*, 1–7.
Jung, J., Wang, Y., & Barrioluengo, M. (2024). A scoping review on graduate employability in an era of 'technological unemployment'. *Higher Education Research & Development, 43*(3), 542–562.
Kaas, M. (2024). The perfect technological storm: Artificial intelligence and moral complacency. *Ethics and Information Technology, 26*(3), 49.
Karapantelakis, A., Nikou, A., Kattepur, A., Martins, J., Mokrushin, L., Mohalik, S., Orlic, M., & Feljan, A. (2024). A survey on the integration of Generative AI for critical thinking in mobile networks. *arXiv:2404.06946.*
Kouritzin, S., Ellis, T., Ghazani, A., & Nakagawa, S. (2023). Gigification of English language instructor work in higher education: Precarious employment and magic time. *TESOL Quarterly, 57*(4), 1518–1544.
Liu, J., Riesch, S., Tien, J., Lipman, T., Pinto-Martin, J., & O'Sullivan, A. (2021). Screen media overuse and associated physical, cognitive, and emotional/behavioral outcomes in children and adolescents: An integrative review. *Journal of Pediatric Health Care, 36*(2), 99–109.
Mahfoodh, H., & Hashim, S. (2021). Integrating employability skills in EFL speaking and writing curricula through digital platforms. *Tesol International Journal, 16*(1), 66–87.
Malinka, K., Perešíni, M., Firc, A., Hujňák, O., & Januš, F. (2023). On the educational impact of ChatGPT: Is artificial intelligence ready to obtain a university degree?(2023). *arXiv preprint arxiv:2303.11146.*
Mejia, S. (2023). The normative and cultural dimension of work: Technological unemployment as a cultural threat to a meaningful life. *Journal of Business Ethics, 185*(4), 847–864.
Motoki, F., Pinho Neto, V., & Rodrigues, V. (2023). More human than human: Measuring ChatGPT political bias. *Public Choice, 198*, 3–23.
Muppalla, S., Vuppalapati, S., Pulliahgaru, R., & Sreenivasulu, H. (2023). Effects of excessive screen time on child development: An updated review and strategies for management. *Cureus, 15*(6), e40608. https://doi.org/10.7759/cureus.40608
Nyaaba, M., Wright, A., & Choi, G. (2024). Generative AI and digital neocolonialism in global education: Towards an equitable framework. *arXiv:2406.02966.*
Pack, A., & Maloney, J. (2023). Using generative artificial intelligence for language education research: Insights from using OpenAI's ChatGPT. *TESOL Quarterly, 57*(4), 1571–1582.
Pollock, F. (1957). *Automation: A study of its economic and social consequences*. Frederick A. Praeger.
Rega, V., Gioia, F., & Boursier, V. (2023). Problematic media use among children up to the age of 10: A systematic literature review. *International Journal of Environmental Research and Public Health, 20*(10), 5854.
Rensfeldt, A., & Rahm, L. (2023). Automating teacher work? A history of the politics of automation and artificial intelligence in education. *Postdigital Science and Education, 5*(1), 25–43.
Saltman, K. (2020). Artificial intelligence and the technological turn of public education privatization: In defence of democratic education. *London Review of Education, 18*(2), 196–208.
Schroeder, J. (2020). Hannah Arendt's machines: Re-evaluating marketplace theory in the AI era. *First Amendment Studies, 54*(1), 28–51.
Selwyn, N. (2022a). The future of AI and education: Some cautionary notes. *European Journal of Education, 57*(4), 620–631.
Selwyn, N. (2022b). Less work for teacher? The ironies of automated decision-making in schools. In S. Pink, M. Berg, D. Lupton, & M. Ruckenstein (Eds.), *Everyday automation: Experiencing and anticipating emerging technologies* (pp. 73–86). Routledge.
Selwyn, N. (2024). On the limits of artificial intelligence (AI) in education. *Nordisk Tidsskrift for Pedagogikk og Kritikk, 10*(1), 3–14.

Selwyn, N., Hillman, T., Rensfeldt, A., & Perotta, C. (2021). Digital technologies and the automation of education: Key questions and concerns. *Postdigital Science and Education*. https://doi.org/10.1007/s42438-021-00263-3

Singh, M., & Huang, X. (2013). Bourdieu's lessons for internationalising Anglophone education: Declassifying Sino-Anglo divisions over critical theorising. *Compare: A Journal of Comparative and International Education, 43*(2), 203–223.

Singh, M., & Lǐ, X. (2024). Bourdieu and Sayad's multilingual disposition and practical research skills: Postmonolingual theorizing as a method of transknowledging. In G. Stahl, E. Weininger, P. Ayling, & G. Mu (Eds.), *The Bloomsbury handbook of Bourdieu and educational research* (pp. 60–73). Bloomsbury.

Singh, M., & Nguyễn, N. (2018). *Localising Chinese language education: Educating teachers through international service-learning*. Palgrave Macmillan.

Suiter, J., & Culloty, E. (2021). *Disinformation and manipulation in digital media: Information pathologies*. Routledge.

Teng, F. (2023). Scientific writing, reviewing, and editing for open-access TESOL journals: The role of ChatGPT. *International Journal of TESOL Studies, 5*(1), 87–91.

Teo, S. (2024). Artificial intelligence and its 'slow violence' to human rights. *AI and Ethics*, 1–16.

Thiga, M. (2024). Generative AI and the development of critical thinking skills. *Iconic Research and Engineering Journals, 7*(9), 83–90.

Veldhuis, A., Lo, P., Kenny, S., & Antle, A. (2024). Critical artificial intelligence literacy: A scoping review and framework synthesis. *International Journal of Child-Computer Interactions, 43*, 100708.

Watanabe, A. (2023). Exploring totalitarian elements of artificial intelligence in higher education with Hannah Arendt. *International Journal of Technoethics (IJT), 14*(1), 1–15.

Zarifis, A., & Efthymiou, L. (2022). The four business models for AI adoption in education: Giving leaders a destination for the digital transformation journey. In *2022 IEEE Global Engineering Education Conference* (pp. 1868–1872). https://ieeexplore.ieee.org/abstract/document/9766687

Zuboff, S. (2022). Surveillance capitalism or democracy? The death match of institutional orders and the politics of knowledge in our information civilization. *Organization Theory, 3*(3), 26317877221129290.

Michael Singh (BEd (Hons), PhD) from Western Sydney University, Australia, has an international track record for advancing methodological knowledge about research principles, objectives, strategies, and tactics. Professor Singh has investigated what democratic principles mean for research methodologies by exploring postmonolingual theorizing as a research method for thinking critically in doctoral education. Pedagogically, his objectives are to add intellectual value to doctoral candidates' multilingual capabilities and enhance their contributions to knowledge. Strategically, Professor Singh works with multilingual teacher-researchers to capitalize on their repertoire of divergent languages by generating funds of conceptual knowledge from divergent intellectual cultures. Tactically, Professor Singh works with translanguaging communities to explore claims of intellectual equality. m.j.singh@westernsydney.edu.au.

Lìpíng Niú (牛丽苹) graduated from the University of Sydney with a Master's in Teaching English to Speakers of Other Languages (TESOL). Ms. Niú gained valuable teaching experience working in education in China as an English language teacher. Her research interests include language acquisition, teacher education, and teacher professional development, focusing on TESOL-related research problems. Ms. Niú works to enhance her expertise in teaching practice and education research through collaborative self-study, participating in teacher-research projects, and contributing to publishing research reports. With the ongoing developments in generative artificial intelligence, she plans to explore the problems these create for TESOL educators and the development of the field.

Xiǎo-Lí Lǐ (李晓黎), (B.A., M.A., PhD.) is a Lecturer in Early Childhood Education at Crown Institute of Higher Education, Australia. Her teaching and research focus on the founding principles, contemporary issues, curriculum design, and Indigenous Australian perspectives for early childhood education. Committed to research-informed teaching/learning practices, Dr. Lǐ engages in collaborative teacher-research that contributes to curriculum decision-making, language education, and inquiry-based teacher professional learning in early childhood settings. Her research into methods of thinking through critical, relational analyses provides insights into curriculum design for crisis knowledge and integrated multilingual early childhood education. Dr. Lǐ's research foregrounds practices that support the meaningful integration of preservice early childhood teachers' experiential knowledge from their divergent intellectual cultures and languages with academic knowledge through pedagogies of knowledge co-construction.

Part VII
Conclusion

Chapter 22
Educators and GenAI: Harnessing a Power, Not Bowing Down to Some Cryptic Deity

Guy Tchibozo

Abstract Generative AI is constantly evolving. New developments are being made every day. The aim at this point is certainly not to draw final conclusions about education in the age of GenAI. Rather, it is to contribute to a reflection staging point.

Generative AI is constantly evolving. New developments are being made every day. The aim at this point is certainly not to draw final conclusions about education in the age of GenAI. Rather, it is to contribute to a reflection staging point.

Generative AI involves risks. A wealth of recent literature describes these issues. The successive chapters in this book have focused on some of the risks to which educators and learners are particularly exposed and sensitive. In Part VI of the book, Singh et al. delivered a systematic and thorough critique of the multiple threats that generative artificial intelligence poses to learners, educators, and educational systems.

Educators are aware that they are caught in the middle. They know that GenAI poses a recurring risk of becoming technologically sidelined. They are aware that integrating GenAI into education requires the continuous updating of skills. However, for those who upskill, using GenAI then entails the risk of insidiously slipping into ever greater dependence on it and ending up dependent, and hence paradoxically deskilled.

Educators also sense that GenAI carries a somewhat comparable risk for their students. Using GenAI allows the learner to skip and overlook certain aspects of the learning process. This undoubtedly saves learner effort and speeds up assignment production. However, the corollary is that, by the same token, the use of GenAI jeopardizes the completeness and depth of learning, which, all things considered, slows the learner's progress in mastering these aspects, and is ultimately detrimental to autonomy.

G. Tchibozo (✉)
LISEC UR2310, University of Strasbourg, Strasbourg, France
e-mail: editor@analytrics.org

G. Tchibozo (ed.), *International Perspectives of Generative AI in Education*, Advances in Artificial Intelligence in Education 3,
https://doi.org/10.1007/978-3-031-99804-1_22

Both educators and learners are aware—as also are other users outside education—that GenAI carries risks of breaching ethics, data confidentiality, research integrity, social justice, and ecological sustainability. All are aware that GenAI can pose problems of reliability, bias, misinformation, malicious use, and toxicity. And that individuals might end up no longer being able to think for themselves.

Educators were quick to recognize the risks associated with GenAI, but many also welcomed it with excitement. This is not surprising from a profession that, while cultivating a critical mind, is keen on new knowledge and is curious about new know-how. Many have sensed that GenAI has a great potential for education.

The work presented in this book suggests the diversity and scope of the positive effects that could result from expanding AI and GenAI in education. In early and elementary literacy curricula, Choi and Min (Chap. 8) have highlighted how GenAI can support image and video generation for responsive multimodal instruction. In physical education, AI can improve the conditions of motor skill demonstration and monitoring student performance (Chap. 7). In teacher education, AI-based mixed-reality simulations can compensate for the shortcomings of traditional pre-service practicum training and improve the preparation of future teachers in pedagogy and classroom management (Chap. 11). Other chapters have analyzed how GenAI can support education in academic discourse articulation (Chap. 5), research writing (Chap. 9), and lesson planning (Chaps. 13, 14, and 18), particularly in terms of time savings, creativity, streamlined processes, compliance with standards, course differentiation and student engagement, and reduced stress. In addition, GenAI can also support teachers in rubric creation (Chap. 18) and in the assessment of written assignments and feedback provision (Chaps. 15, 16, and 18). GenAI can help educators increase their productivity, thus freeing up time for them to refocus on the quality and essentials of the educational process, while avoiding burn-out, which could help counteract teacher shortage trends. All chapters have illustrated how GenAI can facilitate personalized learning, scaffold learning, encourage critical thinking, and support educators in thinking through new approaches. These results are just the beginning. Future research will shed further light on the possible positive contributions of generative AI to education.

Key Points for Stakeholders

The book's key findings offer numerous suggestions to education stakeholders, including educators, teacher trainers, school administrators, policymakers, AI developers, and educational technologists. The book's contributions also call for further research.

Educators

As demonstrated by Thibaud (Chap. 19), Bewersdorf and Wittingslow (Chap. 6) and Singh et al. (Chap. 21), generative AI poses risks to student development; the production, validation, and use of information; and education as a whole, encompassing learners, teachers, and education systems. GenAI can compromise students' mastery of skills related to social interaction, communication, emotional literacy and regulation, dialectical critical thinking, rational abilities, sense of responsibility and agency, self-confidence, and autonomy. These skills are essential to students' identity development. Therefore, Thibaud advocates that educators approach GenAI with sufficient caution in their attitude, use, and teaching, to avoid harming students' identity development processes.

The appropriate use of GenAI tools and the risks they pose in terms of the manipulation and misuse of information also require attention. Bewersdorf and Wittingslow recommend updating information literacy curricula to reinforce learners' reference practices for searching, evaluating, and producing information. Learners should be trained to understand how GenAI systems work, are built, trained, and tested, including why they are predisposed to produce biased content; understand the ethical and legal aspects of using GenAI tools; and understand how GenAI can be misused by bad faith actors and how to identify, evaluate, and thwart malicious uses of it.

Educators are also called upon to take up the challenge that GenAI poses to educational systems, learners, and themselves. Singh et al. invite them to develop their critical GenAI literacy. This involves questioning not only the processes and outputs of GenAI, but also how it disrupts the work of educators, how it affects socially important educational issues, how it threatens equity and social values, how it shapes social relations as well as domination in international relations, and how it weighs on the future of society.

Teacher Educators

Teacher trainers influence educators' skills, mindset and attitude towards GenAI. Therefore, they occupy a central position for the integration of generative AI into education. Several contributions in the book, in particular those by Nyaaba (Chap. 12), Ray and Ntuli (Chap. 13), and González Cerna (Chap. 20), emphasize that while GenAI looks promising for education, it is essential that teacher trainers position it in their teaching as a tool, not to be confused with a substitute teacher. Teacher educators need to clarify to prospective, beginning, and practicing teachers that GenAI tools should be used as teacher aids and, as such, should not be expected to do the work for them.

Most contributions also emphasized the idea that teacher educators need to train their students not only in the technical use of GenAI tools and prompt engineering, but also in GenAI ethics and critical digital literacy.

Educational Institutions and School Administrators

González Cerna (Chap. 20) and Hau et al. (Chap. 3) specifically addressed the responsibility of educational institutions and administrators to provide the educational community with ethical guidelines related to the use of generative AI. González Cerna also stresses that the successful integration of AI in education requires supportive learning environments. He also advocates adapting curricula to induce a future in which the role of AI and technology in general is increased, but where other teaching methods and tools are still used to achieve the goals of holistic education.

Policymakers

Education policy has a key role to play. The contributors reiterate that if the integration of GenAI into education is a political goal, policymakers must establish the corresponding legal frameworks and ensure that educational institutions receive appropriate support. Another important message is that successfully integrating AI into education also requires balancing the benefits and risks of AI with societal values and goals.

AI Developers and Educational Technologists

Wilton et al. (Chap. 4) point out that AI tools are often difficult to decipher: "many of them are proprietary and the AI functionality is not well-explained". Product descriptions sometimes lack transparency and clarity, "can be complex, limited or even difficult to find". "Many applications include a disclaimer where the often difficult to understand terms of service may change at any time without notice". In addition, "the handling of privacy was often unclear. […] At this time, most information provided by the developers of AI products appears inadequate for understanding ethical issues".

This situation affects learners', educators' and administrators' understanding of the learning potential, reliability, and risks of AI tools. These barriers to understanding, in turn, pose a threat to the critical analysis of AI and AI tools, AI literacy, and the integration of AI into education.

Wilton et al. therefore recommend that developers increasingly adopt the practice of providing model-card information in understandable language. They also suggest that those responsible for developing AI technologies and standards increasingly involve educators in the process.

Directions for Future Research

This book is an exploratory undertaking to unearth as many aspects as possible of the potential and challenges of generative artificial intelligence in education. Since this is an exploratory research, it is only logical that it should lead to the identification of avenues for further research. Several promising avenues for future research are highlighted here.

Integrating AI and GenAI into education requires the landscape of mindsets in the background to be designed and shaped beforehand, so that it provides a favorable context in which AI can take root and develop. Drawing on the Palestinian case, González Cerna (Chap. 20) highlights the need to reflect on how to improve community acceptance and attitudes in communities where prevailing mentalities are traditional or out-of-step with respect to responsible use of GenAI: "parents and the community at large […] do not tend to prefer technology-based teaching approaches to traditional face-to-face ones. […] In the current […] mindset, the best possible education definitely is the one that is given by a teacher in front of a classroom, while the effectiveness of other methods tends to be called into question. […] 'even if you offer new methods, people won't believe they will work' […]". Other views "associate the idea of AI with general fears about technology […] 'My dad hears about AI and thinks about robots taking over the world'. […]". In contrast, there are others "for whom grades are the only important and valid measure and outcome of education, and who might encourage their children to use and even abuse AI beyond any ethical consideration, as long as it gets them good grades on their report cards." While creating a favorable environment is the responsibility of policymakers, these also need the insight of research into the drivers and processes of social acceptance and advancing mentalities.

The mindsets and attitudes of educators themselves matter. Hau et al. (Chap. 3) observed that educators' feelings about AI and GenAI range from optimism to apprehension, the latter due to concerns about loss of control resulting from their feeling of being technologically outdated, the opacity of AI, fears of plagiarism, and threats to their jobs. There may be differences between disciplines. In their sample of secondary school teachers in Luxembourg, Hau and her colleagues noted (Fig. 2.1) that while STEM teachers were evenly split between positive, neutral, and negative attitudes, Language teachers were overwhelmingly neutral or negative (perhaps because of concerns about machine translation). By contrast, Arts and Humanities teachers were massively neutral or positive, perhaps acknowledging the creative potential of AI. These authors emphasize the need to consider the emotional context prevailing in each academic discipline in terms of prejudices, acceptance, and willingness toward AI when it comes to implementing AI technologies. Research should explore a wider range of school disciplines, further investigate where these differences between disciplines originate, and reflect on whether and how these differences imply more targeted AI tools, AI-teaching programs and strategies, and approaches to AI integration, that align with the specificities of each discipline.

Further research is also needed on the possible uses of AI and GenAI tools. Cumming et al. (Chap. 11) have shown the potential of AI-based mixed-reality simulations (MRS) for teacher education. Research on mixed-reality simulations is still underdeveloped. Further research is needed to explore the calibration of MRS interventions (number, timing, frequency and duration of sessions; class size; etc.); the transferability (and persistence) of MRS-learned skills to real-world classroom settings; and the potential of MRS for specific subject areas.

GenAI tools can also be effective in supporting lesson planning, rubric creation, and knowledge assessment. Spadoni and Solano (Chap. 14) and Grosso and Solano (Chap. 18) have shown that GenAI tools enable greater creativity, better course differentiation, increased student engagement, and better adherence to standards. These studies also show that using GenAI streamlines the lesson planning process, saves teachers time, reduces stress and burnout, and increases productivity. However, these are only small-scale studies. Their positive results encourage further research at a larger scale to better evaluate the potential of AI-based productivity assistants for lesson planning, rubric creation, knowledge assessment, and teaching in general. Spadoni and Solano insist on the need to compare student outcomes according to whether AI-created lesson plans were used in their classrooms, and analyze AI-created lesson plans in terms of student engagement, perceived effectiveness, standards alignment, impact on promoting creativity, and accommodating different learning styles.

Finally, research is also required to investigate how to address the risks and challenges posed by GenAI. Väkevä and Partti (Chap. 9) suggest that research should examine whether and how users can address, influence, or mitigate biases in GenAI outputs, for example, through appropriate prompting techniques. Laroudie and Tchibozo (Chap. 10) observe that unless learners complete their assignments in controlled environments, many tend to limit themselves to having GenAI perform their tasks, with little risk of being discovered. In the specific context of research-based teaching, they recommend further research to design pedagogical and knowledge assessment frameworks that limit summative assessment to GenAI-proof research tasks. Further research on the respective places of GenAI-proof and GenAI-substitutable learning activities in knowledge assessment is also needed in the broader educational context. The lines drawn by Laroudie and Tchibozo invite an exploration of how, unlike research-based teaching which must exclude GenAI-substitutable research tasks from summative assessment, researcher training might need to include GenAI-substitutable tasks in summative assessment (given that researchers also need to master the use of GenAI), while basic education up to tertiary undergraduate education may need to both educate learners in the proper use of GenAI and exclude GenAI-substitutable activities from summative assessment.

Ultimately, Thibaud (Chap. 19) draws attention to the fact that GenAI may compromise students' mastery of skills related to social interaction, communication, emotion literacy and regulation, dialectical critical thinking, rational abilities, sense of responsibility and agency, self-confidence and autonomy. Still, these skills are essential for identity formation. Research should pay more attention to reflect on how to take these risks into account and how to approach GenAI tools with sufficient caution to avoid harming identity development.

Adopting the Right Posture

Educators cannot turn their backs on AI and GenAI. Their role is to prepare future generations for the world in which they will have to live. And it is clear that this world will be profoundly influenced by AI and GenAI. But then, it is crucial for educators to adopt the correct posture. They will have to dominate AI and GenAI, not be dominated by them.

Dominating AI and GenAI means first learning about them and understanding them in depth. As Wilton et al. suggested in Chap. 4, this will undoubtedly require closer cooperation with AI engineers and developers, as well as with the industry, in order to be at the heart of tool design and influence its direction. Educators should master the use of these new tools, knowing their strengths and weaknesses, the problems they raise, the challenges they pose, and the risks they engender.

As Thibaud (Chap. 19) pointed out, educators should equip themselves intellectually, philosophically, ethically, and technically, to have sufficient confidence in their own expertise, and be able to position themselves as dominating AI and GenAI, rather than being dominated by them. The initial and in-service teacher training should be reinforced accordingly. Sound ethical training should be put in place.

Properly trained, educators will be able to, confidently and effectively, play their role as learners' guides. The educator will have a clear idea of the tools available, the reasons for using them, the objectives to be achieved, the right tools for each case, the risks, pitfalls and possible drifts, and the ways to avoid them. The educator will be able to assess the relevance of the answers provided by GenAI, take advantage of proposals that make sense, spot and reject hallucinations, and in turn pass on this mastery to the learner.

Ray and Ntuli (Chap. 13) observed that some educators may tend to expect AI and GenAI tools to do their work for them, and then be disappointed when they realize the inadequacies of the results they achieve. The opposite attitude should prevail. It is essential that educators recognize that AI and GenAI are tools that they need to master, rather than bend toward them. Only then will educators be able to make the most of these tools, fulfill their own educational mission, and avoid being replaced by AI and GenAI.

Index

A

Academic writing, 7, 81, 92–94, 151, 154, 289
Action research, 195, 211, 247–248, 251, 287, 290
Adaptive learning, 5, 9, 29, 55, 84, 240, 241, 373
Administrative burden, 208, 305
Adobe AI Image Generator, 135, 136
AI acceptance, 19–37, 39, 338
AI adoption, 20, 22
AI effectiveness, 285–294, 388
AI grading, 55, 248
AI in Education (AIEd), 3, 4, 20–23, 27–34, 36, 37, 39, 40, 48–51, 53, 54, 65–67, 69, 70, 101, 145, 289, 293, 299, 317, 328, 345–353, 386
AI integration, 20, 22, 29, 30, 33–36, 150, 303, 317, 387
AI literacy, 7, 48–70, 333, 339, 360–376, 386
AI pedagogy, 49, 51, 153, 158–163
AI readiness, 49, 53, 54, 66, 67
AI tools, 8, 13, 14, 20, 21, 32, 34, 36, 49, 51–53, 55–59, 61–67, 69, 130, 131, 135, 140, 141, 143, 145, 149, 160, 240, 245, 256–258, 260, 265, 289, 293, 294, 299, 300, 303, 304, 308, 312, 317, 333, 336, 337, 348–351, 386, 387
Amazon CodeWhisperer, 12, 13
Analytics, 5, 55, 288, 299, 301
Artificial neural networks (ANNs), 6, 12
Artistic research, 156, 157, 159, 160
Art-related research, 157, 158, 160, 163
Assessment, 5, 22, 51, 84, 103, 116, 171, 193, 212, 228, 248, 264, 285, 299, 309, 349, 362, 384
Australia, 191, 194, 196, 201, 366
Autoencoders, 6
Automating education, 218, 287, 360, 361, 364, 366–369, 371–376
Automation, 13, 267, 304, 305, 337, 361, 363, 372, 374, 376
Autonomy, 20, 32, 179, 180, 183, 191, 267, 298, 303, 304, 331, 339, 360, 383, 385, 388

B

Bard, 264, 265, 269, 274
Bias, 20, 28, 36, 52, 54, 63–66, 68, 104, 108, 158, 160, 161, 257, 265, 288, 338, 360, 361, 363, 375, 376, 384, 388
Biliteracy, 130–145
Bing, 106, 264, 265, 269
BookCreator, 135–137
Bourdieu, P., 365–367, 374
Brainstorming, 96, 136, 151–153, 237, 238, 289, 302, 314, 316, 318
Burnout, 8, 246–250, 254, 256, 258, 287, 297, 298, 302–305, 388

C

Canada, 308, 369
Canva, 58, 130, 133, 135, 136, 300, 303, 308
CapCut, 130, 137, 142, 143

G. Tchibozo (ed.), *International Perspectives of Generative AI in Education*, Advances in Artificial Intelligence in Education 3,
https://doi.org/10.1007/978-3-031-99804-1

ChatGPT, 13, 25, 48, 57, 67, 87, 88, 90, 91, 95, 101, 106, 135, 136, 178, 214, 216, 228, 233, 238, 247, 250, 251, 257, 264, 286, 287, 289–292, 300, 302, 303, 305, 308, 309, 313–318, 332, 333, 348, 362, 373
China, 264, 366, 370, 373
Classroom management, 116, 187–203, 371, 384
Class size, 116, 117, 208, 213, 298, 388
Code generation, 12, 13
Codex, 12, 13
Cognitive tool, 267, 280, 329
Collaborative learning, 50, 53, 216, 220, 229
Colombia, 45
Colvin's Escalation Cycle, 197
Communities of practice, 163, 189
Context window, 153
Copilot, 228, 264, 265, 269, 274
Creativity, 8, 32, 33, 36, 48, 131, 145, 257, 300–302, 304, 337, 353, 384, 388
Critical AI literacy, 65, 369
Critical GenAI literacy, 4, 9, 360–376, 385
Critical thinking, 7, 9, 28, 29, 32, 33, 35, 36, 48, 63–65, 82, 90, 95, 97, 103–105, 170, 183, 208–212, 216, 218, 219, 241, 300, 336, 337, 353, 360–365, 369, 374, 384, 385, 388
Curipod, 250, 301–303
Curriculum, 7, 28, 30, 32, 33, 63, 69, 101–103, 106–111, 130–145, 170, 191, 193, 208, 210, 212, 216–219, 229, 231, 238, 239, 256, 259, 269, 280, 301, 302, 304, 333, 352, 384–386

D
DALL-E, 25, 133, 300
Data privacy, 20, 26, 28, 158–160, 305, 360
Decodable books, 130–134, 145
Deep learning (DL), 6, 12, 309, 365, 368
Democracy, 9, 103, 109, 364, 374
Depth of learning, 9, 383
Developing countries, 8, 211, 212, 214, 216
Differentiation, 29, 49, 192, 194, 231, 238, 246, 255–257, 275, 303, 304, 315, 384, 388
Duolingo, 26, 59, 241

E
Early childhood education, 360
Ecological sustainability, 149, 158, 161, 384
Eduaide.ai, 299, 300
Educational change, 20, 228, 352
Educational technology, 69, 172, 187, 237, 299
Equity, 48, 63, 135, 145, 161, 210, 289, 353, 385
Error detection, 13
Ethics, 3, 5, 7–9, 31, 37, 48, 49, 51, 53, 54, 56, 63–65, 68–70, 97, 158, 183, 195, 202, 203, 230, 235, 240, 286, 293, 369, 376, 384, 385
Exploratory approach, 4

F
Feedback, 8, 12, 13, 56, 57, 65, 83, 84, 92, 95, 97, 105, 117, 118, 122, 143, 153, 156, 162, 175, 178, 180, 183, 189, 191–197, 200, 201, 210, 217, 229, 231, 248, 249, 251, 258, 263–282, 288–295, 302, 304, 305, 309, 333, 334, 350, 351, 384
Finland, 167
France, 178, 264

G
Gaza, 345, 346, 350
Gemini, 136, 153, 228, 264, 265, 274
GenAI-proof tasks, 174, 177, 178, 180, 181, 183
GenAI-substitutable tasks, 5, 388
Generative adversarial networks (GANs), 6
Generative pre-trained transformer (GPT), 151, 216, 265, 309
Ghana, 208–214, 216, 218, 219
GitHub Copilot, 12, 13
Global South, 161, 208–220
Grading, 8, 59, 213, 214, 230, 233, 236, 246, 248, 249, 256, 265, 270, 273–275, 285–295, 299, 301, 302, 312, 350, 351, 372
Grammarly, 59, 95, 151, 289, 373
Grounded theory, 347

H
Hallucinations, 65, 152, 172, 317, 361, 363, 389
Hands-on learning, 214, 217, 218, 220
Higher arts education (HAE), 7, 149–163
Hong Kong, 344

I
Identity, 4, 8, 34, 83, 135, 139, 145, 327–339, 353, 385, 388, 389
Image generation, 6, 130, 131, 145
Inclusivity, 161
Individualized learning, 5, 29, 240
Information literacy, 4, 7, 101–112, 385
Intelligent learning, 54
Intelligent tutoring, 5, 12, 54, 57, 83, 288
Invideo, 137, 142, 143

K
Khanmigo, 299, 300, 303, 305

L
Large language models (LLMs), 6, 12, 52, 65, 101–112, 149–163, 240, 265, 280, 328, 332, 333, 336
Latent Dirichlet Allocation (LDA), 56, 63
Learnification, 334
Learning analytics, 55, 84, 288
Lesson planning, 8, 140–141, 209, 214, 227–240, 246, 247, 251, 254–258, 287, 299, 301–304, 307–318, 384, 388
Linguistically responsive teaching (LRT), 135, 139, 144
Literacy education, 7, 79, 80, 82, 85, 89, 90, 93, 95, 96
Low-code platforms, 12
Luxembourg, 7, 19–37, 387

M
Machine learning (ML), 6, 58, 80, 83, 84, 228, 240, 372
MagicSchool.ai, 247, 249–252, 254–258, 287, 290–292, 299–301, 308, 309, 313–318
MAXQDA, 24
Mediation, 80, 81, 96, 183, 361
MidJourney, 58, 300
Mixed reality, 5, 7, 187–203, 384, 388
Model card, 52–54, 63, 66–67, 386
Motor skills, 116, 117, 124, 384
Multilingualism, 371
Multimodality, 80
Multimodal learning, 96, 142, 145

N
Natural language processing (NLP), 12, 13, 54, 59, 84, 287, 309, 372
Nearpod, 299
No-code platforms, 12
Norway, 269, 274
Norwegian Teacher Self-Efficacy Scale (NTSES), 195, 197–198
Novice teachers, 8, 227–240

O
OpenAI, 12, 13, 151, 373

P
Palestine, 345–351, 353
Pear Deck, 299
Pedagogical innovation, 5, 208, 214
Pedagogical modeling, 8, 208, 209, 211–220
Pedagogical strategy, 32, 51, 83, 95, 191
Perplexity.ai, 250, 309, 310, 313, 315, 317, 318
Personalized learning, 29, 52, 188, 194, 215, 228, 249, 250, 299–300, 303, 305, 308, 309, 353, 384
Personal knowledge management (PKM), 155
Photomath, 26
Physical education, 7, 384
PodLever, 87, 88, 93
Pollock, F., 361, 363, 373, 374
Practical-based teaching, 217
Pre-service teachers, 7, 131–145, 192, 201, 220
Productivity, 8, 9, 13, 26, 228, 248, 307–318, 368, 369, 384, 388
Professional development, 30, 31, 33, 39, 63, 69, 85, 170, 188, 203, 209, 213, 214, 219, 220, 230, 240, 250, 289, 293, 300, 303, 305, 308, 317, 353, 369
Programming, 11–14, 361
Project-based learning, 92
Prompt, 7, 12, 37, 87, 106–108, 136, 140, 153, 172, 218, 220, 227, 233, 235, 238, 239, 246, 249, 265, 266, 268–280, 289, 302, 309, 313, 347, 351, 360, 361, 366, 376, 385

Q
QuillBot, 59, 250, 289, 373

R
Read-aloud, 130, 142–145
Repetitive tasks, 299, 305
Research-based teaching, 5, 7, 170, 171, 174–183, 388
Research education, 7, 149–163, 181
Research integrity (RI), 149, 158, 159, 384
Research writing, 7, 149–163, 364, 384
Resistance to change, 8, 28, 29, 208–210, 213–214, 217, 219
Routine tasks, 29, 301, 303–305, 310, 317
Rubrics, 8, 85, 214, 230, 233, 248–253, 255, 258–260, 265, 269, 270, 273, 276–279, 282, 287, 290, 292–294, 301, 302, 307–318, 384, 388

S
Scaffolding, 80, 83, 135, 139–141, 143, 162, 246, 315, 333
Secondary education, 7, 38, 349
Sentiment analysis, 54, 56, 63, 64
SimLab, 189, 195–197
SimSchool, 192, 193
Simulation, 5, 7, 58, 187–203, 287, 300, 384, 388
Singapore, 116, 117, 308
Situated learning theory, 189–190
Snyk Code, 13
Social justice, 158, 161, 384
Social media, 86, 88, 90, 91, 94, 95, 109, 339, 352, 360, 371
Software development, 14
Sora, 130, 133, 135, 136, 140
South Korea, 116, 130
Student engagement inventory (SEI), 122–123
Student equity, 158, 161
Sustainability, 161
System usability scale (SUS), 123, 124

T
Tabnine, 13
Teacher burnout, 8, 248, 249, 258, 287, 297–305, 310
Teacher development, 244
Teacher education, 7, 122, 130, 188, 190–193, 197, 201–203, 208–220, 234, 239, 367, 369–371, 376, 384, 388
Teacher preparation, 187, 188, 192, 194, 208, 209, 304
Teacher productivity, 230, 248–249, 317
Teacher-research, 360–376
Teacher support, 263–280
Teacher training, 9, 36, 187, 188, 190–192, 203, 210–211, 215, 240, 353, 389
Teaching and Learning International Survey (TALIS), 116
TeachME™ Lab (TML), 192
Technology acceptance, 20–22, 33, 34, 36
Technology integration, 131, 310, 353
Technology Pedagogical Content Knowledge (TPACK), 68, 310, 311, 317
TESOL, 147, 379
Text-to-video, 130, 142–145
Transformer models, 6
Translation, 12, 26, 40, 59, 135–137, 139–141, 143, 144, 155, 264, 303, 368, 370–373, 387
Transmediation, 79–97
Turing, A., 11

U
Unemployment, 218, 219, 363, 371, 372
UNESCO, 49–54, 68, 69, 158, 332
United States, 35, 50, 85, 130, 194, 232, 245, 247, 286, 298, 308, 361
Universal design for learning (UDL), 142, 143

V
Veed.io, 137, 142, 143
Vygotsky, L.S., 80, 81, 230, 231, 234

W
Wolfram Alpha, 26

Z
Zoom, 86, 87, 92, 196, 200, 265, 270, 281

MIX
Papier aus verantwortungsvollen Quellen
Paper from responsible sources
FSC® C105338

If you have any concerns about our products,
you can contact us on
ProductSafety@springernature.com

In case Publisher is established outside the EU,
the EU authorized representative is:
Springer Nature Customer Service Center GmbH
Europaplatz 3, 69115 Heidelberg, Germany

Printed by Libri Plureos GmbH
in Hamburg, Germany